THE BRITISH ISLES

THE BRITISH ISLES

A History of Four Nations

HUGH KEARNEY

Amundson Professor of British History,
University of Pittsburgh

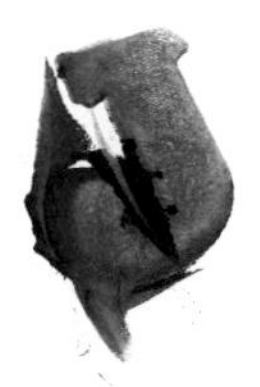

CAMBRIDGE
UNIVERSITY PRESS

Published by the Press Syndicate of the University of Cambridge
The Pitt Building, Trumpington Street, Cambridge CB2 1RP
40 West 20th Street, New York, NY 10011-4211, USA
10 Stamford Road, Oakleigh, Melbourne 3166, Australia

First published 1989
Reprinted 1993

Printed in Great Britain at The Bath Press, Avon

British Library cataloguing in publication data

Kearney, Hugh
The British Isles: a history of four
nations.
1. Great Britain, history
I. Title
941

Library of Congress cataloguing in publication data

Kearney, Hugh
The British Isles: a history of four nations/Hugh Kearney.
p. cm.
Bibliography.
Includes index.
ISBN 0 521 33420 9
1. Great Britain – History. 2. Ireland – History. I. Title.
DA30.K38 1989
941 – dc 19 88-20291 CIP

ISBN 0 521 39655 7

BS

For my wife, Kate

In this Ocean there happen to be two very large islands which are called Britannic, Albion and Ierna, bigger than any we have mentioned.

Aristotle, *De Mundo* c.iv

Contents

Plates

Acknowledgments

Plates 1a, 1b, 2, 3, 4, 5, 6, 7, 8, 9, 10, 11, 13, 18, 24, 25, 26, 27, 28, 30, 31, 32, 33, 34, 35, 36, 42 and 48 are reproduced by permission of the Cambridge University Collection of Air Photographs. Plates 12, 17, 29 and 39 are reproduced by permission of the Royal Commission on the Ancient and Historical Monuments of Scotland; 14 and 15, the British Museum; 16, 19, 20, 21, 22 and 23, the National Museum, Dublin; 37, the National Monuments Record for Wales; 38, 40, 49 and 50, Britain On View (BTA/ETB); 41, the British Tourist Authority; 43 and 44, Borde Fáilte Photo; 45, the National Trust; and 46 and 47, the Wales Tourist Board Photo Library.

Maps

Preface

In the course of writing this book I came to owe a great deal to various friends and colleagues. In particular I wish to thank Rees Davies of University College, Aberystwyth, David Dumville of Cambridge University and Harry Dickinson of the University of Edinburgh for the time they gave to reading various portions of the typescript. I am especially grateful to the Master and Fellows of Peterhouse, Cambridge, and to the Governing Body of the University of Wales, who awarded me visiting fellowships in 1985. My stay in Aberystwyth was made particularly enjoyable thanks to the hospitality of Rees Davies, Gareth Williams, John Davidson, Martin Fitzpatrick and their wives. I wish also to express my gratitude to the University of Pittsburgh for granting me leave of absence during the Fall Term 1985. At various times, I benefited from the encouragement of Janelle Greenberg of the University of Pittsburgh, John Pocock of Johns Hopkins University, Joseph Lee of University College, Cork, James Shiel of the University of Sussex and Lord Dacre of Glanton, erstwhile Master of Peterhouse. Brian Wormald, my friend and old supervisor at Peterhouse (1942–3), gave me many hours of his time forty years later. James Shiel provided the epigraph. Like many others I have incurred a debt to Linda Randall, Hazel Dunn and Maureen Ashby. Mr William Davies of Cambridge University Press has displayed patience and sympathy beyond the call of duty. My deepest debt, however, is to Kate, my wife of over thirty years, who encouraged me to persevere in an enterprise which underwent several strange metamorphoses.

For help and advice with the illustrations I wish to thank the following: Dr Breandan Ó Ríordáin, Director, National Museum of Ireland; Dr Oliver Snoddy, History Section, National Museum of Ireland; Professor George Eogan, Department of Archaeology, University College, Dublin; Dr Barry Raftery, Department of Archaeology, University College, Dublin; Dr Prys Morgan, History Department, University College, Swansea; Mr Tony Parkinson, Royal Commission on Ancient and Historical Monuments (Wales); and especially Mr David Wilson, Curator, Aerial Photography Unit, University of Cambridge.

Bury St Edmunds HUGH KEARNEY

MAP: the British Isles

Introduction

This is not a piece of national history, though it owes a great deal to the work of nationally minded historians. It is an attempt to examine, within short compass, the interaction of the various major cultures of the British Isles from the Roman period onwards. The emphasis throughout is upon the British Isles, in the belief that it is only by adopting a 'Britannic' approach that historians can make sense of the particular segment in which they may be primarily interested, whether it be 'England', 'Ireland', 'Scotland', 'Wales', Cornwall or the Isle of Man.

To concentrate upon a single 'national' history, which is based upon the political arrangements of the present, is to run the risk of being imprisoned within a cage of partial assumptions, which lead to the perpetuation of ethnocentric myths and ideologies. Herbert Butterfield, in his essay, *The Whig Interpretation of History* (1931), stressed the importance of trying to see all sides of past conflicts. The modern world in his view arose from both Protestant and Catholic, not from one or the other. In the same way, no single 'national' interpretation, whether English, Irish, Scottish or Welsh, can be treated as self-contained. A 'Britannic' framework is an essential starting point for a fuller understanding of these so-called 'national' pasts.

This point might hardly seem worth stressing, were it not for the fact that, in its continued use of a 'nation' paradigm, the historiography of the British Isles still bears traces of its late nineteenth-century origins. The professionalisation of history brought with it the acceptance not only of Leopold Von Ranke's critical methods but also his stress upon the role of 'nations' in history. Ranke believed that the 'nation' was the divinely created unit at work in universal history, with each nation having its own appointed moment of destiny. So far as England is concerned, the publication of William Stubbs' *Constitutional History of England* (from 1866 onwards) marked the introduction of history on the Rankean model. Stubbs' *History* was acceptably 'modern' in its critical use of primary sources. There was also no doubt that Stubbs saw the 'nation' as the appropriate unit for a historian to concentrate upon.

Nation-based history became the basis around which the new academic subject of history expanded. The *English Historical Review* was founded in 1886 and in due course national history reviews were founded first for Scotland (1904) and then for Ireland (1938) and Wales (1970). In the new elementary and secondary schools of the late nineteenth century, history was taught on national lines as a means of inculcating the virtue of patriotism. Libraries took 'nations' as the appropriate cataloguing division for the 'subject of History'. During the twentieth century, long after the original impulse from Ranke had been lost sight of, the writing of history along 'national' lines came to seem axiomatic.

The extent to which the writing of history was so strongly nation-based was disguised by the way in which English historians shifted between the use of 'British' and 'English' as if the two were somehow equivalent. Three examples of this tendency may suffice, all taken from major historians.

> The historical development of England is based upon the fact that her frontiers against Europe are drawn by Nature and cannot be the subject of dispute ... In short, a great deal of what is peculiar in English history is due to the obvious fact that Great Britain is an island. (L. B. Namier, *England in the Age of the American Revolution* (London, 1930), pp. 6–7.)

> In the Second World War, the British people came of age ... The British people had set out to destroy Hitler ... No English soldier who rode with the tanks into liberated Belgium ... The British were the only people who went through both world wars from beginning to end ... The British empire declined ... Few even sang 'England Arise'. England had risen all the same. (A. J. P. Taylor, *Oxford History of England, England 1914–45* (Oxford, 1966), p. 600.)

> Nevertheless, something can be learned about the British political system ... The early attainment of national identity is one of England's most distinctive features ... To this extent British political development may be plausibly regarded ... If we are to understand the reasons for the peculiarities of the English political system ... Quite apart from all the consequences that have flowed from Britain's imperial role. (Keith Thomas, 'The United Kingdom', in Raymond Grew, ed., *Crises of Political Development in Europe and the United States* (Princeton, 1978), pp. 44–5.)

These examples indicate that a single nation-based approach is insufficient. Much as the historians concerned wish to keep within an 'English' framework, they are led in spite of themselves to refer to a wider dimension.

There was, however, an earlier tradition of historiography whose practitioners had been willing to consider the histories of Ireland, Scotland and Wales as an essential part of the story. Thomas Babington Macaulay may have entitled his master work *History of England* (1848–61) but it was, in effect, a history of the British Isles during what he saw as the crucial period of modern history, the Glorious Revolution of 1688. James Anthony Froude is best known for history of England in the sixteenth century but his study of *The English in Ireland* (1872) together with his novel *The Two Chiefs of Dunboy* (1889) reveal a remarkable understanding of Ireland. W. E. H. Lecky's *History of England in the Eighteenth Century* (1878–90) included Ireland and Scotland as well as England within its overall perspective.

Elie Halévy's *History of the English People* (1913), despite the limitations of its title, took a wide view of its topic, with extensive treatment being given to Ireland and Scotland. Halévy apart, the influence of these writers tended to decline in the early twentieth century because their narrative approach, their use of the concept of 'race' and their handling of sources was thought to be unprofessional. With them, a 'British Isles' approach declined also. Even in the case of Halévy, it is worth noting that the modern French historian François Bedarida, modelling himself on Halévy some years later (1979), confined his attention largely to English history. For much of the twentieth century, indeed, within the British Isles, history has been taught and written along national lines, and hence tied, often unconsciously, to national ideologies and nation-building. In the United States, also, ethnocentric attitudes among immigrants from the British Isles have encouraged the production of 'national' histories geared to specific ethnic tastes.

The concept of 'nation' provided modern historians with a convenient framework around which to organise their materials but a price had to be paid. What became later national boundaries were extended backwards into a past where they had little or no relevance, with the consequence that earlier tribal or pre-national societies were lost to sight. The border between 'Wales' and 'England' is a case in point. It is now assumed that Herefordshire and Shropshire are part of 'England' and that their inhabitants are 'English', with all the appropriate 'mental furniture' to go with that term. In fact these border counties have been the scene of intermingling between 'Welsh' and 'English' cultures over a long period of time. The same point may also be made about the border between 'England' and 'Scotland', which was drawn at one time to include the (now Scottish) Lothians within England and at another to include Celtic Cumbria within the kingdom of Strathclyde. The modern distinction between Ulster and south-west Scotland did not exist in the later middle ages, since the channel dividing the two areas served as a unifying element for the seaborne post-viking society which occupied the 'Isles'. To make sense of so much variation over time requires a 'Britannic' framework.

This point may be reinforced if it is borne in mind that episodes which are generally recognised as having been of decisive importance in the history of the various 'nations' of the British Isles in fact transcended the national boundaries of a later date. The Roman Conquest, the Barbarian invasions, the viking raids, the Norman Conquest, the Reformation and the Industrial Revolution were all 'events' which affected the British Isles as a whole and brought about crucial changes in the relations between the various Britannic societies of the period concerned. To deal with any one of these episodes requires in every case something wider than a national framework. The only possible exception is perhaps that of the Roman Conquest, from which Ireland was excluded, but even here recent research has revealed the importance of Roman contacts with Ireland. There is in any case the influence upon Ireland of the Latin culture of the later Roman empire introduced through the medium of Christianity.

The present author is not alone in pressing for a 'Britannic' approach. Several recent examples of a similar impatience with the straitjacket of exclusively national categories come readily to mind. Michael Hechter in his stimulating book *Internal Colonialism* (1975) used the concepts of 'core' and 'periphery' in an attempt to elucidate the relations between England and what he termed, misleadingly, the 'Celtic Fringe'. Hechter's main point was that England established a colonial relationship with other parts of the British Isles, from which it alone benefited. John Le Patourel's study *The Norman Empire* (1976) was a successful attempt to avoid a narrowing concentration upon Norman England by examining the impact of the Norman Conquest within the British Isles as a whole. Hugh Trevor-Roper's fine essay 'The Unity of the Kingdom' (though open to criticism for its use of 'race' as a historical concept) stood out from other contributions within a collection entitled *The English World* (1982) by its willingness to move beyond a merely English perspective. Finally, John Pocock in his powerful article 'The Limits and Divisions of British History: In Search of an Unknown Subject' (*American Historical Review*, April 1982) attempted to define a field of study that might properly be called 'British History'. Pocock emphasised the political aspects of 'British Isles' history in an essay, which, though brief, ranged widely in time and space.

My own efforts to deal with the problems raised by 'national' histories have led me to see what I have called the 'Britannic melting pot' in terms of a complex of interacting cultures. 'Culture' is an amorphous concept but it has the advantage of enabling the historian to raise questions about life-style, customs, religion and attitudes to the past in a more fluid way than if confined to a one-dimensional framework. Cultures change over time, are influenced by other cultures, cross national boundaries and often contain sub-cultures within themselves. 'Nation', in contrast, is a term of rhetoric used to evoke feelings of unity in response to a particular situation. When Churchill spoke of 'Britain's finest hour' or De Valera referred to the struggle of a small nation for its independence over seven centuries, they were attempting to sway the emotions of their audiences, not to expound a detached piece of history. It is very doubtful whether the term 'nation' can escape these emotional overtones. One sees this most clearly perhaps in the case of post-colonial Africa where the use of 'nation' all too often conceals the true realities of tribal cultures. From this point of view, it is an accident of history that several states (nations?) eventually made their appearance in the context of British Isles history. The realities with which the historian should deal are the cultures which lay behind the label nation/state. The concept of 'nation' stresses the differences between a particular society and its neighbours. A Britannic approach, in contrast, would emphasise how much these cultures have experienced in common.

With this in mind there is still a good deal to be said for approaching the history of the British Isles during the immediate post-Roman centuries along traditional lines, as a conflict for supremacy between 'Celts' and 'Anglo-Saxons'. It should be made clear, however, that these terms do not refer to distinct 'races' but to broad linguistic and cultural differences. The Celtic and Germanic languages are both Indo-European. Both sets of peoples came from central Europe. In their tribal organisation they closely resembled one another. There is nothing to be gained by using the outmoded nineteenth-century concept of 'race'. We should do better to see the British Isles from the fifth century onwards as an arena in which several Celtic cultures and several Germanic cultures competed with each other. In Ireland there were differences between north and south, in Scotland between 'Irish' and 'British'. Among the Anglo-Saxons, similar contrasts long existed between Northumbria and Mercia and Wessex, as well as within each kingdom. What is clear about the immediate post-Roman centuries is that some 'Britannic' framework is necessary to do justice to a situation in which the Briton (and Celtic-speaking) Saint Patrick brought Christianity to Ireland (most probably the northern areas of it) during the fifth century and Irish monks in turn became missionaries to the inhabitants of 'Scotland' and north Britain. Historians of art devised the term 'Hiberno-Saxon' (now largely replaced by 'insular') to create a broader framework than traditional national categories. It is time for historians at large to follow their example and to break way from the concept of 'nation' which they inherited from nineteenth-century historiography, and which is too rigid to use when dealing with the complexities of the post-Roman centuries.

The same judgment may be made with equal force about the three 'Scandinavian centuries', from the ninth to the eleventh, when large areas of the British Isles fell under the control of first raiders and then settlers from Denmark and Norway. Modern historians play down the importance of this period but it is clear that the cultures of the British Isles underwent profound changes during these years. After this common experience, 'England', 'Ireland', 'Scotland' and 'Wales' all emerged as very different societies in the second half of the eleventh century from what they had been earlier. Marc Bloch saw this as the first phase of feudalism, but whatever term is used the old structures of the 'Celtic' and 'Anglo-Saxon' worlds undoubtedly underwent radical changes. Were it not for the clumsiness of phraseology, terms such as 'Anglo-Scandinavia', 'Hiberno-Scandinavia' and 'Scoto-Scandinavia' might be appropriate.

A new period began with the coming of the Normans (in the mid-eleventh century so far as 'England' and 'Wales' were concerned; in the twelfth century, in the case of 'Scotland' and 'Ireland'). The British Isles were drawn away from Scandinavia and into closer contact with northern France as a consequence, though it was not until the mid-fourteenth century (perhaps later) that the links of northern 'Scotland' with Norway were finally severed. Continental-style feudalism now took root marked by self-conscious knightly institutions, and a greater emphasis upon links with the Crown. In the Church, the authority of the hierarchy became more pronounced. Although 'Normanised Scotland' established its independence within this Britannic framework during the fourteenth century a Britannic approach is still necessary if attitudes and assumptions then are to be understood.

During the early sixteenth century, further profound changes took place within the British Isles deriving largely from continental influences. Reformation and Counter-Reformation were the common experience of all the societies of the Britannic melting pot. Though European in origin these movements became closely connected with the expansion of the influence of the English Crown, throughout the British Isles. The creation of a Protestant English empire was one of the main features of Britannic history during this period, leading to the extension of the influence of a biblically orientated culture throughout the British Isles, and the coast of North America. In due course, Scotland was also to be associated with the enterprise when, after the Union of the Crowns in 1603, Scottish and English settlers took part in the plantation of Ulster. The effects of this proved to be of lasting significance not merely within the British Isles but also in British possessions overseas. In Canada and Australia the conflict of the 'Orange' and the 'Green', like so much else, requires a Britannic framework for its elucidation.

With the Industrial Revolution of the eighteenth and nineteenth centuries, a further series of major shifts took place within the British Isles. A new industrialised and urbanised culture took root in northern England. Large-scale movements of population took place in response to the opportunities offered by an expanding industrial society. In addition to migrants from local areas, English emigrants were drawn into south Wales and Ulster, Scottish Highlanders and Irish into Glasgow and its environs, Irish and Welsh into the Liverpool area. The major cities of the British Isles became multi-ethnic societies in which varied ethnic groupings competed for economic security, social status and political influence. During the closing decades of the nineteenth century, the diversity of this multi-ethnic society was still further increased by an influx of Jewish refugees from eastern Europe into London, Leeds, Manchester and Glasgow. Emigrants also arrived from other areas including Spain and Lithuania. The name of Wolfson College, Oxford, commemorates the success of one of these newcomers. It was not an isolated case.

It was during these years of industrialisation at home that a new British empire was created overseas in Canada, Australia and New Zealand. Though they formed part of the 'history of the English-speaking peoples' (to use Churchill's phrase), these emigrants were by no means all English. The new empire was 'Britannic', drawing for its population upon Scottish, Irish and Welsh as well as English. In due course, after the Second World War, the former colonies became even more multi-ethnic as a result of the arrival of a new wave of immigrants from Europe.

A paradoxical and quite unexpected turn to the imperial story was to occur after 1945 with the arrival in Britain of large numbers of immigrants from the West Indies, India, Pakistan and parts of Africa, at a time when the former Indian empire and the former colonial empire were ceasing to exist. The full significance of this wave of immigration has yet to be fully assessed. In the 1980s cultural tensions between the various immigrant groups led to serious outbreaks of rioting. It may be, however, that the creation of a multi-ethnic society in some parts of Britain is merely one of the ways in which the various societies within the British Isles are coming to resemble the United States. The partial Americanisation of popular culture within the British Isles had begun in the 1930s with the influence of American films. Since then other aspects of American culture have also taken root on both sides of the Irish Sea. Future historians may come to see this as a more important development than entry into the European Economic Community (1973).

It remains to mention the changes which have taken place in the twentieth century in the wake of two world wars. In the years immediately after the end of the First World War, the United Kingdom felt the impact of a successful nationalist revolution. The result of the conflict was the creation of an independent state in southern Ireland, leaving the remaining six counties of the north-east as a semi-autonomous 'province' within the United Kingdom. There was now a political border within the British Isles for the first time since the seventeenth century.

One of the consequences of the creation of an Irish Free State and later (1949) of the Republic of Ireland was the partial elimination of Ireland from historical interpretations of British history. It was almost as if British historians had come to believe that it was possible to write a history of their own 'nations' without mentioning the Irish Republic or the historical territory which it occupied. In the case of the *Oxford Illustrated History of Britain* this tendency had the unfortunate effect of a map being printed in which Northern Ireland appears in some detail while the rest of Ireland remains a blank even though the period under discussion is well before the partition of 1920. The same criticism of course may be made of Irish histories in which Ireland appears in isolation and not as an island linked historically with Britain for well over a thousand years.

In fact, of course, close economic and cultural ties continued to exist between the United Kingdom and the Irish Free State. Informal cultural ties did not disappear. Universities in the Republic drew, as before, upon the United Kingdom for external examiners. Dublin civil servants in the Department of Finance remained in touch with their London counterparts. Links were not as close as they had once been but they were nonetheless real. During the 1950s and 1980s Irish immigration took place into England on a scale unequalled since the 1880s. During the 1960s, as 'Eire' emerged from its self-imposed isolation under De Valera, contacts increased still further. During the 1970s, both states joined the European Economic Community. They were also drawn into close communication as a result of the continued crisis over Northern Ireland. In spite of themselves, the two governments were forced to recognise the existence of a 'Britannic' dimension.

The viewpoint adopted in this book is that the histories of what are normally regarded as four distinct 'nations' appear more intelligible if they are seen first within a general British Isles context and secondly if they are seen in terms of 'cultures' and 'sub-cultures'. Upon closer examination what seem to be 'national' units dissolve into a number of distinctive cultures with their own perceptions of the past, of social status ('class' is here seen as subordinate to culture), of religion and of many other aspects of life. As with any historical approach, however, the problem is complicated by the inevitability of historical change. Cultures change and interact over time. Where nationally minded historians tend to stress a continuity over time between, say, the 'Scots' or the 'Irish' of different periods, a cultural approach involves the recognition that the perceptions of one period are radically different from those of another.

At the present moment (1988) it may be argued that at least eight cultures co-exist in the British Isles. In Wales, the gulf between the Welsh-speaking, Calvinist Methodist north-west and the more cosmopolitan, English-speaking south indicate the drawbacks of speaking in terms of a single Welsh nationality. The Welsh-Jewish poet Danny Abse is best seen as a product of Cardiff rather than of 'Wales' as such. The Welsh nationalist, Saunders Lewis, reacted against the environment of his Merseyside birthplace to become the spokesman of the Welsh heartland. In Scotland, the situation is even more complex. Here the south-west, centred on the Clydeside conurbation, may be seen as a culture in its own right. The western Highlands and the Hebrides constitute a sub-culture, as do Orkney and Shetland. However, the exploitation of North Sea oil since the 1970s has clearly been a source of profound cultural change in both of these areas as well as on the east coast. By 1985 what had seemed like a clear contrast between east and west had begun to dissolve into new cultural patterns. Finally, in England, the decline of the industrial north and the growing prosperity of the south, linked to the E.E.C. markets, has accentuated the cultural differences between these two areas. Overall, the influence of London and the south-east seems to have increased more than ever, thanks to such factors as television, motorways, the growth of the London market and the influence of the E.E.C. Towns such as Brighton, Bath and Cambridge, 50 or more miles from London, have become part of a southern commuter-belt in which people live while working in London. There is thus a good deal to be said for regarding the United Kingdom in the twentieth century as consisting of a dominant metropolitan culture (itself exposed to transatlantic influences) and a number of provincial sub-cultures.

Where do the cultures of Ireland stand in all this? Protestant culture in Northern Ireland seems more closely linked to Glasgow and to Dublin than it is to London (though clearly the influence of a London-appointed Secretary of State cannot be discounted). As for the rest of Ireland, cultural influences deriving from southern England and from the United States contend for supremacy. Tourism, the common law, English newspapers, English T.V., English-language books, contact with recent Irish emigrants to London and Birmingham and a growing involvement with the affairs of Northern Ireland all combine to make the Republic if not a sub-culture of the English south-east at least one heavily exposed to English influences. This is particularly true for the years after the 1960s when a long period of self-imposed cultural isolation came to an end.

Outside the British Isles the direct influence of the English south-east seems to have waned. In Australia, films such as *Breaker Morant* and *Gallipoli* illustrate a growing Australian nationalism. In both Australia and Canada, a large influx of European immigrants after 1945 has also helped to weaken cultural connections with Britain, a tendency accentuated in Canada by its proximity to the United States and by the growth of French-speaking nationalism in Quebec. In South Africa, the English-speaking culture of Cape Town province and Natal has been largely overshadowed by Afrikaner culture. Even in New Zealand strong emotional links with Britain have begun to weaken in the 1980s. By the 1970s throughout the former British empire, in India, Pakistan, Africa and the Far East, it seemed as if British Isles culture would be mediated through the United States. Within the British Isles itself, American influence in the form of a military presence, fast-food chains, T.V. programmes and films continued to grow. To an observer at the end of the twentieth century it might well seem that the various cultures of the British Isles would be submerged in a vast transatlantic cultural aggregation. In such a situation, the 'national' categories of the nineteenth century appear to be of ever-diminishing value to the historian.

1

The Celtic societies of the British Isles

John of Gaunt in Shakespeare's *Richard II* speaks of

> this scepter'd isle ...
> This precious stone set in a silver sea ...
> This blessed plot, this earth, this realm, this England ...

These powerful lines may be seen as representing the unspoken assumption of so many historians that 'England' is for all intents and purposes an island. It is, of course, merely part, though now the most populated part, of the larger island of an Atlantic archipelago situated off the coast of north-west Europe. Shakespeare's poetry, however, may be taken as reflecting the almost total dominance which English culture, more properly perhaps the culture of south-eastern England, has achieved throughout the British Isles in the modern period. The typical inhabitant of the British Isles is today English-speaking (though a minority may speak Gaelic, or Urdu, at home).

The dominance of English culture marks the culmination of a complex and prolonged process, which is far from complete even today. As a historical starting point, however, it must be set on one side. For the purpose of 'making sense' of the history of the British Isles, we must go beyond the Anglo-Saxons and the Romans to the Celtic Iron Age, which left a lasting stamp upon the languages, place-names and cultures of these islands.

A full prehistory would need to go much further back, possibly to 250,000 B.C. A more limited approach might well begin with the mesolithic period of c. 7000 B.C. when human beings returned to the British Isles in the wake of a retreating Ice Age before land bridges between the islands and between Britain and the continent were finally washed away. This period – of hunting, fishing and food gathering – was followed (c. 4000 B.C.) by the introduction of agriculture and the establishment of settled communities by migrants from the Mediterranean. This was the so-called Neolithic Revolution. Megalithic tombs erected during this period indicate the high priority which these societies accorded to the after life. It has been suggested that the building of Stonehenge (begun c. 2500 B.C. but extending over a prolonged period of several hundred years) required 30 million man-hours to complete. (The long barrows of the early neolithic period needed a mere 10,000 man-hours.) The Irish passage-graves, built at much the same time as Stonehenge, suggest the allocation of resources on the same scale, possibly under the dictates of a theocratic priestly class. For much of this period it is clear that the Irish Sea served not as a barrier but as an avenue linking related societies. Passage-graves, such as Bryn Celli Du, on the Isle of Anglesey, are markedly similar to those found on the east coast of Ireland in the Boyne valley and Lough Crew.

During the Bronze Age (of roughly the second millennium B.C.) similar Britannic patterns may be discerned. The introduction of metal-working in bronze led to the creation of economic conditions in which trade across the Irish Sea in Irish copper and Cornish tin (the metals required for the production of bronze) took place on a regular basis. The Middle Bronze Age saw the creation of an axe industry which one archaeologist has described as 'neither English nor Irish but Britannico-Hibernian'. In the Late Bronze Age tools and ornaments from the British Isles reached a wide European market.

In many ways, the coming of the Iron Age may have represented an economic setback. During the first millennium B.C., from c. 750, the Bronze Age communities of the British Isles faced the challenge of a more efficient and cheaper technology based upon iron. Widespread changes took place, though it is not clear how far they were due to invasion and how far to adaptation by native communities. The spread of massive hill-forts in southern Britain, for example, suggests the growth of larger political units based upon the dominance of a military aristocracy. Until recently, an 'invasion' hypothesis, distinguishing between three periods from Age A, B and C, each marked by a different group of invaders, held the field. Since the 1960s, greater emphasis has been placed upon the response made by indigenous elements, though the influence of some groups of newcomers on the east coast and in the south-east must be allowed for. Whatever the explanation, there is no doubt that the communities with which the Romans came into contact in the first century B.C. were Celtic-speaking, iron-using societies organised on a tribal pattern.

Place-names may be seen as illustrating a common Britannic cultural framework during the pre-Roman period. The place-name 'Brent' associated today with the London suburbs of Brent and Brentford is linked with the river 'Braint' in Anglesey and with northern British tribal groups, known as the Brigantes. The name of the Brigantes is paralleled in Europe in such place-names as Bregenz and Brienne. It is also associated with the goddess Brigantia in Britain and with the Irish goddess Brigid, 'the exalted one', who was patron of poetry, healing and metalwork. In due course, Brigid the goddess was to be transformed into St Brigid. The parallels provided by Brigantia, Brent and Brigid clearly point to the existence of common cultural links throughout the British Isles, not merely in a 'Celtic fringe'.

In addition, the art and language of these societies indicate that they shared a common culture with the Celts of continental Europe, groups of whom crossed the Alps and sacked Rome in 390 B.C. The Celts did not form a race, any more than the 'English-speaking peoples' constitute a race today. Nineteenth-century historians may have looked upon the Celts as a race with distinct physical features but there is no sound basis for this view. When discussing the Iron Age societies of the British Isles during the first century B.C. the most we can say is that they spoke one or other of the dialects of a common Celtic language, that their religious beliefs show a common pattern associated with such attitudes as a reverence for rivers and wells and the cult of the severed head, that their social ideals tended to be those of a military aristocracy (though not all the societies of the British Isles were equally military in their outlook) and their art, at this date (c. 100 B.C.), was heavily influenced by the free-flowing 'La Tène' style.

Cult-objects provide a source of evidence for such links. As Anne Ross has shown in her book *Pagan Celtic Britain* (1967) similar types of ritual-artefact are to be found throughout the British Isles. The head was the Celtic symbol par excellence. The Celts seem to have regarded the human head with particular reverence as the seat of the human spirit. It is not surprising, then, that carvings of heads should be found in northern and southern Britain as well as in Ireland. The most famous Celtic head is the Medusa mask in the Roman baths in Bath. Other striking examples are to be found in Ireland. There is little doubt that the cult of the head was widespread throughout the British Isles. In modern times, it has survived at St Winifred's Well (Holywell, north Wales) where a healing spring is said to have appeared after St Winifred was beheaded. Second only to the cult of the head was the devotion paid to the horned fertility god Cernunnos, who was the 'horned god' of the Brigantes. Horned heads from Gloucestershire, Cumberland, Kent, Norfolk and Ireland all testify to the widespread character of this cult. Sword-hilts using the head as a main motif are a further source of evidence.

The most lasting evidence of this cultural affinity is language. Celtic languages still survive in Wales, the western part of Ireland and Scotland, the Isle of Man and Brittany (colonised from the Celtic south-west of Britain under pressure from Anglo-Saxon invaders). These languages are now largely in retreat. To the historian, however, they provide an invaluable reminder of the period when Celtic languages were spoken throughout the British Isles. Before the mid-nineteenth century, and the onset of literacy in English throughout Ireland, Wales and Scotland, the Celtic-speaking section of the population was far more numerous than is the case today. It is ironical that the average student of British history is more likely to have an acquaintance with Latin than to have the faintest glimmering of any Celtic language. The survival of such river-names in southern England as 'Ouse' (from *uisce*, water) and 'Avon' (from *afon*, river) is a reminder, as valid in its own way as more physical evidence, of the earlier presence of Celtic-speaking societies in what became Anglo-Saxon England. Hill-forts such as Ditchling Beacon on the Sussex Downs and Maiden Castle in Dorset, which now bear English names, owe their existence to this Celtic phase in Britannic history.

Finally, there is the evidence of art. The influence of the La Tène style, so widespread throughout the Celtic world, was also powerful throughout the British Isles. It is to be seen in such objects as the Torrs pony-cap (Kirkcudbright), the Turoe Stone (Co. Galway) and the Battersea Shield. Gold torcs, thought to have been worn by chiefs, were to be found in both Britain and Ireland at this time. The La Tène style, though more varied in its local manifestation than might appear at first sight, testifies to the influence of a common Celtic culture throughout the British Isles.

To draw attention to this fact is not to say that there was political and social uniformity throughout the area. The existence of tribal groupings in both Britain and Ireland is an indication of political differences at the local level. The Romans, to whom we are indebted for Latin versions of tribal names in the absence of their original Celtic forms, distinguished over twenty tribes in Britain south of the Forth. In Ireland, where political aggregation had not gone as far as it had elsewhere, the number of tribes seems to have been much larger.

The most powerful cause of variety was geography, in particular the contrast between Highland and Lowland Zones. It was Sir Cyril Fox who argued in his book *The Personality of Britain* (1932) that the Lowlands would usually be exposed to forces of change before the Highlands. The Highland/Lowland contrast certainly makes good sense when applied to Britain, where north and west form a distinctive geographical area, including a good deal of land over 400 metres above sea-level. Poorer soil and climatic conditions made agriculture more of a challenge in the Highland Zone than it was in the south and east. In a British Isles context, however, the Highland/Lowland contrast is not quite so clear. Ireland, which has been compared to a saucer in which the rim represents the hills and the flat base the central plain, is not, geologically speaking, a Highland Zone. At this particular period, however, it may be seen as forming part of a 'cultural Highland Zone', cut off, for better or worse, from the influence of the rising military power of Rome.

Geographical determinism should not be pressed too far, however. It can also be argued that, under certain conditions, the Irish Sea provided a channel of communication linking the Highland Zone with Armorica, Spain and the Mediterranean. This seems to have been what happened during the neolithic period and the Bronze Age. It also seems to have been the case during the fifth and sixth centuries A.D. when Christian communities on both sides of the Irish Sea retained their links with Christian Europe at a time when the eastern half of Britain was being overrun by Germanic settlers. The Irish presence in Scotland in the sixth century A.D. and in parts of Wales illustrates the same point. (Scottish Gaelic and Irish Gaelic are in origin the same language.) The name of the Lleyn peninsula in north Wales links it with Leinster.

For the immediate pre-Roman period, Fox's contrast between a Lowland Zone exposed to innovation and a conservative Highland Zone (including Ireland) provides a good key to the situation. Caesar wrote of the coming of the Belgae to south-east Britain during the first century B.C. The archaeological evidence, now more plentiful thanks to recent excavations, supports the view that the Thames estuary and the territories around it were the centre of an innovative Belgic culture, sometimes termed the Aylesford-Swayling culture from key sites associated with it. The newcomers soon began to expand at the expense of their neighbours until by the early first century their influence had reached as far north as the Trent and as far west as the Severn.

The Belgic kingdoms involved in this expansion were the Trinovantes and the Catuvellauni (to use their Roman names) with their capitals at Verulamium (the modern St Albans) and Camulodunum (the modern Colchester). To the north, the outlying tribes affected were the Iceni and the Coritani, in what are today's Norfolk and Lincolnshire respectively, and to the west the Dobunni in the Cotswolds. The Atrebates to the south lost a good deal of territory to the newcomers and were soon confined to the narrow coastal strip of modern Sussex. It is not surprising that these four tribes seem to have welcomed the coming of the Romans as a lesser evil. The limit of Belgic expansion to the south-west was the tribal territory of the Durotriges centred on today's Dorset. Here the refortification of such hill-forts as Maiden Castle took place in the first century B.C., presumbly as a defensive measure against the Belgae. The forts were still in active use when the Romans arrived in A.D. 43 and formed the basis of temporary resistance to the legions of Claudius.

Another contrast between the Highland and Lowland Zones was almost certainly demographic. No firm statistical evidence exists but several strong indicators suggest that there was a considerable increase of population in the Lowlands from the fifth century onwards, well before the Belgic invasions. A good deal of internal colonisation seems to have taken place during this period. Regularly shaped field systems existed in the areas surrounding hill-forts which suggests that organised schemes of land clearance were being carried out. The thrust of agriculture lay in the direction of improved tillage, presumably in response to the needs of a growing population, though perhaps also with a market in view. Sheep farming also seems to have been practised on a large scale with the aim of providing the manure necessary for newly cleared land. Crops too became more diversified. Demographic growth may have led to land-hunger and to competition over rights to land. If this were the case, it would provide a plausible explanation for the building of hill-forts as the central points of larger political units. Such hill-forts were in effect urban centres with substantial populations. Thus it has been estimated that Hod Hill, Dorset, had nearly 300 houses within its fortifications and a population of 500–1,000. In the territory of the Atrebates, Calleva (on the site of the later Roman town of Silchester) and Venta (later Winchester) were all substantial urban centres. Clearly even before the coming of the Belgae the Lowlands of the Iron Age were undergoing change.

During the first century B.C. the most striking developments occurred in the Thames valley and its environs. Here there was a shift away from an earlier concern with settlement on hill-top sites, such as those at Wheathampstead (Herts) and Bigbury (Kent) towards larger urban units on the plains of which Verulamium, Camulodunum and Durovernum Cantiacorum (Canterbury) were the most important. This was more than a geographical decision. These towns were in effect the capitals of powerful new kingdoms, controlling a wider area than the traditional tribal organisation. Though the details are not clear it would seem that the Trinovantes and the Catuvellauni formed a confederacy under a single king, Cunobelinus (the Cymbeline of Shakespeare). The Romans were able to make good use of the resentment which this monarchy aroused, to make alliances with the southern Atrebates, the Cantiaci (of Kent), the Iceni and the Dobunni, when they invaded Britain after Cunobelinus' death (he died in A.D. 41).

Other signs testify to the importance of the changes which were taking place in the south-east at this time. Perhaps the most important of these was the widespread use of coins. The survival of coins in quantity indicates the existence of a cash market and a certain level of numeracy and literacy, at least among some segments of the population. Coins bearing the image of the king bear witness to settled political conditions. All the signs are that the societies of the south-east were developing economic ties with Rome. Indirect Romanisation had already begun.

In sharp contrast with all this, the political organisation of the Highland Zone (including Ireland) remained very much at a local level. Hill-forts in this area were both smaller and fewer in number, less than a hundred as against the several hundreds of south-east England. The characteristic unit of the area seems to have been the enclosed family homestead, the so-called ringfort. In Ireland and elsewhere in the Highland Zone, 30,000 of these ringforts have survived, and their existence, together with the relative absence of hill-forts, suggests that it was possible, as a consequence perhaps of a relatively static population, for small-scale political units to enjoy substantial independence. Warfare was probably a local affair. Tribal kingdoms existed (Irish *tuatha*) but the powers of the kings were limited. The large number of kingdoms, compared with the Lowland Zone, also suggests that they were small in size. The complete absence of coinage and of urban concentrations is another pointer in the same direction. What appear to be at first sight large hill-forts at Tara, Emain Macha and Dun Ailinne turn out on closer inspection to be ritual sites, built during the Bronze Age and later probably used for annual assemblies.

There can be little doubt that this broad social and economic contrast between Lowland and Highland Zones was also reflected in culture. An obvious next step, therefore, would be to consider the extent to which such matters as law, religion and general problems of 'meaning and value' differed between one Zone and another. The question, however, is easier to ask than to answer, at least for the Lowland Zone. The Roman Conquest, later to be followed by large-scale Anglo-Saxon colonisation, obliterated almost all traces of Celtic cultures in the south and east of England. In contrast, a great deal survived for Ireland. Thus we are in the paradoxical position of knowing more about the 'traditional' era of the Celtic world than about its 'modernising' sector.

Our knowledge of early Irish society derives largely from the evidence of the Brehon Laws first committed to writing in the sixth or seventh century A.D. but undoubtedly, thanks to the conservatism of the jurists, casting light upon some social assumptions of pre-Christian times. Professor Binchy, the editor of the laws, has characterised this society as 'tribal, rural, hierarchical and familiar'. Hence, it may be seen as contrasting with the monarchical and urbanised societies of the Lowland Zone.

Within the context of the British Isles, the relatively traditional character of Celtic societies in Ireland is suggested by several features. They were, in the first place, oral cultures. The localised and static character of these societies is also implied in the importance which was attached to kinship. Power and prestige rested with the kinship group, *derbfine* (*fine* being the term for family). This did not mean that ownership of land was communal. It seems clear that the actual cultivation and ownership of the land rested with individual nuclear families.

The localised character of these societies suggests that a sense of national identity was lacking. Hence the use of the word 'Irish' in reference to this period, though convenient, may be misleading. (The same difficulty will appear later in references to Anglo-Saxon England.) The largest political unit at this period was the tribe (*tuath*) under its king (*rí*). The earliest political terms refer to tribal units, e.g. the Ciarraige (the people of Kerry) or the Muscraige (the people of Muskerry). There were tribal kings with limited powers, but in general the structure of these societies was aristocratic rather than monarchical.

Within the individual kinship groups there was, no doubt, a rough and ready equality, tempered by deference to age and seniority. But kinship groups themselves were not equal. The laws indicate the existence of different grades or *gráda* (perhaps 'castes' might be a more appropriate term) each with its own standard of compensation in the case of injury. The basis for differentiation was the assumption that priestly and warrior kinship groups were superior to the farming groups. By this time, a 'middle class' of smiths and leeches (medicine men) had managed to infiltrate into the social hierarchy, their claim being legitimised on the basis of the craft having allegedly been founded by a particular god.

Aristocratic assumptions may also be seen in the prestige associated with the owning of cattle. It is often, and wrongly, assumed that Irish society rested upon cattle raising to the exclusion of arable farming. There is no doubt that arable farming was practised, but the evidence of the laws and other sources indicates that cattle raising was regarded as a superior form of social activity. Wealth was reckoned in herds of cattle, not acreage. Cattle raids were seen as an appropriate activity for the young nobility of a kingdom. In quasi-feudal arrangements which developed between wealthy patrons and needy clients, grants of 'fiefs' involved cattle not land. The unit of exchange in society was the *sét*, a unit estimated as being equivalent to one heifer. The ritual division of the year into two halves derived from the regular movement of cattle to winter and summer pasture. Bull symbolism also plays a large part in the Ulster epic *Táin Bó Cuailgne*. All these details suggest the cultural dominance of a cattle-raising aristocracy which relegated arable farming to lower social status.

These societies were not localised in any absolute sense. At the level of the elite groups of druids and warriors there seems to have been a common culture. It is easy to overstress the importance of this, however. Most of the gods and goddesses of Ireland were extremely localised personages with a local clientele, as the early Christian saints were to be several centuries later. Trade was confined to annual fairs within each kingdom. The pattern of settlement, based as it was upon isolated 'ring-forts' rather than nucleated settlements, also indicates heavily localised societies. Behind the apparent unity of the Brehon Laws Professor Binchy has detected the existence of local codes. In the fourth century A.D. a considerable degree of political change occurred leading to the formation of several large kingdoms. During this earlier, pre-fourth-century period, however, there seems little doubt that small-scale societies were typical of Ireland, and of the Highland Zone generally.

There was, however, some social change. Kinship groups may have been the norm but the rise of relationships based upon clientage shows that some form of feudal relationship might exist between individuals. Thanks to the researches of Professor Binchy, it is possible also to discern a shift from earlier legal assumptions involving the sanction of taboos to a social world in which the law was enforced by kinship groups or by a powerful patron or king. The earliest level of thinking survived in such practices as *troscad* in which litigants fasted, possibly unto death, in order to bring pressure to bear upon the offending party. Such fasting was probably regarded as a magico-religious activity, capable of transferring the physical suffering of the faster to the person being 'fasted against'. By a later period *troscad* seems to have become largely obsolete as a legal remedy though it was still apparently an option open to the weak and powerless who lacked the backing of patrons or kin. If what we have said about the localised character of these societies is correct, it may also be expected that, within Ireland itself, some areas would be more traditional than others, the practice of *troscad* being a case in point.

The only other substantial body of 'Celtic' law about which something is known derives from the area now known as 'Wales', though there were presumably analogous legal systems operating throughout the rest of the British Isles. Welsh 'tribal' societies came into the direct contact with Rome and there are good reasons for thinking that the legal practice of south Wales, within the orbit of the Roman military base at Caerleon (near Newport, Gwent) was influenced by Roman codes. Elsewhere in Wales pre-Roman social structures seem to have survived to influence assumptions about land-holding. In Welsh local cultures, as in Ireland, specific tracts of land were regarded as belonging to aristocratic kinship groups and hence inalienable by individuals. These assumptions prevailed into the sixteenth century and beyond. Welsh society in the pre-Roman period as later was heavily pastoral and like Ireland, organised around a transhumance pattern of summer and winter grazing. Elsewhere in the Highland Zone we may assume the existence of an 'Irish-Welsh' style of social structure reflected in law, religion and general culture.

It is regrettable that no equivalent sources of evidence exist for the Lowland Zone.

Even for tribal names we have only Latinised equivalents. Had such sources survived we might expect them to reflect in some way the central position occupied by agriculture, the growing importance of trade and the extensive power enjoyed by such kings as Cunobelinus. Warfare, the consequence of invasion as well as of competition for land, was probably more prominent in Lowland culture. All this is a matter for speculation. What seems certain is that the 'Celtic' social arrangements revealed by the medieval Irish and Welsh evidence was more traditional in character than the equally 'Celtic' societies of south and eastern Britain.

The British Isles, on the eve of the Roman invasions, thus present a broad contrast between the urbanised, monarchical societies of the south and east and the rural, tribal and aristocratic societies of Highland Britain and Ireland. For Lowland Britain, the Roman invasion was the latest in a series which had subjected that area to violent change over several centuries. Even before the Romans arrived, the political ambitions of individual kingdoms had led to shifts in the balance of power in the south-east. For some hard-pressed groups, such as the Regni (of what is now west Sussex), the Romans were almost certainly a lesser evil. Perhaps they anticipated that the invasion of Claudius in A.D. 43 would be similar to those made by Julius Caesar in 55 and 54 B.C., raids in force leaving Rome's allies in possession of the field. If so, they were wrong. On this occasion the Romans arrived with the intention of staying permanently. So powerful was their impact that it is only by a great effort of the imagination that we see the need to go beyond the lasting monuments of Roman rule to the scattered relics of the Celtic societies which everywhere in Britain preceded it.

2

The impact of Rome on the British Isles

The tribal societies of southern Britain, already in direct contact with Rome, would have found it difficult to avoid being drawn into a system of 'informal imperialism'. The social and economic consequences of this can only be guessed at, but clearly the expansion of trade and cash-crops together with the spread of literacy would have led to changes in social structure, modifying without necessarily destroying traditional institutions. 'Modernisation', as we have seen, was in some respects well under way. In the event, however, the Romans decided upon a course of conquest and colonisation, which led to the total destruction of the Celtic societies of the south.

What was the overall effect of this upon the British Isles? The North Sea province underwent a social and cultural revolution. South of a line between Lincoln and Lyme Bay, the various Celtic kingdoms lost their independence and were incorporated within an imperial administrative framework. British Celtic language, religion, law and social institutions totally lost their elite status and henceforth were to bear the stigmas of the conquered. The southern Lowlands forming a military province were the most Romanised section of Britain. North and west, a military zone existed over which the policy of Rome was to exercise military control rather than to administer as a civil province.

English historians of the Roman Conquest have seen it, on the whole, through the eyes of the victors, an understandable attitude in a society with its own strong imperial traditions. From the Renaissance onwards, indeed, the Roman model has been looked upon as one which the English should copy. Not surprisingly, English accounts of Roman Britain, even the most recent, give the Romans the benefit of the doubt. We are assured, for example, that the Romans brought 'firm government' (S. S. Frere, *Britannia* (1967), p. 370). They are seen as having 'put Britain on her feet once more and restored her self respect' (p. 111) and inaugurating 'a new era in the province with far reaching advances both in the military sphere and in that of cultural development' (p. 115). We are told that 'the early third century was a period of social advance and that the settlement of Roman veterans near Hadrian's Wall resulted in a much greater community of sentiment between

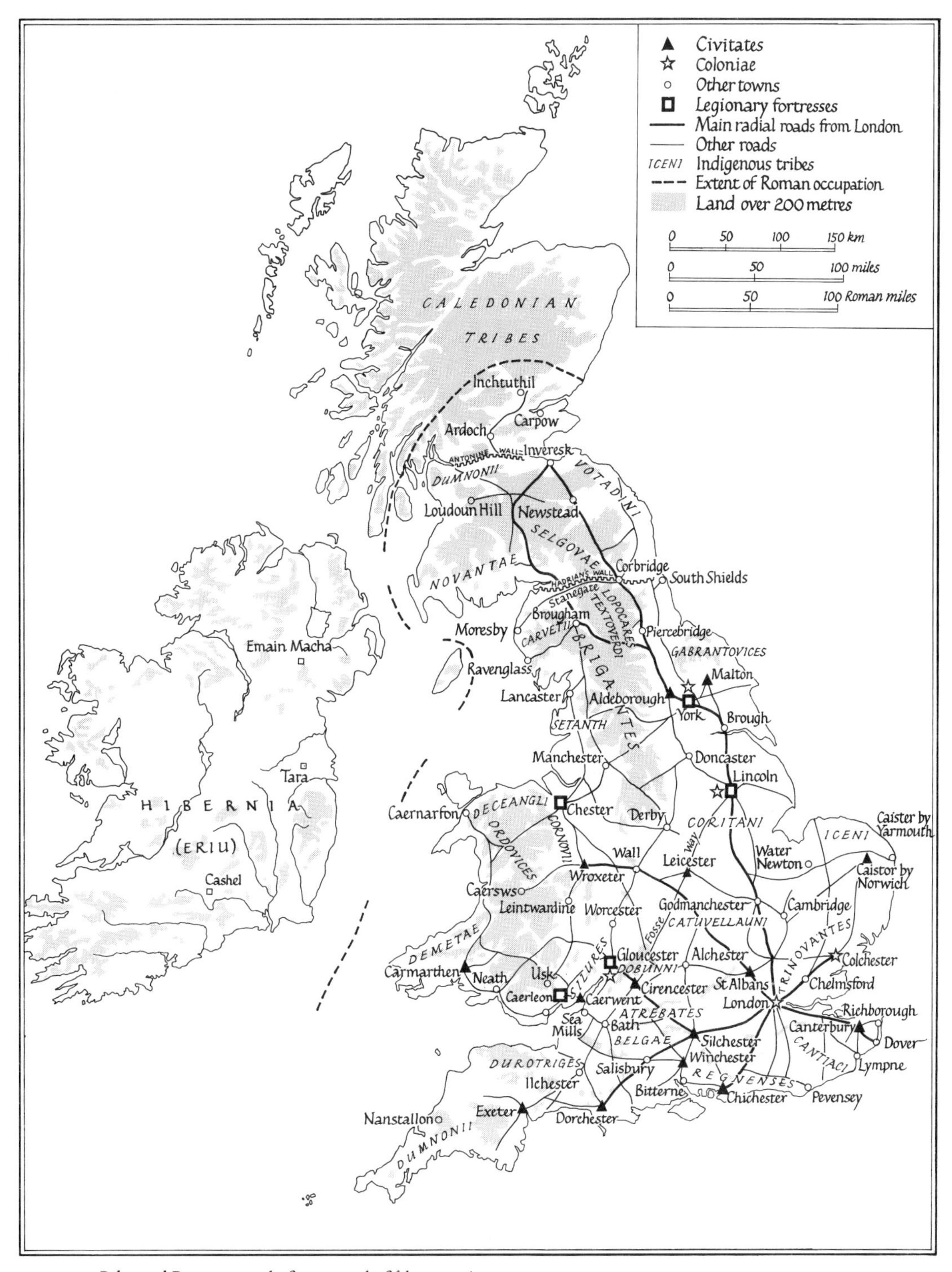

MAP I Celts and Romans, early first to early fifth centuries A.D.

Source: after Christopher Haigh, ed., *The Cambridge Historical Encyclopedia of Great Britain and Ireland* (Cambridge, 1985), p. 11.

the garrisons and the local tribesmen' (p. 214). In the more recent Oxford History (P. Salway, *Roman Britain* (1981)), similar judgments are made. Rome, it is said, imposed relative peace by preventing inter-communal warfare. 'The very presence of a large army and civil establishment and other attractions which the new society held for local leaders cannot have left the humblest family untouched' (p. 236). The Romans, another scholar tells us, aimed to unite Britain with an economy and a culture superior to anything previously known there. For the first time the whole country was united under one government, made possible by a splendid road system. The Roman Conquest is seen as creating a new situation tending to peace and order which greatly stimulated rural development.

The problem with such judgments is that they tell the story from the viewpoint of the coloniser. There were, clearly, other interpretations of events, even though we may never discover them. The work of E. M. Forster or Joseph Conrad (or even in the late twentieth century of Thomas Keneally in his sensitive study of the Australian aborigines *The Chant of Jimmy Blacksmith*) is enough to justify the placing of a question-mark against one-dimensional accounts of the Roman Conquest of Britain. What is clear about the Roman invasion of Britain is that it imposed one culture upon another. What is unclear is the extent to which the colonised inhabitants themselves came to welcome this as 'modernisation'; and how far we ourselves are entitled to make the judgment that the Conquest was 'all for the best'. The overwhelming weight of the evidence, in the shape of inscriptions, pottery and buildings predisposes us to make a judgment in favour of the Romans. On the other hand, the survival of such objects as the Battersea Shield and of later Irish works of art, influenced by La Tène traditions, is a reminder that Roman-style modernisation involved loss as well as gain.

As we have seen, the Celtic societies of Britain were by no means wholly traditional in character on the eve of the Roman Conquest. Social change, at least in the south, was taking place in the direction of larger political units, urbanisation and a wider market economy. The thrust towards 'modernisation' was greatly accelerated, however, after the Claudian invasion of A.D. 43. By the end of the first century A.D. the tribal monarchies of southern Britain had given way to one in which power rested with a literate bureaucracy, ruling according to the standards of a cosmopolitan empire, from urban centres, which were linked by a centralised road system.

The key instrument in bringing about the radical changes which transformed much of Britain was the Roman army. The role played by the army in the initial phases of the occupation was inevitable. What was unexpected was the prolonged nature of the military occupation. Control of the Lowlands proved to be relatively easy. The Highlands, however, were never completely subdued and even maintaining a Roman presence there involved an inordinate amount of expenditure. Unrest among the Brigantes of the Highland Zone (Yorkshire and the Pennines) drew the Roman army into a never-ending series of campaigns. What the government originally envisaged as a buffer zone turned into a dangerous frontier area. The construction of

Hadrian's Wall, with all the diversion of resources which this involved, was a clear admission of the seriousness of the problem. Britain in fact demanded a larger outlay of military resources than any other province within the empire.

In such a situation, in which the army played a key role in decision-making, 'modernisation' took on a military colouring. Military decisions lay behind the establishment of garrison towns at Exeter and Lincoln with a military road, the Fosse Way, linking them. More such decisions lay behind the foundation of York and Caerleon as the main military centres of the Highland Zone. Most urban foundations in Roman Britain had a military origin. Some such as Lincoln or Colchester were colonies of army veterans. Even Bath, with its warm springs, catered largely for the needs of army officers, on leave or in retirement. Roman towns, true to their military origins, resembled barrack-like blocks in their regularity of pattern.

The army was not an end in itself, however. It formed part, but the most essential part, of a wider colonial society. Britain was a Roman colony, run for the benefit of the empire and its representatives. It is this undoubted fact which makes such judgments as 'putting Britain on her feet' so wide of the mark. Rome modernised the various tribal societies of Britain with the intention of exploiting its resources and raw materials. A centralised colonial economy replaced the various local economies of tribal society.

Within the new order the army was by far the most important single market. Its needs for a constant supply of corn, iron, leather, wine and pottery led to the mobilisation of a large labour force. The army was also responsible for the exploitation of silver mines, an imperial monopoly. The 'splendid' road system also required a plentiful supply of stone. All this was achieved not by the payment of wages but by the imposition of slavery combined with the 'pressing' of local labour. Convict labour was used in the mines and, in some cases, labourers were kept underground. The traditional status system resting upon membership of kinship groups was replaced by one in which the army was at the top of the social hierarchy with a largely unfree labour force constituting its base. Slavery existed in the tribal societies of the pre-Roman period but there was a clear difference between that situation and one in which slavery was a central institution.

There is little direct evidence about the transference of a colonial surplus abroad to the continental empire. The existence of an imperial bureaucracy, however, indicates that such a surplus existed, for otherwise the civil servants would have had no raison d'être. The aim of the bureaucracy was the collection of taxes. The officials responsible for tax collection as well as for supplying the necessary quotas of forced labour needed to maintain 'public works' were the *decuriones*. It was they who supervised the collection of the *annona*, the compulsory levy of wheat which was placed in a central state store before being distributed to the army.

In all of this, the demands of the Roman state were paramount. Army, bureaucracy and towns formed parts of a wider imperial organisation. It seems likely also that the Roman villas formed part of this structure. The 600 villas discovered so far were once thought to have been essentially rural in character, but it now seems clear that they were located relatively near urban centres. Far from being places of leisure or retirement, the villas, or most of them, were units of agricultural production, akin to the hacienda of colonial Mexico, or the 'big houses' of eighteenth-century Ireland. The likelihood is that they were run by slave labour, though the evidence is not absolutely conclusive. At Hambledon (Bucks) the numerous remains of female infants suggests that infanticide was practised with a view to maintaining a largely male work force.

The nature of the evidence in Roman Britain means that we know far more about the colonists than about the colonised. Historians have concentrated their attention upon the task of working out the details of how the army was organised or the bureaucracy was run. It is only by placing Roman Britain within the wider context of the British Isles that we are reminded that these institutions rested upon a conquered Celtic-speaking population. Such was the power of Rome that Celtic culture was almost lost to sight in southern Britain. Only in the north and west and in Ireland, which the Romans did not attempt to conquer, may clear glimpses of alternative social arrangements be discerned.

The impact of the Roman empire upon the Highland Zone is difficult to gauge. Roman roads and the accompanying system of Roman forts tended to attract clusters of native settlements. Hadrian's Wall was also an economic magnet in its own right. Apart from these points of contact there is little reason to doubt that Celtic social institutions survived over much of what is now northern England. York, with its cosmopolitan population, must be seen as a garrison town in a largely Celtic 'Yorkshire'. The 'Jackson map' of Celtic river-names offers further evidence of the survival of Celtic culture in what we now think of as England. Celtic religious beliefs undoubtedly survived and perhaps revived in the course of the fifth century or earlier as the Celtic temple in Lydney (Glos) suggests. Even in the Lowland Zone, excavation has revealed the existence of temples on Celtic sites. We may also assume the survival of 'native' law in many cases.

When due allowance has been made for the survival of Celtic culture, there still remains the factor of Roman power to be taken into consideration. In recent work (*An Early Welsh Microcosm: Studies in the Llandaff Charters* (1978); *Wales in the Early Middle Ages* (1982)), Wendy Davies has suggested that over large areas of south Wales, Roman style land law, based on the 'estate', survived for many centuries after the Roman withdrawal. Clearly, considerable 'Romanisation' had taken place in what was part of the Highland Zone. There is also the vexed question about the extent to which the Highland Zone had been Christianised by the fifth century A.D. It was indeed this Church which produced Patrick, the Apostle to the Irish, and the first clearly recognisable individual personality in British history (more so than 'Arthur'). If Christianity is taken as an index of Romanisation, the survival of Christian communities in the Highland Zone after the Roman withdrawal is of considerable significance.

What was the position of Ireland during this period? Conventional interpretations have tended to stress its total isolation. Recent re-assessment of the significance of such evidence as pottery, coinage and other material suggests that this may be too rigid a view, at least for the northern and eastern coasts of the island. Allowing for the fact that Irish raiders brought back silver and coins as booty, there does seem to have been some degree of peaceful contact during the first and second centuries A.D. and again, after a long unexplained interval in the third century, in the fourth and early fifth centuries. Irish material found in south Wales may derive from colonies of an Irish tribe (the 'Deisi').

Of all Romanising influences, however, the most important was undoubtedly Christianity. The coming of St Patrick to northern Ireland and of other missionaries (who may have preceded him) to the southern half of the country is normally seen in exclusively religious terms as part of the history of the Christian Church. In cultural terms, however, it marked the opening up of Ireland to the values of Rome. During the fourth century A.D. Christianity had become the established religion of the empire and as a consequence had organised itself on the Roman administrative model. The Church was no longer a network of sects but an organisation made up of dioceses (the secular term for the imperial administrative unit) ruled by bishops in a monarchical system in which the Emperor as well as the Pope exercised a great deal of power. Latin was the sacred language of the Church and its centre was Rome. The Christian missionaries to Ireland in the course of the fifth century were thus agents of Romanisation. The Church which St Patrick founded was linked with sub-Roman Britain and presumably run on Roman lines.

The religion of the druids was heavily embedded in an oral culture. If later practices of the poets (*filid*) are taken as a guide, candidates for the individual priesthood had to undertake a prolonged course of memorisation extending over many years. Secrecy was all-important and membership as a consequence seems to have been confined to certain kinship groups. Christianity, in contrast, was a religion of the book. It brought literacy in its wake, though no doubt of a restricted kind. The new culture was Latin in its orientation, though the view that Columbanus, the Irish pilgrim of the late sixth century, was familiar with the Latin classics, seems to be unfounded.

The Christian Church which had taken the imperial organisation as its model was monarchical in structure. Its laws were seen as deriving from the authority of duly ordained rulers rather than from the local communities. In principle at least it aimed at uniformity. In doctrine also the Church aimed at orthodoxy, defined in as precise a manner as possible according to Greek philosophy. This too was in contrast with the loose polytheism of traditional societies within Ireland.

This process of Romanisation was by no means an instant success. Indeed, historians have tended to exaggerate the speed at which Christianity made headway in Ireland. The decline of the western empire in the fifth century also played its part in slowing down the rate of change. Many traditional aspects of Irish life survived for centuries to come. In spite of these qualifications, however, there is no doubt that the isolation of Ireland was broken down during this period. During the fifth century, in an episode which is still obscure, Irish colonists from Ulster established themselves in Argyll. During the same period links were established across the Irish Sea between Ireland and Wales. So far as Wales is concerned, the story was to peter out inconclusively. In Scotland, however, the Irish, known by their Roman nickname of 'Scotti', came to exercise lasting influence, since it was from their kingdom of Dalriada that Christian missionaries eventually came to evangelise the Anglo-Saxons of Northumbria in the mid-seventh century.

Scotti

Looked at in broad perspective, the British Isles c. A.D. 400 present a contrast between cultural areas. England south of a line from the Thames estuary to the Bristol Channel was heavily Romanised. Though little or no written sources have survived, physical testimony in the form of the remains of towns, forts and villas indicates that this part of Britain was very much part of the Roman empire. Here was a bureaucratic, centralised administration, capable of responding to military and naval threats by the building of forts at strategic points along the coasts. Roman barracks indicate a rigidly standardised approach to the problems presented by military occupation. Law, we may assume, was administered according to the dictates of the imperial code, with its emphasis upon private property. In the fourth century, the Christian Church, based upon the town and the diocese, administered by bishops, reflected in its unformity the outlook of the empire in which it found itself. Despite this Romanisation, the majority of the population almost certainly spoke British Celtic.

The second cultural area may be seen as a stretching from the territory of the Uotadini with its 'capital' at Traprain Law (near modern Edinburgh) to the tribal kingdoms of Wales and Ireland. In this area societies were heavily localised in their outlook. Laws based upon the dominance of local kinship groups prevailed. The feud and the compensatory fine were the sanctions on which these local societies relied. We may also assume that perceptions of the past adopted by these cultures reflected their local perspective. We are very far here from the universalist outlook of the Roman empire. In these cultures, the patronage of local aristocratic elites still prevailed. As suggested above, the influence of Christian missions brought these societies in Highland Britain and in Ireland into more direct contact with the Latin culture of the late Roman empire. For many, Latin became their sacred language. But the institutions of these societies based upon what was seen as immemorial custom could not be easily swept aside. Christian teaching, as the evidence of a later period suggests, probably remained a veneer in societies which still retained their own rites of passage and attitudes to kinship and, perhaps, human sacrifice.

Over much of the British Isles, the Celtic-speaking world survived the arrival and the departure of the Roman legions. The vitality of local oral cultures led to the invention or re-editing of origin legends, legal tracts and genealogies and narrative histories which were eventually committed to writing in an acceptable form by the monastic scribes of the early middle ages. These cultural traditions in due course gave rise to the fables of Arthur, Fionn MacCumhail and the Mabinogi. Celtic perceptions of the past survived to provide an alternative version of events which continued to exercise a powerful fascination in Wales, Ireland and Scotland and even in Norman England, thanks to the influence of Geoffrey of Monmouth.

3

The post-Roman centuries

Within the British Isles the period between the departure of the Romans (c. 400) and the coming of the vikings (c. 800) was marked by the interaction of four distinct cultures, British, Pictish, Irish and Anglo-Saxon. At the beginning of the period British culture (the culture of the P-Celtic-speaking peoples) was dominant over most of the island of Britain south of the Forth. Much of this culture in what is now southern England and south Wales was heavily Romanised. Roman towns and general organisation survived well into the fifth century. Farther north, for example in the territory of the Uotadini between the Forth and the Tweed, the extent of Roman influence had been much less. North of the Forth, the culture of the Picts (originally known to the Romans first as Caledonii and from the fourth century as Picti) was dominant. We know less about the Picts than any of the other three major cultures of the British Isles but place-names and other evidence indicate that there were two main groups, the southern Picts south of the Mounth and northern Picts north of the Mounth and in Shetland and Orkney. About A.D. 400, the two remaining cultures showed no sign of their coming significance. During the Roman centuries the Q-Celtic-speaking cultures of Ireland had been placed in a position of relative isolation, which was being broken down by the arrival of Christian missionaries from Britain and the continent. Germanic culture was the least important of all four since it was largely confined to eastern and southern Britain where auxiliaries of Teutonic origin had been introduced to serve as protective garrisons for towns – for example, York, Caistor, Cambridge, Leicester, Winchester and Dorchester-on-Thames.

By the end of the period a dramatic change had taken place. At the close of the eighth century, Anglo-Saxon colonists controlled an area stretching from the Forth to the south coast and as far east as a line stretching from the Dee to the Tamar. In an almost equally remarkable turn of events Irish culture had become dominant in the Western Isles of Scotland and in the area of western Scotland north of the Clyde. (The name of this Irish kingdom, 'Dalriada', derived from the north-east Ulster homeland of the newcomers.) Irish culture also established itself in the east of what is now Scotland, among the Picts who were introduced to Christianity

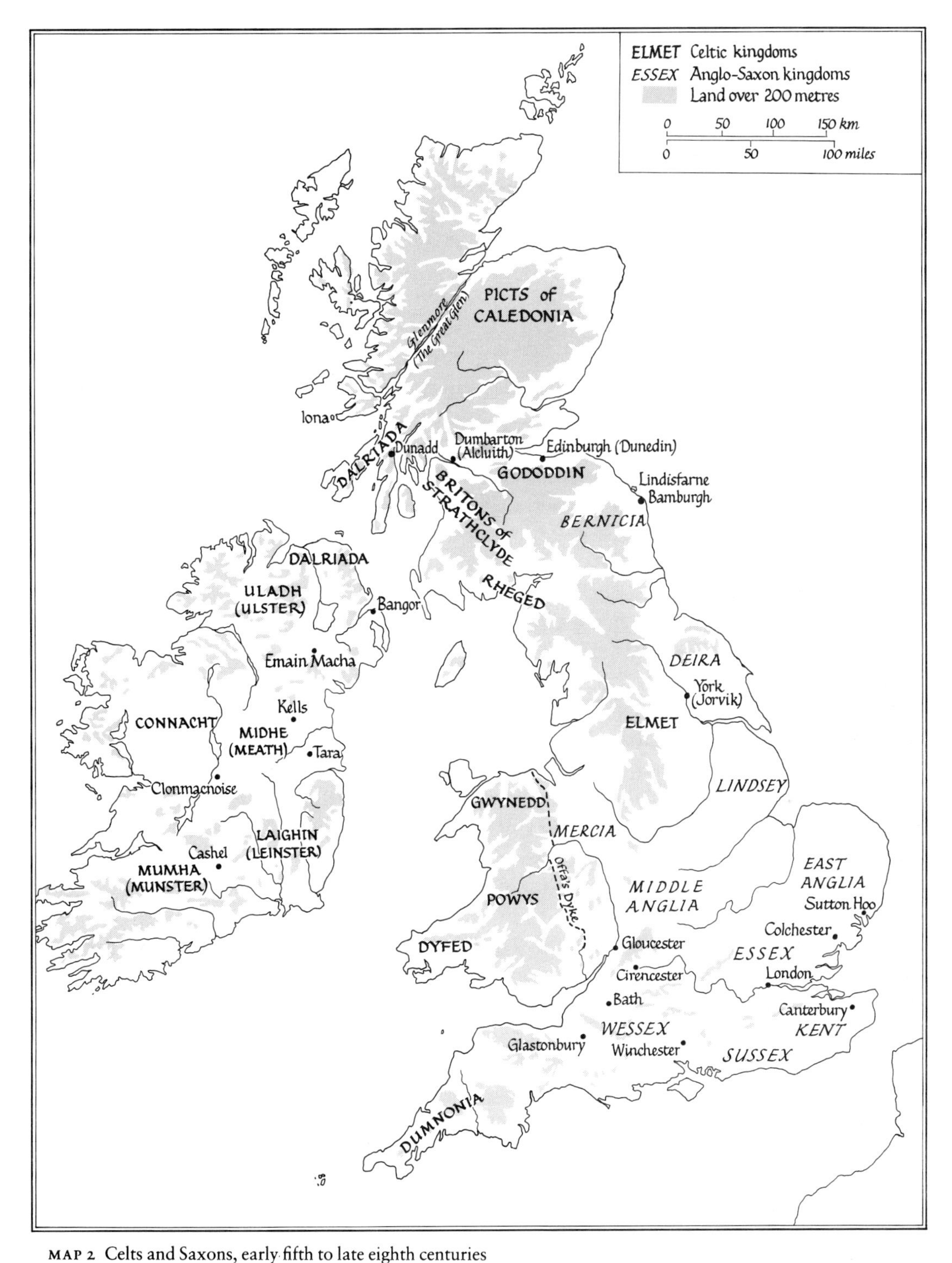

MAP 2 Celts and Saxons, early fifth to late eighth centuries

Source: after Christopher Haigh, ed., *The Cambridge Historical Encyclopedia of Great Britain and Ireland* (Cambridge, 1985), p. 55.

by Irish missionaries from Iona led by Colmcille (Columba). During this period Irish culture also penetrated, but transiently, into south Wales, where kings with a Gaelic pedigree ruled over Dyfed, and to the Isle of Man. Perhaps the most surprising development of all was the influence of Irish culture in the Anglo-Saxon kingdom of Northumbria, which stretched from the Forth to the Humber. By 800 the cultural map of the British Isles had been completely transformed in ways that it would have been difficult to foresee 400 years earlier.

As the Anglo-Saxon and Irish cultures rose in importance during these centuries, the Pictish and British cultures declined. Pictish culture remains one of the great unsolved problems of insular history. The language of the Picts, known only from two dozen inscriptions, has not been deciphered and their general culture, known only from art and place-names, remains wrapped in obscurity. The fate of British culture (P-Celtic) is better known, but even here there are unanswered questions. By the end of this period British culture survived only in the kingdom of Strathclyde with its capital at Dumbarton, in the disputed area of Cumbria (a name which is the same as the Welsh *cymry*, 'fellow-countrymen' and Cymru, 'Wales'), in the several kingdoms of what the English called 'Wales' (meaning 'foreign') and in Cornwall, which may once have been part of the British kingdom of Dumnonia (it preserves the name of the British tribe, the Cornouii). The only area in which British culture expanded during this period was into north-west France where much of the Armorican peninsula came to be called Brittany (Little Britain) and to speak 'Breton', a variety of P-Celtic. It was not until the ninth century, when 'Britannia (minor)' doubled in size that the peninsula as a whole became Breton.

Our interpretation of these centuries has been dominated by the work of the English monk Bede (673–735) who completed his *Ecclesiastical History of the English People* in 731. As a consequence of the genius of Bede we are well acquainted with the Anglo-Saxon version of events. There is, however, no rival version from the point of view of any of the other three cultures, although there are individual sources which go some way towards making up the deficiency. For the Britons there is the work of Gildas, *The Ruin of Britain*, written in the mid-sixth century and the anonymous *History of the Britons* written in the early ninth century. For the Irish, the sources include Adomnán's Life of Columba, as well as less tractable material such as annalistic chronicles, laws, genealogies and saints' Lives. For the Picts, there is almost nothing. The accessibility of Bede's *Ecclesiastical History*, available in paperback in English translation, has added to the influence of his viewpoint in modern times.

Bede's theme is not the clash of cultures, though we may see this mirrored in his general account, but the conversion of the 'English' to Christianity. As a Christian historian of the events of the fifth, sixth and seventh centuries he was presented with the paradox that his own people, the Germanic newcomers, were pagan, while their victims, the Britons, were Christian. Bede solved his problem by attributing the English victory to the working of Divine Providence. 'The fires kindled by the pagans proved to be God's just punishment of the sins of the nation, just as the fires once burned by the Chaldeans destroyed the walls and palaces of Jerusalem.' The alleged slaughter of 1,200 monks in the early seventh century was due to the fulfilment 'of Bishop Augustine's prophecy that the faithless Britons who had rejected the offer of eternal salvation would incur the punishment of temporal destruction'. There is no echo in Bede of the description of the pagan Saxons as a 'people more ferocious than even German ferocity'. In Bede's eyes, the English had become a nation chosen by God. As a consequence of this emphasis we may tend to overestimate the impact of Christianity upon Anglo-Saxon culture. In this regard the pagan burial of Sutton Hoo (c. 625–50) and the pagan aristocratic ideas expressed in the epic poem *Beowulf* may serve as a reminder that there was no 'instant Christianisation' of the Anglo-Saxons.

Of the relationships between the Anglo-Saxons and the three other cultures the evidence of Bede suggests that the one with the Irish was for a time the most harmonious. Bede refers to the presence of 'many English nobles and lesser folk in Ireland who had left their own land during the episcopates of Bishops Finan and Colman, either to pursue religious studies or to lead a life of stricter discipline ... The Irish welcomed them kindly and, without asking for payment, provided them with books and instructors.' Bede also celebrates the role of Irish monks in the rebirth of Christianity in Northumbria, monks from Iona who with King Oswald's encouragement established themselves at Lindisfarne. (It is unfortunate that later devotion to the English St Cuthbert of Lindisfarne has tended to obliterate these early links with Ireland.) Aldfrith, king of Northumbria in the late seventh century (685–705), also had close links with Ireland. Three of the first four bishops of Mercia were either Irish or Irish-trained. Bede also mentions the work of an Irish missionary, Fursu (St Fursey), in East Anglia. These cultural links did not exclude political tension, however, when the interests of the Anglo-Saxons and the Gaels clashed. One crucial turning point in this respect was the battle of Degsastan in 603 when Aethelfrith of Northumbria defeated Aedhán MacGabhrain, king of Dalriada.

The art of the period also indicates the existence of close links between the Anglo-Saxon kingdom of Northumbria and the Irish kingdoms both in northern Britain and in Ireland itself. The late seventh-century copy of the Gospels, known as the Book of Durrow, juxtaposes 'carpet-pages' of Germanic and Irish ornamentation. The Lindisfarne Gospels of the eighth century illustrate an intermingling of Irish, English and Mediterranean styles. Parts of the Ardagh Chalice, which is of Irish provenance, were influenced by Germanic wood-carving techniques. The Book of Kells itself (c. 800) may even be a product of this interaction between Irish and Anglo-Saxon cultures. In his *History* Bede devotes a good deal of attention to the clash which developed among Irish and English churchmen over the dating of Easter before the Synod of Whitby (664). Such tensions undoubtedly existed but they highlight rather than obscure the close relationship which developed between Ireland, 'British' Dalriada and Northumbria until the coming of the vikings and which was symbolised in the prominence of the island-monastery of Iona.

In contrast, the relationship between the Anglo-Saxon and British cultures, between colonists and colonised, was permanently antagonistic. Bede believed that 'it is the habit of the Britons to despise the faith and religion of the English and not to co-operate with them in anything more than with the heathen'. Bishop Aldhelm complained that

> beyond the bounds of the River Severn the priests of Dumnonia, taking excessive pride in the elegance of their own observance, hold our communion in such contempt that they will not deign to celebrate the sacred offices of prayer with us in church, nor in like measure will they share the dishes of the festive board with us at table.

Within the British community, forty days' penance was required before 'an English Christian' was accepted. We must also assume that the massacre of monks which Bede regarded as providential appeared in a different light to the Britons, who presumably looked upon it as an act of barbarism. The most spectacular piece of evidence for the existence of prolonged and continuous hostility between Britons and Saxons is Offa's Dyke, built during the eighth century and stretching from the Dee to the Severn estuaries. It was presumably the need to protect English settlements from British attack which explains the construction of an earthwork nearly 150 miles long, though other interpretations have been offered.

Bede provides us with the viewpoint of a historian for whom the crucial events of the seventh century were the conversion of kings and the miracles of saints. What is lacking in Bede is a sense of the steady process of colonisation which led to the almost total dominance of Anglo-Saxon culture in the Lowland Zone of Britain. Military conquest came first. By the end of the sixth century the Anglo-Saxons had seized the Romano-British centres of Gloucester, Bath and Cirencester, and had advanced to the estuary of the Severn. More permanent than military victory was the persistent advance of agrarian settlements. Modern scholarship has demonstrated how the progress of the west Saxons into the British territories of Devon and Somerset was based upon the creation of nuclear settlements, and no doubt the extermination of the population. Further north, the so-called 'midlands system' of villages and open fields illustrates the same forces at work. The Anglo-Saxon conquest of the Lowland Zone rested upon the demographic preponderance which the village and its open-field agriculture made possible. Where this numerical superiority was lacking, the foundations of Anglo-Saxon society proved less secure. The kingdom of Northumbria, for example, despite its artistic achievements, failed to survive the onset of the viking invasions. In contrast the kingdom of Essex with a larger population was better placed to meet the challenge.

Anglo-Saxon society attributed a much greater importance to descent within the nuclear family and much less to the role of a wider kindred. The Britons created compound words to indicate second, third or even more distant cousins whereas the Anglo-Saxons were content with a single vague term. In Sir Frederick Pollock and F. W. Maitland's *History of English Law* (1898), Maitland commented long ago on the difficulty of establishing where kinship loyalties lay in Anglo-Saxon society, where descent in both male and female lines was acceptable, as compared with the stress upon patrilineal links among Britons and Irish.

The reason for this difference may well be sought in the colonial nature of Anglo-Saxon society. The colonists were ethnically mixed, from several Germanic cultures. In this new, mobile society, unlike the situation in more static societies, the protection afforded by the lord or the king seems to have been more important than that of the kindred. The 'right' to newly acquired land was more likely to be safeguarded by a king than by a possibly distant kindred. Not surprisingly, monarchical institutions became more powerful in this type of society than in the lineage-based society of the Britons and the Irish. In Anglo-Saxon law, the development of *bookland*, land which was protected by a royal charter and which could theoretically be disposed of at will, indicated a profound difference from the assumption of inalienability in 'Celtic' law. The importance of trade within Anglo-Saxon society, indicated by the existence of such ports as London and Southampton (Hamwih) and by the use of coinage, may also be related to a more fluid social structure in which trading was a socially acceptable activity. It was not until the viking period that coins made their appearance in Ireland.

Bede wrote of the 'English People' and it has been convenient so far to refer to Anglo-Saxon culture as if it were a single entity. In fact, however, sharp differences seem to have existed between one group and another. The most obvious difference was that between the smaller, older kingdoms of the east and south coasts (Lindsey, East Anglia, Essex, Kent and Sussex), and the newer, more powerful expanding kingdoms of the north, the midlands and south-west (Northumbria, Mercia and Wessex). Historians have noted a contrast in eleventh-century social structure between the two areas, with slavery being a more prominent feature in the west. Conquest seems to be the most likely explanation of this phenomenon, since, among the Anglo-Saxons, the word 'wealh' could mean either 'Welshman' or 'slave'. The task of establishing a frontier with the British kingdoms to the west was clearly a perennial problem, which the Mercians attempted to meet by building Offa's Dyke. As suggested earlier, the challenge presented by the need to protect newly colonised territories may have led to a greater emphasis upon royal power in Mercia and Wessex than had been the case in the east.

In sharp contrast to the advances made by the Anglo-Saxons, the history of British culture during this period was one of catastrophic decline. By the eighth century much of what had been British territory was securely part of the various Anglo-Saxon kingdoms. P-Celtic culture survived only in widely separated units along the west coast in the kingdom of Strathclyde, the kingdoms of 'Wales', in Cornwall and in Brittany. It was the loss of the British kingdoms of what became northern England, symbolised in the use of the term 'Gwyr y Gogledd' (the 'Men of the North'), which seems to have had the greatest impact upon British consciousness. The heroic poem

The Gododdin told the story of the defeat of a group of northern warriors by the English at Catterick. So complete was the overthrow of Celtic culture in northern Britain that the epic survived only in Welsh translation. Welsh genealogical tracts of the thirteenth century attempted to establish links with northern dynasties of the sixth. Poems written in Powys in the mid-ninth century looked back with bitterness to the defeats of an earlier period in the north. The figure of Tristan (Drystan), like other personages in Arthurian romance, seems to emerge from a northern background. Even though we lack the precision of dates and events to be found in Bede it seems clear that the fragmented British cultures in the west preserved the memory of an earlier period when British kingdoms existed in what became Northumbria. The only large exception to this story of decline was the survival of the kingdom of Strathclyde whose rulers won decisive victories over the Irish of Dalriada in 642. The building of Offa's Dyke in the eighth century also suggests that British resistance in what became the Welsh marches was far from over.

The 'cult' of Arthur may be mentioned in this context. It is not surprising that a culture in defeat should seek compensation in the story of a warrior who would return to drive the Anglo-Saxons into the sea. Such seems to have been the significance of Arthur for many Britons during this period. The actual historicity of Arthur is very much a matter for debate, indeed there is no evidence for his existence. Gildas does not mention him though he does refer to a certain Ambrosius Aurelianus, a 'Roman' under whom the Britons won their first victory against the Saxons. Even if Arthur did not exist, there is no doubt that the myth of Arthur formed part of British historical consciousness during these centuries. There is a reference to Arthur in *The Gododdin*. The Welsh Triads also refer to Arthur. It was only in the twelfth century, thanks in part to Geoffrey of Monmouth's History, that stories about Arthur began to reach a wider audience until, ultimately, he became a figure of European romance. During this early period, however, the story of Arthur, along with that of *The Gododdin*, may be seen as providing us with an insight into British attitudes towards the past.

If the Anglo-Saxons were divided, so too were the Britons. Perhaps the most obvious of these divisions was that between the various kingdoms of what later became 'Wales'. Culturally, north and south offered (and still offer) a contrast. The British kingdom of Gwynedd in north-west Wales looked to northern Britain for its origins. Bardic historians of this area linked its second ruling dynasty with a certain Cunedda who was said to have driven Irish intruders from that part of Britain. (Place-names such as Lleyn which have an Irish origin, in this case Leinster, certainly indicate an Irish presence in north Wales at some time.) Bede's History also indicates Venedotian involvement in the affairs of north Britain.

In view of these links it is not surprising that memories of former British kingdoms in northern Britain should have survived more vividly among the bards of Gwynedd than in south Wales. The cultural horizons of the kingdom of Powys in mid-Wales and of Gwent and Dyfed in the south seem to have been very different. In Powys the evidence of Eliseg's Pillar, set up in the mid-ninth century, suggests that the ruling dynasty looked back to one Gwrtheyrn as its founder. In the kingdom of Dyfed, place-names, Irish-style high crosses and ogham-stones suggest that the dynasty looked west across the Irish Sea rather than east or north. In the south-west, the kingdom of Gwent centred on Caerwent may well have looked back to the days of Rome. Lastly, on the other side of the Bristol Channel, the kingdom of Dumnonia, now reduced to Cornwall, should not be considered separately from south Wales since links across the Severn had always been close and it is probable that the British kingdoms of 'south Wales' had more in common with their counterparts on the other side of the Bristol Channel than with the kingdoms of 'north Wales'. The alleged role of Glastonbury as a British holy place in Somerset before it had been taken over by the west Saxons deserves consideration in this context, though there is no clear evidence. The paradox of Arthur as a figure in Cornish culture also becomes more intelligible if the Severn is thought of as a unifying factor, linking the Britons of the south-west with their countrymen ('cymry') in what is now 'Wales'.

The third of our four cultures is that of Ireland, which enjoyed what is generally regarded as a 'Golden Age' during this period. An expansion of Irish culture into 'Scotland' and 'south Wales' took place, which may be seen as part of a general movement which took Irish missionaries led by Colmán (Latinised as Columbanus) into western Europe. During the fifth century under the impact of the mission of Patrick and others, Christianity had made considerable headway in Ireland, though there could be no 'instant Christianisation'. The druids were eventually replaced by Christian clergy but other key institutions in Irish society remained unchanged. The practice of polygamy, for example, did not disappear for many centuries. Other native ways of life, such as that of cursing one's enemies, seem to have been taken over by Christian holy men. But there is no doubt that Christian teaching evoked a powerful response among some sections of the population. The missionaries whom Ireland produced during these centuries may be compared perhaps with the fundamentalist sects of our own day. They preached a simple message which we find embodied in the stone carvings of biblical scenes on the high crosses at Moone and elsewhere.

In many ways, however, Ireland, though converted by St Patrick and though it influenced Britain through its own missionaries, remained remarkably unaffected by changes on the other side of the Irish Sea. The course of events might have worked out differently if Roman control of the neighbouring island had remained intact. A century after the departure of the Romans from Britain, however, the localised character of Irish society asserted itself. The monastic communities, which became typical of the Irish Church, were essentially local lineage groups in a religious setting, in which the abbot as the kinsman of the saint-founder of the monastery enjoyed the realities of power while the bishop played a secondary role. This pattern of 'coarbs' (i.e. 'heirs' of the saint) lasted in some areas of Ireland until the seventeenth century It was this system, contrasting so sharply with the centralising ecclesiastical structure of Rome which the Irish missionaries introduced into parts of Britain. Its strength lay in the establishment of strong local roots. The rulers of the new Anglo-Saxon kingdoms, however, expanding into Celtic-speaking areas, found episcopal organisation more appropriate as an instrument of government.

It would be a mistake to exaggerate the extent of Irish localism during this period, however. Pre-Christian Ireland, which (as we have seen) was 'tribal, rural, hierarchical and familiar', underwent considerable political change from the fifth century onwards. The fifth century saw the decline of the system of independent small kingdoms and the rise of two major over-kingdoms, that of the Uí Néill in the north and midlands and that of the Eoghanachta in the south. In the north, the expansion of the Uí Néill led to the decline first of the Laigin and ultimately of the Ulaid. The defeated parties found some compensation in the possibilities opened up by expansion into north Britain (what later became known as Scotland). 'Old' and 'new' Dalriada remained linked politically until the seventh century but long after that date close cultural ties persisted. The men of Dalriada brought to Scotland the system of royal lineages which found expression in 'Cenel Loairn' and 'Cenel Gabhrain' (the lineages of Loarn and of Gabran) which played a prominent part in the history of north Britain during these centuries.

The localism of Irish society did not remain unchanged during the centuries of Uí Néill ascendancy in the north of Ireland. When they had gained control of Armagh, the Uí Néill attempted to use its early associations with St Patrick as a means of gaining control of what had been independent monasteries. In this way the monastic centres at Clonard and Clonmacnoise fell under Uí Néill influence. The Uí Néill also sponsored new lives of St Patrick by Muirchú and Tírechán in which the life of the saint was to some extent rewritten perhaps to accord with the political ambitions of the dynasty. The Brehon Laws were also committed to writing, especially in the seventh century, despite a long tradition of secrecy practised by a profession which passed on its learning by oral transmission. There were also attempts to introduce a taxation system based upon the rights of Patrick over monastic houses which he was said to have founded. In all this the Uí Néill were not acting so very differently from their counterparts in Anglo-Saxon Britain, and though we know much less about them it seems likely that the Eoghanacta in southern Ireland were also building up an overlordship on similar lines. No more than in Britain, however, was there any sense of 'nation-building' during this period.

It remains to mention Pictish culture. Ideally we should like to have the literary evidence which is available for Anglo-Saxon, British and Irish cultures during the period. In the absence of this, the historian must be largely content with archaeological material and with references to the Picts in non-Pictish sources. As I suggested earlier, it seems probable that Iona brought Christianity to the Picts, though references in Bede suggest that a certain Ninian, a north British bishop, may have done so already in the fifth century. Irish-style high crosses, to be found in the west of Scotland, the Isle of Man and south Wales, are absent from Pictland, which suggests that Irish influence may not have been as widespread here as it was in the west. However, there is no doubt about the influence of Christianity among the Picts as Pictish cross-slabs and such pieces of metalwork as the Monymusk reliquary indicate. An important discovery (1958) of a silver hoard on St Ninian's Isle, Shetland, provides us with an insight into the wealth of a northern Pictish chief (or perhaps an ecclesiastic) on the eve of the viking invasions. This and other pieces of archaeological evidence indicate that Pictish craftsmen were in contact with Anglo-Saxon as well as Irish culture. Literary evidence also refers to the Pictish King Naiton expressing his willingness to accept Northumbrian guidance about the Roman dating of Easter as well as asking for an architect to build a church on the 'Roman' model. In general, however, Pictish culture remains more of a historical 'problem' than a presence.

Throughout the 'post-Roman centuries' from the fifth to the eighth the image of the late Roman empire exercised a continuing influence upon the cultures of the British Isles. The British kingdoms of western Britain were conscious of their links with Rome, which the myth of Arthur symbolised. In Ireland, the 'Romanising' tendencies of the Uí Néill have been noted. It was among the Anglo-Saxons, however, that Rome seems to have had most influence. The association of Christianity with the power of Rome probably made the acceptance of the new religion and the rejection of ancestral pieties more aceptable. Literacy itself was associated with the Romans. King Aethelberht of Kent is said by Bede to have ordered his laws to be written down 'according to the manner of the Romans'. The dedication-inscription to Ecgfrith, king of Northumbria, is in Latin and takes its dating from the Roman Kalends. The church at Brixworth, which has been described as 'the most notable example of church building north of the Alps during the seventh century' takes its design from the Roman basilica. In the Sutton Hoo ship burial many of the key objects are of Roman inspiration. Not the least consequence of the viking invasions was the weakening of the power of the Roman image. With the vikings the 'post-Roman centuries' come to an end and a new period begins.

4

The vikings and the fall of the Old Order

During the early ninth century, the equilibrium which existed between the cultures of the British Isles was disturbed by the onset of a new, seaborne power, the vikings. The first viking raids took place in the last decade of the eighth century when Lindisfarne was sacked (793). From then on the peoples of the British Isles as a whole were subjected to increasing pressure. Thanks to their longships, a crucial invention, the vikings were able to dominate for long periods much of the Irish Sea and the North Sea. A completely new situation was created, as a consequence of which viking settlements were established along the coasts of Britain and Ireland as well as neighbouring islands including the Isle of Man, Shetland, Orkney and the Hebrides. Though their political power eventually declined, partly as a consequence of political divisions, the communities which they set up remained ethnically distinctive for centuries. With the coming of the vikings a new period may be said to have begun in the history of the British Isles, one which marked a sharp breach with the past.

The term 'viking' originated in a term for 'pirate', but as with the Saxons earlier, piracy eventually gave way to colonisation. The Irish Sea from the Hebrides southwards was largely dominated by the vikings, though it would be a mistake to assume that there was political unity among the various groups. (The Irish distinguished 'dark strangers' *dubhgaill* from 'fair strangers' *fionngaill* whence came 'Fingal'.) During the course of the ninth century, trading posts were established at Dublin, Cork, Waterford and Limerick. The Isle of Man became an important strategic centre. The North Sea also fell under Danish influence. The capital of Northumbria, York, was transformed into a major viking entrepôt, rivalling Scandinavian Dublin in its importance. From the mid-ninth century (856) large-scale Danish colonisation took place along the east coast. In the English east midlands, large areas of Mercia were soon controlled from the five Danish boroughs of Lincoln, Leicester, Derby, Nottingham and Stamford, all of them accessible by river from the North Sea. On the Irish Sea coastline, a secondary expansion occurred in north-west England. In this case the settlers came from the Scandinavian colonies in western 'Scotland' and the Western Isles. During much of the tenth century, struggles for power took

MAP 3 The impact of the vikings, late eighth to early eleventh centuries

place between various groups of vikings. Hence came the spectacle in the tenth century of the Norse kings of Dublin attempting to gain control of the Danish kingdom of York, though ultimately without success.

Conventional interpretations, particularly of English history, tend to underplay the significance of the vikings. Many textbooks of English history assume the continuity of an Anglo-Saxon England from the the fifth century to the Norman Conquest. The French historian Marc Bloch, however, looking at western Europe as a whole, argued that the viking invasions induced responses which led to revolutionary changes in social and political structures. Daniel Binchy also, in his study of Ireland during this period (in *Proceedings of the Dublin Congress of Celtic Studies* (1962)), has spoken of 'the Fall of the Old Order'. In the context of the British Isles, a view which stresses radical change rather than continuity makes the better sense. Both directly in their own actions, and indirectly in the responses which they evoked, the vikings may be seen as agents of revolution rather than as the cause of a minor break in a general process of political evolution.

If we deal with eastern Britain first, the revolutionary effect of the viking invasions is clear. The vikings originally set up puppet-kings in Northumbria and Mercia, but in the first half of the tenth century these kingdoms ceased to exist. The Christian Church which these kings had supported also suffered severe blows. Politically, the result of this was to leave Bernicia, Northumbria north of the Tweed, isolated and exposed to attack from the north. The future of this area was to lie with the Gaelic-dominated 'Kingdom of Scots'. Farther west, Anglo-Saxon settlements in Cumbria, made at the expense of the kingdom of Strathclyde, were submerged. In Deira (south Northumbria) and farther south in Lindsey, East Anglia and Mercia, Danish settlers moved in in large numbers, often, it would appear, establishing themselves alongside the Anglo-Saxons. As the Celts had become second-class citizens in this part of Britain, so too in their turn did the Anglo-Saxons. The Anglo-Saxon elite, if we may go by the evidence of the graves, was a military aristocracy. The new social order was more broadly based upon farmers. Not surprisingly, the aristocratic artistic tradition of Northumbria was weakened though it did not perish entirely. Along the east coast of Britain 'Anglo-Saxon England' ceased to exist in any meaningful sense. The Christian literate culture of Alcuin of York linked to Rome and the Carolingian empire, was replaced by a pagan, oral culture, which looked to Denmark and Norway.

The new society which came into existence in this area during the ninth century was more market-orientated than the society which it replaced though the contrast was not absolute. Anglo-Saxon coins (*sceattas*) testify to the existence of trade between London and the Rhineland during the eighth century. The port of Hamwih (near today's Southampton) enjoyed some prosperity. The trading inclination of the vikings, however, was of a different order. York became an international trading centre, rivalled in the British Isles only by Dublin. Other substantial commercial centres rose along the east coast at Lincoln, Thetford and Norwich. London had a thriving community of viking merchants. On the west coast, Bristol in due course became an important port specialising in trade with Ireland. Trade with the French coastal regions also increased.

In the early years of the viking raids piracy and trade were inextricably intermingled. Their trade was piracy and piracy was their trade. The Cuerdale coin hoard of over 7,000 coins, including some Kufic *dirhams*, shows the 'trading' links which existed between the Scandinavian-controlled areas of England and the Baltic trading zone with its own contacts with Russia. Another index of the commercial changes associated with the Danes is the sudden appearance in the mid-ninth century of excellent wheel-thrown pottery (misleadingly termed 'Saxo-Norman' by archaeologists). The use of this pottery spread everywhere where the Danes had settled. The demand for it suggests the existence of a 'mass market' rather than a restricted aristocratic one such as existed in pre-viking Northumbria. In contrast, pottery in Wessex remained largely hand-made, a sign of that kingdom's more conservative social structure. It was no accident that (on the evidence of Domesday Book) the eastern half of Britain, now under Danish dominance, was wealthier and more heavily populated than other parts of England.

It was suggested above that even during the post-Roman centuries the eastern half of England enjoyed a less rigid manorial social structure than the midlands. The vikings almost certainly added to the proportion of freemen. Maitland commented long ago on the higher proportion of *liberi homines* or 'sokemen' in the east in contrast with the villeinage characteristic of the midlands and West Country. Not all of the freemen need have been descended from vikings but the existence of over 10,000 in Lincolnshire, 5,000 in Norfolk and nearly 2,000 in Leicestershire, areas of major Scandinavian settlement, is a strong argument for some correlation. The feudal tie of lord and vassal does not seem to have been characteristic of viking society. The typical viking, if we may speak of such a person, seems to have been a farmer in arms, not a warrior seeking to control unfree labour. Viking farmers had a tradition of carrying arms in their local assembly as the name *wapentake* indicates. Active participation in political decision-making was encouraged at regular meetings termed *things* (hence such place-names as Thingwall).

Local historians have noted how, even in the thirteenth century, well after the Norman Conquest, and when the trend towards manorial control was at its height, eastern Norfolk possessed a social structure which was unusually flexible and free. Partible inheritance was widespread and most villeins had already established the right to alienate land. Resort to the common-law courts by tenants was not uncommon in this part of England. It is also significant that after their military successes against the vikings (c. 900) the Wessex monarchs did not succeed in establishing the 'hundred' and the 'tithing' in Scandinavian areas. In Wessex, each member of a hundred was obliged to belong to a tithing (a group of ten or twelve men) and to accept responsibility for the behaviour of fellow-members. The absence of such institutions in the Danelaw suggests the extent to which viking society was less authoritarian than the rest of England.

The military revival of the west Saxon monarchy from the early tenth century onwards did not restore Anglo-Saxon cultural, political and social dominance north of the Humber. The royal itineraries of the Wessex kings, which are a good guide to the extent of their real power as opposed to a temporary 'showing of the flag', were largely confined to an area south of the Thames. For a long time to come, considerable differences existed between the Danelaw and the rest of England, not least in language, law, religion and art. The east was very much a distinctive society whose autonomy the west Saxon monarchy was forced to respect. The revival of viking raids in the later tenth century and the establishment of Danish supremacy over all England during the reign of Cnut (1016–35) can have done little to reduce this sense of separateness. Even under the Normans, the Danelaw was to retain much of its own character.

The Scandinavian invasion of the east coast of Britain brought about the fall of the Old Order and the creation of a new society in its place. Had the colonising impetus of the Danes been maintained, 'England' might well have been transformed into a 'New Denmark'. For various reasons, including the shifting of interest to other areas and the divisions which existed among the Scandinavians, the conquest of the Anglo-Saxons was never completed. Indirectly, however, the challenge presented by the newcomers led to revolutionary changes in the south, where Wessex had managed to escape the fate of Northumbria and Mercia. Under a succession of able kings, Alfred (871–99), Edward the Elder (899–924), Aethelstan (924–39), Edmund (939–46), Eadred (946–55), Eadwig (955–9) and Edgar (959–75), Wessex achieved a remarkable period of dominance. The tenth century was very much the 'Age of Wessex'.

These successes were not achieved without paying a price. Wessex, and the areas which came under its control, became more centralised and military in character. For Mercia and East Anglia, indeed, 'liberation' by Wessex meant the exchange of one master for another. It is all too easy to ignore these internal cultural divisions in an interpretation which stresses the movement of history towards the making of the 'English nation'. In due course, despite the military successes of Wessex against the Danes, Mercia was to show itself restive under the west Saxon monarchy. During the earlier eleventh century, indeed, the earldom of Mercia enjoyed a good deal of autonomy.

The new monarchy, from Aethelstan onwards, represented itself as the instrument of the Divine Will, and, as a consequence, enjoyed a superior status over and above any opposition based upon 'tribal' considerations. Edgar in particular seems to have regarded himself as possessing quasi-priestly status. His well-staged coronation at Bath in 973 marks a new point in the development of monarchical ideology. The officiating clergy asked Christ to 'anoint this king to his reign as you have anointed priests, kings, prophets and martyrs'. Somewhat earlier, Alfred had translated works of Gregory the Great and Boethius, probably with an ideological aim in view.

Before the tenth century, kingship was more in the nature of over-lordship. Thus the taxation document of seventh-century Mercia, known as the *Tribal Hidage*, reveals the existence of distinctive 'tribal' groupings beneath the monarchical façade. In contrast, the new west Saxon monarchs, on the basis of their conquest of the Danelaw, in theory enjoyed the power of direct disposal of land which had formerly been 'tribal' territory. A large royal demesne and a reservoir of Church land at royal disposal formed a basis of royal power in the conquered areas. Royal charters provided legal backing for newcomers to these areas. Wessex, once military success had been achieved, absorbed (or attempted to absorb) the former kingdoms of Mercia, East Anglia, Essex, Sussex and Kent. This west Saxon expansion had been made possible by the viking invasions.

If the Danes had created a society in which traders and farmers were preponderant, the west Saxon kings, building upon the demands of the situation, brought a military state into being. As modern research has shown, the administrative units of 'shire' and 'hundred', which were to be so much a part of English history, had a military rather than a civil function. The royal army (the 'fyrd') was not the popular folk-levy of nineteenth-century imagination but a quasi-feudal body bound to the king by the ties of vassalage. The royal boroughs which Alfred and his successors set up as part of their response to the Danes were essentially a system of fortified centres, military rather than commercial in character, and hence quite unlike the Danish towns of York, Lincoln and Norwich. The conquest of Danish Mercia also made possible the reorganisation of former tribal territories into Wessex-style 'shires', under ealdormen, who were not the civil officeholders, which the modern associations of the term (aldermen) might suggest, but primarily military governors. This was not a completely new departure for the kings of Wessex. In large measure it was an extension of the policy and practice employed in the subjection and colonisation of Devon, Somerset and Dorset at an earlier period, under Ine (+726). The military ambitions of the dynasty were eventually to lead them well beyond Anglo-Saxon territory – into Scotland; the year 973 was the high point, when Edgar is said to have been rowed down the river Dee by eight client kings.

If 'feudalism' is taken to mean the holding of land in return for military service, the new monarchy brought a feudal society into existence. The Danish threat created the need for a class of specialised warriors, whose position rested upon a manorial system of unfree labour. Hence came the paradox that during the years of 'liberation' the status of the Anglo-Saxon peasantry seems to have declined even further towards servitude. In those areas which were under west Saxon control, 'tribal society' was replaced by 'seigniorial society'. The new shires which were created in west Mercia bore no relation to the traditional 'tribal' units of an earlier period. The document, known as the *Burghal Hidage*, dating from the early tenth century, indicates the extent to which change had taken place since the earlier *Tribal Hidage*. The new shires were organised around urban centres under royal control and took their names from them (for example, Gloucestershire, Derbyshire) and not from their tribal affiliation as they did in Wessex proper (as in Somerset and Dorset). On the basis of these new centres and of associated smaller fortresses (*burgs*), what amounted to a west Saxon empire was created. As the *Burghal Hidage* makes clear, these military settlements rested upon compulsory levies of men and material assessed according to the unit known as the 'hide' (a family-size holding varying in extent with the area). Thus Winchester was assessed at 2,400 hides. In this new society, kinship ties were giving way to feudal ties imposed from above. In law also, royal justice, in the hands of royal judges, was beginning to assume a new importance.

In this new society, kinship ties, already weak, gave way still further to feudal duties imposed from above. The process of weakening was carried still further as royal justice, administered by royal judges, began to assume a new importance. The change may be seen in the creation of artificial groups of ten or twelve men called 'tithings', which were made responsible for the behaviour of their members. Failure to observe the royal command was punished not by the penalties appropriate to a kinship group but by flogging by order of the king's representative. Law imposed from above was beginning to replace customary law based upon mutual interaction between groups.

The ecclesiastical aspects of the new monarchy especially illustrate the far-reaching character of the changes involved. The 'Tenth-Century Reformation' was a movement which introduced a new style of monasticism into Wessex, Mercia and East Anglia under royal auspices. The three leaders of this reform movement, Dunstan (d. 988), Aethelwold (d. 984) and Oswald (d. 992), all monk-bishops and all men of intellect and vigour, were closely associated with the royal court of Edgar (959–75). Their reforming criticisms were levelled at the married clergy, whom they termed 'lascivious clerks', and their reforms were aimed at reducing the power and influence of local kinship groups. With the backing of the king, they were able to establish well-endowed monasteries which owed little to local aristocratic support. It was during this period that over thirty monasteries were founded, some of them, such as Peterborough (966) and Ramsey (c. 971), in 'liberated' East Anglia, others in Mercia. The most spectacular event associated with the 'Tenth-Century Reformation' was the replacement in 964 of the clergy of Winchester Cathedral with monks from the new monastery of Abingdon. The new monasteries with considerable estates attached to them by royal grant became centres of royal influence. Small wonder that at Edgar's imperial coronation at Bath in 973, the queen should entertain abbots and abbesses, together with monks and nuns.

The reign of Edgar also witnessed a revived emphasis upon episcopal power at the expense of local interests. In Mercia, Oswald, with the backing of the king, greatly expanded the territorial base of the church of Worcester. Against a background of royal expansion, the new monks became the backbone of the episcopate. Monastic bishops were in effect royal bishops. When Edgar died, however, there was a strong reaction in south-west Mercia against the monks, and local nobility who had seen their influence curtailed were able to expel the newcomers and restore their own clerks.

Equally significant was the role of the reformers as propagandists for new-style national monarchy. Dunstan, Aethelwold and Oswald all saw the 'Godly Prince' as the chosen instrument of regeneration. The Anglo-Saxon Chronicle spoke of how 'God had helped him [Edgar] to subdue kings and earls who cheerfully submitted to his will.' The *Regularis Concordia Anglicae Nationis*, the code drawn up c. 970 to govern monastic life in England, allowed great influence to the king. Abbots were to be 'freely' elected but subject to the royal prerogative. In the early eleventh century Wulfstan, successively bishop of London, bishop of Worcester and archbishop of York (+1023), was a particularly strong advocate of royal authority, even though by now the king was the Danish Cnut.

In both Church and state during the tenth century, what later generations would call a social and political revolution had taken place. If the picture given here is correct, there was no simple evolution. The viking era brought about the downfall of the 'Old Order' and created conditions in which a new-style monarchy could extend its power from Wessex over English Mercia, and the Danelaw. What we do not know is the extent to which this 'empire' was accepted by its newly assimilated inhabitants. The problems which it ran into in the reign of Aethelred the Unready (978–1016) suggest that Wessex-style monarchy with its heavy burden of taxation, its military-style government, its 'reformed' monasticism and its depressed peasantry did not enjoy as much universal support as conventional interpretations would have us believe.

The new monarchy in fact did not long outlive Edgar. Political problems seem to have arisen, associated with the succession. There was, in addition, a good deal of hostility towards the newly powerful monks. Finally, from 980 onwards, Danish raids were renewed. Aethelred proved unable to deal with the many problems of his inheritance. In 1002 he was driven to the desperate but impracticable remedy of ordering the massacre of all Danes resident in England. His reign saw a prolonged struggle between the Wessex king and the kings of Denmark for control of England. In 1016 Aethelred died and was ultimately succeeded by the Dane Cnut (1016–35). 'England', now divided into four provinces, each ruled by a representative of Cnut, now became in effect a colony of Denmark. Though Edward, Aethelred's son, returned to the throne in 1042, some years after Cnut's death, English links with Denmark remained strong. The Danelaw was still very much a Danish province with its own law and culture. Kings of Norway also maintained a claim to the English throne. In the mid-eleventh century, the period which had begun with the viking raids of 793 showed little sign of having come to an end. It still looked very much as if the future of the English North Sea province would be linked with Scandinavia.

The events of the late tenth century and the first half of the eleventh bring out the problem of conceptualising the whole of the period from c. 500 to 1066 in terms of 'Anglo-Saxon England'. By the early eleventh century, it was the Danish colonists who were in control of events, and the term 'Anglo-Saxon' to some extent becomes a hindrance to our understanding the realities of the situation. We may therefore continue to think in terms of several sub-cultures each with its own distinctive traditions, though not uninfluenced by the rest. In some ways, the art of the period – with its distinction between the viking motifs of the east coast and the Carolingian trends of Wessex – helps to bring this out more clearly than more conventional forms of historical evidence. There was no English 'nation' at this time in any real sense, a fact which made the Norman success of 1066 so much easier.

Viking influence in the western sea-channels from Orkney southwards had the effect of creating new links between Ireland and Britain, which replaced the cultural ties which had developed since the sixth century. Scandinavian culture now dominated Orkney, Shetland and the Outer Hebrides. Viking cities – Dublin, Cork, Wexford and Wicklow – dominated the western side of the Irish Sea. The Isle of Man, on which viking control had replaced British rule, possessed a strategic importance during these centuries which it was not to enjoy again. The viking kings of Dublin entered into alliances with native Welsh rulers, with Cornish princes attempting to resist the spread of Anglo-Saxon colonists and with the Gaelic rulers of the 'Kingdom of Scots'. If our attention is confined to England it is possible to treat the coming of the vikings as a relatively short-lived threat which was dealt with effectively by Alfred the Great and his successors. When seen in the context of the British Isles it is clear that viking culture added a distinctive element, which remained unassimilated in many areas until the demographic crises of the fourteenth century.

The impact of the vikings upon the Celtic-speaking cultures of the British Isles was in many respects similar to that which they had upon 'England'. The loose kinship-based structures of the sub-Roman period gave way to feudal polities which we may see as a response to the viking threat. Marc Bloch in his study of feudal society (*La Société féodale* (1939; English transl. 1961)) denied that feudalism spread to Celtic areas. In his view 'Celtic' societies remained non-feudal in character for the simple reason that kinship groups in these societies were strong enough to meet the viking challenge. Modern Irish scholarship (and we know more about Ireland than about either Wales or Scotland) is less sure. It now seems that the older political divisions of Ireland gave way to a number of territorial kingdoms. By the first half of the twelfth century the political realities of Ireland revolved around new kingships which had arisen on the ruins of the old. These included the kingdoms of Leinster (much smaller in size than the modern province), Connacht (more limited in area than the modern province), Breifne (including modern Cavan and Leitrim) and in the south the kingdoms of south Munster (Desmond) and north Munster (Thomond). The ruling dynasties of these kingdoms were the families of MacMurrough, O Connor, O Rourke, MacCarthy and O Brien. By then the kingdom of Midhe in the hands of the Uí Néill had become 'the sick man of Ireland'; but at an earlier date under the aggressive leadership of Mael Sechlainn I (+862) of Clann Cholmaín it too may be numbered among these new-style kingdoms. By 1150, Ireland was very different from what it had been in the eighth century. Bloch, like many other historians, exaggerated the unchanging structure of 'Celtic' society.

One further fact may also be noted. The Normans did not reach Ireland until a century after they had overrun England and much of Wales. The Irish kingdoms, and to some extent those of Scotland, were given time to develop in the context of an 'Irish Sea province', independently of Norman pressures.

The process by which these new regional monarchies emerged is still something of a mystery to historians. It was not part of an inevitable pattern of political evolution but the outcome of a struggle between two concepts as to what constituted an acceptable transfer of power. On the one hand political power was conceived of as residing within a wide lineage, distinguished by the possession of royal blood, on the other as belonging to a much narrower dynastic family. On the former pattern, political power did not descend directly from father to son but to a candidate chosen by the kinship group at large. This was the basis of 'tanistry', from *tánaise* ('the awaited one'), a candidate chosen in each generation with the right of succession. Hereditary feudal monarchy rested upon a different basis, according to which the choice of successor rested with the ruling king. Clearly two different conceptions as to what constituted a 'just' succession were involved.

Perhaps the best known example of the bitter conflicts to which this situation might give rise is provided by a society whose history in many ways parallels that of Ireland. In eleventh-century Scotland, MacBeth killed the reigning king, Duncan, and took the kingship himself. Shakespeare's account of this episode, though excellent drama, is misleading historically. In fact, MacBeth was the older man, with a traditional claim resting upon traditional kinship right. It was the younger man, Duncan, grandson of the feudalising monarch Malcolm II, who represented the new tendency towards hereditary monarchy. In Scotland, as in Ireland, such an episode was not merely a power struggle, though it could also be that, but a conflict between two cultures, each with its own justification.

As we saw earlier, the rights and duties of lineages (that is, kinship groups which acted as a unit) were based upon long-standing local possession. In Ireland, as in much of western Europe, the vendetta (*fíoc bunaid* in Irish, *galanas* in Welsh) seemed part of the 'nature of things'. In the absence of a central authority it was the ultimate sanction of law. Kinsmen had the duty to resort to it, if all else failed. Fear of causing a vendetta which might extend over several generations was clearly a powerful factor in persuading an offending party, pushed from behind perhaps by his own kinsmen, to seek out a member of the injured lineage and offer compensation. The guarantee for due performance would be a powerful person willing to act as surety. In all of these proceedings, the lineage and not the individual was the basic unit. To injure one was to injure all. To be injured by one, was to be given the right to injure all.

Monarchical government, in contrast, stood for law enforcement from above and for exemplary punishment, not compensation. The king or the royal justices decided whether a crime had been committed and carried out the punishment, which could include hanging or mutilation. From the monarchical viewpoint the vendetta represented anarchy. To those adhering to the traditional kinship code, monarchy might well stand for savage and institutionalised injustice.

In Ireland, as in western Europe generally, the coming of the vikings was an undoubted factor in the rise of the new monarchies. The impact of the vikings on Ireland was as severe as it was upon other parts of the British Isles. During the ninth century the vikings raided monasteries on the eastern and southern coasts and established a fortress at Dublin. In the course of the tenth century they established centres at Waterford, Limerick and Cork. In Wicklow the vikings ('dark foreigners', *dubhgaill*, from which the modern Irish surname 'Doyle' is derived) were kept to a narrow strip of land between hills and sea. This section of the Irish coast, now a tourist attraction for the growing conurbation of Dublin, was then a wilderness which attracted the monks of Glendalough as well as the Céili Dé of Tallaght and Finglas. As they did on the coast of Lancashire at Formby and Ainsdale the vikings brought land into cultivation which the native inhabitants could not themselves reclaim, or did not wish to.

In some parts of Ireland and for some aspects of Irish culture, the initial impact of the vikings was devastating. During the first half of the ninth century the north-east, the old kingdom of the Ulaid, suffered severely. The monasteries of Bangor on Strangford Lough and Moville on the Ards peninsula were destroyed. The loss of these monasteries, which formed the western end of a cultural unit stretching from Iona to Lindisfarne in Northumbria was a blow from which the insular culture did not recover. Further down the coast the establishment of a viking settlement at Dublin marked the beginning of a new age.

The second phase of viking expansion, in the south of Ireland, was marked both by a greater emphasis on trade and by a more decisive reaction on the Irish side. After some initial success the viking colonists ('Ostmen', men from the east) at Limerick, Waterford and Cork found themselves compelled to come to terms with the local rulers and in effect became client states forced to dance to an internal pattern of politics. Tensions between the two cultures endured for a long time. In the late eleventh century, for example, the bishops of Dublin sought consecration from Canterbury rather than from their Irish neighbours.

Earlier historians, following the evidence of the annals, may well have exaggerated the destructive role of the vikings. Another source of distortion derived from twelfth-century chronicles anxious to provide propaganda for their patrons. *The Struggle of the Gael against the Foreigner* (*Cogadh Gaedhel re Gallaibh*), for example, described Brian Boru leading a campaign to drive the vikings out of Ireland. In the view of some modern Irish scholars, the *Cogadh* now appears as very much a piece of official history written two centuries after the event to glorify the O Briens. The battle of Clontarf (1014) was fought not between Irish and viking but between the forces of Brian Boru and an alliance of the kings of Leinster and Dublin vikings, joined in an attempt to resist what they saw as the unwelcome intrusion of the O Briens of Munster. In such a context, the term 'Irish' can be as misleading as 'Anglo-Saxon' in the history of the North Sea province.

So far from having a totally negative effect upon Ireland, and Europe generally, some of the vikings at least seem to have been traders and farmers, not just marauders. Recent excavations in Dublin have produced unmistakable evidence, in the form of coins and of manufactures such as shoes, for this aspect of viking activity. The vikings, indeed, may be seen as having opened up to commerce a culture which had been landlocked. The result, it would appear, was the rise to prominence of those parts of Ireland which hitherto had been of minor economic and political importance. The ports of Dublin, Wexford and Waterford eventually brought the kingdom of Leinster to a leading place among the new kingdoms. The same may also be said for the effect of Cork upon the MacCarthy kingdom of Desmond and of Limerick upon the O Brien kingdom of Ormond. The economic and financial resources which such centres represented provided the new monarchs with sources of revenue which helped them to build on a much larger scale than had hitherto been possible. The link between the new monarchies and the vikings is also indicated by the way in which Scandinavian motifs dominated 'Irish' art in the late eleventh and early twelfth centuries.

The new patterns of monarchy first made their appearance in the southern half of Ireland during the tenth century. A hitherto subject people of the Eoghanachta, the 'Dál Cais', took advantage of the weakness of their overlords in the face of the vikings to establish a kingdom of their own. Their leaders, Brian Boru and his elder brother, were 'new men' but it was not long before an appropriate genealogy had been manufactured, tracing the descent of the Uí Briain, as their successors were to be called, back to the Sons of Míl. Brian died in 1014 at the battle of Clontarf but his dynasty continued to be the leading force in the south for the next century and more. Unfortunately we know little about the machinery by which this kingdom was kept together, since historians have tended to concentrate their attention upon a largely mythical high kingship. As will appear later (see pp. 51–3), the O Briens, to give them their more familiar name, behaved not as 'high kings' but as regional monarchs of a new pattern, to be found elsewhere in the British Isles. Where they differed from the Eoghanachta was in their adoption of hereditary descent (or where an heir was too young, in granting the right to succeed to a close relative) and of territorial borders.

The best studied of the new kingdoms is Leinster, the last native king of which, Diarmaid MacMurrough (+1171) invited the Normans into Ireland. Until the viking period 'Leinster' consisted of a number of groupings of *tuatha* (petty kingdoms) most of them under the tutelage of the Uí Néill. In the early eleventh century, Diarmaid MacMail na mBo (+1072), king of a newly powerful branch of the Uí Cheinnsellaigh, gained control of the Liffey valley hitherto ruled by the Uí Dúnlainge from their 'capital' at Naas. From then onwards (despite some setbacks) the dynasty of Diarmaid ruled as kings of an expanding Leinster, sometimes backed by other kingdoms as a client against the Uí Néill. In an elaborate analysis of the regnal succession in this area over several centuries, Professor Ó Corráin has shown how 'contest' forms of succession between widely diffused kinship groups eventually gave way to a much more concentrated form of dynastic succession. The prize for the victors was prestige, power and land. A similar type of development took place in the several other kingdoms which emerged from, or perhaps more accurately were carved out of, the 'Old Order' by leaders of ability, whose ambitions were to found their own dynasty.

The implications of the new patterns went well beyond regulations concentrating royal succession within a particular family. Feudal-style changes implied control from above, in ways which were unprecedented in Irish society. The new spirit is to be seen most clearly in the ecclesiastical sphere. Hitherto, as we have seen, the monastic Church was loosely organised upon principles of kinship and clientage. Such attempts at centralisation as did take place were not based upon territorial unity but around networks linking monasteries which were divided by geography. The dispersed jurisdiction of a saint and his heirs may be seen as to some extent the ecclesiastical counterpart of the loose political organisation of the Uí Néill and of the Eoghanachta. Kinship groups on the traditional pattern of hereditary professions enjoyed remarkable continuity in their control of monastic endowments.

One of the most significant internal changes introduced by the new kings was the introduction of bishops as a weapon of 'reform' from above against the old-style 'kinship' monasteries. Thus within their kingdom of Munster the O Briens backed the creation of a diocese of Killaloe, which corresponded in extent with their own territory. In Connacht, the O Connor kings took over former O Flaherty territory and made its 'capital' Tuam (from *tuaim*, 'mound') into the see of a new diocese. Tuam in due course was to become the centre of an archbishopric. A similar development took place in the kingdom of Leinster where Ferns, on the site of an ancient monastery, became the seat of a new diocese, co-extensive with the territory controlled by the Uí Cheinnselaigh kings. In what is now Co. Cavan, Kilmore became the episcopal seat of the O Rourkes, kings of Breifne. Such changes in Ireland paralleled what was taking place in Wessex, England and Europe generally where bishops received their croziers from the king in a feudal ceremony. The bishops, as royal men, could be called upon to support royal authority within territories, which from one point of view were kingdoms and from another dioceses. Diarmaid MacMurrough made his brother-in-law, Lorcán Ua Tuathail/Laurence O Toole, archbishop of Dublin, when he wished to control that city; but he was not alone among Irish monarchs in cementing close links with the episcopate. As in the 'Tenth-Century Reformation' in England, the new bishops became an additional arm of the secular power.

In architecture, the spread of the new Romanesque style supplies a further indica-

THE IRISH SEA PROVINCE IN PREHISTORY

Cultural contacts between various parts of the British Isles extend well back into prehistoric times. Megalithic tombs dating from c. 3500 B.C. are to be found on both sides of the Irish Sea. The two passage-graves illustrated here are Newgrange on the east coast of Ireland and Barlodiad-y-gawres on the Welsh coast (Anglesey).

1a Passage-grave at Newgrange (Co. Meath) situated in the Boyne valley near the east coast of Ireland.

1b Passage-grave of Barlodiad-y-gawres (Anglesey)

In the immediate pre-Roman period, hill-forts were the strongpoints of rival kingdoms.

2 Maiden Castle (Dorset) was sacked by the Romans shortly after the invasion of A.D. 43. Nearby was built the town of Dorchester.

3 Iron Age hill-fort, Baltinglass Hill (Co. Wicklow).

4 White Catherthun (Angus), a Pictish hill-fort with stone walls which may well have been 40 feet thick. Of all the cultures of pre-Roman Britain the Picts, whose language is unknown, but who were probably Celtic-speaking, were the least exposed to Roman influence.

5 A hill-fort at Moel-y-Gaer (Denbighshire) set in the Welsh hills. Under the Roman occupation, this part of Britain was controlled from Chester.

THE ROMAN PRESENCE

The Romans might have attempted to conquer the whole of the British Isles, but in fact did not move much further north than the river Tay (in modern Perthshire). This northern line is illustrated by the aerial photograph of the Roman fort at Ardoch (Perthshire), whose rectangular outline contrasts sharply with the oval hill-forts. As similar Roman forts indicate, there was a strong Roman military presence north of the Trent and west of the Severn. In the north, Hadrian's Wall marked the frontier from the mid-second century A.D.

6 Ardoch (Perthshire): one of the best preserved forts of the Roman period. It was abandoned c. A.D. 105 when the Romans moved the frontier further south.

7 Segontium (near modern Caernarfon) was a Roman fort on the Menai Strait controlling the crossing to the island of Mona (today's Anglesey). The aerial photograph reveals the rectangular outline of the barracks to the right of modern houses.

8 This illustration of Caerwent may serve as an example of the numerous small towns of southern Britain during the Roman period. The outlines of the town of Venta Silurum, the capital of the Silures of south Wales, may be seen along the edges of the modern town of Caerwent. Ten miles away was the major Roman base of Isca (today's Caerleon).

9 Emain Macha (Navan Fort) near modern Armagh. Although the Roman legions did not reach Ireland, Latin Christianity eventually arrived in Ireland c. 432 in the person of the Roman Briton, Patrick. Later traditions have linked Patrick with Tara (Co. Meath). The likelihood is, however, that he confined himself to the kingdom of the Ulaid with its capital at Emain Macha.

After the departure of the Roman legions in the early fifth century revolutionary changes occurred within the British Isles. In eastern Britain Anglo-Saxon settlers moved north and west of East Anglia and Kent, eventually establishing the new kingdoms of Northumbria, Mercia and Wessex. On the north-west coast of Britain, Irish settlers from Ulster established themselves in Argyll (so-called from the Gaelic *earraghaidheal* – the coastland of the Gaels). In south Wales a line of Irish kings ruled the kingdom of Dyfed. The Britons were confined to western areas in what is now Strathclyde, Cumbria, Wales and Cornwall. Colonies of Britons were also established in the Armorican peninsula in what is now modern Brittany (Little Britain).

10 Dumbarton was capital of the British kingdom of Strathclyde, stretching from the Clyde as far south as Cumbria. 'Dumbarton' takes its name from the Gaelic 'fort of the Britons'. Its British name was 'Ath Clut' (Clyde Rock). Dumbarton fell to the vikings in 870. The rock in the foreground was the original 'Dumbarton'.

11 Dunadd (near Kilmartin, Argyll) was capital of the Irish kingdom of Dalriada. After the establishment of a 'Kingdom of Scots' unifying Picts and Irish under Kenneth MacAlpin (d. 858) the political balance shifted eastward. Dunkeld replaced Iona as the ecclesiastical centre of the new kingdom and Scone replaced Dunadd as its political capital. The British are termed 'P-Celts' (their word for 'head', for example, is 'pen'); the Irish were 'Q-Celts' ('head' in Irish is 'ceann'). Scots Gaelic (e.g. Kintyre) and Manx (e.g. Kermode) are Q-Celtic. Breton is P-Celtic.

12 The Celtic monastery of Iona off the coast of Argyll (founded c. 565) was a crucial religious link between Ireland and north Britain. Its founder was Colmcille (Columba) of Derry (521–97), who brought Christianity to the Irish colony of Dalriada (Argyll) and thence to Pictland. After the viking invasions, Iona fell into decay and in the early thirteenth century was converted into a Benedictine monastery. The surviving buildings date from the fourteenth century. During the later middle ages Iona became the centre of an important school of stone cross carving within the lordship of the Isles.

13 Lindisfarne, a Celtic monastery on an island off the coast of Northumberland, was established by Aedan, a monk from Iona, who came at the invitation of King Oswald of Northumbria. Christianity in Northumbria was a mixture of Celtic and Roman traditions which came into conflict at the Synod of Whitby in 664. The buildings shown in the illustration were built on the site of the original Celtic monastery during the Norman period long after it had been sacked by the vikings (793).

Germanic settlers on the east coast formed part of the wide movement of European peoples which we term the 'Barbarian invasions'. The kingdom of East Anglia was one of a number of small Anglo-Saxon kingdoms which were often under pressure from their more powerful neighbours. It was in East Anglia that the Sutton Hoo ship burial, dating from the mid-seventh century, was discovered in 1939. It proved to be one of the most remarkable archaeological finds ever made in Britain.

14 The Sutton Hoo ship burial. The ship burial at Sutton Hoo was almost certainly that of a mid-seventh-century East Anglian king. It was primarily pagan in character though there were some Christian elements. There were clearly great differences in the degree of Christianisation of the various Anglo-Saxon kingdoms.

15 The magnificent buckle found at Sutton Hoo. Its interlacing motif was to be taken up by artists and stone masons in the Celtic tradition, as the evidence of the Irish high crosses indicates. The presence of hanging bowls of Irish design at Sutton Hoo also suggests links between Ireland and Anglo-Saxon England at the artistic level.

16 The Ardagh chalice, now in the National Museum of Ireland, is perhaps the greatest artistic treasure of the Irish Golden Age. Despite its unmistakable Celtic provenance, the ornamentation of the stem was influenced by Germanic 'kerbschnitt' woodcarving. Thus in art, as elsewhere, due attention needs to be paid to a British Isles context.

tion of the activity of the new royal patrons. Early monastic churches had been on a small scale. The Romanesque churches were larger and more expensive, as befitted symbols of royal power. The most spectacular example of the new style is Cormac's Chapel built on the Rock of Cashel by Cormac MacCarthy and consecrated in 1134. Cashel had hitherto been associated with the Eoghanachta. The new chapel symbolised the coming of a new political order.

But Cashel did not stand alone. A building similar in style was constructed at Clonfert for the O Connors. At the older monastic sites of Clonmacnoise and Glendalough larger buildings indicate the establishment of royal control. At Glendalough, for example, a new monastic 'city' was constructed well down the valley from the original site of St Kevin. It was here that a cathedral was built, which still displays its twelfth-century chancel. The king whose power this celebrated was Diarmaid MacMurrough. MacMurrough's hand was also to be seen in the building of a Romanesque church at Killeshin (Co. Carlow) on the site of an earlier foundation. Clonmacnoise, once a centre of Uí Néill influence, became an object of interest to the O Connors in the twelfth century. Turlough O Connor was buried there in 1156 and his son Ruaidhrí in 1198. Here, as elsewhere, building in the Romanesque style marks a new departure. Thus the Nuns' Church built (1167) by the celebrated Derbforgaill, wife of Tighernán Ua Ruairc, in the Romanesque style, is very much part of a general pattern of royal patronage. The gap between such works as this and the earlier churches is immense. One of them belonged to a new European feudal world, the other to one which was far more localised.

In view of all this 'modernising' activity in the southern half of Ireland, it is not surprising that further initiatives for ecclesiastical reform should also come from that area. In 1111 the first reforming Synod, that of Raith Bresail (near Cashel), was held under the auspices of Gilla Espuic, bishop of Limerick, who was backed by Muirchertach Ua Briain, king of Munster. Malchus of Lismore, a protégé of the MacCarthys, was another southern reformer. Reform, however, was not confined entirely to the south. At Armagh, Cellach (+1129) and his protégé, Malachy (+1148), were the spearhead of a movement to weaken the grip upon Armagh of the hereditary coarbs of Clann Sinaich, to which Cellach belonged. Malachy, after successes at Armagh, retired in 1137 to become bishop of Down. Here as elsewhere, 'reform' implied the extension of episcopal authority with the backing of secular power. Another Synod held at Kells in 1152/3 instituted the four provinces of Armagh, Tuam, Cashel and Dublin. In so doing, it recognised political realities as well as the imperatives of reform. An earlier plan called for two archdioceses, based on Armagh and Cashel. The addition of Tuam and Dublin indicated the powerful influence of the O Connors and of Diarmaid MacMurrough. The new order in the Church marked a further decline in status of traditional monastic centres, such as Clonmacnoise, Emly, Kells and Clonard, and for the system of kinship-based monasticism which they symbolised.

The process of kingdom-building involved the growth of monarchical centres of power in ways which were analogous to the building up of territorial dioceses at the expense of local monasteries. The process has been insufficiently studied as yet by historians but enough has been done to provide glimpses of what was involved. Thus, the growth of the O Connor kingdom of Connacht led to expansion from their base in Roscommon and the subsequent 'takeover' of the great plain of Galway around Tuam. The sufferers in the story were the O Flahertys who were forced into west Connacht. Similar internal conquest took place at the expense of the O Kellys of Uí Mhaine when the O Connors seized the strategic site of Athlone and erected a castle there; studies of the rise of the other kingdoms show a similar development. What had been local centres of power could no longer survive in a changing world. The choice lay between becoming the feudal vassals of the new kings or facing dispossession. Some local groups may have welcomed the protection of one king rather than another. Others may have had feudalism thrust upon them.

Many interrelated developments point to the rise of centralising kingships at the expense of traditional, diffused, political structures. In Ireland, as elsewhere in the British Isles and western Europe, monarchy involved castle-building, the setting up or a royal household as a bureaucratic base, the establishment of professional armies and the raising of taxation to pay for them, the promulgation of law on the basis of royal authority rather than as the expression of local custom and, not least, the development of an 'ideology' of kingship.

No doubt the attacks of the vikings, in Ireland as elsewhere, exposed the weaknesses of the *ancien régime* and made new developments possible. By the eleventh century, however, internal struggles had become the chief factor behind change. Control of Ireland's richest resource, land, was the reward for success. Kings were able to offer freshly acquired land to their followers and, in return, to receive homage. As we have seen, Church 'reform' offered possibilities in this direction. Thus Brian Boru's brother, Marcán, was the pluralist abbot of several monasteries on the Shannon. To make a grant to the Church in such circumstances was merely to transfer wealth from one branch of the family to another. But grants of land were also made on a large scale to loyal political followers. Thus Turlough O Connor granted away a large part of Meath to O Rourke who presumably, in his turn, granted it to his own followers as a means of making possession secure. Such Irish kings had little to learn, in this respect, from the Normans.

Where the kings retained control of new territories in their own hands, they appointed a governor or viceroy (*airrí*) on whom they could depend. At a level below these was the royal steward (*rechtaire*) and household-officials (*lucht tige*) normally drawn from less powerful segments of the royal lineage. Territorial kingship required royal 'capitals'. Thus the O Briens had as their seats Kincora, Killaloe, Dún na Scaith and not least Limerick which, from the mid-eleventh century, was a seat of O Brien power. The O Connors for their part had Tuam, Athlone and Clonmacnoise. Castles, professional troops to man them and fleets of ships also made their appearance at this time. The need to finance such a political and military structure led naturally to taxation on a new scale.

From this period dates the rise of new bardic families who took the place of the *filid*, and of the monastic *fir teighir*, as six centuries earlier the *filid* had benefited from the fall of the druids and had become the custodians of secular traditions. What lay behind this change is still a matter for research but it would seem that the bards formed the basis of a new 'establishment', many of whose members were drawn from weaker segments of the major royal kindreds. Such families as the MacBrodys, historians to the O Briens, are typical of the new intellectual class which, like many of the humanists of the sixteenth century, produced propaganda for their patrons. Among the typical literary products of this establishment culture were the bardic poems.

Ideological backing for the new monarchies took several forms, one of the most subtle of which was genealogical in character. Under the influence of royal genealogists the genealogical tracts were 'ruthlessly edited', to use Professor Ó Corráin's words. Whereas thirty-one lines of descent within the ruling house of Ciarraige had been recorded in 750, by 1100 the focus had been narrowed to one line, that of the O Connors. Such a concentration upon a single royal line indicates more clearly than any other single fact how far access to political power shrank during this period. The rise of royal 'surnames' at this time also illustrates the same process at work. Older broad lineages gave way to narrower family loyalties indicated by the adoption of a 'surname'. Kinship loyalty remained strong but it was no longer defined within a clear structure but survived rather as a vague commitment to the *sliocht*.

Propaganda of a more obvious kind was provided by such treatises as *Cogadh Gaedhel re Gallaibh* (*The Struggle of the Gael against the Foreigner*) for the O Briens and *Caithréim Chellacháin Chaisil* (*The Wars of Cellachan of Cashel*) for the MacCarthys. The *Cogadh* stressed the role of the king as a dispenser of justice and keeper of the peace, while the *Caithréim* gave a picture of the ideal vassal. In an age which was largely illiterate, changes in ritual perhaps reached a wider audience.

Behind these changes lay a profound transition in attitudes to law. The evidence of the pre-Viking Age Irish law tracts suggests that in early Irish society law concerned the settlement of disputes between different kinship groups on the basis of compensation. From the tenth century onwards in Ireland, as in other parts of the British Isles, a new emphasis upon law as the imposition of authority from above makes its appearance. Christian teaching certainly played a significant part in this. An eighth-century canon-law collection quotes with approval a text stating that 'the word of a king is a sword for beheading, a rope for hanging, it casts into prison, it condemns to exile'. The churchmen called upon the king to use capital punishment in defence of their interests, clearly a sharp contrast with the theory of early Irish law. Clerical teaching, indeed, was upon the duty of the king to exercise authority and not upon the limitations of his power.

Much of the significance of all this has been concealed from view by the fact that the Irish law tracts of a much earlier period continued to be copied down in the central and late middle ages. It seems clear, however, that continuity with the past, which such copying symbolised, was largely fictitious. Rudolf Thurneysen, the leading twentieth-century student of the law tracts, described the work of the later commentators as

> creating an amalgam in which contact with the world of fact is abandoned in favour of elaborate calculations, minute casuistry and strange construction which often lead to impossible results and can never have had any significance for the practical administration of the law . . . the dreams of bookworms, of pedlars of antiquarianism.

The realities of legal practice which lay behind the smokescreen of the law tracts are suggested by brief references in the chronicles to royal lawyers. One of them was called 'ollam breithemnuis Érenn' ('professor of the jurisprudence of Ireland') but in practical terms he was a royal judge of the O Briens. Many of the new study-lawyers were churchmen, a fact which at this date suggests that they were both literate and sympathetic to the enforcement of law by royal authority. No doubt kinship groups imposed great limitations upon the full exercise of royal power, but the evidence certainly indicates that these developments were making their mark. The Irish high kingship may have been a 'will o' the wisp' as indeed was the regal vision of Alfred the Great's successors in Britain. But the realities of Irish kingly power cannot be denied.

Between the coming of the vikings and the Norman invasions beginning in 1169 it is clear that Irish society underwent a radical transformation. The old order of two ruling federations, each resting upon loosely organised networks of autonomous *tuatha* and locally based monastic communities gave way to new-style territorial kingdoms held together by quasi-feudal ties and supported by a reformed episcopate, centralised religious orders and subordinate towns. The impact of the vikings may have been partially responsible for this change but internal causes seem to have been as important. Perhaps because the vikings did not affect Irish society as much as they did English, the swing towards monarchy was not as marked as it might have been. Many aspects of the old order of kinship and clientage survived, though with reduced status and at a more informal level. The recognition of permanent feudal ties between lord and vassal, the introduction of cash relationships and a new emphasis upon the duty to obey a king or a bishop were new developments in Ireland but they did not eradicate all traditional ties. Local cults still retained their force. Local memories remained tenacious about the intrusion of newcomers even when the official historians told a different story. The vendetta remained even at the level of kinship. When Diarmaid MacMurrough abducted O Rourke's wife Derbforgaill in 1152 he created a feud which was still reverberating over a decade later.

England and Ireland provide the most convenient and best-studied examples of the impact of the vikings upon the cultures of the British Isles. Unfortunately we know much less about northern Britain and 'Wales'. The problem presented by ignorance is made worse by the manner in which national historians of 'Wales' and 'Scotland' (as indeed those of 'England' and 'Ireland') create a framework which presents the 'emergence' of these 'nations' as the primary fact in which we should be interested. Indeed, we deal better with the intricacies of historical development if we leave 'national' categories out of the picture as much as possible. In both northern and western Britain, we may assume, several distinct cultures continued to exist with their own sense of identity and their own view of 'their' past. What later generations see as the emergence of a nation involved the superimposition of one culture upon another. In what we know as 'Scotland', an Irish Q-Celtic culture succeeded in imposing itself upon Picts, Britons and Anglians. But this occurred only in the south and east; in the north and west, viking culture was to achieve its own dominance. Thus the net result of the viking invasions was a new division of northern Britain into distinctive cultural areas. In 'Wales', the viking presence was less marked than it was elsewhere in the British Isles but the consequences were severe enough to induce profound changes.

One of the main results of the arrival of the vikings in the Irish Sea was probably to make contact more difficult between the various P-Celtic communities of west Britain though there is no evidence that links with Brittany and Ireland were cut, rather the reverse. Such links came to be symbolised in the figures of St Samson of Dol (+565) who was believed to have left south Wales for Brittany and St Illtyd, the founder of the monastery in south Wales which came to be known as Llantwit Major (viz., Llanilltud Fawr, the principal church of Illtud), who was believed to come from Brittany. The close links of the kingdom of Dyfed with Ireland are also evident during the sub-Roman period. From the ninth century onwards, however, viking control of the Severn Sea (indicated by over forty Scandinavian place-names in south Wales) and of the Dee estuary divided the P-Celtic cultures of the west more sharply than had been the case before. Some historians believe that the result of these changes was to make possible the emergence of 'Wales' as a distinct British geographical area, separated from Cornwall, Brittany and Strathclyde.

But 'Wales' still remains an elusive concept. There is a Bismarkian assumption about much modern Welsh historical writing as if 'unification' were an end toward which the history of western Britain should have been moving. Thus the ninth-century king, Rhodri the Great, and the tenth-century king, Hywel the Good, once earned approval from historians for their attempts to bring unity to the disparate parts of 'Wales'. The fact that they did not succeed should give us pause. Clearly they met with opposition from their fellow-countrymen who, on nationalist assumptions about the past, should have been the first to welcome their efforts. The term 'Wales' provides a clue as to why such opposition should exist. 'Wales' ('foreign') did not exist save in the minds of the Anglo-Saxons to the east. The P-Celtic-speaking inhabitants of the west saw themselves primarily as 'Britons' belonging to one or other of the various sub-Roman kingdoms or tribal groupings into which the area was divided.

To do some degree of justice to the complexity of the situation during this period we should do well to think of western Britain as being divided into at least three sub-cultures, one (Gwynedd) looking north to Strathclyde and the other 'Gwyr y Gogledd' (the 'Men of the North'), another (Powys) oriented more towards Mercia in the east but still retaining through its bardic poetry the memory of ties with northern Britain, and a third (Dyfed, Glamorgan, and Gwent) linked southward towards the Severn Sea, Cornwall and Brittany. There was no sense of unity in 'Wales'. Attempts by any of these sub-cultures to assert dominance over the others were resisted, even to the extent of seeking help from the Anglo-Saxons. Thus in the ninth century the southern kingdoms of Dyfed, Glywysing and Gwent sought help from Wessex in an attempt to stave off pressure from Gwynedd.

The cultural differences between north and south probably went back to tribal loyalties which the Roman empire had done little to weaken. There was also a 'hidden Wales' in the border counties of Cheshire, Shropshire and Herefordshire, about which we know little but which almost certainly continued to haunt memories on the 'Welsh' side of the border. In the tenth century, as the poem *Armes Prydein Vawr* (*Prophecy of Great Britain*) indicates, some Britons at least were hoping, in alliance with the vikings, the Scots and Strathclyde, to drive the English into the sea. Had the battle of Brunanburh (937) turned out differently, some Welsh border territory might have been recovered. As late as the eleventh century many English settlements well to the east of Offa's Dyke bore the mark of British raids, as Domesday Book itself indicates in references to 'vills laid waste'.

It was during this period of profound change that an 'invention of tradition' took place comparable to that which occurred in England and Ireland. The *History of the Britons* lays particular stress upon the role of the northern kingdom of Gwynedd and was perhaps written as a piece of 'official history' to provide backing for the new dynasty of which Rhodri Mawr (the Great) was to be the main representative. The *History of the Britons* also contains references to the sixth-century bards, Aneirin and Taliesin, presumably as an attempt to provide further 'historical' backing. Aneirin may well have been the author of *The Gododdin*, the heroic poem dealing with events in north Britain during the sixth century. The emergence of episcopal sees at St Davids in Dyfed and Bangor in Gwynedd probably also represents an attempt by the new kings to 'modernise' the Church in their own territories at the expense of the localised monastic institutions of an earlier period. In these various ways, the new dynasties which the viking period brought into existence created a sense of legitimacy for themselves.

As elsewhere in the British Isles, in Wales the coming of the vikings led to the downfall of the 'Old Order'. New men, the Welsh equivalent of the O Briens, carved out kingdoms for themselves. In the north, during the ninth century, the new dynasty of Merfyn Frydi (its first king, 826–44) and Rhodri the Great took over Gwynedd.

In the south in the tenth century a great part of south Wales came to be known as Morganwg (the 'Glamorgan' of a later period) from one of its most successful rulers, Morgan (c. 930–74). New men also seized the ancient kingdom of Gwent. In the south-west, Hywel, known to history as Hywel Dda, acquired control of the kingdom of Dyfed. He also briefly became king of Gwynedd (942–50). Faced with a choice between viking and Anglo-Saxon Hywel chose the latter, rejecting the policy of resistance which the poet of *Armes Prydein Vawr* advocated.

In northern Britain at the end of the eighth century cultural patterns were more variegated than was the case further south. North of the Humber, Anglian culture was dominant up to the Firth of Forth, P-Celtic culture still survived on the Clyde and the Solway Firth, the Q-Celtic Irish of Dalriada controlled Argyll and the Isles and had extended their influence north-eastwards; and on the east coast the Pictish kingdom maintained a precarious independence. Four cultures, four languages and four legal traditions contended for supremacy with the balance perhaps favouring the Anglo-Saxons and the Q-Celts. All this was to be radically changed from the end of the eighth century as a result of the viking invasions. In the north, the vikings seized control of the territory of the northern Picts in Orkney, Shetland and Caithness. The hill land to the south of the plain of Ross came to be called 'Sutherland' (South-land), a geographical perspective which reflected the viewpoint of the newcomers. The place-name 'Dingwall' near the Moray Firth is the same as 'Thingwall' on the coast of Lancashire, both names illustrating the influence of the vikings in northern Britain.

In the west of 'Scotland' the repeated sacking of Iona by vikings from 793 onwards marked the failure of the rulers of Dalriada to protect their holy places and increasingly control of the Western Isles was taken over by the Gall-Gaedhil ('Foreign Gaels') raiders of mixed culture, who spoke a form of Q-Celtic. Viking influence was dominant from the Outer Hebrides southwards (the place-names of the Isle of Lewis are heavily Scandinavian). The kingdom of Strathclyde effectively lost its independence after the taking of Dumbarton in 870 and became a client state of the 'Kingdom of Scots', whose rulers connived at the murder of the last of its independent kings. Strathclyde maintained a precarious separate existence into the eleventh century but was never again a major local power.

Change was equally marked in the east where from the mid-ninth century the kingdoms of the southern Picts fell under the control of a 'new man' of obscure background, Kenneth MacAlpin. MacAlpin's career resembles that of other new-style kings in other parts of the British Isles. A 'Kingdom of Scots' now arose based upon the conquest of Pictland, Strathclyde and of Anglian Bernicia. The dominant culture of this kingdom was at first the Irish culture of Dalriada from which Kenneth came. It is tempting to assert that, as was the case with the new dynasties of Wales and Ireland, a fictitious genealogy was soon concocted, linking him with the early rulers of Dalriada, Cenel Gabhrain, but it is not clear that he belonged in fact to that lineage. Finally, further south, the collapse of the Anglo-Saxon kingdom of

Northumbria in the face of viking attacks led to the setting up of a viking kingdom of York. The ninth century saw the establishment of a viking empire in north Britain, which in its heyday influenced the course of events within the British Isles from 'capitals' at Dublin and York.

There is a general tendency among historians of Scotland (as also among English and Irish historians) to play down the importance of the role of the vikings in the history of northern Britain as if it were historically pre-determined that the Scottish nation should emerge under the leadership of the south-eastern-based 'Kingdom of Scots'. The fact that the vikings came to speak Gaelic and to adopt the kinship-based framework of Celtic society has tended to obscure the viking presence in the Highlands and the Hebrides. The 'MacDonalds' and 'MacDougalls' of Highland history take their names from the 'Donald' and 'Dougall' who were grandsons of Somerled, the Gaelic-Scandinavian chief who carved out a kingdom for himself in Argyll. (The name 'Dougall' itself derives from *dubhgall* ('dark foreigner') which as we have seen appeared as 'Doyle' in Ireland.) 'Somerled' itself was also gaelicised into 'Somhairle' and eventually anglicised into 'Sorley' in the late sixteenth century. (Sorley Boy MacDonnell, the Ulster chieftain who came into conflict with Elizabeth, was Somhairle Buidhe – Sorley the Blonde.) Indeed, the military traditions of the Highlands probably derive from the vikings rather than from the so-called 'wild Irish'. It has even been suggested that the bitter rivalries between Campbells and MacDonalds derive from the overthrow of the Christian kingdoms by the pagan viking newcomers in the ninth century and a long-lived legacy of hatred which was its result.

A permanent Scandinavian presence in Britain north of the Humber was one of the main consequences of the invasions of the ninth and tenth centuries. Another indirect consequence was the establishment of a Gaelic empire, the 'Kingdom of Scots', in what had been the independent territories of southern Pictland, Strathclyde and (northern) Bernicia. In effect, this brought about, for a time, the dominance of Gaelic culture in these areas leaving Pictish, British and Anglian cultures in a subordinate position. The Welsh *Brut y Tywysogion* (*Chronicle of the Princes*) states that 'the men of Strathclyde ... had to depart from their country, and to go to Gwynedd'. In later stories it is stated that Kenneth MacAlpin came to be king 'after violent deaths, after violent slaughter'. Thus the 'Kingdom of Scots' did not emerge as part of a providential development in which 'Scotland' came to take its place among the nations of the earth but, at least in the eyes of its sub-cultures, as a process analogous to that by which the vikings established themselves elsewhere.

The novelty of these developments in the 'Kingdom of Scots' was indicated by the way in which the new dynasty came to cut its links with Iona and to give its patronage to new holy places at Dunkeld and St Andrews. The introduction of St Andrew, an apostle without any apparent connection with Britain, as a cult-figure in eastern Pictland was an important symbolic change. These changes were not, however, accompanied by a shift towards episcopacy, a development which in Scotland did not occur until 1100 at the earliest. Though it was called the 'Kingdom of Scots' there were in fact relatively few 'Scots' (viz., Gaels) in the new kingdom save as a ruling elite (the English ascendancy in eighteenth-century Ireland offers a possible comparison). Of all the political units of the British Isles, the 'Kingdom of Scots' had the least homogeneous cultural foundations.

On the eve of the Norman Conquest of 1066 the future of the British Isles seemed to be largely linked to Scandinavia. Seaborne trade in all areas was in viking hands. The ports of the east coast of Ireland and of the eastern and western coasts of Britain were essentially viking centres. The vikings were also solidly entrenched in many areas of the British Isles from the Shetlands south to Galloway, Lancashire and East Anglia. A new period, this time of French-speaking ascendancy, was about to begin. Over the British Isles as a whole, however, the decline of Scandinavian influence was a much slower process than was the case in England. It was not until the mid-thirteenth century that the kingdom of Norway relinquished its rights over Scotland but viking traditions still remained strong in Orkney, Shetland and Caithness as well as in the Western Isles. In Ireland the viking towns long preserved their own sense of cultural identity. (Waterford, for example, later took as its motto *urbs intacta*, 'intact' in this instance meaning 'intact' from Irish incursions.) In north Britain also, viking cultural traditions survived (within what had been the Danelaw) long after the Norman Conquest. Had the battle of Hastings turned out differently the future of the British Isles for many centuries might have lain with Scandinavia, an alternative course of events which the historian cannot dismiss as an impossibility.

5

The Norman ascendancy

The victory of the Normans in 1066 brought revolutionary changes in its wake, not merely for southern Britain but in due course for the rest of the British Isles. Its effects were most immediate in 'England'. William, who was crowned at Westminster Abbey on Christmas Day, lost little time in establishing himself and his followers. So complete was the Conquest that it is tempting to think in terms of a united kingdom. But the situation as it presented itself in the aftermath of the battle of Hastings was not yet so very different from what it had been earlier. Southern Britain was still divided into its distinctive cultures and these would continue to exist.

The itineraries of Cnut (+1035) and Edward (+1066), when mapped by a modern cartographer, make it clear that the heartland of the west Saxon monarchy was still the area south of the Thames. 'Wessex' was distinguished by large concentrations of royal and ecclesiastical land and by wealthy monasteries open to royal influence. In this region, royal writs and charters were effective and an efficient administration collected geld. This was also a society with a large percentage of unfree labour. There was some resistance in Wessex to the newcomers, at Exeter in 1069 for example, but for a long time to come this part of England was to provide a secure foundation for monarchy.

In the east, where Scandinavian influences were strong, there was a different story. In 1069, a Danish fleet arrived at the abbey of Ely which had close ties with the Danish monarchy. For a short time, under Hereward the Wake, there was to be active resistance to the Normans. Farther north, the earldom of Northumbria still enjoyed a tradition of independence from Wessex, most recently displayed when Harold's brother Tostig had been displaced as earl. Northumbria, which comprised the former Danish kingdom of York and former Bernician 'Anglian' territory north of the Tees, could hope for help from Scotland or Norway or Denmark in resisting the Normans. William himself seems at first to have avoided direct intervention in this sensitive area but its opposition to the payment of geld led him towards a more aggressive policy. In 1069, after a period of crisis during which the Normans experienced defeat and a Danish army took Hull, William intervened to administer a severe lesson. After the 'harrying of the North', the independent character of the

MAP 4 The Norman Conquests, 1066–1169

northern Danelaw was largely undermined. Its place was to be taken by 'Yorkshire', reconstructed on the southern manorial model. Norman castles at Newcastle (at the strategic Tyne-crossing), Durham, York, Norwich and Lincoln symbolised the effective presence of the Norman monarchy on the east coast.

In the north and west, there had been something of a Celtic resurgence early in the eleventh century as a result, in part, of a period of weakness of the west Saxon monarchy. In the north-west, Strathclyde recovered parts of Cumbria which had been lost to the English. In Wales, under the leadership of Gruffydd ap Llywelyn, the frontier with Mercia was pushed back beyond Offa's Dyke. In 1055, Hereford was sacked and English villages such as Knighton were abandoned. In all this, Gruffydd could rely upon help from the vikings of Dublin and Wexford and, in a complex political situation in which Mercia was opposed to Wessex, upon an alliance with Aelfgar, earl of Mercia. A successful campaign in Wales by Harold of Wessex brought this to an end in 1063. Gruffydd's head was sent to Harold by his own followers as a symbol of surrender and his place was taken by client kings.

In Wales, changes were apparent even before 1066. Norman influence was already being felt in Herefordshire in the person of Richard FitzOsbern, who had been called in by Edward the Confessor to defend this exposed frontier. But the Conquest began in earnest in the decades following. By the end of the century the Normans were in complete control of south Wales. On the borders the earldoms of Chester, Shrewsbury and Hereford controlled Mercians and Welsh alike. In the northern kingdom of Gwynedd there was a more complex situation. Here, with the backing of the Scandinavian kingdom of Dublin, Gruffydd ap Cynan halted the Norman advance. In 1098, the fleet of Magnus Barefoot, king of Norway, on a raiding expedition from the isle of Man, appeared off the coast of Anglesey and took the Normans, under the earl of Shrewsbury, by surprise. As a result of this defeat, the Normans seem to have decided to be content with 'indirect rule' in Gwynedd and Powys, tolerating the existence of Welsh princes, provided they did not constitute a threat.

In Scotland, Norman influence was also exerted indirectly through the sons of Malcolm III Canmore (1058–93). Malcolm himself was a 'modernising' monarch, on the lines of the OBriens in Ireland, and in supporting his sons the Normans were taking the side of strong monarchy against aristocratic lineages. They did not become fully involved, however, until 'invited' to do so by Malcolm's youngest son David I (1124–53), who had been educated and knighted at the court of Henry I. David encouraged Normans to settle in lands north and south of the Forth and under William the Lion (1165–1214) the process was taken further. In effect, a Norman settlement took place under the auspices of the Scottish Crown. Lothian and Strathclyde were particularly affected, but there was also Norman penetration farther north in Fife and Moray. Such 'Scottish' families as Fraser, Haig, Bruce, Wishart (Guiscard) and Stewart (many of them today complete with tartan and kilt) first made their appearance in Scotland as a result of this episode.

The various kingdoms of Ireland remained unaffected by Norman power until 1169, although, as we have seen, they were by no means unaffected by 'modernising' tendencies in Church as well as state. The viking towns of the east coast were in control of the Irish Sea and in contact with Scandinavian settlements on its west coast from Galloway southwards. In 1169–70, this situation changed dramatically when the exiled king of Leinster, Diarmaid MacMurrough, asked the Norman lords of south Wales to help him regain his kingdom. In many ways, Diarmaid's decision to seek Norman aid resembled that of David of Scotland, earlier in the century. In Ireland, however, the Normans encountered stronger opposition. Even so, by the end of the century, they were in control of much of the country.

The Norman successes created a French-speaking ascendancy throughout the British Isles. By the end of the twelfth century the various kingdoms and provinces which had been independent entities were ruled by an aristocracy, which in its turn was linked by ties of vassalage to a single monarch. Even the king of Scotland with large estates in midland England (the Honour of Huntingdon) was in a measure incorporated within the system. The kings of Gwynedd in the thirteenth century did homage to Henry III. For a time, in the late twelfth century, the British Isles formed part of a wider empire which also included Aquitaine.

Throughout this period, French culture was a symbol of belonging to the political and ecclesiastical elite. The result was to downgrade the status of the various languages and cultures of the North Sea and Irish Sea provinces. To speak these languages could be a mark of bondage. Lanfranc, the Norman archbishop of Canterbury, referred when writing to Pope Alexander II to his own ignorance of the language of 'barbarous peoples'. In religion, the Normans saw themselves as reformers. They replaced what they regarded as a superstitious attachment to local saints with 'uncouth' names by the veneration of saints of the universal Church. Churches dedicated to St Peter, St Thomas, St Andrew and others replaced saints with possibly dangerous or unfashionable local attachments. The Normans also left their mark on the language of the people whom they ruled, as the following selection of French loanwords in Middle English indicates.

1 ADMINISTRATION, LAW: Crown, parliament, reign, royal, state, city, council, court, evidence, fine, fraud, gaol, prison.
2 DRESS: apron, bonnet, boot, brooch, chain, collar, jacket, jewel, (boot-)lace, ornament, petticoat.
3 FAMILY: aunt, cousin, nephew, niece, uncle.
4 FOOD, MEALS, FRUITS: bacon, beef, mutton, partridge, pheasant, pigeon, poultry, sausage, sugar, tripe, veal, dinner, feast, supper, date, fig, grape, lemon, orange, raisin.
5 HOME, HOUSEHOLD, FURNITURE: chamber, pantry, parlour, scullery, blanket, coverlet, curtain, cushion, quilt, towel, chair, dresser, wardrobe.
6 MILITARY: army, battle, guard, navy, peace, soldier, spy (also military ranks).

7 RANKS: clerk, duke, farmer, master, mistress, prince, servant, sir.
8 RELIGION: abbey, convent, lesson, mercy, parson, pity, prayer, preacher, saint, sermon, sexton, vicar.
9 MISCELLANEOUS: dozen, flour, flower, (cart) grease, hour, litter, mange, more, oil, ounce, pasture, people, person, pocket, quarry, quart, quarter, rein, second, squirrel, stallion, stranger, tailor, tune.

In all areas of the British Isles, the instruments of empire were the castle, the Church and the borough. In England alone, it has been estimated, the Normans built nearly a thousand castles, though few of these were on the grand scale of royal castles. There were well over three hundred in Wales. Castles were fewer in the west Saxon heartland but many were needed in the former Danelaw and in the marcher lordships of Wales. Scotland, too, had its quota of castles on the Norman model. In Ireland Norman mottes and baileys controlled the rich lands of Meath and Tipperary. But castles were not a completely new feature in Ireland. Some Irish kings were building them in the modern idiom before the Normans arrived.

The Church was an integral part of this system, not least because the large ecclesiastical estates were expected to provide their due quota of knights for the royal army. With the Normans came a new emphasis on spectacular building. Edward the Confessor prefigured the trend with his abbey at Westminster. After the Conquest, such cathedrals as Durham and Ely with their imposing message of dominance may be taken as symbols of imperialism. All this was accompanied by the introduction of French religious orders and French colonies of monks. Norman abbeys benefited from grants of English and Welsh land. The military orders of the Temple and of St John took root in marcher areas: the most prominent of the new religious orders, the Cistercians, also came to play a role in this process. The Norman Conquest did not involve the movement of peoples on the grand scale as had occurred during the Anglo-Saxon and Scandinavian/viking invasions. In some areas, however – in particular eastern Ireland, south Wales and parts of Scotland – it did promote a considerable degree of selective, sponsored colonisation. For this the instruments to hand were the borough and the nucleated settlement. Throughout the British isles the borough was a sign of effective Normanisation. By offering the relative freedom of borough tenure, both king and lords were able to attract settlers from Flanders to Wales and in due course to Scotland and Ireland. When land-hunger grew in the thirteenth century a further incentive was added. In north Wales, Edward I's royal boroughs became the points around which colonisation of the countryside was organised.

If some assessment of the significance of three centuries of Normanisation is attempted, it may be argued that the effect of the Normans was felt most strongly in the Irish Sea province. In Wessex, the Normans had inherited an existing system and, though they undoubtedly introduced major changes, they did not transform the social structure. In the Scandinavian areas of eastern England, the trading centres soon recovered. Here, as elsewhere, the Normans superimposed their own culture, though the existing divisions between the 'command' society of Wessex and the 'market' society of the east remained. In the Irish Sea province, where the Normans met with severe resistance, they destroyed existing kinship structures and replaced them with a hierarchical, centralised framework. 'Modernisation' on continental lines was already well advanced in the Irish kingdoms and in Scotland under Malcolm Canmore. What the Normans did was to carry it forward in a revolutionary manner. Feudal relationships were imposed from above, not sought from below.

The general tendency of English historians has been to domesticate the Norman Conquest. In the late nineteenth century Stubbs saw it as an example of a 'masculine' race disciplining and educating a 'feminine' race. The mid-twentieth-century medievalist David Knowles admired the vigour and strength of the Normans. The American sociologist George Homans felt that England was 'fortunate' in being ruled by the Norman aristocracy. The fact remains, however, that the Normans behaved as conquerors and remained conscious of the origins of their power for long after 1066. Late in the thirteenth century William de Warenne spoke of 'how his ancestors came with William the Bastard and conquered their lands by the sword'.

The result of the Conquest was to create a two-class society. It is true that Richard FitzNeal spoke of the mingling of races at the end of the twelfth century, but he restricted his comment to freemen. What he had to say may well have been true of London, but over the great mass of rural England there is little doubt that, for a long time to come, conquerors and conquered remained separate. At the top of the social scale, it is clear that the most powerful families married within the ranks of the baronage. At a somewhat lower social level, marriage between Norman and English took place but only as an exceptional event. The situation was to change only from the mid-fourteenth century onwards as a result of demographic shifts following upon the Black Death, not as the consequence of royal or baronial policies.

There was in fact no 'English' history for long after the Conquest. What is normally spoken of as 'English' political history during these centuries relates almost exclusively to controversy and conflict within the ascendancy. The Becket tragedy, Magna Carta, the baronial wars of the mid-thirteenth century were all essentially matters relating to the French-speaking elite. As Stubbs pointed out, the influence of French culture increased rather than diminished in the thirteenth century. A Frenchman, Simon de Montfort, played an active role in ascendancy politics during the thirteenth century. Edward II took his coronation oath in French. Henry de Beaumont, to whom Edward II gave the Isle of Man, was the son of Lewis de Brienne, viscount of Beaumont in Maine. His brother, the bishop of Durham, is recorded as having said on one occasion under stress: 'Par seynt Lewis, il ne fut pas curtays qui est parole icy escrit' ('By Saint Louis, the word written here is discourteous'). Under Henry III, French became the language of written law, and under Edward I the language of the courts of law. The continued strength of the ascendancy in spite of its internal division is indicated by the survival of such names as de Bohun, Bigod and Mortimer, dating from the Conquest.

The colonial nature of this society needs to be stressed if its true character is to be understood. The followers of William took great risks in the enterprise and their rewards were correspondingly great. Settlers continued to arrive well into the twelfth century, displacing English sub-tenants who had survived the first generation of conquest. For the younger sons of Norman families (and 'Norman' here must be understood to cover much of the north-western coastline of the continent, including Flanders) England was a 'frontier' which offered the chance of social advancement, a fact of which the historian Orderic Vitalis was well aware when he referred to those 'whom Henry had raised from the dust'. It was not uncommon for Norman lords to bring over tenants from their own estates. In modern terms, England resembled a Texas in which the Anglo-Saxons came to occupy second-class status. The Yankees in this case were the Normans.

Such a large-scale process of conquest and colonisation could hardly be successful without a continuing display of military force. Here lay the importance of the Norman castles (not 'English' castles as they are sometimes referred to). The function of the castle was the same in England, at least initially, as it was in the marcher lordships and elsewhere in the British isles – to overawe a subject population. This may seem to be overstressing the obvious, but in most accounts of English history the key importance of the castle tends to be underplayed. Following the lead of the great nineteenth-century historians, modern scholars still concentrate upon such facts of supposedly 'national' concerns as Magna Carta. The castle exemplified the realities of local power. For the great majority living in the unfree condition of villeinage it, not parliament or king, was the dominant institution in their daily lives.

The structure of the colonial aristocracy was never uniform, nor did it remain unchanged from 1066 to the mid-fourteenth century. On the marcher shires of the Welsh border and on the Scottish border from the late thirteenth century, defensive needs were uppermost and, as a consequence, lords needed manpower as much as income. In the east and south, there was no similar military need and as a consequence the military aspect of lordship declined, though it never disappeared. The popularity of tournaments (William Marshall took part in over 500), the Crusades, campaigns in France and the cult of chivalry, all testify to the importance of the military ideal. As control of the colony came to be taken for granted, however, the economic exploitation of the landed estate took on greater significance. The growth of population from the twelfth century onwards, land-hunger and rising prices led the magnates to pay greater attention to the opportunities offered by the market.

These economic activities took several forms. On some estates, attention was concentrated upon raising rents or entry-fines (required when a tenant entered upon his holding). Others encouraged the 'colonisation' of new land from which they were now able to draw rent. In the thirteenth century, Roger Bigod brought tenants from his Norfolk estates to his newly acquired land in Ireland. Other lords took an active interest in demesne farming with the market directly in mind. The earl of Leicester owned vast herds of cows, and from such estates as his the towns of Boston and Lynn exported butter and cheese by the ton. This great rise in economic activity, associated especially with the thirteenth century, is often seen in 'national' terms as if it were 'English' cheese and bacon which was being exported. The great mass of the population, however, does not seem to have benefited. On many estates, landlords attempted to hold on to or even increase the labour services to which they were 'entitled'. If we are to follow Professor Postan's assessment (in *The Medieval Economy and Society* (1975)), the chief beneficiaries of this rise in economic activity were the great magnates. In contrast, the lesser baronage and gentry may have lost ground, a fact which would help to explain the restiveness of this class during the thirteenth century.

Colonialism was not confined to the secular world. It was to be seen also in the field of religion. Like many conquerors, the Normans felt that God was on their side. Walter Espec is reported as saying at the battle of the Standard, 'Why should we despair of victory when victory has been given to our race by the Most High, as it were in fee?' They also saw themselves as reforming a decadent Church. A local, hereditary priesthood was to be replaced by a celibate clergy. Parishes were to be created as the basis of new communities, with tithes as their economic basis. Canon law was to be tightened up with regard to marriage. More churches were to be built. Rural areas were to be more actively evangelised. In all of this, the criterion of reform was to be decided by the new colonial rulers.

One instrument of change was a Normanised episcopate backed by the Crown. Of the sixteen English bishoprics, only one was not held by a 'Norman' at the end of the eleventh century. Professor Le Patourel has shown (in *The Norman Empire* (1976)) that well into the twelfth century the bishops of England were all foreign-born with the exception of two, born in England of Norman or Flemish extraction. The new departure was emphasised in some cases by a shift from an Anglo-Saxon site with traditional associations to a new site. Selsey, for example, linked with St Wilfred and the former kings of the south Saxons, gave way to Chichester.

Another instrument of Normanisation was the monastic order. Many English churches were donated to Norman or French monasteries. Over twenty Norman monasteries were recorded as possessing English manors by 1086. Soon, Norman and French monks were being invited over to England to take part in the work of reform. William de Warenne asked for Cluniac monks to found a house at Lewes. Other prominent monastic houses with a French affiliation were established at Chester, Tewkesbury and Evesham. The abbot of Glastonbury in the early twelfth century was the Norman Henry of Blois. Evesham also had a Norman abbot. Hugh of Avalon, who founded the first Carthusian house in England, came directly from La Grande Chartreuse. The introduction of the French-based Cistercian order into northern England took place under the auspices of Thurston, archbishop of York, who was born in Bayeux. The place which the monasteries enjoyed in the colonial ascendancy may go some way towards explaining their unpopularity at a later date.

How autonomous, then, were religious values within this colonial society? It would be clearly mistaken to see all members of the monastic order as exponents of a colonial ideology. At the level of bishops and abbots, however, Church and colony were closely connected, since both types of prelate were expected, as tenants in chief, to provide the Crown with its due quota of knights. Peterborough abbey, for example, was responsible for sixty knights and Glastonbury for forty. Also, the role of churchmen in administration was fundamental.

The Church in the first century after the Conquest could not have escaped the impress of its colonial situation even if it had wished to do so. Perhaps the real problem is to discover when the situation changed enough to allow the admittance of 'natives' into the higher echelons of the Church. The coming of the Friars in the early thirteenth century seems to have marked something of a turning point. The Franciscans, in particular, drew upon lower social groups within the towns, which were more likely to be English-speaking than French-speaking. However, it was only with the rise of the Lollard movement in the late fourteenth century that an unmistakably English religious movement appeared.

The third element in the colonial structure was the borough. During the years immediately after the Conquest, 'Norman' colonists were introduced into at least six towns, including Nottingham and Shrewsbury. More significant, however, is the fact that many new towns were established during the late eleventh, twelfth and thirteenth centuries. Between 1066 and 1130, forty new towns were founded (not including eighteen in Wales). During the civil wars of Stephen's and Matilda's reign (1135–54), the rate slowed, but it picked up again in the second half of the twelfth century. During the period 1191–1230, nearly fifty new towns were planted. The creation of new towns was thus a remarkable feature of post-Conquest England and Wales.

In seeking an explanation for this phenomenon, historians have tended to stress the rise of trade. From this standpoint, the history of towns forms part of 'English' economic history and, as with 'English' castles and 'English' monasteries, so too there have been studies of 'English' towns. If we look at who founded these towns and why, it is clear that the initiative came mainly from the Norman colonial elite. Some towns, Newcastle, for example, were royal foundations but most owed their existence to the initiative of local lords.

The attraction of such institutions for the lords lay in the fact that towns were, in effect, controllable markets where the output of estates could be turned into cash. The rents which burgesses paid in a lord's town were another source of cash. Trade conducted within a town paid toll. Mills were another source of income. Though the details of boroughs varied from place to place, the object remained the same, to add to the wealth of the colonial ascendancy. The earls of Gloucester acquired a quarter of their total income from the tolls of Bristol. Leicester provided the earls of Leicester with a third of their income. These were large and prosperous urban centres which had existed before the Conquest. More typical were towns of middling importance. The bishops of Worcester founded Stratford. The earls of Chester founded Stockport and Salford. Control of the town of Coventry was disputed between the local feudal and ecclesiastical lords. Under the auspices of the bishop of Norwich, the town of Lynn expanded (to be known first as Bishop's Lynn and then late as King's Lynn). Hugh de Gonneville founded the town of Chipping Camden as an outlet for the Cotswolds wool trade. The same story was repeated many times, sometimes with success, sometimes with failure.

During this period, the towns of England were not independent manifestations of the commercial spirit, but sponsored institutions controlled by the colonial ascendancy. It was only when this started to decline in the second half of the fourteenth century that towns began to achieve some measure of independence. Maitland noted how 'in some great boroughs, seignorial justice was a hardy plant' (in Sir Frederick Pollock and F. W. Maitland, *History of English Law* (1898), p. 646). He was referring to the situation in the town of Stamford in 1275, where various lords, ecclesiastical and secular, claimed rights over their tenants. But Stamford was typical at this date. At Stockport and Salford, the lord's steward presided over the portmanmoot. At Tavistock, the abbot closely supervised the borough which the abbey had founded: the abbot's steward presided over the borough court, levied a percentage on corn ground at the town mill, collected inheritance dues and controlled various services due from 'his' burgesses. At Bury St Edmunds, the abbey wielded wide powers over the economic life of the borough, controlling its court and its market and collecting tolls. The abbey also enjoyed a considerable privilege, in that its own produce was exempt from tolls. It also took precedence in making purchases of grain.

Towns which had existed before the Conquest lost whatever autonomy they had possessed earlier. This may be seen most clearly in the shift in the control of urban churches. In such towns as Bristol, Stamford and Lincoln, churches had been built by local patrons. At Winchester, most of its fifty-six churches had been built in this way. After the Conquest, ownership was vested with the Norman bishop or with the local Normanised monastery. Thus at Leicester, the earl transferred six churches to his new foundation of Augustinian canons. In such an instance we may see how castle, monastery and borough formed a network of institutions supporting the colonial ascendancy.

There is, finally, the key institution of the manor, described by Professor Postan in *The Medieval Economy and Society* (1975) as 'the most powerful, the most ubiquitous and the most characteristic institution of medieval economy and society'. The manor may be seen as consisting of the lord's demesne, worked by an unfree labour force, which in turn for its services was allowed to cultivate its own holdings. Over much of England, it was associated with the so-called open fields in which the peasantry cultivated 'strips'. The economic arrangements of the manor, however, varied widely from place to place and from time to time. In 'Wessex', the tenants were more likely to be unfree than in East Anglia. The same person could pay rent for one holding and be required to pay in labour for another. Rentals on manors in a newly colonised area were likely to be less onerous than those in more settled parts. Recent research also suggests that the tenants were often more mobile than was once supposed. In theory, the peasants were bound to the soil. In practice, the needs of a market economy often meant that some degree of flexibility was permitted by the bailiffs of the estate.

The Normans did not invent the manorial estate. Such estates were already well established in 1066. Indeed, some scholars suggest that their origins may have to be sought in the villas of late Roman Britain. What the Normans did do, however, was to develop the economic potentialities of the manor. Land and tenantry were exploited at a more intense level in an economy increasingly orientated towards the market. New land was brought into cultivation, often at the expense of peasants who had hitherto relied upon 'waste' for fuel or as grazing-land for pigs.

In the colonial situation which existed in England after the Conquest, it was not surprising that royal lawyers should work hard to sharpen a distinction between the 'natives' and the newcomers. By the thirteenth century, it was held in law that villeins could not bring cases to the royal courts. The 'common' law was in effect confined to the ascendancy and those associated with it. A royal writ (*de natiuo*) was devised to help in the repossession of natives who had fled their lord's estate. In the light of these realities, it is ironical that one of the classical works of historiography in the field should be known as *The History of English Law* (not 'Norman Law').

So far we have concentrated our attention upon the Norman elite, a mode of procedure which the great wealth of official records and the traditions of English historiography thrust upon the historian. In comparison with the amount of material relating to the ascendancy, evidence about the majority is minimal. What, then, can be said about them? It is tempting to assume that we are at last dealing with the 'English people'. The survival of regional dialects, however, suggests that local loyalties were still strong. During the Middle English period (1100–1450) earlier cultural divisions into Northumbria and Mercia (both with Danish minorities) and Wessex may be seen as surviving in the form of dialect areas, now known as 'Northern', 'Midlands' ('East' and 'West'), and 'Southern'. The south seems to have been more Normanised than the north, if the evidence of Norman loanwords is a safe guide. In the north-west, the incorporation of former Gaelic-Scandinavian areas and of Strathclyde south of Carlisle into the Norman colony meant that new subcultures now existed within 'England'. To these may be added Shropshire and Herefordshire, now part of the Norman kingdom but inhabited in their western sections by a population of Welsh background. In Herefordshire the existence of the enclave of 'Archenfield' (Erging, in Welsh) with its own Welsh laws and language symbolised the cultural diversity of this area. There was, finally, Celtic-speaking Cornwall, which was incorporated into 'England', governmentally if not culturally.

As well as cultural diversity, there was considerable social differentiation within the majority. The basic unit of society was the vill (a term used to suggest something simpler and often smaller than the village) but, as modern research has shown, the relative poverty of these small-scale societies did not exclude differences of status and wealth. There were clear class divisions between richer and poorer peasants, and in the light of modern colonial societies it would be unwise to assume that common hatred for the foreign lord outweighed the bitterness of local conflict. Studies of nineteenth-century Ireland have shown how hostility between farmers and labourers could be more significant as a cause of violence than that between landlords and tenant.

There was, in the third place, the contrast between the relatively commercialised east and the more manorialised parts of England, particularly the west midlands and the southern counties. This was a distinction which went back to before the Conquest, but it seems to have become more marked in the post-Conquest period, as the growth of London and of the ports of the east coast indicates. In the west the rise of Bristol and of Chester point to the commercial development of the 'Irish Sea province', as well as the new trading links with south-west France. By the mid-fourteenth century, the east coast and (in the west) the Bristol hinterland were the wealthiest regions of England. Such commercialisation makes it understandable how the dialect of the east midlands, with its centre at London, should become the language of the new society which emerged after the decline of the colonial ascendancy.

On the eve of the Norman Conquest of England, there were four major Welsh political units – Gwynedd in the north-west, Deheubarth in the south-west, Morganwg in the south to south-east and Powys in the east surrounded by a number of smaller lordships over whose fate the dominant kingdoms contended. Some historians have been eager to see the rise of a Welsh national consciousness during the pre-Norman centuries, but there was little sign of unity. As a result of the divisions imposed by geography and by their different historical experiences, Gwynedd looked towards the Gaelic-Scandinavians of the Wirral and the viking kingdom of Dublin, Deheubarth had been drawn at least spasmodically into the sphere of Wessex and the fortunes of Powys had been linked with Mercia. Despite these divisions, however, 'Wales' had survived the challenges of the viking centuries. The west Saxon and Anglo-Danish kings had been content with asserting a general suzerainty over Wales, whenever this was possible. With the coming of the Normans, however, a new period began, marked by military control and large-scale colonisation.

The full impact of the Normans was not felt immediately. William seems to have been content to establish control of the Welsh borderlands, with the probable aim of containing unrest in Mercia. At this date, the three great Norman earldoms of Chester, Shrewsbury and Hereford may be seen as largely defensive in character. In the last decades of the eleventh century, however, with the opportunity offered by the death of Rhys ap Tewdwr, king of Deheubarth (+1093) a more forward policy of conquest and colonisation began. The coast of south Wales with its easy access by sea from Devon was an inviting target for those younger sons who had missed earlier opportunities in England. In the north, an approach from the Dee estuary offered similar possibilities, though it was to be much less successful. Not until the campaigns of Edward I in the late thirteenth century was the kingdom of Gwynedd in the north finally brought under control.

The Norman Conquest of Wales is a dramatic story. What was less dramatic but equally significant was the process of colonisation which accompanied it. The first plantation of Flemish colonists took place in Pembrokeshire in the early twelfth century but the really decisive factor in the Norman success was the supply of English colonists. Much of Wales was mountainous but there were many substantial pockets of fertile land along the south coast and in the valleys of the Severn, the Usk and the Wye. In the north, the vale of Clwyd and the Isle of Anglesey were similar areas. Herefordshire, today a part of England, was another attractive target for the colonist. All these lands were to fall to English colonists during the twelfth and thirteenth centuries. The demographic upsurge which was so marked a feature of English society in the twelfth and thirteenth centuries provided the impetus behind the colonisation of Wales. Without the numerical backing of English tenants, it would have been impossible for the Normans to make the inroads which they did. By the early fourteenth century much of the best land in Wales was occupied by the Normans and their tenants. Each lordship had its 'Englishry' of good land, and its 'Welshry' of poorer land. In the one, the Norman law operated, in the other Welsh. A colonial society was delineated in Wales more clearly than anywhere else in the British Isles.

As in England, the combination of castle, borough and Church provided the framework around which Norman control was organised. Several hundred castles were built, mostly of the motte-and-bailey type. Castles, as at Chepstow, provided the nuclei towards which smaller castles could look for support. It was a sign of the hostile environment within which the colonists operated that castles were much thicker on the ground in Wales than was the case in English counties, such as Somerset. Another sign was the *de facto* independence which the Crown permitted the lordships to enjoy. Royal law did not operate in the marcher lordships, which numbered about forty during the heyday of the colony.

Boroughs were also created to meet the needs of the castle and the settlers. Some of them, such as Cardiff and Monmouth, developed into fully fledged towns. Others, such as Whittington and Chirk, remained scarcely more than villages. In the later thirteenth century, Edward I established Flint and other boroughs as part of a conscious policy of colonisation. Though at a later period such towns became indubitably 'Welsh' in their outlook, to live in a town during the Norman period was a sign of belonging to the English colony. The Welsh were in fact excluded from them. The square towers of many urban churches were intended to serve a defensive function, and no new town was established far from the protection of a castle. The towns existed primarily to serve the needs of the Englishry.

The Norman Conquest had a particularly marked effect upon the Welsh Church.

In Wales there had been no equivalent of the English 'Tenth-Century Reformation' with its policies of centralisation. As in other areas of the Irish Sea province, earlier patterns of local control based upon kinship groups had prevailed against a system based upon government by bishops. There were four Welsh bishoprics (St Davids, Llandaff, St Asaph and Bangor) but in the countryside episcopal surveillance counted for little against the entrenched traditions of abbeys with strong local roots, symbolised by an attachment to a local saint. In the Church, as in secular society, the kinship group was an enduring institution.

Wherever they established themselves, the Normans almost immediately 'reformed' this system out of existence. At Brecon, where he established a castle, Bernard of Neufmarche established a monastic cell linked to Battle Abbey (Sussex). West of Cardiff, Richard of Granville set up a monastery of Neath linked with the French order of Savigny. Other lords became patrons of monastic houses linked with Le Mans and Saumur. Another maintained ties with Glastonbury. (In parts of Wales less affected by Norman pressure, local kings established Cistercian monasteries with similar 'reforms' in mind.) In Norman-controlled Wales, the Church became closely identified with the 'Englishry'. This was as true of the bishoprics as of the monasteries. The see of Glamorgan had been 'anglicised' for some time before the Conquest, but the see of St David had been completely Welsh. After the Conquest, both bishoprics were reorganised on lines acceptable to the newcomers.

There was, finally, the manor, with the accompanying nucleated settlements and open-field system. Within the Englishry of the various lordships, the presence of the new colonists was marked by agrarian arrangements characteristic of England not Wales. The main difference lay in the fact that such land was held from a lord in return for services rendered, and not by virtue of membership of a kinship group in return for reciprocal services. Enjoying better land, thanks to the backing of their lords, the Englishry could regard itself as superior to the Welshry. Outside the immediate circle of the lord's control, however, Welsh custom based upon partible inheritance continued to be practised. Also, customary law relating to the feud (*galanas*) and the principle of compensation to relatives for a crime committed against one of the kindred's members survived in many areas. Marcher lords themselves were willing to enforce the law of *galanas* in the Welshries in return for a fee.

A distinction may be drawn between the early colonisation of Wales in the immediate post-Conquest period and the later, more centralised attempt to colonise Gwynedd during the reign of Edward I. Gwynedd had succeeded in maintaining its autonomy during the twelfth century and much of the thirteenth, though at the cost of its rulers formally accepting the overlordship of the English king. A period of relative independence during the baronial wars of the mid-thirteenth century was followed eventually by defeat at the hands of Edward I. In 1282 Llywelyn of Gwynedd died in battle and his brother David was executed a year later. In 1284 Edward held a 'parliament', as a result of which the Norman criminal law enforced by Norman-style sheriffs was introduced into the three shires which now constituted the former kingdom of Gwynedd.

As in the south, the classical combination of castle, borough and Church was relied upon to provide the framework of the colony. Edward's castles at each end of the Menai Strait and down the coast at Harlech still stand as a monument to his policy. More effective, at least at first, were the newly founded boroughs of Flint, Denbigh, Holt, Rhuddlan and Ruthin. These are thoroughly Welsh today but they were originally intended to be islands of colonial privilege in the Welsh countryside. Welshmen were forbidden to live within them and were excluded from taking an active part in their trading activities. A policy of plantation was also adopted in connection with these boroughs and as a consequence good land in the vale of Clwyd was confiscated for the benefit of new settlers while the Welsh were 'compensated' with poorer land on the hillsides. The Greys of Ruthin were one of the families who benefited from their part in this colonisation.

The Statute of Rhuddlan, which was drawn up under Edward's guidance, made clear that colonisation and 'civilisation' were thought to go hand in hand. Edward saw himself as retaining certain good customs of the Welsh while abandoning those like *galanas* and fosterage which seemed undesirable. Archbishop Pecham of Canterbury, who regarded *galanas* as a travesty of justice, also wished to reform Welsh custom with regard to marriage and legitimacy. In theory, this should not have led to discrimination. In fact, Englishmen settling in Wales were often promised that they would be tried only by Englishmen, if accused of a crime. Welshmen were often prohibited from buying land held on English tenure without the licence of the lord concerned.

The Welsh castles of Edward I reveal the extent of his imperialism. Of the major castles which were to be built along the Welsh coast, Caernarfon was singled out for particular emphasis as a symbol of empire. The site itself was the Segontium of the Romans. The bailey of the late eleventh-century castle was retained as a reminder of the early years of the Normans. The Eagle Tower of the castle was intended to recall Constantinople. Finally, the queen made a special journey to Caernarfon in order that her son, Edward, should be born there. In the context of the history of the British Isles, Edward I appears as much the English Augustus as the English Justinian.

Unfortunately for this imperial vision, the demographic conditions which might have made it possible did not survive the first quarter of the fourteenth century. Traditional institutions of kinship were still to be found in Gwynedd (now part of the principality of Wales), and other areas such as Clun which did not feel the full brunt of colonisation, into the fifteenth century and beyond. The three political units of the pre-Conquest period each had different historical experiences. Deheubarth and the south had been most affected by colonisation. Powys had faced a more peaceful penetration. Gwynedd had not been affected fully until the late thirteenth century. Beneath the Norman ascendancy, distinctive cultures still existed.

The Norman Conquest of Wales was to have an indirect effect on Ireland as well as England. An invasion of Ireland may have been planned in the late eleventh century. It took place in fact in the late twelfth, when Normans who had taken an active part in the Conquest of south Wales crossed the Irish Sea. The descendants of Gerald of Windsor, the steward of the earl of Pembroke, became the FitzGeralds of Munster. In due course the Irish Sea province became part of a Norman empire in the British Isles. The lords of the Welsh marches also played an important role in English politics from the twelfth century onwards. With military forces at their disposal, they were always in a position to intervene in England, should they be called upon to do so. Indeed the part which they and Llywelyn played in the wars of Simon de Montfort probably persuaded Edward to adopt a more active policy towards Wales.

Scotland, like Wales and Ireland, was very much a 'geographical expression' at the end of the eleventh century. Broadly speaking, it appears divided into an Irish Sea Province and a North Sea province, though the distinction must not be pressed too hard in view of the fact that Norway controlled Shetland, Orkney, the islands of Lewis and Skye and the Isle of Man. The Inner Hebrides had in the early twelfth century been formed into a kingdom by Somerled (+1164) and his descendants continued to rule the area. Galloway, closely tied to the north of Ireland, was ruled by Gaelic-Scandinavians, whose power south of the Solway had given way before the expanding Canmore monarchy. It is difficult to be certain about the political and social arrangements of the Gaelic-speaking lordships but it would seem that a kinship system still survived, modified by feudal ties between lord and vassal. The vikings who colonised Argyll and the Isles became gaelicised, and took over Gaelic forms of legitimation. Donald and Dougall, the sons of Somerled, used the Gaelic patronymic 'Mac' (son of) which came to be the basis of the MacDonald and MacDougall clans. But the stone castles, which were built at key anchorages in this seaborn society, pointed to the influence of ideas which were not very far removed from those of the Normans.

The Irish Sea province looked towards the western seas and for some time after the Norman Conquest of England was to be left to its own devices. It was the North Sea province of 'Scotland' which was drawn first into the Norman sphere of influence. The reigns of David I (1124–53) and of William IV (the Lion, 1165–1214) were decisive here. Where Malcolm Canmore had been largely concerned with extending his influence into what had been Bernicia and was now northern Northumbria, his sons and grandson moved north into Gaelic-speaking Moray and Buchan and south-west into Galloway. This could hardly have been successful without the support of the Normans. The kings of the twelfth and thirteenth centuries were, all in their different ways, dependent upon the Norman kings. Without this support the rise of Edinburgh to political importance is difficult to explain. A Norman ascendancy was thus established in Scotland but more indirectly than was the case in Wales or Ireland.

The instruments of Normanisation were the same as those employed elsewhere in the British Isles – castle, borough and reformed Church. It has been estimated that there were twenty-eight mottes in Annandale, twenty-six between the Nith and the Cree and eleven to the west of the Cree – well over fifty in the south-west alone. Some of these mottes, like the motte of Urr, were major undertakings. In addition to these baronial castles, there were royal castles, such as those at Stirling and Inverness. The building of castles in such numbers makes clear what may not be apparent at first sight, that the establishment of the Canmore dynasty rested upon the fact of conquest; however, traditionally, historians have preferred to see it in terms of 'the making of a kingdom' according to the 'best European models'.

Resistance to the newcomers continued for some considerable time. In the late twelfth century, and in the early thirteenth, risings took place in the north-east in the name of MacWilliam, the presumed son of Duncan II. The Normans took these risings sufficiently seriously publicly to beat out the brains of a supposed MacWilliam female infant in the square at Falkirk.

In Galloway, the practice known as *surdit de serjeant* illustrates the conflict which existed between notions of justice derived from kinship obligation in the feud (*galnes* in Cumbric) and royal justice dispensed from above. *Surdit de serjeant* empowered the royal officers (serjeants) to indict those whom they suspected of being criminals and to hang them if caught red-handed. Unfortunately we know little about this type of law enforcement at the local level. The experience of such royal justice, however, may go some way towards explaining the continued restiveness of Galloway under the new regime. The viking background of Gallowegan culture must also have been a factor.

As elsewhere in the British Isles, the Norman borough played a crucial role in the working of the Norman ascendancy. The aim was to establish local trading monopolies which could levy tolls and hence raise cash for their owners, whether king or local baron. Many boroughs, such as those of Renfrew and Prestwick, were founded by local barons, but most, in keeping with the prominent role played by the Scottish Crown in the changes of the twelfth century, were royal. Such ventures are frequently depicted as part of an enlightened commercial policy designed to develop trade, but the complaints made by the monks of the Isle of May, about their loss of freedom in selling fish as a result of the establishment of a royal borough, indicate that changes were not always regarded as reforms. As was the case in Wales and Ireland, the new boroughs were often mini-colonies of Flemish or English immigrants dependent upon the king or their lord for survival. The names mentioned in borough records are overwhelmingly foreign at this date. Thus, taken in conjunction with the restrictions which were imposed upon the movement of the peasant population, the boroughs appear as part of a system of regulation imposed from above.

There was, moreover, the reform-minded Church which also occupied a prominent place in the process of Normanisation. The picture emerges most clearly in the north-east, where viking traditions were strong. Here, new dioceses were created for Moray, Ross and Caithness. These were the ecclesiastical counterparts of the earldoms now under royal control. In Moray, the royal burgh at Elgin became the site of a cathedral which was built in the thirteenth century. This new centralised structure of Church government brought a new bureaucracy into existence, together with a system of Church courts, to replace the loosely organised system of local churches in which kinship groups had been dominant. Hundreds of parish churches were eventually established, each, in theory at least, staffed by a priest whose livelihood depended upon the collection of 'teinds' (tithes). The introduction of new monastic orders was also a feature of the first half of the twelfth century, thanks to the extraordinary zeal of King David I. The monastery at Holyrood was staffed with monks from Merton in England and the abbey at Jedburgh with monks from Beauvais. The new monasteries, staffed by foreigners and often committed to expanding revenues for building purposes, admirably fulfilled the purposes of the ascendancy. We can only guess at the local response to their foundation.

By the end of the twelfth century all the elements of a Norman ascendancy were in place in the east and south of Scotland. During the course of the next century, Alexander II (1214–49) and Alexander III (1249–86) attempted with some success to bring the west under the control of the monarchy. By the late thirteenth century, the Stewart family, with its castle at Rothesay in Bute, was the most powerful Norman family in this area. Alexander II challenged the authority of Norway in the Isles, but his unexpected death brought expansion to an end for a time. In 1266, after a struggle in the course of which a Norwegian fleet was dispersed by a storm (1264), the kings of Norway agreed to convey the sovereignty of the Isles, including the Isle of Man, to the kings of Scotland. The MacDougalls and MacDonalds also came to terms with Alexander III.

In 1278, when Alexander III was compelled to go to Westminster to do homage to Edward I, the Norman ascendancy within the British Isles seemed secure. In 1286, however, as a result of the unexpected death of Alexander III without a male heir, new problems began to appear. The Norman lords in Scotland agreed to accept the 'Maid of Norway', Alexander's granddaughter, as queen, but her death in 1290 brought to a head a struggle for power, which had been brewing for some years.

The main protagonists in the struggle were the factions of Bruce and Comyn, each with its candidate. The Bruce candidate was Robert Bruce of Annandale; the candidate of the Comyns was John Balliol, brother-in-law of the Comyn baron, and a new arrival in Scotland. In due course, with Edward I's active participation as the overlord of many of those involved, the court which had been appointed to decide gave its verdict in favour of Balliol. In 1292 Balliol became king, with the support of over half of his fellow-magnates. There was little trouble until 1294, when Edward called upon his vassals to aid him in defending Gascony against the attacks of the French. Edward's magnates in England were reluctant to do so, and it is not surprising that John Balliol and his supporters should also refuse. Edward's response was to make war in the Scottish Lowlands and to treat with unusual severity any of his opponents who might be captured. William Wallace (whose name with its 'Welsh' overtones recalls the old British kingdom of Strathclyde) rose in the name of King John and enjoyed some success before being captured and executed in 1304. Comyn and Bruce already had made peace with Edward in 1301. When in 1306 Robert Bruce quarrelled with John Comyn in the Greyfriars church at Dumfries and stabbed him to death, it looked as if Edward had little to fear in the future, despite the fact that Bruce had himself crowned at Scone. Edward's death in 1307, however, and the weakness of his successor in the face of baronial opposition, made it possible for Bruce to survive and eventually, in 1314, to defeat his enemies at Bannockburn, near Stirling.

Confusion is often caused by the use of the concepts 'English' and 'Scottish' in dealing with these events. In fact, issues of national identity have little place in a situation which at the highest political level was dominated by ideas of lordship and vassalage. What occurred in the years following 1294 was not a conflict between 'England' and 'Scotland' (though it became so later) but a struggle for power within the Norman ascendancy. As such, it was little different from the civil wars of the mid-century. The contenders in the struggle, with the exception of Wallace, were all of 'Norman' extraction. Balliol and Bruce (the elder) had been taken prisoner at the battle of Lewes in 1264, fighting for Henry III against Simon de Montfort. Comyn had taken the side of Simon and Llywelyn of Wales. A structure of politics which allowed this to occur took little account of national aspirations. When Bruce was proclaimed king at Scone, the three areas which took sides against him, Buchan, Galloway and Argyll (with their distinctive cultures), were precisely those in which the Canmore dynasty had had most difficulty in establishing its authority. Bruce's support came from his fellow-Normans, and not all of them. Those who gave him their support took their stand against a king who seemed to have shifted his position from that of feudal overlord to one of imperial dominance. Edward I was the revolutionary. They were the traditionalists, defending the local autonomy to which they felt themselves entitled.

Concentration upon the political activity of the Normans tends to distract attention from the fate of the various sub-cultures which co-existed in Scotland in the eleventh century. By the beginning of the fourteenth century, Gaelic was clearly in retreat, except in the west. Its place had been taken by English in the form of the Lothian dialect. The elite spoke French but, below that level, English took over. Why this should be so is not very clear. It may be due to a number of factors, including sponsored colonisation from the Lowlands, of a kind which led to the anglicisation of parts of south and east Wales. After two centuries of Norman ascendancy, the five sub-cultures of Scotland had given way to three, English in the east, Gaelic in the west and Scandinavian in Shetland and Orkney. The latest casualty was Gaelic-speaking Buchan which did not recover from the 'harrying' it received at the hands of the newly crowned Bruce.

Unlike the Norman infiltration of Scotland during the twelfth century, the coming of the Normans to Ireland was sudden and dramatic. On 1 May 1169 a small contingent of Norman knights landed at Bannow Bay near Wexford. A year later a larger force led by Richard FitzGilbert, earl of Pembroke, landed at Waterford. Dublin fell to the Normans in 1171, and soon the two Irish kingdoms of Leinster and Midhe were in Norman hands. In 1171 King Henry II visited Ireland and accepted the homage of both the conquistadores and of many of the Irish chiefs. He also, in an act of far-sighted policy, established royal castles in Dublin, Waterford, Cork and Limerick. Throughout the feudal period these were to remain symbols of a Crown 'presence' in Ireland. Soon, much of Ireland was overrun by the Normans. In 1175 the Norman newcomer de Cogan (a name which survives as 'Goggins' in modern Ireland) and his followers conquered most of the MacCarthy kingdom of Desmond. In 1177 John de Courcy marched north and seized much of north-east Ulster. Parts of Thomond also fell under Norman control. Connacht west of the Shannon was spared for a time, thanks to the political skill of its O Connor king, Cathal Crobhderg, who negotiated successfully with Henry II and his successors. Much of Connacht too, however, had been taken over by the mid-thirteenth century. Some of these successes proved to be temporary, most notably in the Shannon area, but much of the best land in the east changed hands permanently. Ireland indeed has suffered the same fate as England, Wales, the Scottish Lowlands and other parts of western Europe. The 'blitzkrieg' was not without its horrors. In 1170, for example, by the orders of the Norman commanders seventy citizens of Waterford were thrown from a cliff into the sea after their legs had been first broken.

In Scotland the colonists derived legitimacy from the invitation of King David I. In Ireland they legitimised their invasion on the basis of the invitation from their Irish ally Diarmaid MacMurrough king of Leinster. It was Diarmaid who in effect called in the new world to redress the balance of the old. His aim as revealed in the years before 1169 was to extend the power of the Leinster kingdom from the Scandinavian towns of Dublin, Wexford and Waterford to the Shannon where Ossory was under his control, and from the southern borders of Munster to the Boyne where the ailing kingdom of Midhe was an obvious prize. These ambitions led him into rivalry with the Shannon powers of Connacht and Breifne and in the power struggle which occurred in the 1160s he came off worst. Forced into exile in 1166, Diarmaid's request for help from the Normans was something of a gambler's throw. Henry II himself had enough on his hands with the problems of his own Angevin empire in France and England and showed little enthusiasm for the prospect. It was among the Norman feudatories of south Wales that Diarmaid found support. And the fact that they acted to some extent in defiance of the Crown was to have long-term consequences. The Norman conquistadores always felt that they were independent of royal control. Indeed it was not until the reign of Henry VIII that the title 'king of Ireland' was officially adopted by the Crown. Throughout the medieval period the kings of England were merely 'lords' of Ireland. Nonetheless, royal authority, at least in the thirteenth century, was very much a reality.

Diarmaid also gave an additional cover of legality to the enterprise by arranging for the marriage of Strongbow to his daughter Aoife, though such an arrangement carried little weight in traditional Irish law. In their own eyes, however, the Normans now had a claim to the kingdoms of Leinster and Midhe. Religious reform added a further card to play. Diarmaid was a 'reforming' king who had founded monasteries and had been in contact by letter with the great St Bernard himself. The Norman episcopate in England could be relied upon to support their king. The Pope, Alexander III, also looked upon the newcomers as agents of reform. But, in essentials, the coming of the Normans to Ireland involved a conquest, with consequences as unmistakable as that by the Teutonic knights in east Prussia.

What were the consequences of the coming of the Normans? This is an issue which still deeply divides Irish historians. Eoin MacNeill (in *Phases of Irish History* (1919)) looked upon the invasion as a wholly negative episode as a result of which the development of Irish nationhood was set back for centuries. More recently, Professor Binchy (in *Proceedings of the Dublin Congress of Celtic Studies* (1962)) has argued strongly in favour of regarding the viking invasions rather than the Norman Conquest as the crucial turning point in Irish history. There is also a 'revisionist' school of Irish historians which stresses the positive contribution made by the Normans in some areas. Professor F. X. Martin, for example, has argued that the Normans made possible the introduction of parliamentary institutions into Ireland. Professors Aubrey Gwynn and John A. Watt have seen the Normans as completing the movement of reform in the Irish Church. H. G. Richardson stressed the role of the Normans in bringing Ireland into the mainstream of European culture and though, as we have seen earlier, the Romanesque architecture of the early and mid-twelfth century indicates that pre-Norman Ireland was not isolated, Goddard Orpen, in the standard work on the Normans in Ireland, pre-judged the whole issue by entitling his first chapter 'Anarchic Ireland'. The interpretation which I adopt here is nearest to that of Eoin MacNeill, though not without some reservations.

If what has been said earlier is well founded, the Normans did not introduce feudalism. From the tenth century onwards, Irish kings had conquered territories, built castles, exacted oaths of fealty from vassals and used 'religious reform' to extend their control of newly acquired areas. The punishments inflicted by Irish kings upon the recalcitrant included blinding and the cutting off of hands and feet. The education of these kings was modelled upon a warrior ethic similar to that of the Normans.

In Ireland as elsewhere these new attitudes clashed with traditional attitudes towards the rights of kindred. Even before the Conquest, kings in Ireland were trying to enforce a regnal succession from father to son. Kings, like bishops, found an ideological basis for this in the idea of patriarchal authority. Well before the Norman Conquest parts of Ireland were moving towards a 'modernising' pattern.

It is clear, however, that external conquest by newcomers of a different language and culture and with different assumptions about the role of law brought more far-reaching consequences in its train than internal conquest by those possessing the same language and culture. The former kingdom of Midhe, for example, which was the product of many centuries of political evolution, stretching back to the shadowy Niall of the Nine Hostages in the fifth century, was transformed into the 'Liberty' of Meath. ('Liberty' was a technical term under Norman law for a lordship held from the Crown under which the lord had the right to enforce law and order, with the exception of certain pleas reserved for the Crown courts.) 'Midhe' ceased to exist, except in the memory of the conquered. Meath was now a fief held from the English Crown by Hugh de Lacy in return for the service of 100 knights. De Lacy's castle at Skryne, overlooking the ancient site at Tara, symbolised the dominance of the new order. His vassals, among whom were numbered Petit, Pippard, Tyrell and Rochfort, held their own fiefs as part of the feudal pyramid. A gigantic simplification had taken place. The complexities of an older political culture, with its myths and genealogies, had been relegated to obscurity. The Irish language itself became a mark of servitude within the Norman-controlled area. 'Hibernicus' and 'villein' were synonymous. The coming of the Normans, far more than the coming of the vikings, marked a social revolution, at least in eastern Ireland.

Institutions which had been associated with the traditional order found no place within the new society. Thus, the Norman bishop of Meath, Simon de Rochfort, centralised his diocese upon the new fortified town of Trim. In the process, the older centres of Clonard and Fore, with their cults of the early Irish saints Finnian and Fechin, were downgraded. It may well be that Bishop Simon's motives were mixed and that he saw himself as undertaking genuine religious reform, but the result was to place the Church in Meath firmly behind the new order. Within the Norman-controlled areas, Irish hereditary learned families ceased to have an economic base. Bards and brehons also lost their elite status in this part of Ireland although they probably survived at a popular level. Clearly, Irish culture in these areas received as profound a shock as Anglo-Saxon culture did in England after the Norman Conquest of 1066.

It was as much by colonisation as by conquest, however, that the Normans revolutionised eastern Ireland. Marc Bloch (in *Feudal Society* (1961)) looked upon colonial settlement as one of the features which distinguished the second phase of feudalism from the first. In this the Irish experience formed part of a general European pattern, which derived from population pressures and land-hunger. The same forces, indeed, which led the Germans to establish colonies beyond the Elbe led the 'Franks' into south Wales, the Scottish Lowlands and the east of Ireland. How many colonists came in the late twelfth and thirteenth centuries will never be known, but the incidence in east Leinster of such surnames as 'Walsh' (viz., Welsh) 'English', 'French' and 'Fleming' provide some indication of their numbers. We have a better sense as to why they came. Some at least were drawn to a strange land by the prospect of holding land by free tenure. A number of place-names incorporating 'burgage' or 'borris' provide evidence of this phenomenon (for example, Borris, Co. Carlow).

Burgage tenure was in fact free tenure. Direct pressure from Norman lords in England probably also played a part in 'encouraging' emigration. The Norfolk manors of Roger Bigod, who was lord of Carlow as well as earl-marshal of England, show high rates of emigration during this period.

Once the initial military successes were over, the story was that of painstaking colonisation, particularly of the river valleys of Cos. Wexford, Waterford and Meath. In Wexford, settlers moved up the valley of the Slaney. In Waterford, they colonised the valley of the Barrow from New Ross to Carlow, the Nore valley up to Kilkenny and beyond, and the Suir valley from Carrick to Clonmel and Cahir. In Meath, they followed the course of the Boyne from Drogheda through Navan and Trim to Edenderry. Each stage of the advance was marked by the building of mottes and baileys, walled towns, stone castles and monasteries. Historians and archaeologists have still to examine the chronology of this process, but it seems likely that the valleys of the Boyne, the Barrow and the Nore were the first areas of colonisation followed later by the less accessible valleys of the Slaney and Suir.

Cultivation and clearance of land on this scale was something new in Irish history. The three-field system, with its division into strips cultivated with the heavy plough, probably made its first appearance in Ireland at this time. There was thus an important new economic aspect to the Norman Conquest. The tillage of the heavy soil of the river valleys could not have taken place without a new expertise. Overall, however, the military aspect seems to have been dominant. Great stone castles at Trim, Carlow, Kilkenny, Cahir and elsewhere were the key centres of the new order. The garrisons of these castles provided protection for the settlers and in return received their agricultural surplus. Towns also had an important military function. The Norman settlements at Trim, Thomastown and elsewhere resembled similar Norman foundations at Flint, Denbigh and Rhuddlan in north Wales. In Wales, the natives were (at least in theory) excluded from these towns. In Ireland, the same rule seems to have been applied. In Wales such towns become the target for attack from a resentful countryside. So too, in Ireland, such towns as Carlow suffered a similar fate at the hands of the MacMurroughs, when these erstwhile allies of the Normans turned against them.

The Church itself played an active military role in some areas. Medieval historians have largely ignored the part played by the military order of the Templars and the knights Hospitallers of St John in the Conquest of Ireland. Most numerous among the religious orders during the post-Conquest period were the Augustinian canons with well over a hundred houses. Between them, the Templars and the Hospitallers accounted for at least twenty and possibly as many as sixty. Their role was by no means negligible. The military-style architecture of the monastery at Kells (Co. Kilkenny) speaks far more eloquently about the role of the Church in this area than any written sources. Other monastic houses such as the Cistercian monastery at Dunbrody (Co. Wexford) served the needs of the colonists. The archbishopric of Dublin was also very much a part of the military establishment, with castles at

Swords and Tallaght. Statues of knights in the cloisters of Jerpoint abbey (Co. Kilkenny) make the same point about the place of the Church in colonial Ireland.

From the beginning, indeed, the Church was committed to the support of the Conquest, though ecclesiastical historians often lose sight of this fact by isolating Church history from history at large. Bishops were now royal tenants in chief with military obligations. The bishop of Limerick, for example, was responsible for maintaining the king's peace as a secular judge. Reorganisation of cathedral chapters in the name of reform enabled prebends to be held by royal or other nominees who were not obliged to reside. Churchmen also played a key role in the royal administration, and did not always avoid the seamy side of politics. Recent research has shown the close involvement of Stephen of Fulbourn, bishop of Waterford, in the assassination of the two MacMurrough brothers at the end of the thirteenth century, an incident which did not prevent his later promotion to the archbishopric of Tuam. Another interesting ecclesiastical figure was the military-minded bishop of Ossory who carried the Host about with him on the grounds that any attack on his person would become by definition an act of sacrilege. There is no reason to think, however, that the role of the Church was any different in Ireland after the Conquest from what it was in England, Wales and Scotland. Monastic historians mesmerised by 'bare, ruined choirs' have tended to overlook the way in which castles, cathedrals and monasteries formed part of a single colonial complex, in which French-speaking culture was dominant.

In Munster the Conquest was signalled unmistakably by the building of a large Gothic church on the Rock of Cashel, completely overshadowing Cormac's Chapel. In Dublin the Normans built a Gothic cathedral and dedicated it to St Patrick, thus attempting, as others had done before, to control the saint for their own purposes. At Durrow, Hugh de Lacy attempted to use the stones of the old monastic site to build a castle and was struck down for his pains. At Lismore a castle was built upon the site of the ancient monastery. Other important monastic centres of the traditional order – Emly, Clonmacnoise and Terryglass, which had been active in the first half of the century – were allowed or encouraged to decay. At Fore the older monstery was replaced by a house of Augustinian canons.

Resistance, when it came, was not from these older foundations but from Cistercian monasteries in the valleys of the Boyne and Barrow, where the reform movement had made some headway before the Norman Conquest. Trouble arose at Mellifont, Bective (near Trim) and Jerpoint in the early years of the thirteenth century and had become sufficiently serious by 1211 to warrant the appointment of an official investigation by the Cistercian order. The mission was carried out by Stephen of Lexington, a Norman cleric linked by close family ties with Henry III's administration. As might have been anticipated, the result went against the Irish monks. It was ordered that only French and Latin, and not Irish, should be spoken within these houses. The various monasteries with Irish monks were placed under French or Anglo-Norman supervision. Overall the effect was to undermine still further the position of Irish-speaking institutions within the Norman orbit.

It would be an oversimplification to suggest that the clergy both higher and lower were drawn completely from the ranks of the conquerors. The role of the Crown in ecclesiastical appointments, however, did place the newcomers in a strong position in such sees as Dublin and Meath and the southern half of the archdiocese of Armagh. The amalgamation of the traditional see of Glendalough with Dublin (1216) and the transference of the see of Clonard to Trim (1202) were carried out in the name of reform but clearly benefited the urban partners. With their insistence upon clerical celibacy and stricter adherence to canon law concerning marriage, the Normans had another weapon in their armoury, the reforming papacy of Innocent III. Though the whole topic requires further investigation, it seems likely also that the Normans dedicated their churches to the Holy Trinity, the Virgin Mary or to saints with a wider reputation than those enjoyed by the more localised Irish saints. Churches dedicated to Saints Peter and Paul, St Anne, St Thomas, St Mary, St Michael and St David are examples of this tendency. St Audouen's in Dublin was a Norman foundation. Here again, however, as we have seen earlier, the Normans had been anticipated by the O Connors, the O Briens, the MacMurroughs and other Irish kings.

The oldest traditions did not disappear overnight. Many of the Irish cults survived at a popular level, kept alive by the observance of feast days, visits to local wells, the holding of 'patterns' (patrons) in honour of local saints and perhaps also by the belief in the greater efficacy of prayers to Irish saints. At Ardmore near Waterford, for example, devotion to St Declan flourished for many centuries after the coming of the Normans. It is perhaps not inappropriate to see the Norman clergy in Ireland as an Established Church in a world of Irish-speaking dissenters, divided from them by culture and tradition as well as by economic and political status. There seems little doubt that the outlook of the Norman theologian Richard FitzRalph, who taught at 'Drawda Hall', Oxford, was poles apart from the *mentalité* of rural Meath, though he was born at Drogheda, in the same county.

Outside the areas of direct Norman control, the elite status of the Irish language survived and with it the traditional hereditary professions of bards, brehons and historians. Some hereditary families were driven from one part of Ireland only to take refuge in another. Thus the O Clerys (Ua Cleirigh) moved from near Galway to Mayo. The Duignans (Ua Duibhgennain) originally from Clonmacnoise, settled in Leitrim and Roscommon. The Wards (Maic an Bhaird), formerly hereditary poets to the O Kellys in the Athlone area (Uí Mhaine) became bards to the O Donnells in Donegal. The Maic Conmidhe became poets to the O Neills. The O Breslins were poets to the Maguires. Actual possession of land in some areas was slow to change hands, and it has been suggested that many such families survived as erenaghs (*air-chinnigh*) or lay stewards of lands belonging to traditional monastic foundations. On Devenish Island and Boa Island (Co. Fermanagh) such traditional monastic communities existed side by side with newer foundations.

Irish cultural institutions did not disappear, but they were probably placed on the defensive. Many of the manuscripts which survive are compilations. For better or worse the *Book of Invasions* (*Lebor Gabala*) seems to have achieved canonical status at this time as a record of an Irish past contrasting with that of the Normans. In the field of law the text of the *Senchas Mar* continued to be copied but its original meaning had been lost, not to be recovered until the twentieth century (and then with extreme difficulty). The brehons were carrying on a legal tradition which they did not fully understand. The tradition of keeping annalistic chronicles was maintained, however, and stories around the figure of Fionn MacCumhail multiplied, thus ensuring at a popular level the survival of a version of the remote Irish past. Fionn was in some measure the Irish equivalent of King Arthur, a Celtic leader whose existence implied a pre-Conquest past.

As elsewhere in the British Isles, a particularly sharp contrast existed between the outlooks of conquerors and conquered in the field of law. The Normans assumed that in matters of inheritance the appropriate pattern was from father to son. Irish traditions, though changing to some extent at the royal level in response to a new model of kingship, still stressed the rights of kindred. Such differences did not originate in racial origins nor were they unique to Ireland. They were indeed cultural in origin. As Professor Le Roy Ladurie (in 'Family Structures and Inheritance Customs in Sixteenth-Century France', in Jack Goody, Joan Thirk and E. P. Thompson, eds., *Family and Inheritance*, 1976) has shown in relation to France and the Netherlands during this period, profound differences existed between north-east and north-west France about the rights enjoyed by fathers in the disposal of property. This was not a matter of light and darkness, as historians brought up within a narrow English common-law tradition tend to assume. Rather it originated in profoundly different ways of looking at ends and means. In a father–king-centred paradigm such as the Normans brought with them to Ireland, the kindred and the sons were legally disadvantaged. In the Norman scheme of things, the tendency was towards 'primogeniture' (the right of the eldest son to inherit at the expense of all other claims); entail (the process of controlling inheritance over several generations by a decision of the existing landholder); and the disposal of personal property by will by a father who might conceivably ignore any claims upon his property. In Norman-controlled areas those assumptions tended to prevail, since they had the backing of the Crown and the common-law courts. Thus the FitzGeralds consistently adhered to primogeniture. In Irish-controlled areas the clash between old and new continued for several centuries. The chronicles regularly refer to conflicts over succession which often seem to originate in a clash between these two approaches.

In criminal law Norman emphasis was upon retribution. Thus hanging for theft became a routine penalty. In some Irish areas thieves might well receive exemplary punishment, but the tradition of compensation and of kinship responsibility survived until the seventeenth century. Here again this was not a contrast between civilisation and barbarism, though the Normans tended to see it that way, but a clash between two legal systems organised on different principles. A similar clash existed in the field of ecclesiastical law where Norman views on clerical marriage, polygamy, marriage between prohibited degrees and illegitimacy contrasted with Irish traditions. The struggle between the two was not to be resolved for many centuries. Ecclesiastical historians, however, have perhaps been too ready to take the side of the self-styled reformers.

The gulf which existed between these two legal worlds was not totally unbridged. Five royal lineages (Ua Néill of Ulster, Ua Mael Shechnaill of Meath, Ua Conchobair of Connacht, Ua Briain of Munster, and MacMurrough of Leinster), which had all come to terms with the Normans, were allowed access to royal law courts as a privilege. It was also possible by the second half of the thirteenth century for individual Irishmen living within Norman areas to buy grants of privilege, though this class of person never seems to have numbered more than a few dozen. An attempt was made c. 1277–80 by the archbishop of Cashel to negotiate the purchase of a grant of English law on a wider scale. Though this did not come to anything, it presumably reflected a recognition by churchmen of Irish background that the existing situation carried with it serious disadvantages for the Church as an institution. Archbishop MacCarvell and others like him were, after all, 'reformers' with no great commitment to the traditional Irish kinship system as it extended to ecclesiastical matters.

In general, however, the effect of the introduction of Norman-style law with its relegation of many Irishmen to second-class status may well have been to increase the attractiveness of reliance upon kindred. To whom could an Irishman turn? The Calendar of Justiciary Rolls tells of a group of Irish tenants who after their English lord was slain approached another Englishman and asked to be placed under his protection. He agreed to do this, indicated some waste lands where they might settle and then arranged for them to be massacred en route. Presumably not all such requests for 'avowry' ended in this way, but it may well be that kinship ties seemed a more reliable method of achieving security. If this was so, the introduction of Norman feudalism into Ireland may have had the paradoxical result of helping to keep alive non-feudal ties. There is no doubt, indeed, that the Normans themselves came to recognise the power of kinship links among the Irish – so much so that a technical term from Brehon law, *cin confocuis*, appears in early parliamentary legislation in Ireland during Edward I's reign.

In some parts of Ireland, notably in the south-west, the Normans blended into an existing pattern of alliances. Maurice FitzThomas, who first established the power of the FitzGeralds in south Munster, drew upon the support of the O Briens as well as some of his fellow-Normans. However, perhaps the key difference between the two societies lay in the continuing colonial settlement of the east. Without this factor it is difficult to explain why the MacMurroughs should have become disenchanted with their former allies, the Normans. The MacMurroughs initially benefited from the invasion. It was their hereditary enemies, the O Brenans, who had been driven out of Wexford to take refuge in the uplands of the Nore valley. From about 1270, however, the MacMurroughs showed signs of hostility to the colonists, so much so that Roger Bigod, earl of Norfolk, who had been granted the lordship of Carlow, planned to bring them over to England to meet Edward I, in the hope of negotiating a truce. Bigod himself, however, may have been the cause of the problem, in so far as he encouraged colonisation of his Irish estates. At all events, the threat from the MacMurroughs had become so great that in 1282 the justiciar, Stephen of Fulbourn, bishop of Waterford, took steps to have them assassinated. In folk-memory this murder became an event by which the passing of time was judged.

> That Mary was of the age of twenty-three years on the vigil of St Mary Magdalen last. He knows this by common fame current in this country which was that Mary was born to Philip, of his wife then being in Fyngal, on the day when Art McMurth was slain who was slain on the said vigil. And it is known in the whole country that twenty-three years are passed since Art McMurgh was slain.

If the viking invasions brought about the fall of many aspects of the 'Old Order', the Norman Conquests completed the process. During the viking centuries the British Isles remained divided into distinct but overlapping political and cultural communities, all of them affected to a greater or lesser extent by Scandinavian influences, Norwegian or Danish. With the coming of the Normans, communities of the British Isles were brought together at the aristocratic level, in Church and state, within a single cultural and political ascendancy which looked towards France. For nearly three centuries a French-speaking colonial elite imposed its own cultural norms, with the castle, the borough, the reformed Church and new-style episcopal government as their mainstays. This was very much a 'command' society in which power rested with a military aristocracy. Institutions associated with different forms of society, those based on kinship or on the market, took a second place during this period. The Normans were not interested in trade for its own sake. The dominant ideology of the regime was based upon the notion of the three estates, warriors, priests and peasants, each with its own function. Merchants had no obvious place in this scheme of things. In this society the highest prestige was reserved for the military class with its tournaments and its cult of chivalry. The highest loyalty was reserved for lord or king, not for the kinship group. In religion the same assumptions may be seen at work. The cathedrals of the colonial regime stressed the importance of authority, divine and episcopal. Some historians have detected a shift, from a concern with offences against one's neighbour or kindred to a preoccupation with sin against divine authority, as having taken place during the Counter-Reformation. Something of the same kind, though possibly on a more limited scale, seems to have occurred during this period also.

The use of the term 'Norman' for the whole of this period, from the mid-eleventh to the mid-fourteenth centuries, is, of course, very much an oversimplification. The followers of William the Conqueror were not exclusively Norman. Many were Breton, Flemish and Picard by background. From the mid-twelfth century the line of Norman kings was replaced by that of Henry II Plantagenet and the Angevins. The early settlers of Wales, Scotland and Ireland included many Flemings. But such qualifications, while necessary, do not change the essential fact that a French-orientated ascendancy introduced by the Normans came to dominate most of the British Isles, so much so that the historian loses sight of the varied cultures over which the 'Normans' ruled. It is only by a conscious effort that the historian reminds himelf that the newcomers were very much in a minority. The history of the various cultures of the British Isles during this period still remains to be written, for the localities of England as well as for north and south Wales, Highland and Lowland Scotland and Ireland, east and west of the Shannon. These cultures survived, but few if any of them escaped the influence of the Norman ascendancy.

6

The decline of the Norman-French empire

The end of the thirteenth century saw the greatest extent of what may be termed the Edwardian empire of the British Isles. In Wales, Edward I's castles symbolised the establishment of royal authority over the last autonomous Welsh kingdom. Wales was now divided between marcher lordships in the south and west and a principality in the north-west where royal castles dominated the coastline from Harlech northwards. In Ireland, the royal justiciar John Wogan sitting at Ardfert in Kerry heard a plea concerning land at Dunquin. Royal power was not confined to Dublin and the east coast but extended to remote areas in the south-west. In Scotland, Edward, acting as overlord, had appointed guardians to decide upon the succession to the Scottish Crown. In England, the king seemed well able to cope with any opposition. The main problems seemed likely to arise in Gascony which Edward held as the vassal of the king of France.

As we now know, none of this proved to be permanent. Wogan's court in 1307 was the last royal assize to be held in Kerry for three centuries. In Scotland, Robert Bruce, whose father had fought with Henry III at the battle of Lewes, defeated the forces of Edward II at Bannockburn (1314). The conquest of Wales seemed to have succeeded but even here at the end of the fourteenth century, Owain Glyndwr exposed the shallow foundations of Edward I's success.

With the benefit of hindsight we may decide that the break-up of the Edwardian empire into four 'national' units was inevitable. But this may be to take too narrow a view. In the context of the British Isles, the superiority of the south-east in men and resources was clear. The building of Edward's Welsh castles was a remarkable technical achievement, which depended for its success upon the mobilisation of skilled labour from all over England. The royal administrative system made it possible to levy taxes on a national scale. Given the political will, the assertion of royal authority throughout the British Isles seemed to be an eminently practicable proposition. Twenty years after the defeat at Bannockburn, Edward III gave his support to Edward Balliol's attempt to gain the Scottish throne. Robert Bruce had died in 1329, succeeded by his son David, who was only five years old. There was thus a golden opportunity to avenge Bannockburn and to reverse the terms of the Treaty of Northampton, by which the independence of Scotland had been recognised. In 1333, Balliol gained a decisive victory at Halidon Hill, and in 1334 ceded much of the area south of the Forth to Edward III. Edinburgh was occupied by Edward and remained in his possession until 1340.

What made the conquest of 'Scotland' difficult was the support which the young David Bruce began to receive from the French. In effect, France presented Edward with the option of choosing between Gascony and Scotland. Edward's reply, in 1337, was to claim the Crown of France, a claim which he might well have put forward in 1328 after the death of Charles IV, last of the Capetian kings of France. From 1337 onwards, Edward was committed to a gigantic gamble on the European continent. It was to this that royal resources were to be devoted. Scotland for the time being became an object of secondary importance.

The French wars, as we now know, proved to be a long-term commitment. For over a hundred years, the French enterprise required the expenditure of resources and manpower on the grandest scale. Historians differ about the profitability of the wars, much as they do about whether the British empire of a later date showed a profit or loss at the end of the day. What concerns us here are the political consequences of the wars in the context of the British Isles. There can be little doubt that the prime importance which was given to the dream of an empire in France distracted attention away from what now seemed to be the lesser vision of an empire in the British Isles.

As a consequence, at least in part, of Edward III's involvement in France, the Norman ascendancy dissolved into several constituent parts. The sense of difference was most marked in the Scottish Lowlands where the struggle for independence was prolonged. In Ireland, it arose as the result of the Norman lords being left to enjoy a *de facto* independence over a long period. In Wales, the marcher lords were allowed to retain their privileges as the price of defending the Welsh march. In northern England, a new class of marcher lordships came into existence to defend the border with Scotland. During the fourteenth and fifteenth centuries, a pattern may be seen emerging in the British Isles which was nearer to that of the Iberian peninsula than to France, in the sense that local autonomies prevailed over a wider monarchy.

The future of the Norman ascendancy was also influenced by factors over which Edward III had little control. In 1349, the Black Death reduced the population of England by one third. The result of this and succeeding attacks of plague was to reduce the population pressures which had provided much of the impetus to colonisation. The pressure on land which had drawn many English tenants to seek their fortunes in Wales and in Ireland was reversed. For the remainder of the century and for most of the fifteenth it would be a question of landlords seeking tenants for their land, not vice versa. The Norman colonies in Ireland and Wales now lacked the constant supply of manpower upon which they relied. The demographic links which held the ascendancy together began to dissolve during the fourteenth century.

It was not until the sixteenth century that this period in insular history came to an end. By then the demographic situation had changed. In addition, the Tudors, for their own reasons, were prepared to give much of their attention to the affairs of Scotland, Ireland and Wales. After the Scottish defeat at Flodden in 1513, the Lowlands were left exposed to English pressure and in 1560 Elizabeth was able to intervene on the side of the pro-English party. The victory of John Knox and the Scottish reformers was in effect a victory for English influence. In Ireland, successive monarchs had intervened from time to time though without effective results. Edward III sent William of Windsor over to Ireland in the mid-fourteenth century. Richard II made two largely symbolic visits to Ireland. Edward IV sent over John Tiptoft as lord deputy, with disastrous consequences for the earl of Desmond (who was executed) but without long-term political results. It was not until Thomas Cromwell took action against the young earl of Kildare in 1535 that royal power became a reality. In Wales, the Acts of Union, passed under Cromwell, in 1536 and 1543 brought the marcher lordships to an end. In England itself the defeat of the Pilgrimage of Grace in 1536 led to the establishment of a royal Council of the North, which in effect took over from the marcher lords. In 1314 all this was far in the future. For two centuries the history of the British Isles was the history of its individual communities.

The political history of England during the fourteenth and fifteenth centuries is a tale of violence and revolution made familiar in the work of Shakespeare and Marlowe. In 1327 Roger Mortimer and Queen Isabella deposed Edward II, only for Mortimer to be killed in his turn by the young Edward III in the counter-revolution of 1330. In 1399 Richard II was deposed by Henry of Lancaster, who claimed the throne as Henry IV. In 1461, Henry VI was deposed, restored in 1470, and deposed once more in 1471. In 1485 Richard III died on Bosworth Field in battle against Henry Tudor, the future Henry VII. To this story of violence must be added the violence involved in the Hundred Years War, with its innumerable sackings, sieges and destructive 'scorched earth' marches. The battles of Crécy, Poitiers and Agincourt and the burning of Jeanne D'Arc were incidents in a prolonged war, at the end of which there was civil war in England itself.

From the standpoint of political history, it is difficult to avoid a pessimistic conclusion. Looked at in the context of economic history, however, the fourteenth and fifteenth centuries take on a somewhat different colouring. As a consequence of the sudden decline in population caused by the Black Death of 1348 the second half of the fourteenth century in England witnessed the decline of unfree tenures, accompanied by a shift from labour services to cash rents. A shortage of labour led to the rise of labourers' wages. During the same period, cloth made in southern England began to be exported in large quantities. Industrialisation took place in East Anglia, the Cotswolds and, in due course, in the West Riding of Yorkshire. England which had been a colonial-style economy exporting raw materials turned to manufactures.

The sharp contrast which exists between the political and economic history of the period suggests that we may be justified in thinking that we are dealing with two societies, one of them a military society, in which a military class controlled the use of resources, and the other a market society, in which profit by peaceful exchange was the main objective. During the twelfth and thirteenth centuries the castle dominated the working of the English economy. During the fourteenth and fifteenth centuries, the balance shifted in favour of the merchant community. The continuance of the Hundred Years War, however, ensured that military considerations were often paramount. Thus the Crown, using its right of purveyance, was empowered to buy food for its armies or garrisons at prices which were set by its own representatives. The war necessarily diverted resources from the economy at large for the purposes of achieving political objectives.

The existence of a military society during these centuries was clearest on the border with Scotland. The Scottish wars, which were inextricably intertwined with the wider conflict of the Hundred Years War itself as a consequence of the Franco-Scottish alliance, led to the creation of a military class to defend the north of England. Hence the northern counties of Northumberland, Westmorland and Cumberland became more 'feudalised' than had been the case earlier. The building took place of castles of a type which was no longer needed in the more peaceful south. Such castles were built at Etel (1341), Edlingham (1350), Gleeston (1330) and elsewhere. Smaller 'peel' castles were also erected for the defence of smaller estates. A type of marcher society came into existence in northern England of a kind which had long been familiar on the Welsh borders and in Ireland. The Percys, the Nevilles and the Cliffords came to play a role in English politics which the Mortimers of Wigmore and Chirk had played earlier.

The castle was a familiar feature of military society. The war also brought into existence a new institution in the 'affinity' of indentured retainers. John of Gaunt, one of the sons of Edward III, indentured well over a hundred esquires at a peacetime salary of up to 20 marks a year, provided that they also recruited a man at arms. While it may be going too far to regard the Hundred Years War as a gigantic system of outdoor relief for the English feudal elite, there is no doubt that service with the military nobility during the war provided an attractive and appropriate career for many hard-pressed younger sons of minor landlords. The war in France was a long-term imperial venture, which was the counterpart in the fourteenth and fifteenth centuries of the empire in the British Isles which had drawn the Normans in 1066.

War to such men as Sir John Chandos and Sir John Fastolf was a money-making enterprise. The Hundred Years War, however, was not exclusively justified in financial terms by its participants. In an earlier period, the idea of the Crusade had provided the reason for undertaking military expeditions in eastern Europe, the Holy Land and even in parts of western Europe. The ideological backing for the Hundred Years War was supplied by the cult of chivalry. Edward III consciously cultivated the notion that the war was a romantic enterprise. The torchlight-procession of knights at Bristol in 1358 was not an isolated event but part of a programme of tournaments and other activities intended to convey the chivalric message. In 1348 Edward III founded the Order of the Garter as a community of knights modelled upon the fellowship of King Arthur and the Round Table. The knight was encouraged to see himself as following a higher calling, marked off by the code of chivalry from those who made fortunes by the base method of trade. Presumably those who suffered at the hands of Edward's captains did not share these assumptions.

This romantic approach to war (or pseudo-romantic depending upon one's point of view) was incorporated in the architecture of the castles which were built in southern England. The new-style castles of the fourteenth and fifteenth centuries provided a military façade for what were in fact palatial living quarters. The most spectacular example of such conspicuous consumption was the castle which Edward built at his birthplace, Windsor, between 1350 and 1377. St George's Chapel, Windsor, was built with the Order of the Garter in mind. The cost of the whole enterprise was, by contemporary standards, prodigious. John of Gaunt built a similarly elaborate castle at Kenilworth. Sir John Fastolf, a lesser figure, built in the same vein but on a smaller scale at Caistor, near Norwich. Other examples of the 'chivalric castle' include castles at Raglan, Crew and Tattersall. All were monuments to a particular ideology.

The attractions of a military career may well have seemed greatest to lords and their families who were hard hit by the crisis in agriculture. During the two centuries which followed the Conquest the feudal elite controlled resources through the related institutions of castle, borough and Church. In the fourteenth century, this situation changed radically. As a result of the sudden decline in population which followed the Black Death, the manorial officials were no longer able to control their tenants in the same way. Since land was freely available, it was relatively easy for unfree tenants to move. As labour was now scarce, wages went up on estates which made use of wage-labour. More and more landlords decided to abandon demesne farming, and to cease employing the unfree labour on which the system depended and to rent their land out to tenants. Villeinage declined and the status of peasants rose. There also seems to have been a shift of wealth from the countryside to the towns during this period.

A comparison of the taxation returns of 1334 and 1515 indicates that the balance of wealth shifted from the grain counties of the midlands to the new clothing-industry areas of the south. In 1300 English wool provided the raw material for the cloth industries of Flanders and northern Italy. By 1400, a 'native' cloth industry had come into being, partly as a result of the migration of Flemish weavers to a country in which wool was relatively cheap and water power was abundant. The heavy export taxes on wool exported abroad made the possibility of manufacturing cloth a more practicable proposition than it had been when export duties were light. By 1381 Flemish weavers were conspicuous enough to be the targets of native hostility.

One of the consequences of the rise of the cloth industry was the development of towns and industrial villages in those areas where the industry prospered. In these counties a shift took place from the manor-dominated borough to the independent town. Coventry achieved its independence during the mid-fourteenth century. Other towns followed suit in obtaining their own mayor and council. Ecclesiastical boroughs, which were slow to make the transition, became centres of unrest during the so-called Peasants' Revolt of 1381. What was coming into being was a market-orientated society in the south of England, above all in London.

Military society had its own institutions, as too had the market society, all of them associated with towns. The equivalent of the military affinities were the urban guilds, which were in essence monopolies designed to protect the general interests of their members. The profit motive was understandably uppermost but the guilds also stressed the importance of fraternity. The fraternities, each with their own church, were the equivalent in market society of the indentured retinues of military society. Rituals, patrons, saints, liveries, mystery-plays, all served as symbols of unity within the appropriate fraternity. Conspicuous consumption in this society took the form of church-building or of the establishment of chantries to say masses for the souls of guild members. In the early fifteenth century some London guilds were able to buy town-houses from the nobility and convert them to their own purposes. These economic changes were also responsible for a cultural change of great significance – the emergence of the English language as a socially acceptable medium. English was the language of the trading community and the rise of London, Norwich, Bristol and other towns brought about the elevated social status of English.

The constitutional link between the military and market sectors of English society was provided in parliament. The balance between the two was far from equal, however. For all the wealth of the market society, the exercise of political power was heavily weighted in favour of the landed aristocracy. It might have been better for the towns had a system of estates developed different from that of the English parliament. As it was, the landed interest dominated the House of Lords in the persons of the great magnates and the House of Commons in the representatives of the knights of the shires. It is not surprising that parliaments should have consistently thrown their weight on the side of 'military society'. From the mid-fourteenth century onwards parliament passed a series of sumptuary laws, designed to prevent the 'lower' classes wearing clothes which were more appropriate to the gentry. It was parliament which in 1351 passed the Statute of Labourers in a vain attempt to control wages in the interests of rural landlords. It was parliament which attempted to forbid towns from harbouring villeins who had fled from their masters. In 1413 the Statute of Additions was passed requiring persons involved in law suits to give more precise descriptions of themselves, another measure aimed at restricting social mobility. In 1429, in an attempt to retrict the number of voters in county elections, the vote was confined to forty-shilling freeholders.

The most dramatic example of the control of parliament by military society was the 'Merciless' parliament of 1388, when the five magnates, Gloucester, Arundel, Warwick, Bolingbroke (the son of John of Gaunt) and Nottingham brought about the downfall of Richard II's government. One of the royal counsellors was Nicholas Brembre, mayor of London, who supported the anti-war policies of the Crown. The king was forced to give way and Brembre, along with some others, was executed. A similar crisis occurred a decade later, when Richard II was forced to abdicate by Henry of Lancaster. Richard was committed to a policy of peace with France and had he remained in power the likelihood is that the Hundred Years War would not have been resumed. The political power of the magnates ensured that England was again involved in a long imperial venture under Henry V and his successor which may be said not to have ended until the loss of Calais in 1558.

The political influence of military society was also to be seen in the interventions which the Percys, marcher lords of the north, played in the revolution which brought down Richard II and in events in 1403 which might easily have caused the fall of his successor Henry IV. During the Wars of the Roses a similar role was played by the Nevilles.

There was little sign of the political rise of a middle class during this period. The politically ambitious merchants had to acquire some semblance of gentility in the form of a landed estate before they could hope for a political career. Social differences died hard, however, as John Wiltshire found to his cost when he purchased half a manor and became tenant in chief to the king, with the service of handing the king a towel before dinner on coronation day. The court set up by John of Gaunt to adjudicate on his claim ordered that it be delegated to the earl of Cambridge. Despite such individual problems, however, it has been estimated that marriages between children of gentry and of merchants were common (amounting to between a quarter and a third of surviving cases).

In the context of insular history the partial industrialisation of the southern counties was a significant event, or series of events, which led to the differentiation of this area of England from the rest of the British Isles. The southern counties came to resemble other industrialised areas of western Europe, especially Flanders and northern Italy. In terms of population and wealth they mark a great change. The economic pull of the market society of the south began to influence Wales and Ireland even during a period when the political links between the various communities were in a state of suspension.

At the end of the thirteenth century, the power of Edward I in Wales was at its height. His victories over Llywelyn had led to the creation of the principality which stretched from Gwynedd in the north, down the Welsh coast to Carmarthen in the south. But this was not the only indication of royal influence. During the 1290s, Edward made a point of demonstrating his control over the marcher lords. He sat in judgement on the earls of Gloucester and Hereford, lords of Glamorgan and Brecon respectively. He imprisoned the lord of Ewyas Lacy. He ordered Edmund

Mortimer of Wigmore, who had hanged a villein belonging to the royal lordship of Montgomery, to provide an effigy of the felon which could be hung on the royal gallows. In these and other episodes Edward showed his intention to maintain his rights in the marches, though he was careful not to take more than what he considered his due.

In both the principality and the marches, the foundation of 'Norman' power still rested upon the combination of castle, borough, priory and manor. Castles continued to dominate the countryside. The burgesses of boroughs established close to the castles often served as warriors in the retinue of their lord. In time of political confrontation, the marcher lords were able to parade the military strength which they had at their disposal. In 1313, the Bohun earl of Hereford could rely upon his 'crowd of Welshmen wild from the woodland'. In 1321, the followers of Mortimer of Wigmore paraded 'all clothed in green with their arms yellow'. In the revolution of 1399, Henry of Bolingbroke was met by loyal tenants from his Welsh estates. The marcher lordships exemplified the power of military society.

As was the case in fourteenth-century England, however, the foundations of this society were soon to be eroded by the demographic catastrophe of the Black Death and its aftermath. From mid-century, villages began to be abandoned. The area of cultivated land contracted. Lords found themselves unable to enforce the labour services due to them within the manorial framework. In 1397, the lord of Dyffryn Clwyd complained that his 'natiui' refused to perform their harvest obligations and mill dues. Bondmen fled from their estates, in 'Welshries' as well as 'Englishries'. Many colonial boroughs were penetrated by Welshmen whose presence within their walls had hitherto been forbidden. The Englishry of Glamorgan was recolonised by Welshmen. Reaction against seigniorial attempts to restore the *status quo* was almost certainly one of the causes behind the revolt of Owain Glyndwr in 1400. By the early fifteenth century, the military society was everywhere in retreat, despite the enactment of penal laws which made Welshmen 'second-class citizens' in their own country.

Socially, if not legally, the Welsh 'natives' were the beneficiaries at the expense of the colonists. The situation was by no means a simple one, however. In the 'Welshries', the social structure which had survived Norman invasion broke down in the face of population decline. The kinship-based system of inheritance increasingly gave way to one in which holdings passed from father to son. In the late fourteenth and early fifteenth centuries, Welshmen in large numbers adopted English tenure, with its freer possibilities of alienation, and its allowance for descent to women, in preference to the Welsh system with its defence of the rights of the members of the kinship group. By the end of the fifteenth century, Welsh rural society was heavily 'anglicised' in an economic sense.

The marcher lordships also found it difficult to cope with the new freedom of market conditions. Ideally, each marcher lordship had constituted a single economic unity whose resources were mobilised for the good of the whole (as seen from the lord's point of view). Thus the Mortimer estate in Wales provided supplies for the Mortimer estate in Ireland. The controlled market upon which this rested gave way to a more open system. Market towns, such as Wrexham, replaced the restricted estate boroughs. Fairs became increasingly popular for the freedom of sale which they offered. In south Wales, numerous small ports traded with Bristol and Devon. The wool of the Welsh uplands became an important source of raw material for the growing English cloth industry. Welsh cattle supplied meat for the markets of south-eastern England. South and east Wales, in particular, were drawn into a close relationship with the English economy. The particularism which had been so marked a feature of the economic life of the marcher lordships gave way to a more open system.

The result by the early sixteenth century was considerable social change. The military society, dominated by the castle and its associated institutions, gave way to one in which the squire's manor house, the market town and the individual farmer were typical. The egalitarianism of the kinship group (*gwely*) gave way increasingly to a society stratified by wealth. The bondmen, whose task from early days had been to supply the courts of the Welsh princes with food, disappeared from Welsh life, perhaps to become labourers. In the 'Englishries', the manorial structure gave way to farms and villages.

All these changes preceded the formal incorporation of Wales into the English political, legal and administrative system in the Acts of Union 1536–43 which in effect ratified the social revolution of the preceding century. Differences between English and Welsh codes of law were now abolished. Marcher lordships were incorporated within English-style shires. The Welsh language survived these changes but the culture which came into existence in most parts of Wales was something new, an amalgam of Norman, English and Welsh. The new Welsh squirearchy in many ways resembled its English counterpart. Soon *gwely* and *galanas* were to be forgotten and castles to fall into ruins. Broad differences of outlook between north and south Wales continued to exist, however.

In Scotland, Bruce's victory in 1314 at Bannockburn and the Treaty of Northampton some fourteen years later, recognising Scottish independence, did not bring peace. The border between England and Scotland became in effect a subsidiary theatre in the Hundred Years War. The French alliance, which was the guarantee of independence, by its very nature required the Scots to engage in military operations on the border. Hence what might have been a peaceful frontier turned into an area of continual war. The high points of this were the battles of Neville's Cross in 1346, Homildon Hill in 1402, Flodden in 1513 and Pinkie in 1547. But these were merely the major events in a series of conflicts which went on for over two hundred years.

We have already glanced at the effects which this state of affairs had upon the northern counties of England. The effect was equally far-reaching upon the Scottish Lowlands, and indirectly upon the Highlands as well. The frontier war brought into existence a society which was even more organised for war than that which had existed in the twelfth and thirteenth centuries. In this situation the Scottish Crown was heavily dependent upon a nobility able to put large numbers of retainers into the field at short notice. The most powerful of these was the house of Douglas, rulers of Galloway (the Black Douglases) and through another branch of the family of the east coast (the Red Douglases of Angus). The Douglases also had allies in the north upon whose support they could count.

The power of William, eighth earl of Douglas (1425?–52) was seen most dramatically in his treatment of a certain MacLellan, who refused to serve as a Douglas retainer. MacLellan was imprisoned. A kinsman who came to ask for his deliverance was told, after being served dinner, that '[he had] come a litill to leit; bot zondar is zour sistir sone lyand; bot he wantis the heid; take his bodie and do with it quhat ze will'. This incident well illustrates how the Black Douglas regarded himself as to all intents and purposes an independent ruler with the power of life and death. It also helps to explain how the king with the aid of the enemies made by the Black Douglas was able to bring about the downfall of the family in 1455.

In this military society the castle was the centre of lordship. The Douglas castle at Threave in Galloway, built in the late fourteenth century, had its counterparts in other lordships throughout Scotland. Not until the coming of artillery in the mid-fifteenth century did the balance shift against the castle. With its base in local society the nobility controlled access to higher appointments in the Church and the major abbeys. Even more than in England parliament was dominated by the earls and nobles. In any one parliament it was usual for only a few boroughs (not always the same) to be represented. Boroughs, indeed, despite their theoretical independence were very much exposed to pressures from the local nobility. The baronial courts were the real legal reality in the face of the continued weakness of the royal courts. Sheriffs, in theory royal servants, commonly belonged to the dominant nobility of the region. War, far from uniting society, was a major factor in creating disunity.

One consequence of the overwhelming importance of the defence of the southern borders was the decline of Lowland influence in the west. During the fourteenth and fifteenth centuries, while the attention of the Lowlanders was diverted southwards, the west was able to enjoy a prolonged period of independence. During this period the MacDonalds, Lords of the Isles, were able to extend their influence into Ulster, where a branch of the family became the MacDonnells of Antrim. The military innovation on which this rise in their power rested were the gallowglasses (*galloglaich* = foreign soldiers), highly disciplined companies of swordsmen and axemen who dominated the tactical scene in this area until the sixteenth century. Gallowglasses from the Isles became the indentured retainers of the O Donnells and of the earl of Desmond. The importance of the Lords of the Isles in a British Isles context was illustrated in 1388 when Richard II sent a mission to establish good relations with them. For their part, the Scottish kings were always willing to accept overtures from disgruntled Ulster chiefs.

Royal influence had not entirely ceased to exist in the west, but here as elsewhere the Crown was dependent upon a military nobility which had its own interests in mind as much as those of the Crown. In Argyll, the Campbells had been brought in by Bruce as a replacement for the MacDougalls, the allies of his rivals, the Comyns. In due course the Campbells, who became earls of Argyll in 1458, were to be uncrowned kings of the west. Farther north, the Huntleys and the MacKenzies served as the channels of Lowland influence.

It is possibly a mistake to overstress the difference between the 'two cultures' of Highlands and Lowlands at this date. Such Lowland magnates as the Black Douglases, with their indentured retainers and their power to enforce acceptance of service ('bond of manrent') over a wide area, in many ways resembled Highland chiefs. The inner core of their followers, enjoying the same name as their leader, were bound by ties of kinship as close as any Highland clan. In the absence of a central authority the 'feud' may indeed have been the main sanction behind local law. The clan, for its part, was by this date very much a feudal institution in which military service was rendered to the chief in return for his protection. The *galloglaich*, who served in Ireland, were the Gaelic equivalent of indentured retainers. Feudalism in its late medieval form was no stranger to the Highlands. Many of the customs of the Highlands seemed strange to Lowland eyes, but the political behaviour of the chiefs conformed to the assumptions of the time. John MacDonald of the Isles when he became the ally of the Douglases saw nothing strange in making a treaty with Edward IV of England. The survival of lordship rested upon a shrewd appraisal of the realities of the balance of power. In the long run, however, this was to tilt against the MacDonalds.

The Lowlands proper consisted of a relatively narrow belt stretching east–west between Glasgow and Edinburgh and a coastal strip running north–south from Coldingham to Brechin, and taking in the river valleys of the Forth and the Tay. It was the culture of this area which contrasted most sharply with that of the Highlands. Here English was now dominant even among the nobility. The earl of March, writing to Henry IV, his patron, in 1400, spoke of his preference for English rather than French. The majority of burghs, churches and monasteries was concentrated in the Lowlands. There is little doubt that the level of literacy was higher than in the rest of Scotland. Above all, market relations based on cash were becoming more common in the south-east than in the feudalised west where services in kind remained usual for a long time to come. The shift to a cash economy was to be seen in the commutation of labour service into money rents, a process which occurred during the fifteenth century on the ecclesiastical estates which covered much of the region. The practice of *feuing* (leasing out land for a fixed annual sum), which guaranteed inheritance in perpetuity provided the sum was duly paid, was a feature of the Lowlands. It was unknown in the Highlands where security of tenure was still associated with membership of a kinship group under the chief's protection.

Signs that the autonomy of the Isles might be in danger have been read into the fall of the house of Douglas in the 1450s. It was not until 1476, however, that James III (1460–88) turned his attention to the west. In 1476, John MacDonald, earl of Ross and Lord of the Isles, surrendered his earldom to the Crown after being accused of treasonable relations with Edward IV in the preceding decade. He was soon to be overthrown by his illegitimate son Angus Og, who in his turn was to be assassinated (1490). In 1494 a royal naval base was created at Tarbet on the Clyde, once a castle of Bruce. Early in the sixteenth century several castles in the Isles were bombarded from the sea. Royal artillery, which had proved so effective against Douglas, had been mounted on ships and used against the MacDonalds.

As in Wales and Scotland, the high-water-mark of imperial power was reached in Ireland c. 1300. In 1245 the old kingdom of Leinster had been divided into five feudal lordships, Carlow, Kildare, Kilkenny, Leix and Wexford. The magnates who held these fiefs – Bigod, de Vesci, de Clare, Mortimer and de Valence – were all members of the ruling elite and their 'presence' in Ireland indicated the strength of the imperial connection. Assizes were held regularly at Dublin, Cork and Limerick in the second half of the thirteenth century. As mentioned earlier, the peak of imperial power may be seen in 1307 when the king's justiciar, John Wogan, tried a case at Ardfert (Co. Kerry) concerning land in Dunquin, at the tip of the Dingle peninsula. The imperial connection could go no farther in the south-west of Ireland. It was a brief moment, however, and three more centuries were to elapse before it re-occurred.

The immediate causes which led to the decline of imperial influence in Scotland also affected Ireland. In 1315 Edward Bruce, brother of Robert Bruce, was invited to campaign in Ulster by an alliance of Ulster chiefs and discontented Norman barons. For a time there was a real possibility that Ireland might follow the example of Scotland and become an independent kingdom with Edward Bruce as its ruler. Bruce's defeat at Faughart in 1318 ruled this out but the result of the Bruce episode in the long term was to expose the dependence of the Crown upon the feudal magnates. By the end of the fourteenth century, direct imperial rule in Ireland had been replaced by indirect influence exercised throughout the south of Ireland by three great feudal magnates, Desmond, Ormond and Kildare. Though they held their land in theory from the Crown as earls, the FitzGeralds of Desmond and of Kildare and the Butlers of Ormond in effect ruled their territories as independent units. The FitzGeralds and the Butlers were the equivalent in Ireland of the great marcher houses of the Welsh and Scottish borders tolerated by the Crown for fear of a greater evil.

Future patterns of power in the south were already evident in the first half of the fourteenth century in the tumultuous career of Maurice FitzThomas, who was created first earl of Desmond in 1329. The house of Desmond, once established, became the leading political force in Munster and together with the FitzGerald earls of Kildare and the Butlers of Tipperary and Kilkenny formed an Anglo-Norman bloc, which, despite internal dissensions and repeated clashes with the royal administration remained part of the English nexus. The earl of Desmond for example served as a loyal tenant in chief with Edward III against the Scots. Feudal structures and assumptions survived in the south in spite of the fact that direct Crown control was ultimately confined to the 'Pale' around Dublin and Waterford.

Maurice FitzThomas was a descendant of the Geraldine, Thomas of Shanid, younger son of Maurice FitzGerald and a relatively minor figure in the Norman invasion of Munster in the late twelfth century. By 1300 the family controlled the fertile lands of north Kerry, from its base at Tralee, and much of Limerick, from its castles at Adare, Askeaton and Kilmallock. In effect, the earls of Desmond took over much of the territory which the O Briens had occupied in the tenth century under Brian Boru. They felt, as conquistadores, that they did not owe their position to Crown help, a fact which helps to explain the ambivalent attitude and behaviour of Maurice FitzThomas.

Thanks to the researches of Professor G. O. Sayles ('The Rebellious First Earl of Desmond', in J. A. Watt, J. B. Morrall and F. X. Martin, eds., *Medieval Studies Presented to Aubrey Gwynn S. J.* (1961), we know a great deal more than once seemed possible about FitzThomas. During the thirty years of his active political life he was involved in two prolonged clashes with the Crown (1329–33 and 1339–44) as well as numerous small-scale incidents. In 1329 he was the leader of a conspiracy whose members planned to make him king of Ireland and to divide the country among themselves. During a further period of unrest he was accused of usurping royal authority and of protecting and harbouring rebels. Eventually, in 1343, the royal justiciar marched against him, took the castles of Askeaton and Castle Island and hanged the earl's steward. In 1346 Desmond surrendered and went to London to make his submission. In 1355 he returned, this time as justiciar. In 1356 he died.

Professor Sayle's judgment on all this is that 'for the second quarter of the fourteenth century, the activities of the first earl of Desmond made orderly government in the south west of Ireland very largely impossible'. That is, in effect, the viewpoint of the Crown on 'law and order'. We know, however, from the involvement of the justiciar in the assassination of MacMurrough in 1283 that Crown officials themselves were quite capable of behaving illegally in the cause of 'law and order'.

What is interesting about Desmond's behaviour is that he confined his attention very largely to bringing pressure to bear upon royal officials, centres of royal power and Crown-controlled towns, such as Limerick and Youghal. In 1330, for example, he ordered Sir Thomas FitzGulber to publicise a prohibition that neither the sheriff nor any other servant of the king was to be obeyed. When, a few days later, Brian O Brien slew the sheriff, Desmond made 'great wassail' with him in celebration. Later in the same year, when the deputy justiciar ordered a new sheriff to take action against O Brien, Desmond ordered him to return O Brien's horses and cattle. In 1332 the royal stronghold at Bunratty Castle was destroyed by O Brien and MacNamara, presumably with Desmond's blessing.

It seems clear from this and other episodes that Desmond was attempting to set up a 'palatinate' in which he would be the sole source of political and legal authority. Thus he held a court at Dungarvan at which he issued fines and distraints. He appointed his own constable at Bunratty. He ejected royal bailiffs from the barony of Inchiquin and held his own court there. He issued pardons and ordered executions. He intervened in legal disputes or encouraged others to do so. He seized cattle from a certain John of Byford after John had refused to become 'his man'. All this indicates Desmond's wish not to destroy law and order but to become the fount of law and order in this particular part of Ireland. The alternative to a resident lord was the intervention of royal officials on behalf of an absentee monarch. Judging from the support which Desmond received from Irish and Norman alike his attitude was viewed sympathetically.

Part of the explanation for Desmond's outlook may be sought in the various attempts which were made by the royal administration to 'resume' control of land which, it was argued, had been acquired without appropriate legal authorisation. Desmond, as the husband of an O Brien, was open to charges of intermarriage with the king's enemies. The Statutes of Kilkenny, passed in 1366 but anticipated in legislation passed fifteen years earlier in 1351, were clearly aimed at such lords as the earls of Desmond. From time to time throughout the fourteenth century the Crown through its deputies and eventually in the person of King Richard II made attempts to assert its authority, but without lasting effect. The relative abundance of evidence dealing with parliaments and lord deputies has perhaps tended to mislead historians. There never was a 'royal lordship of Ireland' during the late medieval period. It existed only in the minds of lawyers and administrators. The reality of power in the southern half of Ireland rested with the great feudal earldoms and not with the administration, even though the Crown might 'show the flag' when the situation seemed to require symbolic action. The career of the first earl of Desmond illustrates the success of a 'feudal resurgence' against the Crown. For two centuries and more the key to understanding the course of events in the southern half of Ireland lay in the Geraldine centres at Askeaton and Maynooth and in the Butler-controlled castles at Cahir and Kilkenny.

In the northern areas of Ireland, there was no semblance of an 'imperial presence' after the Bruce episode. Power rested to a great extent with the rival dynasties of O Neill and O Donnell, each of which would look back to a shadowy Uí Néill genealogy. The realities of power rested, however, not upon descent but military retinues. The O Donnells came to power and retained it thanks to gallowglasses imported from the Isles. The MacSweeneys, MacSheehys, MacDowells and other clans of *galloglaich* played the same role in Ireland as indentured retainers did in fifteenth-century England. Their reward was land, in the MacSweeneys' case, on the estuary of the River Moy. In 1373 when O Neill negotiated a treaty he was accompanied by MacDonnell, 'captain of the Scots dwelling in Ulster'. One of the O Connors married a MacDonnell and received 120 *galloglaich* as his dowry. At the end of the fourteenth century, gallowglasses moved into the Glens of Antrim and set up a lordship at Dunluce. In the early seventeenth century the MacDonnell earl of Antrim took his name 'Somhairle' from 'Somerled', the twelfth-century ancestor of the MacDonalds and MacDougalls.

It seems clear that during this period the north of Ireland fell within a sphere of influence whose centre was the lordship of the Isles. Ulster, in fact, was the Irish equivalent of the border area between England and Scotland. In such a twilight zone, the O Neills and the O Donnells who were themselves hereditary enemies, were able to play off one side against the other. When Manus O Donnell wrote to James IV of Scotland, asking for assistance he referred to his father's earlier association with the Scottish Crown. James, in his reply, described O Donnell as his 'most devoted subject'. The O Neills for their part looked to the English monarchy for support. This situation persisted until the beginning of the seventeenth century, when, in a fundamental political shift, James VI of Scotland became also king of England, and the raison d'être of these marcher lordships disappeared.

The symbolism of these Gaelic regimes was 'traditional' in character, though the tradition may have been recent in origin. The Gaelic lords were careful to legitimise their behaviour by surrounding themselves with the cultural trappings of an earlier age. Thus learned families from south and west Ireland were able to find employment with the northern chiefs. Few episodes are more revealing, however, than the installation of a new MacWilliam under the auspices of Hugh Roe O Donnell in 1595. O Donnell summoned the eight claimants to the chiefry to meet him at Tyrawley. The rath where the 'election' took place was surrounded by four lines of troops, O Donnell's own personal guard, the troops of Tir Connell, the gallowglasses of the MacSweeneys and 'the men of Connacht'. O Donnell's own nominee was selected and three of the seven defeated candidates were placed in bonds. O Donnell seems to have chosen other chiefs in similar fashion, on other occasions.

As in Scotland, there were significant differences between north and south. The north was the Irish equivalent of Highland society and it was here that the main clusters of Irish hereditary learned families were to be found in the later middle ages. Each of the Gaelic elite families, like the MacDonalds of the Isles, had its own bards, senachies and brehons. Thus the O Cleirigh family, one of whose members was to take his part in producing the Annals of the Four Masters, were historians to the O Donnells. It was Luigh O Cleirigh who produced an official life of Hugh Roe O Donnell in the early seventeenth century. One of the last families to survive the Cromwellian debacle were the MacFirbisigh, bards to the O Dowds. The last representative of this culture was Roderick O Flaherty in the remote parts of west Galway.

In the southern half of Ireland there was a different situation thanks largely to the dominance of the powerful Norman lordships of Kildare, Desmond and Ormond. In certain areas, there was indeed an 'Irish resurgence' in the sense that local Gaelic-speaking elites gained control of territory once occupied by the Normans. But the concepts both of 'Irish' and of 'resurgence' are misleading if they are taken to imply either nationality or the regaining of land by the original holders. Much of the best land remained in the possession of the Normans. Relatively poor areas, though large in acreage, were now controlled by such families as MacCarthys, MacMurroughs, O Mores and MacGiolla Padraig. There was a marked contrast for example between the MacCarthy territory of Duhallow in the narrow upper valley of the Blackwater and the attractive Norman land of Mallow and Charleville in the lower valley. A similar contrast existed between the MacCarthy land of Muscraige in the upper Lee valley and the good land further down. In the Barrow valley, further north, the bleak moorland of Fassadinin offered shelter for the O Brenans, while the fertile valley remained in the hands of the colonist. The 'Celtic Rally' was more of a 'Celtic Survival'.

At the end of the thirteenth century, the political future of the British Isles seemed to be directed towards a unified Norman ascendancy. In the event, the ascendancy dissolved into a number of independent or semi-independent units. The 'Norman Scots' declared for a kingdom of Scotland. In Ireland, their equivalents settled for a real autonomy beneath a vague royal overlordship. In Wales, the great marcher lords after meeting the challenge of Edward I survived for another century or more. All this was made possible by the decision of 'England' to seek an imperial future in France, a venture which turned into the Hundred Years War.

The characteristic unit of society during this period was the 'Norman' feudal lordship, or, in the west of Scotland and over much of Ireland, feudal lordship in its Gaelic guise. Though it is tempting, and perhaps unavoidable, to refer to 'Ireland', 'Scotland' and 'Wales', each of these 'polities' was in fact remarkably fragmented. Even England, with its marcher areas in the north and west, was far from unified. The 'paradigm' which governed political attitudes is best characterised as 'feudal' in the sense that security was felt to lie not in allegiance to a distant and perhaps ineffective Crown but in the service of a local magnate or those linked to him.

Change in the direction of a new set of political assumptions came first in south-east England, with its great trading metropolis of London. 'Progress', associated with literacy and with the growth of market relations, seemed to lie with a more powerful monarchy. The same phenomenon was also to be observed in south-east Scotland. By the early sixteenth century few areas of the British Isles can be said to be entirely immune from the influence of such agencies of change, though felt least in the west of Scotland and the north of Ireland. Such factors as the growth of population, the increased use of artillery and warships made further change possible.

The shift which was taking place has been characterised by sociologists and historians in various ways, though usually with some implication of 'modernisation'. Clearly, profound changes were likely to take place. What was not clear was the direction. It was by no means inevitable, for example, that Scotland should fall under English dominance. Nor was it inevitable that the English government should decide to attempt a second conquest of Ireland. Models for possible futures could have resembled those offered by Switzerland, the Habsburg empire and Italy as much as those of France and Spain. As much was to depend upon decision-making as upon 'historical trends'.

In this chapter little emphasis has been placed upon the 'Wars of the Roses'. Shakespeare in his history plays made these a central feature of English history, marking the transition from the anarchy associated with usurpation to the blessings of Tudor monarchy. From a 'British Isles' standpoint the 'Wars of the Roses' may be seen as the final chapter in the decline and fall of the Norman-French Empire. During the late fifteenth century, Scotland, Ireland and Wales were left largely to their own devices and even smaller communities such as the Isle of Man and Cornwall, which deserve more attention than has been given to them here, enjoyed a good deal of independence. In a fuller British Isles version of the Wars of the Roses, the role of the two Yorkist pretenders, Lambert Simnel and Perkin Warbeck, would be given more emphasis. Both landed in Ireland, in 1487 and 1491 respectively. Simnel was crowned in Cork. Warbeck, with the support of the Fitzgerald earls of Desmond and Kildare, claimed to be the duke of York, son of Edward IV. Warbeck's travels in search of the crown during the 1490s took him to Scotland and Cornwall and again to Cork in 1497. He was executed in 1499. Warbeck, like Richard II before him, and James II later, was attempting to play the 'Irish card' as a means of gaining power. When the English 'core' was divided, as it was during the Wars of the Roses, the 'periphery' could be of considerable political importance.

7

The making of an English empire

In the early sixteenth century, a new period began in the history of the British Isles. It was characterised by the emergence of an 'English empire', or, more precisely, an empire based on the wealth, population and resources of southern England over the rest of the British Isles, and, in due course, over the east coast of North America and the West Indies. During the fourteenth and fifteenth centuries, after the decline of the 'Norman empire', independent centres of local power existed in many areas of the British Isles. By the mid-seventeenth century these were incorporated within a larger whole. Even Scotland, which had been independent for so long, was conquered by Cromwell's armies in 1650 and eventually brought into a parliamentary union with England in 1707. During the years 1580–1640 large-scale emigration, which had been characteristic of the twelfth and thirteenth centuries, was resumed. Ireland was now once again to be the prime attraction for colonists from Scotland, Wales and England.

This imperial control was exercised in different ways. For much of the sixteenth century and the first half of the seventeenth, the north of England was governed by a specially created council. Wales also, though joined to England in the Act of Union of 1536, was still thought enough of a special problem to merit government by the Council for Wales. In Ireland, the English government was represented by a lord deputy, ruling with the aid of a parliament which was eventually dominated by the new colonists. In Scotland, the government of Elizabeth, having brought John Knox and the reformers to power in 1560, enjoyed a good deal of indirect influence in the second half of the sixteenth century, which was increased when James VI of Scotland succeeded to the English Crown in 1603. If the later middle ages in Scotland had been marked by a Scottish link with France, the early modern period witnessed the gradual incorporation of Scotland within a London-based empire.

There were several factors which made the emergence of an 'English empire' possible. The rise of the English cloth industry in the south created a society which was more prosperous, more heavily populated and better endowed with towns and markets than the rest of the British Isles. The south of England also enjoyed the

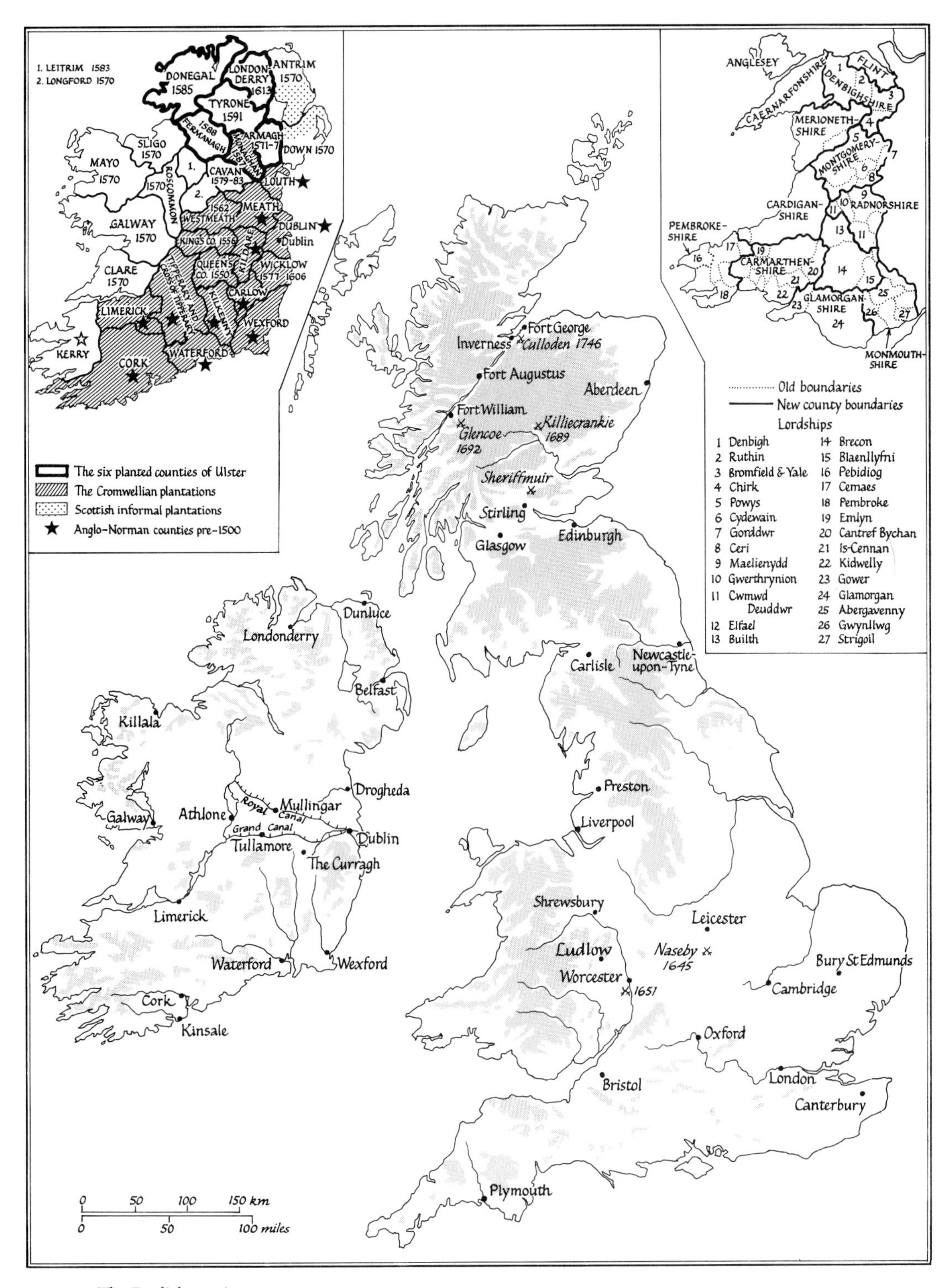

MAP 5 The English empire, 1536–1690
(a) Tudor and Stuart Ireland
(b) Tudor Wales
Source: after Christopher Haigh, ed., *The Cambridge Historical Encyclopedia of Great Britain and Ireland* (Cambridge, 1985), p. 163.

advantages of political, administrative and economic centralisation around the capital, London. Indeed it would be hard to overestimate the significance of London as a centre of power, with its population ten times that of its nearest rivals, Norwich and Bristol. The commercial wealth of London made it possible for governments to draw upon financial resources which were totally beyond the range of other societies within the British Isles. Now that the long imperial adventure in France was over, southern England was in a position to impose its authority upon the rest of the British Isles, should its rulers wish to take that course.

An observer in 1500 might well have forecast that the ties linking southern England with the rest of the British Isles would remain largely commercial in character. Already it was clear that the markets of London and other large towns such as Norwich and Bristol were attracting raw materials from Ireland, Scotland and Wales. Irish and Welsh wool, Scottish and Welsh cattle, coal from the north of England were being drawn to the south. What could hardly have been foreseen were the political and religious changes which led to much closer English involvement (or, re-involvement) in Ireland and Scotland.

So far as Ireland was concerned, the choice facing Whitehall was whether to be content with a policy of 'sober ways, politic drifts, and amiable persuasions' exercised indirectly through a great Anglo-Irish magnate like the earl of Kildare or to intervene more directly through an English lord deputy. It was under Thomas Cromwell, Henry VIII's chief minister during the 1530s, that the decision was taken to overthrow the Kildare ascendancy and to rule, so far as possible, from London. In 1537 six of the FitzGeralds including 'Silken Thomas', who had risen in revolt in 1534 against Cromwell's policy, were hanged at Tyburn.

After some hesitation, the administration pressed ahead with an 'anglicising' policy of 'surrender and regrant' in those areas of Ireland where the Irish system of landholding based upon the rights of the kinship group prevailed. An English-style system was to be introduced in which the rights of the kin would be converted into freehold transmitted by primogeniture. Though there was some alternation between force and persuasion during the middle years of the century, there was as yet no hint of a fullblooded policy of conquest and colonisation. For much of this time the pro-English landlords of the east coast (sc. 'The Pale') enjoyed a good deal of indirect influence at court and their voice was raised in favour of the peaceful extension of anglicanisation. It was not until the 1570s, largely in response to a growing threat from Philip II's Spain, that the die was cast in favour of a more forceful policy, under the auspices of Sir Henry Sidney and his followers.

The model for this Irish policy was Wales. Wales was seen by these men as an example of a 'backward' society successfully 'modernised' under English auspices. Sidney was lord president of Wales, an office which he held until his death in 1586. Perrot, who served as lord president of Munster before his appointment as lord deputy in 1584, came from Haverfordwest in 'anglicised' Pembrokeshire. To Sidney and Perrot the success of English policy in Wales lay in replacing a traditional landholding system based upon kinship and gavelkind with an English-style squirearchy and freeholders. Reforms were backed by a strong executive in the shape of a Welsh equivalent of the Star Chamber, the Council for Wales, with the power to appoint sheriffs and justices of the peace. Ireland was to be ruled in a similar fashion by lord presidents appointed to replace the great magnates and by an Irish equivalent of Star Chamber ('Castle Chamber') in Dublin.

This extension of southern English criteria of 'law and order' to northern England, Wales and Ireland after two centuries of withdrawal was not a simple task. It was made more complicated by being interconnected with the religious changes of sixteenth-century Europe. Thomas Cromwell, the administrative reformer, was also a religious reformer of Lutheran views. It was during Cromwell's years of power that the influence of the London government was placed behind a Lutheran-style Reformation in England under a 'Godly Prince'. With Cromwell's backing, a 'magisterial Reformation' based upon reform from above was introduced into Ireland and Wales and, after the failure in 1536 of the Pilgrimage of Grace, into northern England. The symbols of change were the royal supremacy, the translation of the Bible into the vernacular and the dissolution of the monasteries.

For the first half of the sixteenth century, Scotland, as a client state of France, remained largely untouched by these changes. Thirty years after defeating the Scots at Flodden (1513), the English monarchy still found it difficult to exercise political influence in the Scottish Lowlands. During the 1540s in a campaign known as the 'Rough Wooing' an English army invaded Scotland, but at the end of it French power seemed to be as strong as ever, under the Regent, Marie de Medici. The heir to the Scottish throne, Mary, was sent for her education to France, where she was betrothed to the Dauphin. What made a Scottish revolution possible was the outbreak of the wars of religion in France, which left the way open for Elizabeth to support a pro-English faction in Scotland. During the 1560s the balance turned decisively in favour of the Reformation in the Scottish Lowlands. Henceforth, the future of Scotland was closely associated with that of England.

The history of England during the sixteenth and seventeenth centuries has been distorted by a tendency among historians to write about England without relation to other cultures of the British Isles. There has also been an additional and related tendency to assume that there was a single, national, 'English' culture. Indeed the contemporary rhetoric of the period has lent itself to Anglo-centric interpretation. At least three influential currents of political and religious rhetoric were couched in terms of a single English nation. In Shakespeare's play, *Henry V*, the king's speech before Agincourt links the history of the monarchy and the nation as Henry cries 'God for England, Harry and St George'. There was, secondly, the religious rhetoric of John Foxe's *Book of Martyrs* which spoke of 'England' as an 'Elect Nation' singled out by God as an instrument of Divine Providence. In the third place there was the rhetoric of the common lawyers which looked upon the 'Ancient Constitution' of 'England' as the legacy of the Anglo-Saxons. Monarchy, Reformation and common law were all powerful symbols of a national unity which was believed to have existed over many centuries.

As is often the case with nationalist interpretations of the past, however, such rhetoric concealed a more complex situation. The culture of London and the south-east with relatively high rates of literacy, growing numbers of grammar schools, the expansion of colleges and halls at Oxford and Cambridge, a growth of industry in the clothing villages of the south and east and the development of London as a financial and trading centre was taking on a character different from that of the north and west.

The growing importance of London and the south-east had been concealed during the Wars of the Roses, which were in effect a civil war between rival factions of the feudal nobility in the north and west (including the border counties of Wales). The reaction which followed upon the Wars of the Roses made possible the rise of a monarchy based upon the power of London and the south-east. The law courts had of course long been centred upon London. To them were to be added during the early sixteenth century the courts of Star Chamber, and the court of Wards and Liveries. Star Chamber, though in theory a court, drew for its membership upon the privy council. It was indeed the government acting as a court in matters which were regarded as serious breaches of the peace. The court of Wards and Liveries was a department of state created for the financial exploitation of the Crown's position in the feudal hierarchy by controlling the disposal of the estates and marriages of tenants in chief.

There were in addition the House of Commons and the House of Lords. The Commons was far from being a political institution reflecting the outlook of 'England' as a whole. It is true that members were elected for each of the shires of England but the boroughs which elected the great majority of members were concentrated largely south of the Trent. The composition of the Lords also came increasingly to reflect the political and cultural dominance of the south-east, since after the dissolution of the larger monasteries, many of them in the north, their abbots ceased to be members of the House of Lords. After the Reformation the bishops became, even more than had been the case before, spokesmen for the south. The role of new laymen in the Lords such as William Cecil, Lord Burghley, Robert Dudley, earl of Leicester, Charles Brandon, earl of Suffolk, reflected the dominance of London and the south. There was also the educational preponderance of the south symbolised by the colleges of Christ Church at Oxford and Trinity College at Cambridge. Other foundations and grants such as St John's College at Oxford linked the universities more closely with London.

The growth in the influence of the south would no doubt have taken place in any event. Until the growth of an 'Atlantic economy' in the seventeenth century, English trade and industry was focussed upon the traditional link with the Netherlands. The growth of the cloth trade in the fifteenth century was accompanied by a rise in importance of London and the south-east. The prominent place of the

East Anglian city of Norwich as the second city of the kingdom was a further indication of the important role of England, south of the Humber.

What provided an additional impulse towards the assertion of full cultural dominance by the south over the rest of England and Wales and in due course Ireland and Scotland was the impact of the Reformation. The decisive decades were the 1530s, the 1540s and the 1550s, during which the ideas of Luther, Zwingli and Calvin made rapid headway in the literate areas of the south and east. It is understandable that this should be the case, as it was elsewhere in other areas of high literacy throughout western Europe. Without the support of the government, however, during the 1530s when Thomas Cromwell with his Lutheran sympathies was Henry VIII's chief minister and during the reign of Edward VI when the privy council was strongly Protestant it is unlikely that the reformers would have achieved success so swiftly.

During the 1530s the London-born Thomas Cromwell struck a decisive blow in the establishment of south-eastern supremacy by dissolving the monasteries, a revolutionary step which was completed during the early years of Edward VI's reign by the dissolution of the chantries, institutions dedicated to saying (sc. 'chanting') masses and prayers for the dead. During these years a revolutionary minority controlled the religious and political fortunes of the south. The repressive policies of Mary (1553–8) did not succeed in establishing the *status quo*. On the contrary there was a reaction against the Fires of Smithfield in which hundreds of Protestant martyrs perished. The accession of Elizabeth ensured that religious change would continue at a slower pace, though too slow for many advocates of more radical change, the so-called 'Puritans'.

The key role which was played in the spread of Reformation ideas by radical groups in the south was illustrated during the 1530s and 1540s by the reaction against them in the north and west. In 1536 the gentry of Lincolnshire, Yorkshire and much of England north of the Humber rose against changes in Church and state in the movement known as the 'Pilgrimage of Grace'. It is clear from the demands of the rebels that the north by and large was opposed to the growing religious, political and economic influence of the south. Cromwell's plan to dissolve the smaller monasteries provided the immediate cause of revolt, but the Pilgrims' demands for a parliament to be held at York, for the reversal of enclosures, for the restoration of Princess Mary, for the banning of books which propagated the new ideas and for the overthrow of Cromwell indicate unmistakably that the north was attempting to put an end to what was regarded as southern encroachment. In 1549 a similar reaction occurred in the south-west when Cornishmen revolted against the imposition of religious changes which originated in southern England.

Robert Kett's rebellion in Norfolk (1549) illustrates the contrast between north and south from a different perspective. In Norfolk, rebellion originated in a sense of disappointment with the progress of the Reformation. Unlike the Pilgrimage of Grace and the Cornish Revolt, Kett's rebellion pressed for the carrying out of the more radical aspects of the Reformation, notably by participation in the choice of ministers, wider access to education for the poor and the freeing of bondmen.

During the course of the sixteenth century the south succeeded in establishing dominance over the cultures of the north and west. Victories over the Pilgrimage of Grace of 1536, the Cornishmen's Revolt of 1549 and the Rising of the Northern Earls of 1569 brought under southern control areas of England which during the later middle ages had been largely autonomous. Some modern historians have been tempted to see these developments as a sign of progress. The work of Mervyn James, however, suggests that the values of northern culture deserve more sympathetic treatment than they have been accorded by the victors. Henry VIII's description of the county of Lincolnshire as 'one of the most brute and beastly of the whole realm' need not be taken literally. James indeed suggests that the values of northern society were different from but not necessarily inferior to those of the south. In his view, the lineage culture of the north placed loyalty to 'good lordship', 'blood' and 'name' above loyalty to a bureaucratic southern-based Crown.

As the Reformation made headway throughout England during the second half of the sixteenth century it began to lose whatever unity it possessed. In broad terms what Professor Collinson has termed 'the Religion of Protestants' (in *The Religion of Protestants: The Church in English Society 1559–1625* (1982)) began to polarise between those who accepted the idea of a national Church based upon conformity in ritual and those who demanded something more than external assent. A wide spectrum of possible attitudes existed, ranging from those who recognised some value in the Church of Rome to those who regarded the Pope as Anti-Christ. Perceptions of the English past also covered a wide span, from Shakespeare whose plays show a certain sympathy with the middle ages to John Foxe for whom the thousand years after Constantine was the millennium referred to in the Book of Daniel, when Satan ruled the world.

War with Spain in the last two decades of Elizabeth's reign kept polarisation in check to some extent. The early years of the seventeenth century, however, brought a re-emergence of the Counter-Reformation in Germany and a revival of ritualism in England itself. During the 1620s, when Spanish troops were advancing in the Netherlands and the ritually-minded bishop William Laud enjoyed political influence in England, English culture began to divide between ritualists and pietists, between 'Anglicans' (a nineteenth-century term but a convenient one to use here) and 'Puritans', between those who regarded episcopacy as a necessary foundation of a hierarchical Church and those who merely tolerated it as convenient and, if circumstances warranted, capable of being dispensed with.

A decisive split did not occur until the crisis years of 1640–2 and the civil war which followed left an imprint upon English life which lasted until the early twentieth century. For a time, during the 1650s, the Puritans enjoyed power but the Restoration of the monarchy in 1660 led to the creation of a profound divide between churchmen and dissenters. A penal code passed during the 1660s was not seriously modified until 1828. Dissenters remained 'second-class citizens' until that date and to a certain extent after it.

The events of the mid-seventeenth century thus offer a key to much of English culture during the two centuries which followed. They cannot be understood, however, entirely in English terms. As will be suggested below, the so-called 'English Revolution' was very much an affair of three kingdoms, influencing the course of history in Ireland and Scotland and being in turn influenced by them.

What happened within the English polity during this period was paralleled in Wales and Ireland and to some extent in Scotland. In 1521 the attainder of the duke of Buckingham carried out by Wolsey enabled the Crown to re-assert its influence on the Welsh borders. The dissolution of the marcher lordships made possible the incorporation of the counties of Monmouthshire, Herefordshire and Shropshire into the kingdom of England, and the union of Wales with England during the years 1536–42 led to the opening up of Wales to direct intervention by the Westminster government.

Westminster also became more closely involved in the affairs of Ireland than had been the case in the later middle ages. During the course of the century, from the 1530s onwards, English lord deputies played an ever-increasing role in the running of Irish affairs. From 1541 Irish chiefs were persuaded or cajoled into accepting a policy of 'surrender and regrant', namely, the surrender to the Crown of land held by Gaelic forms of tenure and its re-assignment to the chiefs and their followers under common law.

Full English involvement in Ireland did not come, however, until the reign of Elizabeth. Rebellions in Munster in the 1570s and 1580s and in Ulster during the 1590s were actively encouraged by Spain as a 'tit for tat' for English intervention in the Netherlands on behalf of Protestant rebels. It proved to be impossible for the English to stay out of Ireland and once there to reduce their military commitment.

In addition, active colonisation began for the first time since the early fourteenth century. The situation underwent a further change when James VI of Scotland succeeded to the English Crown. Ulster, which had been a frontier province against unwelcome Scottish intrusions, now lost its military raison d'être (as did the border counties of northern England). The way was open for Scottish and English colonisation of the territories of O Neill and O Donnell after the Flight of the Earls in 1607, the city of London acting as a source of financing for the plantation of Londonderry. The affairs of the three kingdoms thus became closely intermeshed in what by early seventeenth-century standards was a major colonising project. O Neill and O Donnell did not vanish from history, however. In 1641 Sir Phelim O Neill led an insurrection against the Ulster plantation. It was this 'popish plot' plus an apparent massacre of Protestant colonists which had such a dramatic impact upon the English (and Scottish) political scene in 1641. The bitter debate in the House of Commons which led to the passing of the Grand Remonstrance in December 1641 took place in the aftermath of the Ulster rebellion and the 'Irish massacre'. On several occasions during the 1640s the Irish issue acted as an obstacle to successful negotiation between Crown and parliament. It seemed that peace in Ireland was only possible at the cost of concessions on matters of religion and state which were unacceptable to the parliamentary leaders. Sir John Temple's highly partisan account of the 'massacre' kept the memory of 1641 fresh in English (and Scottish) minds.

The close involvement of Irish affairs in English politics had already been a feature of the 1630s when Thomas Wentworth became lord deputy of Ireland. Wentworth saw himself as a reformer in Ireland, completing the anglicisation which had been advocated by Edmund Spenser and Sir John Davies. In the eyes of Puritan leaders such as Pym and Hampden, with whom Wentworth, though not himself a Puritan, had been associated in the 1620s, the autocratic policies of the lord deputy seemed to foreshadow the setting up of an absolute monarchy in England itself. Wentworth's record in Ireland provided much of the basis for his impeachment in 1640 and subsequent attainder and execution. The downfall of Wentworth indeed was a prime example of the way in which English and Irish affairs had become closely intertwined.

The same point may also be made about the relationship between England and Scotland. From 1560 onwards England replaced France as the dominant partner in Scottish politics. In 1568 Mary Queen of Scots fled to England and for the next two decades the Scottish queen became a centre of political intrigue which was only resolved by her execution in 1587. The close involvement of English political leaders in Scottish affairs continued during the 1590s as it became clear that James VI was the most likely candidate to succeed Elizabeth.

James VI tended to keep Scottish and English affairs separate but during Charles I's reign, the English Crown became more closely involved in the 'reform' of the Scottish Kirk on English lines. Archbishop Laud, Charles I's chief minister, was blamed for attempting to introduce 'Popery' into Scotland, and a religious crisis developed which led to the signing of a National League and Covenant by disaffected elements in Scotland. This was followed by a resort to arms which led to the defeat of the royal army and the Scottish occupation of the English border counties in 1640. Opposition leaders in England welcomed the Scottish crisis as a means of breaking the political deadlock.

In 1642 civil war broke out in England between the forces of Crown and parliament. In recent decades historians have tended to discuss it as an 'English Revolution'. To treat it merely in English terms, however, is to lose sight of the ways in which the affairs of Scotland and Ireland raised the political temperature in English politics. The Irish 'massacre' of 1641 in particular played into the hands of the Puritan leaders. The 'no Popery' card was to be played on many occasions throughout the seventeenth century. Since English Catholics were in fact few on the ground, the potency of the cry of 'No Popery' is best explained in the context of the three kingdoms, where Ireland and to some extent Scotland and Wales were looked upon as centres of Papist disaffection.

In the framework of the three kingdoms, the civil wars may be seen as taking on the character of savage 'wars of religion' such as had occurred in France during the late sixteenth century and were occurring in Germany during the Thirty Years

THE VIKINGS

The vikings had a powerful impact upon the cultures of the British Isles. During the ninth century, viking attacks led to the collapse of the British kingdom of Strathclyde, the Anglo-Saxon kingdom of Northumbria and the 'Old Order' in Ireland. Despite the military successes of Wessex during the ninth century, Danish political influence in England was still strong in the tenth century, as the reign of Cnut indicates. The Norman Conquest brought the viking era to an end in England. In Scotland and Ireland, viking power remained strong for much longer. In Scotland it was not until 1266 that formal links between the 'Isles' and Norway were abrogated. In the Hebrides and the Isle of Man, as well as Orkney and Shetland, Norse culture survived until the modern period.

17 The vikings established themselves in Shetland and Orkney in the ninth century. Shetland: Jarlshof (the name given to it by Walter Scott) was a Norse settlement from the ninth century. The original Norse house can be seen running from north-west to south-east.

18 It was from such bases in Orkney and Shetland that the vikings raided the remote monasteries of Iona, Lindisfarne and Skellig Michael, off the coast of Kerry. Skellig Michael was sacked by seaborne raiders at the end of the eighth century.

THE IMPACT OF THE VIKINGS

During the ninth and tenth centuries the Irish Sea became in effect a viking lake with Dublin and the Isle of Man as major strategic points. Recent excavations by Dr Breandan Ó Ríordáin have revealed the economic importance of Dublin. The cultural influence of the vikings is clear from other artefacts and from such well-known works of art as the cross of Cong.

19 A hoard of pewter tokens found at Wine Tavern Street, Dublin.

21 Coin of King Sihtric III of Dublin (c. 944 – c. 1030) from a hoard discovered near Dundalk, 1980.

20 Fragments of leather and portions of shoes from a huge deposit in High Street, Dublin.

22 A bone trial piece in the Ringerike style of eleventh-century viking art from High Street, Dublin.

23 The cross of Cong (twelfth century) is a major piece of Hiberno-viking art in the free-flowing Urnes style of later viking art.

THE NORMAN EMPIRE

Norman influence was felt throughout the British Isles from the mid-eleventh century onwards. In 1066 they conquered England; in the late eleventh century they moved into Wales; and from the early eleventh century they penetrated into the 'Kingdom of Scots'. From 1169 onwards they attempted to subdue Ireland. North Scotland and the Hebrides alone remained outside their direct control.

24 The Norman castle at Chepstow, with its priory and town at the mouth of the river Wye, controlled entry into south Wales. It was some 10 miles distant from Caerwent, the former Roman capital of the Silures.

25 The great motte of Urr (Kirkcudbrightshire) was built by the Normans to control Galloway in the south-west, an area exposed earlier to viking settlements. Similar mottes are to be found in large numbers in the south of Ireland.

26 The Benedictine abbey of Dunfermline, on the north side of the Firth of Forth. It was founded by Margaret, the English wife of Malcolm Canmore, in 1072. She intended it to replace the traditional Celtic monasticism of Scotland. In due course Cistercian abbeys such as those at Melrose and Jedburgh replaced earlier Celtic foundations. Similar 'reforms' occurred also in Wales and Ireland.

27 The Norman cathedral on the Rock of Cashel (Co. Tipperary) overshadows Cormac's Chapel, which was built by the MacCarthys (1128–34).

THE FEUDAL RESURGENCE

The power of the Anglo-Norman monarchy reached its peak within the British Isles under Edward I (1272–1307) and began to decline under Edward II (1307–27). Scotland achieved its independence under Robert Bruce but the Scottish monarchy remained weak, overshadowed by powerful magnates, of whom the most important were the Douglases. In Ireland, Edward Bruce's invasion in 1316–18, in the aftermath of the Scots victory at Bannockburn (1314), undermined the power of the Anglo-Norman monarchy. In southern Ireland the FitzGerald earls of Kildare and Desmond came to enjoy *de facto* independence, as did the O Neills and the O Donnells in the north of Ireland. In western Scotland the MacDonald lordship of the Isles profited from the weakness of the monarchy. In Wales also the marcher lordships were largely free of constraints imposed by the English monarchy.

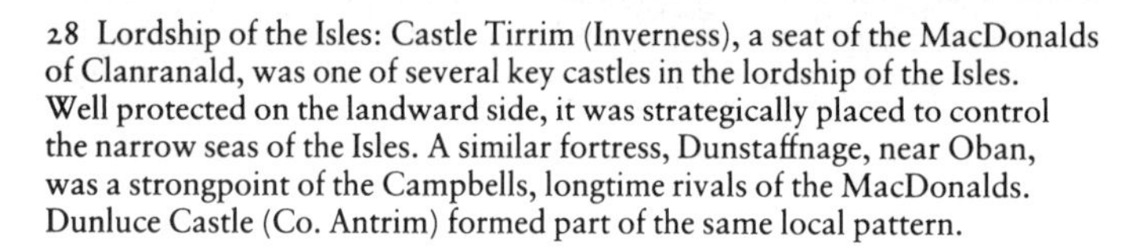

28 Lordship of the Isles: Castle Tirrim (Inverness), a seat of the MacDonalds of Clanranald, was one of several key castles in the lordship of the Isles. Well protected on the landward side, it was strategically placed to control the narrow seas of the Isles. A similar fortress, Dunstaffnage, near Oban, was a strongpoint of the Campbells, longtime rivals of the MacDonalds. Dunluce Castle (Co. Antrim) formed part of the same local pattern.

29 The high cross at Oronsay is a fine example of late medieval art within the lordship of the Isles. Over eighty stone monuments survive on Iona itself.

30 Threave Castle (Kirkcudbrightshire) was built by the third earl of Douglas in 1360–70 as a strongpoint in south-west Scotland. The Douglases during the late fourteenth and fifteenth centuries were a constant challenge to the Scottish Crown.

31 Maynooth Castle (Co. Kildare), centre of FitzGerald power in Leinster, dates from the thirteenth century. The earl of Kildare was regarded as the uncrowned king of Ireland during the late fifteenth century. Maynooth was destroyed by English artillery in 1535 in the aftermath of the rebellion of Silken Thomas FitzGerald.

THE ENGLISH EMPIRE

During the early sixteenth century the power of the Tudor monarchy expanded throughout the British Isles. In 1536 the Welsh marcher lordships were organised into counties, and Wales as a whole was brought into political and legal union with England. In northern England, the defeat of the Pilgrimage of Grace undermined the autonomy of the northern earldoms. In Ireland, the FitzGeralds were defeated, and in due course the position of the northern chiefs, O Neill and O Donnell, was undermined. In the early seventeenth century Ulster was colonised by English settlers and in greater numbers by Scottish settlers. Scotland itself was brought under closer English control, the climax of this process being the Act of Union of 1707. Throughout this period of change religious and political issues were closely intertwined. In the New World a new alternative English society made its appearance.

32 Ireland: Kinsale (Co. Cork), with its magnificent harbour, possessed great strategic importance during the seventeenth and eighteenth centuries. Forts on each side of the harbour were designed to protect it against French and Spanish attacks.

33 Scotland: Fort George (Inverness) was built by Robert Adam in 1748–63 to replace an earlier fort blown up during the Jacobite rebellion in 1745.

War (1618–48). The Irish 'massacre' in particular left an enduring mark. In 1644, for example, Montrose, the royalist general in Scotland, was denounced for having 'joined with a band of Irish rebels and mass-priests, who had, this two years bygone, bathed themselves in the blood of God's people in Ireland'. In 1645, 300 Irish women were butchered after the Covenanting victory at Philiphaugh. In 1646, O Neill's troops at Benburb gave the Scots no quarter. 'The rebels', it was said, 'had never such a heavy day of the Protestants.'

In England itself Charles I came increasingly to place his hopes of a royalist revival upon the arrival of aid from Ireland. Rumours that Charles was prepared to ally himself with Irish Catholic Confederates left him open to charges of 'Popery'. In 1643 it was said after the capture of the royalist earl of Antrim that 'the discovery of this plot did more to work upon most men than anything that had happened during these miserable calamities and civil wars of England, because it now seemed that there was a fixed resolution in the Popish party utterly to extirpate the true Protestant religion in England, Scotland and Ireland'. When news arrived that the earl of Ormond had agreed to a 'cessation' of arms with the Confederates in 1643 it was declared that this 'will tend not only to the utter ruin of themselves, but of all the Protestants in England and Ireland also'. The arrival in Ireland of a Papal nuncio, Archbishop Rinuccini, in 1645 added further fuel to the propaganda war of the three kingdoms.

In 1648, it was the expectation of aid from Irish Catholics and Scottish Presbyterians which led Charles to gamble upon a successful outcome to a 'second civil war'. The rise of Cromwell and the extremist faction in the New Model Army, the exclusion of 'Moderates' from parliament in Pride's Purge and the subsequent execution of the king thus took place against a background of the three kingdoms, not merely of England. It was the expectation of what might happen as a result of Irish and Scottish invasion as much as the fear of English royalism which led to so violent a reaction on the Parliamentarian side. The crisis of 1648 in fact brings out the extent to which Charles saw himself as a king of the three kingdoms, not just of England, facing the problems created by a purely English parliament.

The interaction of the three kingdoms was to continue during the rest of the century. In 1660 it was the attitude of the Parliamentarian General Monck in Scotland and the Puritan leader Broghill in Ireland which made possible a peaceful Restoration. During the post-1660 years the Crown was faced in Ireland with the problem of dealing with a Cromwellian ascendancy, which was determined to hold on to the estates of former royalists. In 1685–8 James II's sympathy for the Irish royalists and his appointment of Richard Talbot, earl of Tyrconnell, helped to weaken his position in England and played an important role in his downfall. In turn the knowledge that he could count on Irish support led James to land in Ireland in 1689 and to use it as a base from which to regain his crown. It was no accident that the decisive battle of the English 'Glorious Revolution' should be fought on the river Boyne in 1690.

Scottish affairs also formed one of the strands of post-Restoration politics in England. Royal attempts to defuse religious bitterness in Scotland by issuing a Declaration of Indulgence establishing a certain measure of toleration led to reaction among the king's ultra-Tory episcopalian supporters.

It is of course possible to deal with the history of England during this period exclusively in English terms. To do so, however, makes it difficult to explain why the civil wars actually took place. Constitutional conflict over such matters as Ship Money appeared to have been resolved by the middle of 1641. What introduced a higher degree of emotion was the Irish rebellion of 1641 with its accompanying 'massacre' of Protestant settlers. This in its turn can only be explained against a background not merely of Anglo-Irish affairs but also those of Scotland as well.

The real 'English Revolution' of this period was in fact the English Reformation, the success of which in England and Wales brought about further involvement in Ireland and Scotland. By the end of the seventeenth century an English empire had come into existence throughout the British Isles. As a consequence the histories of Ireland and Scotland cannot be understood in their own terms. Equally, however, the English were to find in dealing with rebellion in Scotland in 1715 and in 1745 and in Ireland in 1798 that they could not extricate themselves at will from the historical situation which had been created by the decisions taken during the seventeenth century.

The history of Wales during this period is not of such central importance as those of the three kingdoms proper. Nevertheless, the course of events in Wales helps to illustrate by comparison or contrast what happened in Ireland and Scotland. During the early middle ages, Welsh history had been closely interwoven with that of the great Norman barons. When the houses of Mortimer, Lancaster and Clare intervened in high politics they drew much of their power from the resources of their marcher lordships. During this period the border between England and Wales was effectively moved further west from the Severn to the Wye. The political and demographic crisis of the fourteenth century placed the colonial regime in Wales on the defensive (as was the case also in Ireland). The rebellion of Owain Glyndwr in the first decade of the fifteenth century struck a blow from which the 'Englishries' and colonial boroughs did not recover. It is true that after Glyndwr's defeat in 1406 a series of penal laws were placed on the statute book which recall the Statutes of Kilkenny in their severity, but in Wales, as in Ireland, restrictive legislation of this kind was as much a sign of weakness as strength. In theory, the Welsh were forbidden to dwell in boroughs, to take part in trade and to acquire land. In practice it was the 'Englishry' in Wales which declined in strength during the fifteenth century.

During the unsettled conditions of the Wars of the Roses, Welsh marcher lords were provided with the opportunity to intervene in English politics. The battle of Banbury in 1469 was regarded as a peculiarly Welsh disaster. The rebellion of Buckingham against Richard III in 1483 involved south Wales. But the most decisive contribution which Wales made was the support which it produced for Henry Tudor in 1485. Henry landed at Milford Haven and rallied Welsh support at Welshpool. Welsh troops enabled him to defeat Richard III at Bosworth. Welsh versions of British history enabled him to prop up a weak claim to the throne, a move which was followed up later by the naming of his eldest son Arthur. Henry repaid his debt to his Welsh allies by appointing them to key offices in north and south Wales and by naming Welshmen to the sees of St David's and St Asaph. In due course the penal legislation against Welshmen holding office and acquiring land was also repealed, not without protest from the 'Englishry'.

The use of the terms 'Wales' and 'Welsh' is almost unavoidable in dealing with the history of this period. In fact, however, 'Wales' was still very much a 'geographical expression', lacking in cultural and social unity. The various contingents which joined Henry in 1485 were drawn from contrasting areas in Wales itself. The troops of William ap Griffith of Penrhyn and Richard ap Howell of Mostyn were northern clansmen who brought their own droves of cattle with them. The Herberts, in contrast, led feudal levies from the south-east. Rhys ap Thomas drew upon the Welsh-speaking heartland of Carmarthen. Linguistic differences divided Welsh-speakers in north and south. Wales was still a country divided by its history into several sub-cultures each with its own view of past and present.

The reign of Henry VII in many ways marked the end of a period rather than a new beginning. Signs of more radical change came with the rise to power of Wolsey and with the execution in 1521, at Wolsey's instigation, of the duke of Buckingham, the most powerful of the Welsh marcher lords. In 1531 Rhys ap Griffith, the grandson of Rhys ap Thomas, was executed on charges of treason, after incidents which anticipated events in Ireland involving 'Silken Thomas' and the FitzGeralds. In 1529 the young Rhys had challenged the authority of the royal chamberlain in south Wales, Lord Ferrers, who had been appointed to succeed Rhys ap Thomas after his death in 1525. The Crown was clearly challenging the 'Old Order' in Wales, as it was soon to do in Ireland. In 1536 the decisive shift came with the passing of an Act of Union, completed by further legislation in 1542. The Acts of Union completed the attack on feudalism which had been foreshadowed in 1521, with Buckingham's execution.

As with so much else in Henry VIII's reign, the Acts of Union formed part of the 'modernising' policies of Thomas Cromwell, though they were not completed until after his execution. The Norman empire in Wales which had been in existence since the late eleventh century was in effect dismantled. The marcher lordships were henceforth incorporated within an administrative system of already existing shires, such as Carmarthen, or amalgamated into new counties, Monmouth, Brecon, Radnor, Montgomery and Denbigh, freshly created at the Union. The legal autonomy of the lordships was done away with. The English common law was to be enforced throughout Wales, with English as the sole language of the courts though the need for translators long remained. The sheriff and the justice of the peace took over from marcher officials. Primogeniture in theory replaced partible inheritance, though, in actual fact, traditional practice based upon the desirability of sharing land among all the sons remained powerful at the local level for a long time to come. The border between Wales and England was clearly drawn for the first time. The border counties of Shropshire and Hereford were placed firmly within England, though Hereford in particular contained Welsh-speaking communities. Wales itself was now the first province within an English empire.

The Acts of Union were part of an administrative revolution but what was intended in Whitehall did not necessarily happen on the ground. A century later, local aristocrats such as the Herberts and Somersets in south Wales and the Greys and the Wynns in north Wales were still powerful. During the civil wars of the mid-seventeenth century the Somerset earls of Worcester and the Herbert earls of Pembroke were key figures on the royalist and parliamentary sides respectively, and Raglan Castle and Pembroke Castle were both put to military use during the wars. But the earls of Worcester and Pembroke for all their local importance were not marcher lords in the old sense of the word. Their titles dated from the sixteenth century and they, like the earl of Leicester in north Wales, were essentially representatives of the English empire in Wales.

Much changed after the Acts of Union; much also remained unchanged. The distinctive cultures of north, south and west Wales embedded in kinship, land-holding and general outlook did not appear overnight. Powys, already partitioned under the Normans, was redivided between the new county of Montgomery and the existing county of Merioneth though bardic tradition kept the memory of the old kingdom alive. The mountainous area of Gwynedd (today's Snowdonia) was resistant to change. Elsewhere, social divisions between 'Englishries' and 'Welshries' continued to influence behaviour. The county of Flint was divided between its Welsh and its English areas. The town of Hay-on-Wye was split between English and Welsh. The port of Haverfordwest retained its distinctively Flemish character. Parts of Pembroke were known as 'Little England'. Ethnic differences existed in Wales as they did in Ireland and Scotland. The inhabitants of 'English' Shropshire and Herefordshire were conscious of the presence of Welshmen in their midst. During this period, as earlier, the history of Wales cannot be written from a single 'national' point of view.

In Wales, as in England and Ireland, the 1530s were also marked by a religious revolution, the main material result of which was the dissolution of the Welsh monastic houses. The lands of Tintern passed into the control of the Somerset family. The Mansels acquired the lands of Margam. Church wealth in the form of tithes also passed into the hands of wealthy laymen. Far more than the so-called revolution of the 1640s, the Henrician Reformation in Wales was a social revolution which marked a breach between the medieval and the early modern period. The creation of an English interest in Wales, corresponding to similar groups in Ireland and Scotland, dates from these years. The power of these new families, the Wynns, the Vaughans, the Prices, was not to be challenged until the nineteenth century, after industrialisation had wrought its own revolution.

In Wales, as in Ireland, the Reformation initially made little impact at the popular level. A Welsh translation of the Bible was produced in 1588 for use in churches and a smaller edition, the little Bible (*y Beibl Bach*) in 1630, but in so dispersed and rural a society, with many local dialects, no single translation sufficed. In some ways, the Counter-Reformation, thanks to the support of such magnates as the Somerset earls of Worcester, had more success. From their base at Cwm, on the English border near Monmouth, a Jesuit mission operated in the early seventeenth century in conditions comparable to those in the north of England and in Ireland. As with the Reformation, so too with the Counter-Reformation, the challenge proved to be too great for the resources available. As a consequence, rural Wales remained, like rural Ireland and the Scottish Highlands, very much a traditional society in which local institutions such as the 'wise man' of the village, the fair, the wake, and kinship ties retained their hold in the face of attempts at 'anglicisation' by an English-orientated gentry and clergy. It was not until the eighteenth century that these popular cultures finally collapsed in the face of Methodist denunciations. It was then that dancing, harp-playing and fiddling began to give way to a new popular culture based upon hymn-singing and the Sunday school.

During the early modern period, it is probable that the impact of the English food market was as powerful an instrument of social change as either the Reformation or the administrative revolution. In the Welsh Lowlands, farmers responded to the English demand for meat, butter, cheese and wheat. The upland farmers exported thousands of head of cattle to be fattened up in Shropshire and Herefordshire before being sold in the markets of London. The vale of Glamorgan was described as 'the Garden of Wales and for good cattle of all kinds the nursery of the West'. It was estimated that twenty-four Wynn farms in north Wales would sustain nearly 3,000 head of cattle annually. Wales had 245 fairs a year in 1602, over half of them in the five southern counties. As a consequence of growth in demand from England, pressures grew for enclosure on the English model. A class of gentry began to emerge from the general run of yeoman farmers and as the pressure upon pasture increased, traditional tenants complained of being deprived of common grazing, of free access to fuel and of the free use of summer houses for 'transhumance'. By the early eighteenth century, a class of anglicised gentry had come into existence. In some areas, such squires, together with an English-speaking clergy, were largely cut off from their Welsh-speaking tenants and labourers. English became the language of the law, of politics and polite society. The gentry attended the universities of Oxford and Cambridge, though the growing dominance of English culture did not prevent some of the gentry from acting as patrons for Welsh scholarly works.

In Scotland, radical religious and social change came a generation later than in Wales. In July 1560 the French garrison in Scotland returned home and the political connection which had linked France and the Scottish Lowlands came to an end. Henceforth English influence was to be dominant north of the border. Political change coincided with religious reformation. The Scottish Reformation, indeed, was successful in its first stages thanks largely to English backing. John Knox, though Scottish born, had taken an active part in the Edwardian Reformation and it was English arms and money which helped Knox and his allies among the nobles to overthrow the pro-French party in Scotland. The Bible in English was to prove to be a formidable instrument of anglicisation. Puritanism, ultimately defeated in England, had its greatest successes in Scotland.

Scotland in the mid-sixteenth century was a country of two cultures (three if Orkney, Shetland and the Norse counties of northern Scotland, are taken into consideration). The cultural and political balance of power between Highlands and Lowlands still remained. The Gaelic-speaking west was closer to Ulster than to the English-speaking Lowlands. The MacDonalds of the Hebrides and the MacDonnells of Antrim saw themselves as sharing a common history which went back to the Three Colls and Niall of the Nine Hostages. 'Feudal' culture survived in the Highlands well into the eighteenth century long after it had been destroyed in Ireland. With the coming of the Reformation, the cultural differences between the two areas increased. In the Lowlands the long-term effect of the Reformation was to replace 'feudal' loyalty with commitment to a particular religious persuasion. In the Highlands, even where the Reformation did make headway, it was associated with loyalty to a particular chief, such as the earl of Argyll. The Lowlands, thanks to Puritan emphasis upon Bible-reading, became a highly literate society. The Highlands remained an oral culture throughout the early modern period. In the Lowlands, strict observance of the Sabbath was regarded as a sign of godliness. In 1709, for example, the Kirk Session of Edinburgh, 'taking into consideration that the Lord's day is profaned by people standing in the streets ... as also by idly gazing out at windows, and children and apprentices playing in the streets, warn parents and threaten to refer to the civil magistrates for punishment, also order each session to take its turn in walking the streets on the sabbath'. In the Highlands, Sabbatarianism was to come much later.

Within both Highlands and Lowlands, the Reformation intensified internal differences. In the Highlands, conflict between the MacDonalds and the Campbells, which had its origins in the later medieval period, when the Campbells acted as the instrument of an expanding Crown, at the expense of the MacDonald Lords of the Isles, was exacerbated by Campbell acceptance of the Reformation. In the early seventeenth century, the earl of Argyll attempted to plant Kintyre on lines similar to those of the Ulster plantation. In the civil wars of the mid-seventeenth century, the Campbells took up the Covenanting cause; the MacDonalds in contrast, allied with their kinsman, the MacDonnell earl of Antrim, supported the Crown. In 1692, a Campbell regiment was involved in the massacre of a MacDonald clan at Glencoe. In 1746, in the aftermath of the Jacobite rebellion of '45, Captain Robert Duff R.N. reported to Argyll how he had dealt with Argyll's tenants, the Camerons, who had supported Bonnie Prince Charlie against the wishes of their hated landlord.

On the tenth instant [March 1746] at four in the morning I landed Lieut. Lindsay with the detachment of your regiment [the Scots Fusiliers] Captain Campbell with 20 men ... a lieutenant and fiftyfive men from my ship with orders to burn the houses and destroy the effects of all such as were out in the rebellion.

When the land was leased out again, many of the beneficiaries were Campbells. So far as the Highlands were concerned, the Reformation led eventually to the victory of the English-backed clans, Campbells, MacKenzies and MacLeods, over the rest.

In the Lowlands also, existing regional differences seem to have become more marked as a consequence of the Reformation. In the north-east, ancestral territory of the Gordon earls of Huntley, episcopalianism flourished in a general atmosphere of social hierarchy. South of the Tay, where the lairds and towns made common cause, a Presbyterian form of Church government, giving wider scope to a 'middle class', made headway. In the south-west, for reasons which may go back to long-held resentment against a Normanised landowning class, the small farmers became 'Covenanters', stressing godliness above inherited status. During the civil wars of the mid-seventeenth century, the Covenanters supported a theocratic regime which abolished patronage and forced a sinful nobility publicly to admit its moral failures. During the Restoration period the south-west was disturbed by peasant revolts, which in their religious intensity resembled the 'Camisards' of southern France. Throughout the seventeenth century, episcopalians, Presbyterians and Covenanters contended for supremacy. Victory went finally to the Presbyterians, leaving their rivals with the status of 'second-class citizens'.

These internal conflicts, in both Highlands and Lowlands, had their own Scottish flavour. Throughout the early modern period, however, it became increasingly difficult to keep the history of 'Scotland' distinct from that of a wider 'English empire'. In the Lowlands, during the late sixteenth century, contending political groups of nobles depended for success in seizing and retaining power upon English support. The flight of Mary, Queen of Scots, to England in 1568 involved English politicians more closely in Scottish affairs than ever before. For a Scottish noble such as James Douglas, earl of Morton, 'conformity with England' was the key consideration. For James VI, son of Mary, Queen of Scots, the Union of the Crowns was the main long-term aim of political strategy, and when it was achieved in 1603 he came to look upon the episcopal State Church of England as the example to be followed in Scotland. One of the rewards of the Union of the Crowns was the opening up of Ulster to Lowland settlement. From the mid-sixteenth century onwards, Scotland, which had enjoyed independence in the later middle ages, was drawn increasingly into a Britannic framework.

If there were rewards in this situation, there was also a price to be paid. In Charles I's reign, the Crown became a more active instrument of anglicisation than had been the case under James VI. The Lowland nobility were disturbed by secret royal plans to recover Church property and alienated tithes. Presbyterians south of the Tay resented the influence of the episcopalians of the north-east, who had found a powerful ally in the English Lord Treasurer, Archbishop William Laud. The new departure was symbolised in the creation of a bishopric of Edinburgh and the transformation of the kirk of St Giles into a cathedral. In Ireland, Charles I's minister, Strafford, succeeded in uniting Old and New English alike against him. In Scotland, Charles and Laud brought Kirk and nobility into common opposition, based upon a Presbyterian National League and Covenant (1638).

The National League and Covenant did not lead to greater national independence in the long term, however. One of the consequences of successful opposition to the Crown was to draw the Presbyterian leaders in closer ties with the English Puritans. The reformation of the Church of England on Presbyterian lines seemed possible and in 1643, Scottish Presbyterians and English Puritans joined in a Solemn League and Covenant. At the same time, in Ireland, a Scots army under Monro fought to defend the Ulster plantation against the Irish confederate forces of Owen Roe O Neill. In Scotland, Charles looked for aid to the Highlanders under the earl of Montrose, who in 1644 was joined by a force of MacDonalds and MacLeans under Alasdair Coll Ciotach (the 'left-handed', anglicised as 'Colkitto'). These MacDonalds had the backing of the earl of Antrim. In 1648, Charles in the aftermath of defeat hammered out an unlikely alliance between his Irish, English and Scottish supporters despite their religious differences. As we have seen, the so-called English civil war was essentially a war of the three kingdoms.

During the 1650s, after Cromwell's victories at Preston, Dunbar and Worcester, Scotland found itself incorporated within a wider commonwealth, in which England was very much the dominant partner. The situation changed to some extent after the Restoration of Charles II in 1660, when Scotland regained some measure of autonomy, though English influence still remained strong. London backed an episcopalian form of Church government, under which James Sharp, a north-easterner and graduate of Aberdeen, became archbishop of St Andrews. Royal attempts to achieve a general compliance met with little success, however. In the south-west, Sharp was regarded as a traitor to the godly cause which he had once, as a former Covenanter, professed. His murder in May 1679 was a signal for a general rising in the area. The Covenanters' success proved shortlived and with the accession of James II, a long period of episcopalian dominance seemed likely. In Scotland, as in England, however, James alienated his supporters by adopting pro-Catholic policies. The earl of Argyll, whose father had been executed, returned to lead the resistance and after an initial military setback at Killiecrankie (1689), Presbyterianism was once again restored, this time, as it turned out, permanently. The episcopalians of the north-east, now without influence in London, turned to Jacobitism and the hope of a return of the Stuarts. In the south-west, the Covenanters, also a minority, soon broke away from the Established Church to found their own Associate Synod. Thus Scotland remained a deeply divided country, as divided in its own way as Ireland.

The history of Ireland during this period is often regarded as having followed its own distinctive path. In fact, however, the course of events in Ireland to a considerable extent resembled that of other areas which were incorporated within the English empire during the sixteenth century. In Ireland, as elsewhere in the British Isles, this period saw the collapse of feudalism. The resources of the state were mobilised to overthrow the private armies and jurisdictions of the great magnates, both Anglo-Norman and Gaelic. Galloglasses, introduced into Ireland in the fourteenth century, were still a familiar feature of the Irish scene in the sixteenth century. The MacSheehys, the MacSweeneys and the MacDonnells still provided the basis of the military power of the earls of Desmond, and the Gaelic chiefs, O Donnell and O Neill, as they had done for so long. As indicated above, it was on the basis of such armies that chiefs like O Donnell were able to impose their own candidates upon chiefries within their 'sphere of influence'.

It is difficult to recognise any sense of common nationality in this political world. In 1567 the MacDonnells of Antrim beheaded Shane O Neill who had taken refuge with them and sent his head, 'pickled, in a pipkin' to the royal administration in Dublin. Rivalries between the two great Munster magnates of Munster, the earls of Desmond and Ormond, compelled lesser lords to take sides in the interest of self-preservation. Sidney complained that many had 'never heard of other prince than Ormond or Desmond'. 'Feudalism' had in fact gone further in Ireland than it ever had in England or Scotland.

The revolts which took place in Ireland during the sixteenth century were the Irish equivalent of the Pilgrimage of Grace and the Rising of the Northern Earls, in the sense that they were attempts to retain an established feudal world against the unwelcome pressures of a 'modernising' state. What lent the struggle a particular intensity was that to these political and social tensions was added the emotional fervour of the wars of religion. Cultural differences also played their part in leading to charges of atrocity and counter-atrocity. Nevertheless, the success of the English government in reducing the power of the great magnates would scarcely have been possible had they not enjoyed the support of powerful interests within Ireland, notably the towns, which, in Ireland as elsewhere in western Europe, welcomed Crown support. Thus in the rebellions of the 1570s, towns such as Cork and Galway and Kilkenny withstood attacks by local magnates.

The English administration could also count on the support of the landlords of a wide area round Dublin, the 'lords of the Pale', who remained aloof from any involvement in the Desmond rebellion. The O Briens of Thomond and the Burkes of Clanricarde and even the O Neills took a similar attitude. The Ormond interest also could generally be relied upon to support the Crown though some of the Butlers were involved in an attempt to overthrow a local attempt at plantation. Later in the century, in Ulster, traditional enemies of O Neill and O Donnell refused to join in the Nine Years War. The ruling septs of Monaghan escaped plantation as a consequence. Clearly there were many, among the Irish elite, Gaelic as well as Anglo-Norman, who welcomed the defeat of 'overmighty subjects' and were willing to cast in their lot, however reluctantly, with the Crown.

The decline of feudalism in Ireland had begun with the overthrow of the house of Kildare in the 1530s. This still left untouched the great 'pretendid palatinates' of Ormond and Desmond as well as the Gaelic and gaelicised chieftainries of the west and the north. Sidney established lord presidencies in Munster and Connacht, each with a military force at their disposal with the aim of replacing the authority of the magnates with that of the Crown. In 1576 the various 'countries' of Connacht were transformed into the English-style counties of Sligo, Mayo, Roscommon and Galway. In 1583 the power of Desmond was overthrown. In 1585 the Crown arrived at a 'composition' with the lords of Connacht whereby they agreed to pay a rent to the Crown, provide military service and introduce the common law. For a time it seemed that Ulster also would follow the example of Connacht in submitting to peaceful assimilation. In 1595, however, Hugh O Neill who had enjoyed Crown support as earl of Tyrone, took the great gamble of resisting the advance of the English administration into his territories and rose in revolt, with Spanish support. The gamble failed. O Neill's defeat at the battle of Kinsale in 1601 marked the downfall of feudalism in Ireland.

A social and political revolution had taken place comparable to that which had occurred in England and Wales during much the same period. The English common law was soon enforced throughout Ireland, though in fact the courts took account of 'brehon law' where the circumstances seemed to require it. The traditional order of coarbs, brehons and bards which had survived in Ulster gradually collapsed. It was now possible for an Irish parliament to meet which could draw upon representatives of shires and boroughs from all over Ireland.

What then went wrong? Why should there have been a revolt in 1642 among the very pro-English elements which had acquiesced in the overthrow of Desmond and O Neill? The plantation of the territories of O Neill and O Donnell was not in itself a cause of unrest. The Catholic earl of Westmeath benefited from the plantation of Cavan. The greater landowners such as the Dillons accepted English titles. Such septs as the O Hurleys, O Briens and O Dwyers made the transition from Gaelic chieftain to landed aristocrat. Bishop O Hurley of Emly belonged to a family which had a record of loyalty to the Crown during the Nine Years War, and possessed an estate of eight and a half thousand acres. Such landowners had a great deal to lose. The reasons for unrest may be sought in the list of grievances which was presented to the Crown in 1628 and is known as the 'Graces'. On the basis of this, it seems clear that the expectations aroused by the victory of the 'loyal' groupings had not been fulfilled. Economic power in both trade and land was overwhelmingly in the hands of the Catholic 'Old English' (using that term in the sense of 'loyalists', not in any 'racial' sense). Political and administrative influence, however, was passing into the hands of those new Protestant settlers who had arrived in Elizabeth's reign. Administrative devices such as the court of Wards and Liveries had introduced religious criteria as a condition for inheriting land. The plantation of Connacht, attempted during the 1630s by the lord deputy, was further evidence that the English administration intended to continue its policy of anglicisation of the 'Old English' interest. Religious conformity was to be the measure of loyalty, as the full implications of the English Reformation began to work themselves out in Ireland.

In Ulster there was also another source of discontent which arose from the plantation of the lands of O Neill and O Donnell after the Flight of the Earls in 1607. In Ulster, as in Desmond, the aim of Crown policy in the sixteenth century had been to create a class of landlords and tenants holding their estates under the common law. The decision to replace this policy with one of colonisation was to have momentous consequences, especially as the best land was reserved for Scots and English colonists. The rising which took place in 1641, at a moment when the English monarchy faced a severe political crisis in both Scotland and England, was almost inevitable. It was accompanied by widespread killing, though the figure of 200,000 victims was totally inaccurate. The myth of '1641', however, was accepted in England and formed the rationale for the punitive actions which followed under Cromwell in the next decade.

In Ulster, during the 1640s, Old Irish and Presbyterian Scots were engaged in almost continual warfare in which neither gained the upper hand. Elsewhere, in the provinces of Leinster and Connacht and parts of Munster, the 'Old English' party erected a polity which provided a glimpse of one possible future for Ireland. An English-style parliament was set up at Kilkenny, though the term 'Confederation' was used for political reasons. In their statement of aims the Confederates looked back to the 'Great Charter' and declared that the common law 'shall be observed throughout the whole kingdom'. Penal statutes against the 'Roman Catholic religion' were alone exempted from this statement of principle.

There was no more striking monument to the success of the policies of 'surrender and regrant' than the Confederation of Kilkenny. The Confederates had risen in the name of the king and were willing to provide him with military aid provided that their political and religious aims were met. Among these, an independent parliament free of Poynings' Law and the public practice of their religion loomed largest. Negotiations with the king, however, were made difficult by the problems of Ulster, by the failure of the king to promise more than a bare tolerance for the Catholics and, in 1645, by the refusal of the Papal nuncio, Archbishop Rinuccini, to compromise with a heretic monarchy. When agreement was arrived at in 1646 (the first Ormond Peace) it was condemned by Rinuccini and the 'Old Irish' of Ulster. A second agreement (the second Ormond Peace) signed in 1649 proved to be merely the prelude to the Cromwellian conquest of Ireland.

During the confederate period, the divisions between north and south, a feature of Irish history in the later middle ages, once more re-emerged, accentuated now by the plantation of Ulster. Even within the Catholic episcopate there was a marked difference of attitude between the Old English bishops, with social backgrounds in the urban patriciate or the landed aristocracy, and those from Ulster, belonging to the Gaelic nobility, whose families had been dispossessed. Ulster had its own set of problems deriving from the large-scale settlement of Scots in Down, Antrim and Derry. These longstanding differences of *mentalité* survived amid the anguish of defeat, and exile, when one side sought to blame the other for the catastrophe. The historical controversy between the 'Old Irish' Richard O Ferrall and the 'Old English' John Lynch reflected this clash of attitude. Exiled members of the bardic order also took up the same themes.

The Cromwellian conquest brought about the downfall of the 'Old English' interest in Ireland. The real beneficiaries of the conquest, however, were not the Cromwellian soldiers but the 'New English' planters of the pre-1641 period who now styled themselves 'Old Protestants' to distinguish themselves from the Baptists and Quakers ('New Protestants') of the Cromwellian army. It has been estimated that of the 36,000 soldiers who stood to benefit from the original plantation, only 8,000 remained twenty years later. The Protestant ascendancy was very much an 'Old Protestant' ascendancy. The Cromwellian settlement also left intact the hold which the Ulster Scots enjoyed in Down and Antrim.

It had originally been planned to transport all Catholics west of the Shannon. Eventually only landlords suffered this fate, the actual occupiers of the soil being retained in the east as an indispensable labour force. The Catholic urban patriciate also were displaced from the towns, which henceforth became centres of the new colonial regime. From the economic point of view, the effects were catastrophic. Of Galway it was said in 1655 'her merchants were princes among the nations but now the city which was full of people is solitary and very desolate'. The Cromwellian plantation thus did not have the consequences which its exponents hoped for. In the absence of large-scale colonisation from England, neither the extermination nor the conversion of the Irish took place.

As in England, so in Ireland, the mid-seventeenth century marked the peak of Reformation fervour. After the Restoration the Protestant interest was placed on the defensive and even forced into full retreat during the crisis of 1688–9. The victory of William III at the Boyne in 1690 decided the future of Ireland for the next two centuries on the basis of a Protestant landowning ascendancy.

For much of the period that we have been considering the aim of successive governments was to develop unity within different parts of the English empire on the basis of religious conformity. When the political and religious map of the British Isles was stablilised in 1690 religious unity had not in fact been achieved. In England bitter hostility existed between the Established Church and the dissenting sects, each of which had its own version of the events of the civil war. In Scotland Presbyterians of various persuasions contended for control of the Established Church and were often united only in their hatred of episcopalianism and Popery. In Ireland, the population was divided into 'Protestants' (sc. members of the Established Church),

Catholics and Presbyterians. In Wales the Established Church confronted the dissenters. What seems to have occurred during these two centuries was that for many the sense of belonging to a particular Church replaced an earlier cultural identity. The divisiveness of the feudal period gave way to a new form of divisiveness based on religion.

8

The remaking of an empire

In orthodox interpretations of English history, the revolution of 1688 occupies a special place, as a landmark in the history of English liberty. In 1688 the victory of Protestantism and progress was assured by the flight of James II and the peaceful accession of William of Orange and Mary, James II's daughter. In the wake of revolution came a Toleration Act allowing dissenters to erect their own places of worship. Though it was not clear at the time, divine right monarchy had given way to parliamentary sovereignty. In due course, the revolution acquired its permanent appellation of 'Glorious'.

In the context of the British Isles, however, the Glorious Revolution takes on a more complex colouring. It was, in the first place, by no means bloodless, nor was its success inevitable. The future of the revolution in Scotland was still in doubt after the battle of Killiecrankie (1689) which was won by James II's supporters, though the effect of the victory was destroyed by the death of their leader, Claverhouse. In 1715 the revolution, though buttressed now by the Act of Union (1707) was challenged again when the Old Pretender, James VIII, landed in Scotland. Not until after the battle of Culloden (1746) can it be said that the regime set up in 1689 was secure. In Ireland, the fate of the Stuart cause was unclear until after the battle of the Boyne in July 1690 and perhaps not until the surrender of Limerick to Williamite forces a year later. Within the British Isles, the result of William's victory was not toleration but the establishment of an episcopalian ascendancy in Ireland, and a Presbyterian equivalent in Scotland. In Ireland, Catholics and Presbyterians found themselves under episcopalian dominance. In Scotland, Catholics and episcopalians were placed under the control of a Presbyterian establishment.

In England and Wales, the toleration which was extended to dissent was very much a limited one. Religious tests imposed by the Corporation Act (1662) and the Test Act (1673) still remained in force, their object being to prevent dissenters exercising political influence at the local as well as the national level, and various attempts made to repeal them in the eighteenth century failed. Toleration remained confined to religious observance. Outside this narrow range, the legacy of the civil wars of the mid-seventeenth century led to the perpetuation of distrust and hostility between the two cultures of Church and dissent, each with their own interpretation of the recent past, the churchmen looking back to the executions of Charles I and of Archbishop Laud, and the dissenters to their ejection from the Established Church after the Restoration. As Dr Jonathan Clark has recently emphasised (in *English Society 1688–1832* (1985)), an Anglican ascendancy retained control of the institutions of power and influence long after 1688. Episcopalian culture was dominant in the universities, the major public schools and the army and navy as well as in the Church itself. Dissenting culture was forced to create its own institutions of higher education, the dissenting academies in London and the north and west, where they had some numerical strength.

In Scotland, a similar clash of cultures took place though here it was the episcopalians who found themselves in a subordinate position. The Covenanters, now in a position of power, abolished episcopacy as an institution in the Established Church. In the Highlands, the renewed influence of the Campbells, which had been in decline since the Restoration, was signalled by the massacre of the Catholic MacDonalds of Glencoe in 1692. During the first half of the eighteenth century, Jacobitism, drawing support from bitter feelings of discrimination, remained far more of a threat than the Whig historians implied. But the dominant culture, reinforced by the Act of Union of 1707 and enshrined in the power of the Kirk, in the universities and the schools, remained Lowland Presbyterianism. This is not to say that it was united. Throughout the eighteenth century, Covenanting sects broke away from the establishment because it was not godly enough for their taste. In their hatred of Popery and of such historical figures as Claverhouse, however, Presbyterians of all views were at one.

In Ireland, defeat at the Boyne in 1690 marked the final eclipse of the culture of the 'Old English'. James II's general, Richard Talbot, earl of Tyrconnell, took his title from the O Donnells, chiefs of Tir Connail, but his roots lay in the anglicised counties of the Pale. The same may be said of the defender of Limerick, Patrick Sarsfield, whose estate was at Lucan, near Dublin. The Cromwellian confiscations had dealt the Old English a severe blow, from which they had made a partial recovery after the Restoration. The Williamite confiscations, however, together with the penal laws passed under William III and Anne, applied the *coup de grâce.* Henceforth members of Catholic gentry families sought careers as 'Wild Geese' in the armies of France and Spain. The dominant culture of eighteenth-century Ireland was to be that of the 'Protestant' (sc. episcopalian) ascendancy. Dublin, Cork and Limerick became Protestant urban centres, round which the great houses of the new elite were soon to be clustered. In the north-east, Presbyterians, linked closely with Scotland, formed a powerful bloc, though excluded from their full say in political and social life. It was here during the 1790s that the United Irishmen attracted many recruits for a movement which moved towards republicanism, under the influence of the United States as well as France. Among the Catholics, the bitter divisions between Gaelic and Old English cultures, deriving from the outcome of the confederate wars of the mid-seventeenth century, gave way ultimately to a sense of a common Catholicism, which accepted, however unwillingly, a subordinate position in the polity of Ireland.

Our attention cannot be confined solely to the British Isles, however. One of the most remarkable changes which occurred within the English empire during the period after 1688 was the growth of the American colonies. The population of the thirteen mainland colonies grew from c. 250,000 in 1700 to c. 2,500,000 by the 1770s. Trade with the colonies became a new and important feature of the economies of the British Isles. The prosperity of London was in large measure built upon it. The rise of Liverpool and Bristol in the course of the eighteenth century was bound up with colonial trade, including the slave trade. Ireland, though excluded from full participation in the English mercantile system, enjoyed a burgeoning trade with the slave-based societies of the West Indies, which provided a market for Irish salt beef and linens. In Scotland, the rapid growth of the port of Glasgow was connected with the tobacco trade.

Economically, the American colonies were an integral and increasingly important part of the English empire; culturally, also they cannot be left out of account in assessing the relative balance of Church and dissent. The various cultures of dissent were much more strongly represented within the thirteen colonies than was the case in England. In New England, Puritanism formed the basis of the dominant culture though now in more variegated forms than those held by the founding fathers of the early seventeenth century. In the middle colonies of Pennsylvania and New York, which expanded more rapidly during the eighteenth century than the colonies to the north and south, the emigration of Scotch-Irish Presbyterians from Ulster reinforced non-Anglican elements. Throughout the colonies, the impact of various evangelical movements, known collectively as the 'Great Awakening' found a ready response among those opposed to a religious establishment. Taking the English empire as a whole the rise of dissent in the colonies during this period led to a shift in the balance of the cultures of Church and dissent. In England itself there was no doubt about the dominance of the Anglican establishment, but beyond England dissenters could look westward across the Atlantic for moral reinforcement in time of crisis. From this point of view, the American revolution of the 1770s takes shape as a renewal of the seventeenth-century conflict between the two cultures of Church and dissent.

As suggested above, England during the eighteenth century was a society deeply divided on religious grounds. The divisions created by the civil war were still far from healed and the unity created by the fear of James II's Catholicism proved to be only temporary. During Anne's reign successful attempts were made by the High Church interest to reduce the role of dissent on public life. The Occasional Conformity Act (1711) was intended to prevent dissenters from complying with the letter of the law by taking the Anglican sacrament once a year in order to qualify for office. By the terms of the Schism Act (1714) dissenters were to be deprived of their schools and academies. The fact that these two acts were repealed after the accession of the Hanoverians cannot conceal the fact that the rift between the two cultures of Church and dissent remained deep for many decades to come. The dissenting deputies, drawn from each Presbyterian, Independent and Baptist congregation within 10 miles of London, reported regularly upon the pressures of various kinds to which the dissenters were exposed. In 1743 attacks by a riotous mob in Anglesey attracted their attention; in 1748 the refusal of burial to children of dissenters in a Suffolk village; in 1767 the exaction of tolls upon chapel-goers using a turnpike road. Perhaps the main factor tending to keep these tensions under control during the first half of the century was the fear of the return of Popery in the person of the Pretender.

The mutual animosity which existed between churchmen and dissenters derived in large measure from doctrinal and political differences and from rival interpretations of the recent past. Cultural differences of a less intellectual kind also played their part. The dominant Anglican culture embodied attitudes toward leisure which were criticised in dissenting circles. Racing, gambling, theatre-going, card-playing, dancing were all activities tolerated and often encouraged within the dominant culture. At a popular level, the village alehouse was the secular counterpart of the parish church.

The growth of a consumer society provides an indication of the strength of the dominant culture. It was 'at church' that a commentator noted how:

> in a populous city in the north, the macebearer cleared the way for Mrs Mayoress who came sidling after him in an enormous fan hoop of a pattern that had never been seen in those parts. At another church [he] saw several negligees with furbelowed aprons ... but these were woefully eclipsed by a burgess' daughter just come from London who appeared in a Trolloppee of Slammerkin with treble ruffles to the cuffs, pinked and gymped and the sides of the petticoats drawn up on festoons.

Such fashions were unlikely to be seen in dissenting chapels.

In the face of this Anglican ascendancy, dissenters, at least until the 1760s, were on the defensive. In dissenting circles, it was commonly held that 'going to horse races, cricketing and playing at cards etc is not to be practised and in no ways allowed by the professors of the Gospel'. 'Fiddling and vanity and singing vain songs' were also discouraged. There were also some who regarded Christmas and other feasts as pagan feasts, 'dung ... received from Baal' in the words of the sixteenth-century reformer Robert Browne. As some compensation, there developed the practice of communal hymn-singing which was uncommon outside chapel culture until the nineteenth century.

Excluded from the universities, the dissenters sought to preserve their cultural identity by establishing academies. The attitudes of some churchmen towards these institutions was represented in the dedication to Clarendon's *History* (first published during the reign of Anne). 'What can be the meaning of these several seminaries, and, as it were, universities, set up in divers parts of the kingdom by more than ordinary industry, contrary to law, supported by large contributions, where the youth is bred up in principles directly contrary to monarchical and episcopal government?' What it meant in fact is suggested by a remark made later in the century about the teaching of history. 'Eachard, Hume, Smollett and others of their turn, write their histories upon the principle of tyranny for the use of kings ... Wilson, Osborne, Coke, Rapin, Mrs Macauley, Harris etc write for the use of the people.' Joseph Priestley who was educated at Daventry Academy and who taught at Warrington Academy declared that, 'while your universities resemble ponds of stagnant water, secured by dams and mounds and offensive to the neighbourhood, ours are like rivers which taking their natural course fertilise a whole country'.

To analyse English society in terms of two cultures is clearly an oversimplification, however. Within the dominant Church culture itself, there were the two major traditions of High Church and Low Church, the latter being more sympathetic to the dissenters. Within dissent, there were marked differences between Presbyterians, Independents, Baptists and Unitarians. The position was further complicated by the rise of the evangelical movement of Methodism within the Church of England. Methodism was a missionary movement within the Church but in many ways it owed its inspiration to the world of dissent. John Wesley ordered his followers

> to taste no spirituous liquors, no dram of any kind unless provoked by a physician ... to pawn nothing, no not to save life, to wear no needless ornaments, such as rings, ear-rings, to use no needless self-indulgence, such as taking snuff or tobacco unless prescribed by a physician ... To give alms ... To be patterns of diligence and frugality, or self denial and taking up the cross daily.

Their critics indeed looked upon the Methodists as crypto-dissenters whose aim was to subvert the Church from within. Attacks made upon Methodist meetings by church mobs bear witness to the enduring tensions between Church and dissent during this period.

The dominance of the establishment was in many ways reinforced by what was the most remarkable example of social change in eighteenth-century England – the continued growth of London. London was already a metropolis in the seventeenth century. During the eighteenth, however, its dominance became even greater. Daniel Defoe noted in his *Tour of England* that few areas were unaffected by the pull of the London market. The population of London rose from 350,000 in 1700 to nearly 1 million at the end of the century. This market also influenced the economies of the Scottish Lowlands, the Welsh border counties and the counties of eastern Ireland. London also became the centre of a rapidly growing re-export trade, most notably in sugar and tobacco, two of the 'enumerated commodities' which by the terms of the Navigation Acts could not be exported directly from the colonies to Europe. Trade brought in its wake a demand for warehouses, docks and ancillary labour, as well as for credit facilities and insurance services supplied by the 'City'.

London, already an administrative, political and legal centre and now a commercial entrepot on the grand scale, also became a centre of consumption. Shops, theatres, clubs, coffee houses, drinking houses all came to provide facilities for enjoyment. Dissent may well have been overrepresented in circles of trade and finance, though this often-made assumption is by no means beyond challenge, but the values of the city as represented by its architecture and day-to-day activities were an urban extension of a broad-based 'Church' culture. Over much of the metropolitan area the tone was set by the town-houses of the aristocracy in the newly built square near to the palace of St James. It was this life-style which the dissenter Richard Price presumably had in mind in denouncing 'an abandoned venality, the inseparable companion of dissipation and extravagance [which] has poisoned the springs of public virtue among us'.

During the reigns of George I and George II (1714–60), the balance between Church and dissent was held by the Whig administrations of Sir Robert Walpole and his successor, Henry Pelham, relying upon a system of political 'influence' which their opponents denounced as 'corruption'. Several factors made possible this long-term success of the Whigs in the face of what may well have been a Tory majority in the country as a whole. The 'Low Church' Anglican episcopate, appointed under government patronage, could be relied upon to support the government in the House of Lords (at the local parish level, where the parsons were generally Tory, the situation was very different). The long period of war, or fear of war, from 1688 to 1815, sometimes termed the 'Second Hundred Years War', led to the growth of a patronage system linked to wartime requirements. The army and the navy were a source of useful government patronage. Government influence could be brought to bear upon dockyard towns such as Chatham, Gravesend, Deptford and Greenwich. The Whigs were also able to control many small boroughs in the south-west. Dissenters tolerated a government which was much better from their point of view than a possible Tory alternative with High Church affiliations. In counties such as Cheshire and Lancashire in the north-west and in Hertfordshire, Gloucestershire and Essex in the south, where dissenters accounted for one fifth of the electorate, this support could be an important consideration.

In the 1760s this 'Age of Equipoise' came to an end. The accession of George III in 1760 brought his adviser John Stuart, third earl of Bute, to a position of great influence. In 1762 the duke of Newcastle resigned and the long period of Whig ascendancy came to an end. The change was widely interpreted by its critics as a shift to Tory-style government and Bute's policies came under attack on these grounds. For reasons which are still unclear, John Wilkes, a relatively obscure politician, became a symbol of popular discontent in London and in some provincial towns. The arrest of Wilkes for publishing a seditious libel in no. 45 of *The North Briton* was the first in a series of events which led to repeated challenges of the government. He was four times elected as M.P. for Middlesex, each election being followed by a government-inspired annulment. In 1768, several people were shot by Scottish troops at a meeting of Wilkesite supporters, an event known as the 'St George's Fields' Massacre'. In 1774 Wilkes was eventually elected M.P. for

Middlesex. By then, Wilkesite agitation had become a symbol linking political opposition in Britain and America.

The events of the 1760s and 1770s, culminating in the war of 1775–83, are generally conceptualised in terms of the 'American revolution'. It makes equally good historical sense to see them in terms of a civil war between the cultures of Church and dissent and recalling in some of its particulars the first civil war of the 1640s. To some observers, the attitudes of the Americans appeared to be a modern example of 'the principles of the Independents in Oliver's time'. In the 1770s, as in the 1640s, 'No Popery' became a stick with which to beat the government. To some, the Quebec Act of 1774, granting toleration to French Canada, was part of a general conspiracy to plant 'Popery and arbitrary power in America'. It was said that 'the Inquisition may erect her standard in Pennsylvania and the city of Philadelphia may yet experience the carnage of a St Bartholomew's day'. In England a certain Mr Hudson told a pro-government candidate that he would not vote 'for any Popery in Canada and shutting up the port of Boston'. An observer less sympathetic to the American cause commented that

> if this rebellion in America proves successful, it will be in consequence of republican principles of the most levelling kind; and the victors will no doubt aim, with the assistance of their restless friends in England, to overturn that happy limited monarchy, which experience has taught us is best suited to a realm so extensive as ours, and which has long been the glory of Britain and the envy of all the world.

The conflict which developed between the British government and the American colonies after the end of the Seven Years War arose for many different reasons, economic, political, constitutional. It may also be seen as arising from a profound disharmony between the rival cultures of Church and dissent. In the mother country, the Established Church provided the basis of a dominant culture with deference built into the fabric of society. Dissent, with its less deferential traditions resting upon the notion of a 'godly elect', had been, since the defeat of the seventeenth century, a subordinate culture. In the mainland colonies of North America, however, the balance of cultures during the course of the eighteenth century shifted in favour of dissent. In New England dissent in its various forms was a dominant culture. In the middle states of New York and Pennsylvania, both of which expanded more rapidly than the colonies of New England and the south, large-scale immigration of Scotch-Irish and of German Lutherans tilted the balance away from Anglicanism. According to one episcopalian, 'Africa never more abounded with new Monsters than Pennsylvania with new sects who are constantly sending out their Emissaries around.' It was said later of the Scotch-Irish (with some exaggeration) that 'with a very few exceptions, they are United Irishmen, Free Masons and the most God-provoking Democrats this side of Hell'. In Pennsylvania, in 1768, Scotch-Irish led the violent Paxton Boys movement against the Anglican-Quaker dominance of Philadelphia. In North Carolina, resentment arose from the fact that Presbyterian marriages were invalid, a situation not remedied until 1766. The impact of the religious revival known as the 'Great Awakening' also helped to swell the ranks of the evangelicals. In Virginia the culture of the Anglican gentry, revolving around race meetings and other 'festive' occasions, found itself on the defensive.

The crisis within the English empire lasted from 1763 when the government attempted to raise money from the colonies by means of the Stamp Act (1765) to the recognition of American independence in 1783. A series of British defeats from Saratoga in 1777 to Yorktown in 1781 led to what must have seemed inconceivable at the end of the Seven Years War, overwhelming defeat for the mother country at the hands of an alliance between the mainland colonies and the 'Popish monarchy' of France. Only Canada and the West Indies remained of a transatlantic empire which had first come into existence nearly two centuries earlier.

The political and cultural consequences of the rift between Britain and her former colonies were profound, for both societies. The United States became a society without a religious establishment, as Anglican loyalists moved north to Canada or back to Britain. The result was to give the cultures of dissent full play. The Declaration of Independence and the Constitution of the new state were drawn up by men strongly influenced by the values and traditions of 'civic humanism' deriving from Machiavelli and Harrington. There can be little doubt, however, that the Reformation was a more powerful influence upon the future of the infant United States than either the Renaissance or the Enlightenment. The 'Great Awakening' set the tone for much that was to come. As Jonathan Edwards declared half a century earlier,

> It is not unlikely that this work of God's Spirit the awakening so extraordinary and wonderful is the dawning, or at least the prelude of that glorious work of God so often foretold in the Scripture, which, in the progress and issue of it, shall renew the world of mankind ... We cannot reasonably think otherwise than that the beginning of this great work of God must be near. And there are many things that make it probable that this work will begin in America.

This was a note that was to be repeated throughout the nineteenth century and which derived unmistakably from the culture of dissent.

For better or worse, the new state was freed from the restraints of an Anglican establishment. The sect was the characteristic form of religious organisation and it was this which provided the basis of what Tocqueville later analysed in his *Democracy in America*. In its lack of deference, in the absence of a formal hierarchical structure in Church and state, in its egalitarian emphasis, the United States developed along lines which derived from the dissenting tradition. In the American view of history John Milton and Algernon Sidney enjoyed a place which they were denied in the established English interpretation. Not surprisingly Mrs Catherine Macaulay, critic of Hume's 'Tory' history of England, came to visit George Washington in the years after the revolution. The lack of an establishment in America, however, may well have led to a certain anti-intellectualism and scorn for high culture.

Henry James, looking back to the earlier years of the infant republic, was less enthusiastic than Jonathan Edwards when he commented:

No Sovereign, no court, no personal loyalty, no aristocracy, no church, no clergy, no army, no diplomatic service, no country gentlemen, no palaces, no castles, nor manors, nor old country houses, nor parsonages, nor thatched cottages, nor ivied ruins; no cathedrals, nor abbeys, nor little Norman churches; no great Universities nor public schools – no Oxford, nor Eton, nor Harrow; no literature, no novels, no museums, no pictures, no political society, no sporting class – no Epsom, nor Ascot.

In England itself the result of defeat in America was to weaken the culture of dissent and to intensify the defensive attitude of the establishment. In 1787 Pitt and North spoke out against the repeal of the Corporation and Test Acts on the grounds that they were 'the corner stone of the constitution which should have every preservation'. In 1790 the vote against Repeal was larger than it had ever been. In 1794 Joseph Priestley left for America where he died ten years later. The United States as much as revolutionary France was a warning of the type of 'levelling' society which might take root in England. During the half century which followed the end of the American war, 'class' as a concept made its appearance and it may well have been during this period that the hardening of class lines and the growth of deference which foreign observers noted as being characteristic of English society made their appearance. The loss of America may thus help to explain why there was no English equivalent of the French revolution.

In terms of size and population (c. 350,000) the position of Wales within the English empire may be compared, not unreasonably, to one of the mainland American colonies. In Wales, as in colonies like Virginia and Pennsylvania, there was a 'Great Awakening' of 'vital religion' and a conflict between the cultures of Church and dissent, which ended with the triumph of dissent. George Whitefield's Calvinistic Methodism made as great an impact in Wales as it did in America. Wales did not achieve political independence but in a sense the eventual victory of non-conformity provided a substantial measure of cultural and linguistic autonomy, though at too high a cost in the eyes of its opponents. Nonconformity became the religion of the majority in Wales as it did in the infant United States, where Thomas Jefferson said that two-thirds of the population were dissenters. Calvinistic Methodism was particularly strong in Welsh-speaking north Wales. Perhaps it was only by being allied with a popular movement of this kind that the language survived. The alternative was absorption within England as happened in Cornwall (where Cornish died out in the eighteenth century) and in the border counties of Shropshire, Herefordshire and Monmouth, which became heavily anglicised.

At the beginning of the eighteenth century no single culture enjoyed complete dominance in Wales. The squirearchy was Anglican, as were the bishops and parochial clergy, and there were pockets of dissent in the small English-speaking market towns of the borders and the south, but the culture of the rural Welsh-speaking majority was an amalgam of traditional 'festive' culture, varying from locality to locality.

The bardic culture of the elite had been undermined after the Union (1536–42) with the coming of print and the growth of governmental pressures to use English, but at a popular level Welsh oral culture, divided by its local dialects, survived. Wakes, feasts and wassailing, and the practice of certain rites of popular religion, such as the use of charms and holy wells to ward off evil spirits, flourished in the Welsh countryside as they did in Ireland and the Scottish Highlands.

During the course of the century, the situation was transformed, thanks largely to the zeal of churchmen working within the establishment. Missionary activity came from within the Anglican Church, often with the direct support of English clergy. The Society for the Propagation of Christian Knowledge, founded in 1699, took Wales as one of its targets and sponsored the foundation of a number of English-speaking charity schools, most of them in south Wales. The real turning point came, however, when Griffiths Jones, an Anglican parson at Llandowror, turned his attention to Welsh-speaking areas. Jones set up a system of scriptural education, in Welsh where it seemed appropriate, using itinerant (sc. 'circulating') teachers who taught Bible-reading to rural labourers during quiet months of the agricultural year. Hundreds of these schools introduced a primitive form of literacy based upon the Old and New Testaments and the Book of Common Prayer to the rural world of Wales. At much the same time, from the 1730s onwards, an evangelical movement, comparable to the 'Great Awakening' in colonial America, led to the creation of 'Methodist' societies within the Established Church. The leader of the movement was Howell Harris, whose views like those of Jonathan Edwards in New England and George Whitefield were strongly Calvinist. Welsh Methodism thus took on a different colouring from that of English Methodism, which followed the Arminianism of John Wesley.

Much may be attributed to the charismatic gifts of the evangelists but more is needed to account for their long-term success in transforming the *mentalité* of rural Wales. In social terms it would seem that the Methodists managed to adapt for their own purposes some of the institutions of rural society. Methodist societies overcame the challenge of a dispersed rural setting as the formal parochial structure could not. The evangelists remained within the structure of the Established Church until a decisive break came in 1810–11 but, well before this, Methodist institutions were not truly part of the parochial structure. In the face of clerical hostility, the Methodists were often forced to build their own chapels, which became dissenting chapels after the final breach.

Throughout the eighteenth century tensions within the Welsh Church were as bitter as those between the Church and the Old Dissenting bodies. Churchmen complained that the Methodists asserted 'that they and none others are the elect and damn all others in order to terrify the illiterate into their faction. They assure them that their fathers and grandfathers are in hell; and that they see visible marks of damnation in the faces of such as will not become Methodists.' Others protested about 'itinerant preachers who alienated the affections of weak people still further from the Established Church ... [maintaining] that our most excellent liturgy is a dead letter, a heap of Popish rubbish composed by devils'. To the more orthodox churchmen the Methodists seemed to be crypto-dissenters bent upon seizing power for themselves. When the breach came, however, it was the Established Church which suffered the heavier blow. In both north and south Wales it became the Church of a minority, yielding precedence to the Calvinistic Methodists in the north and to the chapels of Old Dissent, most notably the Independents and the Baptists, in the south. The loss of the Methodists was the main cause of this shift, which was to have significant consequences when, thanks to industrialisation, Wales became more important than it had ever been before within the English empire.

Although the language of Calvinistic Methodism was Welsh, the values and attitudes of the movement resembled those of other evangelical movements in England and America. Indeed there was little that was distinctively Welsh in their Sabbatarianism and their dislike of secular amusements. Thus, when every allowance is made for the importance of the Welsh language during this period, the fact remains that Wales became subtly anglicised during this period. Within the context of an English empire, Wales was in many ways a sub-culture, drawing its standards from the metropolis. It was reaction against this, to some, unpleasant, truth which led to the rise of a Welsh Romantic movement, reviving an interest in things Welsh. Support was greatest among the London-based Welsh, themselves a symbol of the incorporation of Wales within a wider political context. The society of Cymmrodorion (still in existence) was founded in 1751. The most active individual was Edward Williams, known usually by his bardic name 'Iolo Morganwg'. 'Iolo' revived the holding of eisteddfoddau, not seen since the mid-sixteenth century. The first meeting was held on Primrose Hill, London, an indication that the movement drew its support from the ethnic enthusiasm of exiles. It was in London that the need to preserve a sense of Welshness was most acute, whereas in Wales itself local identities were still all-important. Edward Williams himself came from an English-speaking background and spent much time in England before returning to Glamorgan. 'Iolo' and his compatriots created a new Welsh past which ignored the complexities of an earlier 'British' past. In so doing they were providing a Welsh equivalent of similar cultural revivals in the Scottish Lowlands and in Ireland.

In the late eighteenth century, several Welsh sub-cultures may be discerned, each operating within a larger imperial context. The first was that of the ruling elite of episcopalian gentry, in whose hands parliamentary politics rested, together with the control of local administration. Within the Established Church a revival took place, with gentry backing, later drawing much inspiration from the ritualism of the Oxford Movement. Overall, however, it was the two forms of dissent which came to exercise dominance. A broad distinction may be made between south Wales, commercialised (albeit with some industry), anglicised and cosmopolitan, and the north, heavily Welsh-speaking and rural. In the south, Anglicanism contended with a wide variety of dissenting sects which had roots going back to the civil war period and among which demands for political reform found a ready response. In the north, it was Calvinistic Methodism, still at this date within the Established Church, which took root among the rural population. Though both were 'Welsh', it is not too much to say that north and south were in essence different sub-cultures.

It was from the cosmopolitan south that Richard Price and Iolo Morganwg came. Both men were heavily involved in the radical politics of the day, especially the issues raised by the American and French revolutions. As freemasons, they were both sympathetic to the ideas of the Enlightenment. Pockets of similar radicalism existed further north but in general it was the south, exposed to the influence of Bristol, which was most sympathetic to opposition causes. Rural north Wales, by contrast, was a more localised culture in which traditional elements were still strong despite the activities of the Methodists. The contrast between the two areas was to increase even more from the end of the eighteenth century with the onset of industrialisation in south Wales.

The changes which took place in Wales during the eighteenth century made little impact upon the other societies of the British Isles. However, the rise of Wales as a factor in wider British politics during the nineteenth century, when Welshmen became involved in the fortunes of the Liberal party, becomes explicable only against the background of the eighteenth century.

In Ireland, the formative period of the Reformation ended with the population divided into three distinct cultures, the episcopalians of eastern Ireland, the Presbyterians of Ulster and the Catholic majority to be found in all four provinces. Among the Catholics the reforms begun during the Counter-Reformation had not progressed very far. The survival of such popular rites of passage as the 'wake' suggests that in the west, particularly, traditional patterns still survived. In times of active persecution, informal religious gatherings such as the 'patron' (the festival of local saints) were one of the few means by which religious identity could be maintained.

The episcopalians, though probably the smallest in numbers, enjoyed the greatest political power at the local and national level, since most of the landowners belonged to the Established Church. The Presbyterians were socially dominant in Antrim and Down but not well represented elsewhere. The Catholics, largely deprived of leadership, had least influence of all. Each of these groups constituted its own self-contained world. The Presbyterians enjoyed close links with Scotland where issues involving the covenant and lay patronage loomed large in the early eighteenth century. Ideological divisions in Scotland inevitably came to influence the various branches of Presbyterianism in Ulster. Episcopalians in contrast were closely involved with affairs in England, as the career of Jonathan Swift suggests. Increasingly, however, the Protestant ascendancy became a society with its own distinctive outlook. Trinity College, Dublin, for example, which had drawn its provosts from Oxford and Cambridge during the seventeenth century, appointed men from its own ranks in the eighteenth. There was, thirdly, the Catholic majority, whose leaders, though deprived of prospects at home, sought military, ecclesiastical or commercial careers on the continent. The outlook of most Irish-speaking Catholics, it is safe to say, were largely bounded by their locality. A letter written by a Cork landlord in 1702 describes how

> The practice has been to let a great deal of land to some Irish gentleman who has nothing of his own so that he may bring in his followers, and while he makes them pay double the rent, he lives idly on the overplus himself. Besides, while all these depend on his protection, they follow his bagpipe, whenever disturbances happen.

In a state now dominated by an English-speaking elite, a largely Irish-speaking society turned in upon itself. The landlords, overwhelmingly English in origin, were content to deal with their Irish tenants through a 'broker', either a 'middleman' or the local priest.

In principle, there was little reason why this cultural balance of power in Ireland should ever change. Indeed, the elaborate system of penal laws was intended to ensure that it did not. Among the remaining rump of Catholic aristocrats there was a steady drift into the Established Church. Among the Presbyterians, emigration to North America seems to have acted as something of a safety valve. The Irish Catholics remained tranquil during the pro-Stuart risings of 1715 and 1745 in Scotland. The Protestant ascendancy seemed to be established on secure foundations. Place-hunting rather than ideology provided the main motive for entering politics.

From the mid-eighteenth century, however, signs of change began to appear. Ireland, like Scotland and Wales, responded to the challenge of the growing markets of England and the colonies: the result was to create three specialised economic areas in the east of the country – the linen producing counties of Ulster east of the Bann, the wheat producing counties of Leinster and the 'dairying' and cattle producing counties of Munster. The growth of economic activity was reflected in the growth of market towns and larger centres, such as Cork City, which became a centre of the export market in butter. Limerick, once a military base, became a large provision market. Ballinasloe was one of several large sheep markets in the midlands. In Leinster, Dublin enjoyed remarkable growth during these years. In Ulster, Belfast became the main market outlet for the linen industry, after the opening up of the Lagan navigation in 1756.

The prime beneficiary of these changes was the ascendancy landlord class, as the architecture of the second half of the eighteenth century makes clear. The great houses of the ascendancy (the 'Big House' of common parlance) were built within reach of the growing ports, on the basis of the newly found prosperity. In Ulster, landlords took the initiative in encouraging the development of linen manufactures of their estates. The marquess of Downshire became one of the richest men in the kingdom as a result of such enterprise. In Leinster, the confidence of the landlords was displayed in the building of the Grand Canal and the Royal Canal as a means of opening up the midlands to the market. The great victory of the landlords came in 1782 when they forced Lord North to grant them a larger measure of political autonomy. During the American war the Volunteers led largely by the landlords proved to be a powerful weapon in the hands of the ascendancy. Political reforms were kept at arm's length. The post-1782 Irish parliament may be called 'Grattan's parliament' but it was largely dominated not by the liberal Grattan but by his opponents, who resisted any change which might weaken the ascendancy.

The landlords were not the only class to benefit from the economic revival. In Munster and Leinster a rural middle class of 'strong farmers' appeared, many of them Catholic. In this development, Irish agrarian society was following the English pattern of change in response to the market, which had brought about the replacement of small farmers by a system based on large tenant farmers and labourers. There was also the rise of a comparable urban middle class, much of it Catholic. Slowly and cautiously these groups began to press for the repeal of the penal laws which, though largely a dead letter in some areas, still remained on the statute book. The Catholic Committee was formed in 1772 as a lobby to bring pressure to bear on the government. As a consequence of this, some important economic grievances were redressed during the period of the American war. Penal prohibitions relating to officeholding, voting and sitting in the House of Commons still remained, however, and were to become a major political issue before the end of the century.

In Ulster, Presbyterian merchants, farmers and shopkeepers had also profited from the expansion of the English and colonial market. Belfast and Londonderry were both prosperous and growing ports. Belfast, in particular, had replaced Dublin as the outlet for much of the Ulster linen industry. Presbyterians did not suffer from the same range of legal disabilities as the Catholics. Nonetheless, they were excluded from playing their full role in political life as a result of the operation of the Test Act of 1704, requiring local officeholders to take the Anglican sacrament. At a local level, Presbyterians saw key decisions being taken by unrepresentative grand juries dominated by landlords or their agents. At a national level, the choice of parliamentary candidates was frequently decided by closed urban corporations, from which Presbyterians were excluded. Though the offending act was repealed in 1782, many grievances still remained.

Many farmers had benefited from the expansion of the market. As in England, however, there were those for whom economic change brought the prospect of insecurity and downward social mobility. The rapid expansion of new-style farming in parts of Leinster and Munster reduced the land available for small farmers and turned many of them into labourers. Agrarian unrest was the consequence, especially in the rich agricultural land of the Golden Vale. This 'Whiteboy' movement of the 1760s was followed by a similar 'Rightboy' movement in the 1780s. Though it is possible to differentiate between the two movements, it seems clear that they were both responses to the pressures of the market. The 'Rightboys' for example complained about the use of cheap labour, the rise in rents and the practice of advertising vacant farms for sale, thus making them available to non-locals. The areas affected were precisely those in which the market economy was making most headway. Connacht, where subsistence farming was the norm, was unaffected. In the north, however, where the farmers were also exposed to market pressures, there were similar outbreaks during the 1770s and 1780s by 'Oakboys' and 'Steelboys', who drew their membership from Presbyterian small farmers. Here the rise in rents, the payment of tithes and increased charges for the use of turf for fuel were major grievances.

Rural violence often took a sectarian form especially where the payment of tithes was an issue. The main outbreak of sectarian violence, however, took place in an area which had been affected by the onset of proto-industrialisation. This was Co. Armagh, where the growth of the linen industry had led to the creation of new industrial villages such as Keady and Newtown Hamilton in parts of Ulster which had hitherto been unaffected by the market. It is still not clear why conflict should have arisen between episcopalian 'Peep O Day Boys' and Catholic 'Defenders', in the 1780s. Perhaps each regarded the other as intruders and a threat to their standard of living. The rural population, largely Catholic, may have seen the new villages as a danger. Whatever the reasons, sectarian violence was a feature of the 1780s in these newly industrialised areas. The antagonisms of the Reformation had returned, this time in a 'modern' environment.

The most serious crisis which the ascendancy had to face came in the 1790s when the United Irishmen, after pressing unsucessfully for political change, rose in revolt in 1798. Fortunately for the landlords, the rebels failed. The rebellion did however prove to be more widespread than the county-wide outbreaks of rural protest which had taken place from the 1760s onwards. In the north, the Presbyterian farmers of Antrim and Down, or some of them, 'were out' in 1798. South of Dublin, in Wicklow, Wexford and Carlow, small farmers also rose in revolt. But most of Ireland, especially the west, where a small French force landed in 1798, was uninvolved.

Tom Paine's *Rights of Man* circulated in the cities of the east coast (Wolfe Tone called it the 'Koran of Belfast'), but sectarian hostility proved to be more powerful than ideals of universal brotherhood. In Co. Armagh, sectarian conflict had already broken out in the 1780s. It became more intense after the outbreak of the French revolution and the rise of the United Irishmen. In 1795 after a violent clash between Catholic and Protestant at the Diamond (Co. Armagh), landlords placed themselves at the head of a 'Church and King' organisation known as the Orange Order. On the strongly episcopalian estates of the north, Protestant landlords and tenants were enabled to unite under the banner of 'No Popery'. Not all landlords followed this course. The Whig earl of Gosford was a notable exception, but it was the general tendency among more conservative landlords.

In the counties south of Ulster, where Catholics were in a majority, the situation was different. Here a Protestant presence was looked upon as an indication that landlords were attempting a policy of 'colonisation'. In Co. Louth, John Foster, former speaker of the Irish House of Commons openly advertised for Protestant tenants. In Wicklow, villages like Newtown Mount Kennedy were newly established Protestant centres in a largely Catholic countryside. Thus the south became a reverse image of the north. In Armagh, a Protestant declared 'Sir, I hate a Papist as I do a toad and none of my neighbours has gone further in their extirpation than I have.' In Cavan, a group of Catholic Defenders stated their intention to 'destroy every Scotchman or Presbyterian they could find'. The worst excesses, however, were reserved for Wexford in 1798. Nearly one hundred Protestants were executed in Wexford town and a number of others were burned alive in a barn at Scullabogue, near New Ross. The shadow of 1798 lay heavily over nineteenth-century Irish history, both in the north, where Scullabogue was remembered, and in the south where the counter-atrocities perpetrated by the militia passed into popular consciousness.

The rebellion of 1798 led Pitt to conclude that a union of Ireland with Britain was a political necessity, in spite of the opposition of the ascendancy. The result of two years of pressure upon the Irish parliament was the Act of Union of 1800 which provided for Irish representation in the House of Commons (100 members) as well as for the election of 25 representative peers to the House of Lords. It was intended that the Act would win Catholic support thanks to an additional measure admitting Irish Catholic M.P.s, but George III refused to give way on what he regarded as an essential element of the constitution. For some time, therefore, the full implications of the Act of Union were concealed. Of the three cultures of Ireland, it was only one, the Anglo-Irish episcopalian interest, which was represented at Westminster. The Irish Catholic bishops gave their support to the measure but reaped no reward. In Ireland, at least for the moment, the ascendancy was victorious.

In Scotland, in the years following the Glorious Revolution, there were three distinctive cultures: the Presbyterianism of much of the Lowlands and those parts of the Highlands under Campbell influence, the episcopalianism of the east coast, north of the Tay, and the residual Catholicism of a few scattered areas, especially those under MacDonald control in the Isles. Of these, Catholicism, despite Presbyterian obsessions with the growth of 'Popery', was the least important. The real struggle in Scotland lay between the cultures of Presbyterianism and episcopalianism, each with their own interpretation of the recent past. The episcopalians who had been royalist in the civil war looked back to the memory of Montrose, whose remains, scattered after his execution, had been recovered and buried with due solemnity at the Restoration. (The Montrose legend, however, was complicated by his Convenanting past.) The Presbyterian version of recent history singled out the 'Killing Time' after the Restoration, when their most zealous members had been persecuted. During the rebellion of 1715, Jacobite commanders asked strangers, whose sympathies were unknown, whether they attended the meeting house (episcopal) or the church (Presbyterian), a clear indication of how the battle lines were drawn.

The Glorious Revolution replaced an episcopalian ascendancy with a Presbyterian ascendancy. In 1690 the victors abolished lay patronage and placed the presentation of ministers in the hands of the presbytery and the heritor (chief landowner) of the parish. The Kirk Session, made up of ministers and elders, became the chosen instrument for the enforcement of Presbyterian views on private and public morality. With the backing of the English government, the newly established Church was able to exercise its authority south of the Forth. In the south-west, Glasgow, Ayrshire and Galloway, the Covenanters were dominant. In Edinburgh, William Carstares, who had once been tortured on suspicion during the Rye House Plot, was the spokesman for William III. Episcopalian clergy in strongly Presbyterian areas were 'rabbled' by hostile gangs and forced to leave their parishes. Others were accused of immorality and ejected by special committees set up by the General Assembly. In Scotland, more so than elsewhere in the British Isles, the Glorious Revolution possessed a revolutionary character, displacing one regime and establishing another.

North of the Forth, among the great landowners and gentry of the east coast, the story was more complicated. Here there was no equivalent of the great cities of Glasgow and Edinburgh. Episcopalian landowners, secure in their estates and the backing of equally well-established relatives or patrons, were able to resist the pressures of the General Assembly. The universities of St Andrews and Aberdeen were purged of episcopalians but even so it was said in 1749 that episcopalian schools in the north-east 'poisoned the greatest part of the Young Gentry of those parts with Principles that have since thoroughly appeared – For as the young gentlemen came to their estates, Nonjuring meeting houses were instantly erected on their Lands: and they were themselves almost to a man the officers in the Rebel army in 1745.' Presbyterian ministers found it difficult to make headway, in the face of gentry hostility, after lay patronage was restored by the Patronage Act of 1712, during the Tory-dominated last years of Anne. In Scotland as a whole the real power of the establishment was confined to the area south of the Forth–Clyde line. Without the backing of the English government, the Presbyterian cause might well have been placed in jeopardy and it was the knowledge of this which created among the Presbyterians a strong commitment to the Act of Union of 1707.

Among the Presbyterians there was a wide variety of opinion ranging from the Cameronians at one end of the spectrum with their distrust of the secular world and the Moderates at the other. The Kirk Session of Morton may be taken as representing one powerful strain in its fierce denunciation of dancing in 1715:

> Considering that the great abuse that is commeted at wedding dinners and in particular by promiscuous dancing betwixt young men and young women which is most abominable, not to be practised in a land of light, and condemned in former time of Presbytery as not only unnecessary but sensuall, being only an inlet of lust and provocation to uncleanness of men and women in this loose and degenerate age, wherein the devil seems to be raging by a spirit of uncleanness and profanity.

Robert Woodrow, historian of the days of persecution, lamented in 1725 that 'Wickedness is come to a new height.' He protested that 'all the villainous, profane and obscene books and plays, as printed in London, are got down by Allen Ramsay and lent out for an easy price, to young boys, servant girls of the better sort, and gentlemen'. The Moderates, represented by such figures as the historian William Robertson, friend of David Hume, took a more detached view of the temptations of secular culture, and it was from this end of the Presbyterian spectrum that the Scottish Enlightenment, or much of it, emerged.

The first open conflict between the two cultures came after the accession of the Hanoverian George I in 1714. In 1715 the episcopalians rose in revolt in the name of James VIII, counting upon widespread resentment against the Act of Union to bring the uncommitted over to their side. For a year, the future of Scotland, and perhaps of the British Isles, was in the balance, much as it had been during 'the troubles' of the previous century. In the event, however, the Presbyterian regime survived, though the gap between the two cultures remained as wide as ever.

The rebellion of 1745, though more celebrated in romantic legend than the '15, was much less of a threat to the government. The Young Pretender found support only among a minority of Highland clans and among a fringe of discontented episcopalian gentry. The initiative for the rebellion seems to have come largely from France as a means of creating trouble in northern Britain. The great magnates and substantial gentry stayed aloof from what they saw as an ill-conceived venture. One of the MacDonald chiefs urged Charles to go back home. However limited the support which Charles received among the episcopalians, one of the consequences of the rebellion was to widen the rift between them and the Presbyterian establishment. The penalties levied on unqualified clergymen were increased in 1746 and again in 1748. Clergymen found breaking the law by preaching to more than four people were made liable to six months' imprisonment for the first offence and to banishment for life after the second. Meeting houses were plundered or burnt down. It was not until 1792, four years after the death of Charles, that these penal laws were repealed.

The tensions between Presbyterian and episcopalian culture were well exemplified in the life of Sir Walter Scott (1771–1832). There were episcopalians in Scott's background but he was brought up by a father who was a strict Presbyterian. Scott recalled how his father observed the Sabbath by preaching three sermons to the household, cross-questioning his audience at the end to see how well they had listened. When one of the family praised the Sunday broth as 'good', Scott's father poured a cup of cold water into his plate, saying 'Aye, too good.' Scott himself reacted against this upbringing. He married an episcopalian and his children were christened by episcopalian ministers. His novels *Waverley* and *Old Mortality* indicate how Scott looked upon the recent history of Scotland as a clash between two cultures.

The battle of Culloden in 1746 was the Scottish equivalent of the battle of the Boyne. Victory gave the Presbyterians a new confidence in their own future, creating conditions which made possible the rise of open divisions within the Established Church, between the 'Moderate' and 'Popular' parties. In the absence of a Scottish parliament, the General Assembly provided the occasion for debates upon issues of the day. In the main, the Moderates could be relied upon to support government policy, notably during the American wars. The Popular party, which was more critical of the role of government patronage in the Kirk, supported the Americans. On a different issue, the passing of a Catholic Relief Act in 1778, the parties also took different sides, the Moderates being in favour of the official policy of toleration. Outside the establishment, lay a number of seceding sects, divided among themselves, and from the establishment, about the correct relationship between Church and state.

The confidence of the establishment was also bolstered by the economic revival of mid-century. The initial impact of the Union had been disappointing. Such economic changes as took place were on a small scale. In the south-west, Glasgow merchants began to take advantage of the opening-up of trade with the American colonies though Edinburgh remained the largest city in Scotland. In the Highlands, first in Kintyre and then, in 1737, on the rest of his estates, the duke of Argyll introduced a system of cash rentals, replacing the indirect link through the 'tacksmen' (the Scottish equivalent of the Irish 'middleman'). But in Scotland, as in Ireland, it was not until mid-century that the various regions began to respond to the stimulus of the growing English and colonial market.

Signs of economic change become much more numerous in the second half of the eighteenth century. The Clyde grew as a centre of trade with the colonies. In Glasgow the building of Virginia Street (1753) and Jamaica Street (1761) was evidence of a growing faith in a colonial future. In Edinburgh, after the draining of the North loch and the construction of the North Bridge in 1767, the building of the New Town began, with its long list of streets dedicated to the British link.

Change was slow to come in the rural world but here also opportunities offered by a wider English market proved difficult to resist. Most of the better land in the Lowlands was enclosed during the second half of the eighteenth century with commercial production as the end in view. Old-style runrig (the equivalent of Irish rundale), with its communal sharing of land, gave way gradually to individual farms on the English model of tenant farmer and labourer. For the farmers this meant prosperity. For the labourers the barrack-like bothies had little to recommend them. 'Improvement' on these lines made headway first in the Lothians of the south-east, with its rich soils. In the north-east the pace of change was slower. It was not until the 1790s that roads up to the new standards began to be built on any scale in Aberdeenshire. In all areas landlords came to see the planned village on the English model as a means of stimulating economic growth on their estates, though in many cases the experience proved less than satisfying. Planned villages such as Gifford and Ormiston survive as a reminder of this phase of Scottish economic history when an 'Anglomania' affected the Scottish landlords as much as it did the French. (In Ireland also at this time, the planned village made its appearance.)

Changes in the Lowlands were undramatic. The most dramatic changes occurred in the Highlands in the aftermath of the defeat of the clans at Culloden in 1746. Traditional dress was banned and hereditary jurisdiction, the source of the legal powers enjoyed by the chiefs, abolished by act of parliament in 1747. The chiefs' estates were put into the hands of Lowlanders who lost little time in replacing traditional land-holding with cash rentals. To some extent these changes had been taking place piecemeal. The '45 rebellion itself may be seen as an attempt to halt the process of change, but overwhelming defeat at Culloden in 1746 left the Highlands defenceless. Planned villages made their appearance in the Highlands, sometimes with the aim of providing quasi-colonial settlements for demobilised troops. When, in 1773, Dr Johnson visited the Highlands in the company of Boswell, he was conscious of seeing a culture in decay.

The middle of the eighteenth century may be taken as marking the end of a period. Two centuries earlier there was by and large a balance between two cultures, Highland and Lowland. The long-term effects of the Reformation, the connection with England and the plantation of Ulster led to a shift in the balance in favour of the Lowlands (now split over the issue of episcopacy). When the kilt and the tartan returned in the nineteenth century, it was as part of the Romantic movement. Lowlanders flocked to identify themselves with the clans from which they had fled less than a century earlier. The cult of 'Ossian' (Oisin was the son of Fionn MacCumhail in Irish legend) added to the confusion. James Macpherson claimed to have discovered long-lost Scottish manuscripts which he claimed were earlier than their Irish counterparts and, though Dr Johnson among others denounced him as a forger, the Ossianic myth continued to exercise an extraordinary fascination. In this way Highland culture survived in transmogrified form in the Lowlands long after the social reality had passed away in the Highlands themselves.

For a good deal of the eighteenth century the significance of Scotland within a British Isles context was political, in the sense that successive governments used episcopalian discontent under the guise of 'Jacobitism' to keep alive the prospect of a 'Popish' king. During the seventeenth century Irish Catholicism had played the part of bogeyman. During the next century the Whig ministry in London cast the episcopalians in a similar role. The long Whig ascendancy after 1714 rested in large measure upon the way in which the Whigs played the 'Jacobite card'. The passing of the Septennial Act in 1716, extending the life of parliament from three to seven years, was made possible by the fear of Jacobitism. Scotland influenced the course of English history in the seventeenth century; it did so equally, if less dramatically, during the eighteenth.

Under the influence of Sir Lewis Namier, historians of the eighteenth century have been particularly prone to see the history of England in narrowly English terms. If the approach adopted here is correct, however, this is a self-defeating procedure. England, as a consequence of decisions made during the Reformation period, had become the centre of an empire, the various cultures of which interacted with those of the mother country as well as with each other. The culture of the English establishment undoubtedly became more powerful than it had been earlier but the fact remains that the cultures of the 'periphery', especially those of Scotland and colonial America, influenced the course of events in England itself. Ireland was more isolated, but even here, as we have seen, the Scotch-Irish came to form part of the story of 1776. In England, the names of Swift, Burke, Goldsmith and Sheridan indicate that the Anglo-Irish element in the culture of the metropolis cannot be ignored. In addition, though the 'Irish Question' did not assume the proportions which it reached during the nineteenth century, unrest in Ireland during the crisis years of 1796–1800 became an object of great concern for Pitt's administration. Pitt was willing to risk alienating Protestant opinion by granting concessions to Irish Catholics in order to make Ireland more secure. The Irish rebellion of 1798 also made possible an Act of Union between Great Britain and Ireland. This was an enactment which proved to have profound consequences for the history of the British Isles during the nineteenth and twentieth centuries.

Over much of the history of the English empire during the eighteenth century there looms the shadow of the Reformation rather than the Enlightenment. In order to understand the outlook of the various cultures which went to make up the empire, it is the events of the century earlier rather than those of the eighteenth century itself which provide the key. In England, the execution of Charles I was still a live issue, in Ireland, the massacre of 1641, in Scotland, Montrose and Claverhouse, in colonial America, the memory of Russell and Sidney. The Glorious Revolution of 1688 was merely one of a number of events which gave meaning to particular pasts.

9

The Britannic melting pot

During the course of the nineteenth and twentieth centuries the balance of cultures within the British Isles once more shifted radically. In England, the social, demographic and economic changes, which are usually subsumed under the portmanteau concept 'Industrial Revolution', led to the creation of a new urban culture in 'the north', a term which may be used to include the industrial areas of the west midlands as well as the areas north of the Trent. 'The north' in this sense comprised the large cities of Birmingham, Liverpool, Manchester, Sheffield, Leeds and Newcastle, the factory towns of Lancashire and Yorkshire and the mining villages of the counties north of Nottinghamshire. Historians have tended to treat 'the midlands' as if it were different from 'the north'. In fact, however, there seems to be no good reason why we should not look upon 'the midlands' as a sub-culture within the north. From this point of view, the midlands, Merseyside, Manchester and its hinterland, the West Riding, Tyneside and Teesside all constituted sub-cultures within an overwhelmingly industrial 'northern' culture. (An exception to this general northern pattern was Cornwall with its tin and copper mining.)

The new economic importance of 'the north' appeared all the more striking when contrasted with the decline of London as an industrial centre. Industries, such as shipbuilding and silk weaving, unable to compete with northern competition, sank into insignificance. Other skilled trades such as coopering and watch manufacture declined, especially after 1850. In 1870, Sir Charles Trevelyan described the metropolis as 'a gigantic engine for depraving and degrading our population' and 'a common sink of everything that is worst in the United Kingdom'. In some occupations, such as dock labour, brewing and transport, wages were driven down by the importation of cheap labour from the depressed agricultural counties of the south-west, from Wales and from Ireland. The immigration of many thousands of east European Jews in the 1880s led to fierce competition in the tailoring and shoemaking industries, already hard-pressed by provincial competition. London retained its importance as a banking and insurance centre but in general it lost ground to 'the north'.

Changes in the cultural balance also took place in other parts of the British Isles largely as a consequence of those which occurred in England. In Scotland, the growth

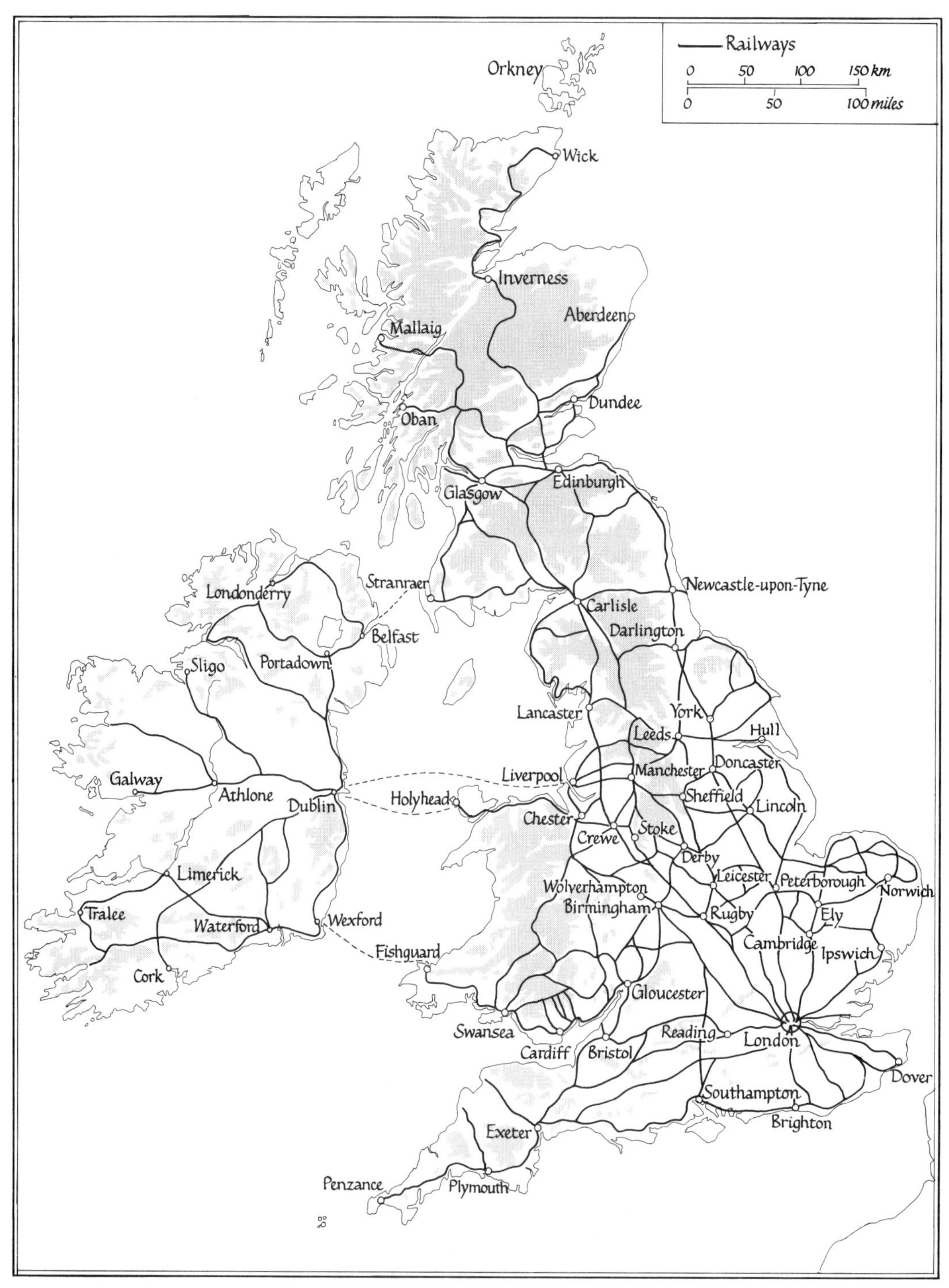

MAP 6 The railway age during the nineteenth century

of Glasgow and the towns which surrounded it led to the rapid rise of Clydeside as a centre of industry and mining, rivalling the English west midlands. Social and economic change were accompanied in due course by religious change, in this case by the split known as the 'Disruption' (1843) within the established Presbyterian Church. In terms of Scotland as a whole the Highlands became less important. The division between Highlands and Lowlands was overshadowed by a new divide, that between the heavily industrial south-west and the more conservative and rural east, with Edinburgh as its capital. As in Wales and Ireland, there was an anglicised gentry in Scotland, which, as an ascendancy class, retained much of its power and influence. Amid all this change there took place the rise of new sub-cultures created by the influx of Catholic and Protestant immigrants from Ulster in search of employment.

In Wales, similar changes took place as a consequence of the industrialisation of south Wales and to a lesser extent of north-west Wales. As we have seen, there had always been regional differences in Wales, but the contrast between the Welsh-speaking rural north and the more anglicised industrial south was intensified by the economic and social changes of the nineteenth century. Cardiff became a 'melting pot' attracting English and Irish immigrants as well as internal migrants from Cardiganshire and rural counties. Welshmen also poured into Liverpool, and any history of Wales which left out the role of Liverpool during this period would be unbalanced. In the early twentieth century a revivalist preacher said that he preferred to speak in 'Welsh Liverpool' rather than 'English Cardiff'. A third culture, that of the English-orientated gentry, lost ground during this period. Gentry families which dominated the parliamentary representation of Wales in 1800 had vanished from view by 1900.

It remains to mention Ireland. Here the counterpart of the rise of northern England, Clydeside and Glamorgan was the industrial expansion of Belfast and the Lagan valley. It was Ulster which benefited from the Act of Union in spite of the initial fears of Orangemen. The south, by contrast, suffered from considerable de-industrialisation and the infant industries which had made their appearance under the wing of the protectionist legislation before 1800 found it impossible to compete with the flood of cheap goods from England. Dublin became an economic backwater as Belfast prospered. Ulster, which had taken very much a second place to the south for much of the later medieval and early modern period, became the centre of a confident, expanding culture. One of the casualties of the nineteenth century was the Anglo-Irish ascendancy, which, like its equivalent in Wales, gradually lost its political grip, outside the province of Ulster.

Historians once argued that the rapid growth of British industrial cities was made possible by a shift of population from the rural south to the industrial north. Their emphasis now is upon the influx into the cities from local areas. Looked at in the context of the British Isles, however, it is clear that there was a good deal of population movement from one cultural zone to another. The result was to create in cities such as Glasgow, Liverpool, Belfast and Cardiff a 'melting pot' effect, marked by inter-ethnic hostility. Football teams such as Celtic and Rangers in Glasgow, Hearts and Hibernian in Edinburgh, Dundee United and Dundee F.C. in Dundee, Belfast Celtic and Linfield in Belfast and Everton and Liverpool on Merseyside drew their support from different ethnic communities. In Wales, internal migrants from the rural north faced the hostility of the southerners who denounced the 'Cardies' from Cardiganshire.

In northern England, Jack Lawson looking back from 1932 described the way in which 'the county of Durham has become a sort of social melting pot owing to the rapid development of the coalfield during the nineteenth century'.

By the time of which I write [1890s] there was a combination of Lancashire, Cumberland, Yorkshire, Staffordshire, Cornish, Irish, Scottish, Welsh, Northumbrian and Durham accents. All these and more tongues were to be heard in a marked way; and not only that, but the families in each group gravitated together and formed a common bond. (Jack Lawson, 'A Man's Life', quoted in W. H. B. Court, *British Economic History 1870–1914: Commentary and Documents* (Cambridge, 1965), p. 97.)

Lawson also commented on the difference between the relatively settled older collieries in the east of the county and the mobile populations of the new collieries in the west: 'A new colliery or a new seam meant bigger money and there was always an emigration followed by the incoming of new people to take their place' (*ibid.*).

One of the main consequences of the intermingling of cultures within the British Isles was the rise of inter-ethnic hostility particularly in relation to Irish Catholics and, in the late nineteenth century, to Jews also. Catholic Emancipation, which was a relatively minor reform proposal in some eyes, aroused strong feelings because it implied the entry of Catholic Irish into parliament. In the 1840s the Maynooth Grant issue became, in Harriet Martineau's words, 'the great political controversy of the day – the subject on which society is going mad' (quoted in E. R. Norman, *Anti-Catholicism in Victorian England* (1968), p. 23).) 'No Popery' and hostility to new migrants became an explosive political mixture. In Stockport in 1842, where the proportion of Irish-born had risen from 7 per cent to 10 per cent, a large crowd carried an effigy of the Catholic parish priest through the Irish quarter and tore it to pieces. William Murphy, leader of the Protestant Electoral Union, surrounded by the bodyguard of 'Stalybridge lads', held a series of violent 'No Popery' meetings in 1867–8. During the 1868 general election at Stalybridge, Conservative party placards were headed

THE QUEEN OR THE POPE
which will you have to reign over you – will you suffer Mr Gladstone to destroy the supremacy of your sovereign and substitute the supremacy of the Pope? Sidebottom calls to English freemen to assert their rights. (Neville Kirk, 'Ethnicity, Class and Popular Toryism 1850–1870', in K. Lunn, *Hosts, Immigrants and Minorities* (London, 1980))

In 1868, English reaction to Irish sympathy for executed Fenian prisoners, known as the 'Manchester Martyrs', led to widespread rioting. The rise of the Home Rule movement in Ireland from the 1880s onwards led to a further intensification of ethnic rivalries throughout the British Isles.

Historians have become accustomed to thinking of the British Isles in terms of four national histories each of which could be dealt with separately in its own terms, English, Welsh, Scottish or Irish. As we have seen, however, there were at least two cultures in England, three in Wales, three in Scotland (four if we include Shetland and Orkney) and two in Ireland (or three with the Gaelic west). A source of additional complexity is the fact in some areas these cultures overlapped, thus introducing problems arising from inter-ethnic rivalries. The influx of east European Jews in the 1880s was another factor in the situation. The early modern period (c. 1500–c. 1700) had been marked by heavy out-migration into Ireland and the American colonies from Britain. The modern period was characterised by large-scale movement of population into the industrial areas of Britain from Ireland and elsewhere. The history of the British Isles during this period resembles that of the United States more than is commonly realised. From this point of view the multi-ethnic character of modern Britain is a continuation of nineteenth-century trends.

There is, finally, the additional complication that the various cultures of the British Isles were an immense source of emigrants to North America, the United States as well as Canada, and to Australia, New Zealand and South Africa. This nineteenth-century migration was much less exclusively English than that of the seventeenth century. The Catholic Irish who had avoided emigration in earlier periods now came to accept emigration as an unavoidable, if unwelcome, necessity. The Scots also emigrated in large numbers both from Highlands and Lowlands. Only the Welsh who had the mines of south Wales as their 'New World' were not represented in proportion to their numbers. The new empire of the nineteenth century was very much the creation of the British Isles as a whole and as a consequence reflected the tensions of the cultural complex from which it originated.

From the late eighteenth century onwards the structure of English society changed radically under the impact of rapid industrialisation and urbanisation. By the early twentieth century over four-fifths of a vastly increased population lived in towns, compared with one third in the mid-eighteenth century. The proportion of the population engaged in agriculture dropped to 5 per cent from well over 33 per cent earlier. In broad terms the continuing 'Industrial Revolution' is the most important fact with which the historian has to deal. It is not the only fact, however. The Act of Union with Ireland (1800) brought the complexities of Irish politics and society into the heart of the Westminster parliament, where they could not be ignored. Irish immigration into England also introduced ethnic problems, which were aggravated by a 'nativist' reaction in particular areas. 'Ireland' during this period became a new feature of the English political landscape at both the national and local level. There was also the fact of religious revival among all the Christian denominations. Though half the population remained uninterested in organised religion, the proportion of religious activists rose dramatically in the course of the century. The most noteworthy change was the rise of dissent from the position of a minority to numerical equality with the Established Church. Class feeling, religious consciousness and ethnic rivalries were interrelated poles around which much of English life revolved.

At the end of the Napoleonic wars the dominant culture was still that of the Anglican establishment, encompassing a wide variety of opinion and life-style. It was agreed by such influential spokesmen as Blackstone, Burke and Paley that an Established Church was essential for the preservation of social order. In the early nineteenth century, as in the eighteenth, membership of the Established Church was needed for full participation in politics, in the army and the learned professions. Anglican control of the universities and the great public schools led almost inevitably to this consequence. At Oxford, acceptance of the thirty-nine articles of the Church of England was necessary for matriculation and at Cambridge, for admission to a degree.

As we have seen, during the eighteenth century, the conflict between the cultures of Church and dissent was a major theme of the history of the English empire, with victory going to the Church in England itself and to dissent in the American colonies. In England, during the nineteenth century, industrial and demographic expansion in 'the north' provided an opportunity of which the dissenting sects took more advantage than the Established Church. The towns of the West Riding were strongholds of nonconformity and in cities such as Birmingham, Liverpool, Leicester and Sheffield, the city council came to be dominated by dissenters after the electoral reforms of the 1830s.

The attention of some historians has been concentrated in recent years upon the 'Making of the English Working Class'. In fact, however, it seems to have been the relative deprivation which the dissenters experienced which fuelled most of the agitation against the establishment during the 1820s and 1830s. The repeal of the Test and Corporation Acts in 1828 and the establishment of University College, London, in the same year testified to the new strength of the dissenters. It was followed by pressure for further political change which led eventually to the passing of the Reform Act of 1832. This in its turn led to a growing demand for the remedy of specific dissenting grievances, especially the payment of tithes, the levying of Church rates to pay for the upkeep of the fabric of the parish church, the legal requirement that dissenters should be married within a Church of the establishment and the continued exclusion of dissenters from Oxford and Cambridge. In 1833 dissenting leaders attacked the union of Church and state as unjust and unscriptural. In 1834 a dissenting conference of 400 delegates under the chairmanship of Edward Baines, a prominent Leeds nonconformist, demanded the disestablishment of the Church.

The animosity between the two cultures of Church and dissent dominated English politics throughout the nineteenth century. During a period of considerable industrial change it might have been expected that 'class conflict' would come to the fore. This was true of some areas during the late 1830s when the Chartist movement reached its peak. In general, however, sectarian animosity seems to have been far more important. In his *Autobiography* 'Mark Rutherford' commented that, 'Generally speaking, there were two shops of each trade; one of which was patronised by the church and Tories, and another by the Dissenters and Whigs. The inhabitants were divided into two distinct camps – of the Church and Tory camp the other camp knew nothing' ('Mark Rutherford' (sc. W. H. White), *Autobiography* (1981), p. 34). Hostility between Church and dissent broke out not infrequently into violence or near violence. At Newark the parson ordered the fire engine to be wheeled out to hose a dissenting preacher. Dissenting chapels continued to seek the obscurity of the back streets in some towns. In Cambridgeshire, dissenters were unacceptable as tenants on the estates of strongly Tory squires. There is no doubt as England became more religious in the nineteenth century in the sense that the power of organised religion grew, a sharper awareness of rivalry developed between the cultures of Church and dissent.

The Lancashire towns of Blackburn and Ashton may be taken as illustrating what the contrast between the cultures of Church and dissent meant in practice. It was said of Blackburn by a critic that

> it is a thorough going Tory community. Strong drink is the secret of its own and Britain's greatness; after that its heart has been given for long year to the Church and cockfighting. Be sober, lead a decent and respectable life and your genuine Blackburner will wax red at the mention of your name and dismiss you as 'a *** Dissenter.

In general, Tory millowners were less interested in inculcating 'improving' virtues and more tolerant of the workingman's beer. In the liberal areas of Blackburn, the most important mills were those of the Pilkington brothers, one of whom, James, was Liberal M.P. for the town. Here the headquarters of the Liberal party at election times were to be found in the Congregational chapel and the schoolroom, both built with Pilkington patronage. In Ashton and Stalybridge, where dissenters were in a majority, workingmen's educational classes and mutual improvement societies were popular, and temperance was much more of an issue. At Ashton the Mason works became a centre of moral improvement with 'library, baths, burial society, mothers class (Sunday devotional meetings), bowling green, gymnasium, brass band and weekly lectures'. The local Tory newspapers regarded all this munificence as an attempt to impose morality by authoritarian means. At a higher social level the passion of Lord Derby for whist, horse-racing and gambling offers an interesting contrast.

The contrast between the cultures of Church and dissent was, to a great extent, one between a largely rural 'south' and a heavily industrialised 'north'. Asa Briggs has remarked that 'a nineteenth century conflict between North and South was as much a leading theme of English as of American history' (*The Age of Improvement 1783–1867* (1959), p. 50). As the dominant Toryism of Blackburn makes clear, however, the dominance of dissent in the north was never absolute. Cobden, spokesman for the 'Manchester school of Free Trade', was an Anglican. John Fielden, the Tory critic of the factory system, was M.P. for the northern town of Oldham, and owner of a cotton mill at Todmorden.

The north was industrialised England, stretching from Newcastle in the north-east to Birmingham in the west midlands. The textile industries in Lancashire and Yorkshire, the metal industries in Birmingham, potteries at Stoke on Trent, and mining in the north-east were the centres of a continuing process of industrialisation. New towns such as Oldham in the first half of the century and Barrow and Middlesbrough in the second made their appearance. The eighteenth-century ports of Bristol and Liverpool, once heavily dependent on the slave trade for their prosperity, found themselves functioning as outlets of the industrial north. Within this region there were large areas given over to agriculture and pastoral farming. The North Riding of Yorkshire and north Lancashire were mainly rural, but the main trend within the north was towards ever greater industrialisation on the basis of its rich deposits of coal and iron. In what was once a relatively unpopulated highland Zone, there were by the early twentieth century five large conurbations: Merseyside, Leeds, Manchester, Sheffield and Birmingham. In Northumberland, one in every four workers was a miner, one in five a worker in heavy industry. In Durham the proportion was one in three and one in four respectively.

'The south', with the large exception of London was, in contrast, dominated by great landed estates, whose landlords were, on the whole, Tory and Anglican. (The existence of Whig landlords does not alter the general validity of this picture.) In rural areas the expectation was that tenants would vote as their landlords wished. In Suffolk a witness declared that 'the individual feeling among farmers is that their vote is their landlords''. In 1841, a landlord stated that 'I did think that interference between a landlord with whose views you were acquainted and his tenants was not justifiable according to those laws of delicacy and propriety which I consider binding in such cases.' Another advised his tenants to vote 'in such a manner as should appear to them to be right and according to good conscience and as most likely to uphold that Church in which the purest doctrines of our religion are taught in the best manner'. In 1831 the duke of Northumberland 'desired' of his tenants to sign a petition against the Reform Bill, asking to know the names of those who did not. In return for rent reductions in bad times, landlords expected some recognition of their generosity at election times. As Sir Frederick Pollock put it in his discussion of the Land Laws,

> The landlord in return expects a certain amount of deference and compliance in various matters from his tenants. Not only does the farmer meet him halfway on questions of shooting rights, and allow free passage to the hunt, but his political support of the landlord is not infrequently reckoned on with as much confidence as the performance of the covenants and conditions of the tenancy itself. In the case of holdings from year to year it may be not unfairly said that being of the landlord's political party is often a tacit condition of the tenancy. (F. Pollock, *The Land Laws* (London, 1883), pp. 150–1)

An attempt to identify a distinctive ideology of northern dissent would need to take into account such figures as Samuel Smiles and John Bright. Though born in Scotland, Smiles lived in Leeds from 1838 to 1858. His best-selling book, *Self Help*, which had sold a quarter of a million copies by 1905, put forward the self-made man as a praiseworthy social ideal. His heroes were the innovators and engineers of the new northern industrial society, Wedgwood, Brindley and Stephenson, whose success he thought could be emulated at a humbler level by the average workingman. Thrift and temperance were habits which could enable workingmen to become capitalists themselves. 'A glass of beer', he wrote, 'is equal to forty five shillings a year. This sum will insure a man's life for a hundred and thirty pounds payable at death or placed in a savings bank, it would amount to a hundred pounds in twenty years.' A man with savings in hand could 'boldly look the world in the face ... He can dictate his own terms. He can neither be bought nor sold. He can look forward to an old age of comfort and happiness.'

John Bright (1811–89), son of a Rochdale millowner, began his political career in 1830 with a speech advocating temperance. In 1840 he fought a successful campaign at Rochdale against the imposition of Church rate upon dissenters. His later denunciations of the establishment cannot be separated from his dissenting background. His view of English history derived from the Puritans of the seventeenth century. He thought Milton was 'the greatest man who had ever lived'. In 1866 he wrote to a friend that 'blows must be struck from this historical standpoint. Our forefathers thought so also, 200 years ago.' He attacked the southern aristocracy. 'The [Anti-Corn Law] League is the foe of aristocratic injustice and the State Church is the creature and tool of the aristocracy.' Bright's radicalism was not typical of all dissenters (the Wesleyans were always more conservative), but his views found a home in the Liberal party which was very much the party of the north against the south.

Puritanism, as the widespread influence of Smiles and Bright shows, was a key element in this northern culture. Bright found Shakespeare unfit to read and only came round to accepting novels after a good deal of heart-searching. Methodists, when in power locally, were likely to suppress the theatre. Fiction was banned from the Methodist school at Woodhouse Green near Leeds. Novels which did enter a Methodist household were described as 'the deceitful bakemeats of some huxtering heathen smuggled into a Levite's tent'. It was such attitudes as these which Matthew Arnold was to criticise in his *Culture and Anarchy* (1869).

If dissent found its spokesmen in such figures as John Bright and Samuel Smiles, the establishment found an eloquent defender in Benjamin Disraeli. Disraeli (1804–81), of Bohemian temperament, middle-class background and Jewish origins, was an unlikely candidate for such a role, but his success was greater than that of a not dissimilar 'outsider', Edmund Burke. Disraeli's opportunity came in 1846 in the parliamentary debate over the Corn Laws. He launched a fierce attack on the 'school of Manchester', of which Cobden and Bright were the prime representatives.

He defended the aristocracy on the ground of history. England possessed a territorial constitution and it was the land which bore the burdens of 'the revenues of the Church, the administration of justice, and the estate of the poor'. He saw his aim, he said later, as 'to uphold the aristocratic settlement of this country. That is the only question at stake however manifold the forms it assumes.' The aristocracy, in his view, was 'the only security for self government, the only barrier against that centralising system which has taken root in other countries'. It was not surprising that he should sympathise with the 'aristocratic' south during the American civil war.

In an industrial age, Disraeli waxed eloquent on the joys of rural life. In 1860 he held a summer fête on his small estate of Hughenden (bought with a loan from his patron Lord George Bentinck in 1846 as an entrée into the world of the squire-archy).

> There are 100 school children, [he wrote] as many farmers with their wives and all the county families for ten miles around – Sir George and Lady Dashwood, Colonel and Mrs. Fane, Sir Anthony and Lady Rothschild and a great assemblage of squires and clergymen. Lord Tredegar who never forgets that I made him a peer sent me a buck. They feasted in the open air and danced until sunset amid trees that were planted in the reign of Queen Anne and when Bolingbroke was Secretary of State.

Later he wrote to a friend, 'We have realised a romance we have been many years meditating; we have restored the house to what it was before the Civil Wars and we have made a garden of terraces in which cavaliers might roam and saunter with their lady loves.' Disraeli's view of English history was clearly very different from that of John Bright. In his Young England days before 1846, Disraeli had admired Laud and Strafford, and this Tory view of history remained an important element in conservative perceptions of the past. In 1910, when the constitutional position of the peerage was under attack, a defender wrote how 'In 1641 the English House of Commons abolished the Second Chamber and the House of Commons became the greatest tyrant to the democracy of England that there has been seen.' In contrast, the 'Whig' interpretation of Stuart history in which Laud and Strafford were the villains of the piece found a more sympathetic audience among the dissenters of the north.

Disraeli, though a self-made man himself, was no admirer of meritocracy. He criticised Gladstone for introducing competitive examinations into the Civil Service and when he was in power himself he wrote, 'I want a man of the world, and of birth, breeding culture and station to be the chief of the Civil Service Commission so that if any absurd or pedantic schemes of qualification are put before him he may integrate and modify them and infuse them with a necessary degree of common-sense.'

Disraeli's political career spanned the years of greatest crisis for the establishment. It began in the 1830s when to an ambitious young politician like Disraeli the future seemed to be with the Whigs. It continued in the 1840s when he became identified with opposition to the policies of the Peelite leadership of the Tory party. In 1845 Disraeli attacked the renewal of the Maynooth Grant. In 1846 he remained with the majority of the Tory party after Peel decided to repeal the Corn Laws. For the next two decades the establishment was on the defensive until Disraeli led it to victory in the general election of 1874.

What requires explanation is how the establishment managed to survive, in spite of the rising power of dissent. To churchmen of the 1830s the outlook for the establishment seemed gloomy. The 1832 Reform Act appeared as the first step in a process of revolutionary change, and the disendowment measures which the Whig government proposed to take with respect to the Church of Ireland had obvious implications for the Church of England. That the establishment did survive during the critical years of the 1830s was due in large measures to four factors. In the first place, the Whig leaders were by no means united on the issue and one of the ablest of them, Edward Stanley, resigned on the Irish Church issue. More important, perhaps were the fears of social and political revolution aroused by the Chartist movement during the late 1830s. The violent rhetoric of the Chartist leaders and the rising at Newport in 1839 played into the hands of the defenders of the establishment. Thirdly, the dissenters themselves were divided. Wesleyan Methodists who were the largest of the dissenting bodies kept clear of advocating disestablishment. Fourthly, what appeared to be the advance of 'Popery' encouraged the cultivation of good relations between evangelical churchmen and their counterparts in the world of dissent. Disestablishment did not go away as an issue, however, and during the middle years of the century it was kept alive by radical dissenters under the leadership of Edward Miall, a former nonconformist minister, who founded the British anti-State Church association, later known as the Liberation Society.

Though it makes good sense of much of English history during this period to see it in terms of a clash of two cultures, English involvement in the affairs of the British Isles cannot be left out of account. Ireland in particular came to occupy a more central place than had hitherto been the case. After the Act of Union there was direct Irish representation at Westminster. The fact that Irish Catholics were excluded from membership of the House of Commons despite the fact that Catholic forty-shilling freeholders could vote fuelled the flame of constitutional agitation during the 1820s. Catholic Emancipation was looked upon as the first step in the overthrow of the constitution. During the 1830s Whig proposals to reform the Church of Ireland led to cries of 'the Church in Danger' within England itself. During the 1840s, the crisis over the Maynooth Grant question and the challenge presented by the Irish Famine led to serious divisions within the governing Conservative party. The long-term effect of the Act of Union was to thrust Irish issues upon the attention of successive Westminster governments, which found it difficult to treat them on their own merits, irrespective of their implications for England.

In April 1848, the following appeared in *The Economist*:

> Thank God we are Saxons! Flanked by the savage Celt on the one side and the flighty Gaul on the other – the one a slave to his passions, the other a victim to the theories of the hour – we feel deeply grateful from our inmost hearts that we belong to a race, which if it cannot boast the flowing fancy of one of its neighbours, nor the brilliant *esprit* of the other has an ample compensation in [a] social, slow, reflective phlegmatic temperament.

The 'racial' interpretation of Irish history appealed to many in the nineteenth century and is still not quite dead even in the best academic circles. As an explanation of the complexities of Irish history, however, it is quite inadequate. In Ireland, as in England, the concept of culture provides a better source of enlightenment as to why Irish history in the nineteenth century took the course it did.

In the late eighteenth century, Ireland, like England, was a society dominated by the landed estate. In any particular locality the inhabitants identified themselves as being within the jurisdiction of a particular landlord or his agent. Estates were made up of 'townlands' which formed the basic rental unit, but, though the townland provided the framework for day-to-day living, it was the landlord or his agent who made the crucial decisions about a particular tenant's future. The 'Protestant ascendancy' was an ascendancy of landlords. The Irish parliament was dominated by the landlord, or the borough representatives which they chose. At the parliamentary level, political differences related to such matters as the 'Absentee Tax' which smaller landlords periodically proposed to levy upon larger, absentee magnates. The siting of roads or canals, important for the prosperity of an estate, was another issue which politics might decide. The perquisite of political power included patronage in the Church, the army and the administration.

The history of Ireland in the nineteenth century thus revolves by and large around the decline and fall of the Protestant ascendancy and its key institution, the landed estate. The 'Golden Age' of the ascendancy is frequently associated with 'Georgian Ireland'. The demise of the Irish parliament, brought about by the Act of Union of 1800, is thought to mark the beginning of the end. In fact, the power of the ascendancy reinforced by urban elements was to last for a century after the Act of Union. The landlords continued to enjoy considerable local power and influence until the Local Government Act of 1898 did away with the Grand Jury. In many respects, it may be argued the ascendancy lasted in Northern Ireland until 1972 when the last of the old-style landlords, Chichester Clark, finally gave way to a businessman, Brian Faulkner.

During the course of the nineteenth century, the balance of power within the ascendancy shifted in favour of the north. Industrial growth was centred on Belfast which rose in population from 37,000 in 1821 to nearly 350,000 by 1901. The population of Dublin which had been 336,000 in 1821 had risen to only 448,000 in 1901 and much of this increase had taken place without any industrialisation. Dublin remained a centre of consumption while Belfast became a centre of production in linen spinning and weaving and in shipbuilding. In Ulster by the end of the century there were 900,000 Protestants, of whom 670,000 lived in Belfast and its hinterland.

Within a radius of about 65 miles around Belfast, Protestants amounted to over 75 per cent of the population. Nearly half the factories in Ireland and over 75 per cent of factory workers were concentrated in the north-east. In the three southern provinces, Protestants, mostly episcopalian, amounted to only 10 per cent of the population, mainly concentrated around Dublin and Cork. The northern Protestants were divided almost equally between episcopalian and Presbyterian but the old animosities between the two groups had died away to a large extent in an environment of industrialism and in the face of a revived Catholicism.

In the south the influence of such magnates as the marquess of Lansdowne and the duke of Devonshire remained. More and more, however, power shifted to the Catholic middle class which found a charismatic leader in Daniel O Connell, lawyer, brewer, banker and landowner. Ireland is often described as a 'peasant society' but this vague concept tends to obscure the complexity of Irish social structure. Catholics were under-represented in the middle class in proportion to their numbers but they cannot be ignored. It has been estimated that in Cork and Waterford they made up one third of all merchants. In 1861, the first year that statistics are available, Catholics formed roughly a third of the medical and legal professions. They also formed a high proportion of 'strong farmers'. Finally, but not least important, the Catholic clergy seem to have been drawn in large measure from the middle class. In 1826 a student at Maynooth declared: 'I conceive my parents to belong to that state of life which we call the middle class of society; and with regard to the generality of students at Maynooth it is my opinion that their parents belong to the same order of persons.' By 'the middle class' he went on to explain that he meant those persons in commerce or agriculture 'who can live independently and who, perhaps, could provide for their children a situation that could be more lucrative than the priesthood'. The president of Maynooth also stated in 1826 that 'our students are generally the sons of farmers who must be comfortable in order to meet the expenses I have already mentioned: of tradesmen, shopkeepers: and not a very small proportion of them are the children of opulent merchants and rich farmers and graziers'. The rise in status of the Catholic clergy during the nineteenth century was symptomatic of the general rise of a Catholic middle class.

Though denied the right to sit in parliament in 1795, the Catholic middle class had held aloof from the rebellion of 1798. Archbishop Troy of Dublin declared in 1793 that 'society implies different classes and orders of men, necessarily subordinate and dependent'. In 1793, Bishop Coppinger of Cloyne and Ross asked 'How can there be cultivation where there are no tillers? And where shall you find tillers if all become gentlemen?'

> Rank and property must go hand in hand, the inequality of both in every civilised country must be as various as the talents of men. Were every individual in the land possessed at this day of an equal share of property, a lapse of twelve months would exhibit numerous gradations. The industrious, the thrifty, the honest, the temperate would soon surpass the idle, the squanderers, and the licentious.

It was anticipated that loyalty would be rewarded after the passing of the Act of Union which the Catholic bishops supported on the understanding that Catholics would be eligible to sit in the House of Commons. In the event, it took two more decades before O Connell, who himself had opposed the 1798 rebellion, was able to force the issue after a good deal of agitation. In 1828, O Connell defeated a popular Protestant landowner in a Clare by-election and the British government finally gave way on the issue of Catholic Emancipation, in the teeth of opposition from the ascendancy. 'Catholic Emancipation' was a success for the Catholic middle class in Ireland comparable to that which the dissenters obtained in 1832 in England. As with 1832, however, the Catholic victory of 1829 left the landlords in possession of much of the field.

Though it would be easy to press the analogy too far it may be argued that the perceptions of the northern English dissenter paralleled those of the Catholic middle class in Ireland. Both groups felt themselves to be excluded from the full life of their society. O Connell's Repeal programme of 1832 which called for the abolition of tithes, Church rates and vestry cess was similar to the reform programme of the dissenters. Like the dissenters, the Irish Catholic middle class objected to the control which the Established Church exercised over higher education and, like them, they established their own university, Newman's Catholic University in Dublin in the one case, and Owens College, Manchester, in the other. In both groups there were strongly 'democratic' sentiments. Tocqueville, on a visit to Ireland in 1835 commented about the political outlook of the higher clergy: 'The feelings expressed were extremely democratic. Distrust and hatred of the great landlords; love of the people and confidence in them. Bitter memories of past oppression. An air of exaltation at present of approaching victory.' He might very well have found a similar outlook among the leaders of northern English dissent. Though poles apart in theology, the Liberation Society of dissenting England and the Catholic National Association of Ireland saw eye-to-eye on the question of disestablishment and agreed to work with one another.

Links between English dissent and the Irish middle class were expanded upon in a letter from John Bright which was read out at a meeting of the National Association in Dublin in 1864. Bright applauded their efforts at land reform and indeed urged them to go further. He went on to say with regard to the State Church:

> [it] is an institution so evil and so odious under the circumstances of your country that it makes one almost hopeless of Irish freedom that Irishmen have borne it so long. The whole Liberal Party in Great Britain will, doubtless, join with you in demanding the removal of a wrong which has no equal in the character of a national insult in any other civilised and Christian country in the world.

(Bright, however, opposed Home Rule in 1886.)

In 1800, there were three cultures in Ireland, episcopalian, Presbyterian and Catholic, each with its own tradition of Christianity, its own ethnic identity and its own version of Irish history. By mid-century, joined by a common fear of resurgent 'Popery', episcopalians (of English background) and Presbyterians (of Scottish background) were tending to merge their differences under the common label 'Protestant', which had thitherto been confined to episcopalians. Among the episcopalians, evangelicalism gained ground. Among the Presbyterians, 'Old Light' unitarianism lost influence in the face of a militant 'New Light' movement, led by Henry Cooke of Belfast. Among the Catholics, Moderates such as Daniel Murray, archbishop of Dublin, were succeeded by Ultramontanes, whose acknowledged leader was Cardinal Paul Cullen.

Another major cause for the continued division between Catholic and Protestant cultures in Ireland must be sought in their contrasting experiences during the years of famine 1845–9. The Protestant north, where oats rather than potatoes were the main element of popular diet, was spared from famine, when the potato crop failed. It was the Catholic small farming and labouring classes in the south and west, heavily dependent upon the potato, which bore the main brunt of famine. As Professor Joseph Lee has shown (in *The Modernisation of Irish Society 1848–1918* (1973)) the labouring class, overwhelmingly Catholic, was decimated by disease and starvation during these years. By 1847, small farmers, also Catholic, who had managed to survive three years of potato failure, were forced to emigrate in large numbers, if they were not to suffer the fate of the labourers. By 1851, Ireland had lost a quarter of its population by emigration or by death, a social tragedy which had its greatest impact upon the Catholic poor. Memory of the Famine became part of the *mentalité* of Catholic culture, differentiating it from that of Protestant Ireland. It was a memory which many emigrants took with them to the New World, where in due course it provided an emotional reservoir for Irish Catholic nationalism.

In the mid-eighteenth century, Wales was in many ways a smaller version of Ireland, its population of about half a million being roughly an eighth of the population of Ireland. Like Ireland, it was a society of landed estates, whose proprietors, or their agents, controlled the political and economic life of their area. There was also an Established Church which was cut off from full communication with the mass of the people by linguistic and social barriers. The cleavage between the episcopalian ascendancy and the great majority was not as sharp in Wales as it was in Ireland, since it was not based upon recent conquest. It was there nonetheless. When one of the Wynn family was thrown from his horse after a hunt, the event coincided with a petition at a Methodist prayer meeting: 'O Arglwydd cwympa Ddiawl Mawr y Wynnstay' ('O Lord, cast down the Great Devil of Wynnstay'). Dissent became the religion of most Welsh religious activists much as a 'reformed' Catholicism became the creed of the Irish majority, and perhaps for much the same reasons. Dissenting ministers, like the Catholic clergy, were able to express openly, or at least to symbolise, the resentments which fear of eviction kept concealed among the tenantry. Political representation, as in Ireland, was in the hands of the ascendancy and the survival of the Test and Corporation Acts on the statute book until 1828 served as a reminder that the dissenting majority was excluded from full participation in national life.

Given these political and social circumstances, it is not surprising that there should have been some reaction in Wales to the revolutions in America and France. Two of the most prominent individuals involved were Richard Price, the Welsh-born minister of a congregation at Stoke Newington and David Williams, a friend of Benjamin Franklin. Price's pamphlet *Observations on the Nature of Civil Liberty* (1776) was an attempt to place American resistance in a wide context of political rights and it was his sermon in 1789, praising the French revolution, which provoked Edmund Burke's *Reflections*. David Williams was closely involved with the Girondins during the French revolution and after their fall he returned to England. Radical ideas were also put forward by the London-Welsh society Gwyneddigion, whose most prolific member was Edward Williams ('Iolo Morganwg'). In Wales itself, however, there was no equivalent of the United Irishmen. When a French landing took place at Fishguard in 1797 it aroused confusion and consternation rather than enthusiasm. To some Welsh Baptists the French revolution presaged the coming of Anti-Christ. There were food riots during the war years as well as anti-militia and anti-press gang riots but these were local demonstrations rather than an indication of widespread revolutionary sympathies. The hatred of the crowd was directed against farmers and corn dealers rather than the landowning classes.

The attitude of dissenting ministers in Wales towards the French revolution was similar to that of most of the Catholic clergy in Ireland. Other parallels may also be drawn. Both groups looked upon popular oral culture as the enemy of Christian morality. In 1791 the great Methodist reformer, Thomas Charles of Bala, wrote to a friend: 'No harps but the *golden* harps of which St John speaks, have been played in this neighbourhood for several months past. The craft is not only in danger but entirely destroyed and abolished.' In another letter he wrote: 'The revival of religion has put an end to all the merry meetings for dancing, singing with the harp, and every kind of sinful mirth, which used to be so prevalent amongst young people here' (quoted in Eric Hobsbawm and Terence Ranger, eds., *The Invention of Tradition* (1983), p. 55). Such statements recall episcopal denunciations in Ireland of 'all unbecoming, disorderly and irreligious assemblages of people at Patrons' from the 1780s onwards.

Another resemblance between Wales and Ireland lay in the resentment felt over the payment of tithes to support what was regarded as the Church of a minority. In Ireland, the expectations aroused by Catholic Emancipation in 1829 had not been fulfilled. The result was the Tithe War of the 1830s in which the Catholic clergy of some areas took a prominent part. In Wales, discontent was aroused by an act of 1836, which in the name of tithe commutation seemed to be raising the obligations of the tithe payers. An unpopular issue was made less tolerable by economic distress. The 'Rebecca Riots' which broke out in 1839 may be seen as the Welsh equivalent of the Irish Tithe War though what finally put the match to the fire of rural discontent was not payment of tithes but the exaction of tolls upon parish roads. (The title 'Rebecca' was said to derive from the scriptural passage declaring that 'Rebecca should possess the gates of her enemies.') Tolls levied at a growing number of toll gates acted as an internal tax system which lay heaviest upon hard-pressed small farmers taking their produce to market. The area originally affected was on the Carmarthen–Pembroke border but it spread in 1842 to other counties. The New Poor Law workhouses were also an object of attack. The Rebecca Riots were firmly put down by the government, but major concessions over the turnpike system removed this particular source of discontent. Tithes still remained a major grievance, as was to be shown in the 'Tithe Wars' of 1886–91.

The course of the rural history of Wales thus clearly offers some parallels with that of rural Ireland during the late eighteenth and early nineteenth centuries. In south Wales, however, from the 1760s, changes were already in train which were to make the counties of Monmouth and Glamorgan one of the most heavily industrialised areas of the British Isles. The booming market for iron during the Seven Years War provided the take-off for the exploitation of Welsh coal and iron at Wrexham in the north as well as Merthyr in the south. The American and French wars and the growing demand for steam power led to further expansion. By 1815 the south Wales iron industry was producing one third of the total of British iron production. Barry and Swansea began to grow as ports during this period, though Cardiff and Newport were still undeveloped. In 1801, the population of the counties of Glamorgan and Monmouth amounted to a little over 100,000 in a population of over half a million. By 1901, the two counties accounted for over half the total population of 2 million. The north-east of Ireland underwent considerable industrialisation during the nineteenth century but the proportion of the Irish population involved was never more than a quarter of the total.

The consequences of industrialisation were very important for Wales since it saved the country from the massive emigration which took place in Ireland. South Wales became a melting pot in which Welsh, English and Irish were intermingled, though the great majority was Welsh. There was no equivalent of the Irish Famine, no mass emigration to America under conditions of great hardship and no Welsh equivalent of the intense involvement which Irish-Americans often displayed in the affairs of their homeland. There was thus no counterpart in Welsh history of Fenianism. A movement for Welsh Home Rule did make its appearance in the 1880s, but its strength lay in the rural areas of west Wales. When it came to the point of setting up an independent Home Rule party on the Irish model the industrial cities of south Wales stood in the way. The parallels with Ireland existed but the industrial sector of Welsh society was much stronger than its Irish counterpart.

There were, indeed, two cultures in nineteenth-century Wales. In the Welsh-speaking counties of the west, wage labour was still relatively uncommon. The social structure in many ways resembled that of parts of the west of Ireland, with its division into large farms (*lle mawr*), small farms (*lle bach*) and cottagers (*pobol tai bach*, people of the little houses). This was a heavily localised world in which there was a good deal of interdependence. Small dairy farmers needed the services of the bull, which only large farms could provide. In return they provided help at harvest time. Cottagers paid with their labour for the potato land which the farmers provided. The gentry, *y gwyr mawr* (the great people), constituted a distinctive sector of society. The problems facing Welsh rural society were related to such questions as security of tenure, rent increases and survival during a time of bad harvests and the price of store cattle and salted casked butter on which most depended for cash. This was the world of Welsh nonconformity. The Established Church found its support among the gentry, and the wage labourers of the border counties.

This culture was in sharp contrast with that of the industrialised, partially English-speaking counties of the south-east, Glamorgan, Monmouth and east Carmarthen, which were to grow in importance throughout the nineteenth century. In due course the ports of Newport, Swansea, Barry and above all Cardiff were to become the Welsh equivalents of the industrial towns of northern England. In the first half of the nineteenth century signs of industrial unrest had already made their appearance in the south. Chartism enjoyed considerable support, notably at Newport, where John Frost led a Chartist rising. During the 1820s and 1830s a secret society known as the 'Scotch Cattle' operated in the iron-mining and coal-mining villages of Monmouthshire. 'Boom' conditions from mid-century on, however, brought prosperity to the south, whose main problem was that of absorbing the large numbers of immigrants who flocked to the mining villages of the Rhondda. It was the grievances of rural Wales which provided the impetus which lay behind the rise of Welsh Liberalism. Disestablishment, tithes and evictions, not trade unions, payment in truck and strikes, were the issues on which Welsh Liberalism was to be based.

The influence of the landlords had survived the 1832 Reform Act in most Welsh counties and with them the privileges of the Established Church. In Denbighshire and Merioneth, the Wynn family retained the political power which it had enjoyed since the eighteenth century. Anti-ascendancy feeling had been expressed in 1859 in Merioneth, where an attempt to unseat a Wynn had been followed by a number of politically motivated evictions. The 1868 election, in which a wider franchise based upon the 1867 Reform Act was in operation, made possible another attack. In Denbighshire, Sir Watkin Wynn retained his seat but the Whig candidate, with whom he had agreed to 'share' the county, was defeated. The 1868 election marked the beginning of a trend which left the Liberals totally dominant in Wales. In 1885, there were thirty Welsh Liberals in the Commons and only four Welsh Conservatives.

The political pressures which led to this change came largely from the dissenting Churches, which in 1851 numbered nearly 400,000 compared with just over 100,000 attending the Established Church. Dissent, like Catholicism in Ireland, was the religion of the great majority. Hence, grievances such as Church control of education in rural areas were felt to be particularly galling. New fervour was added by the religious revival of 1859 which was a 'Year of Grace' in Wales as it was in Ulster.

The growth of Tractarianism within the Established Church also made 'No Popery' an issue. The most significant change, however, was the attempt to bring temperance into politics. The advocates of temperance reform looked upon alcohol as the main cause of social problems and they aimed to control its use by legislative action instead of moral persuasion, as had been the case earlier in the century. It was during the middle decades of the century that temperance together with Sabbatarianism and disestablishment came to be seen by many Welsh Liberals as expressing a particularly 'Welsh' outlook on life.

Though it is tempting to speak of nineteenth-century Scotland as a single unit, there were, at least, three 'Scotlands' during this period, each with their own distinctive characteristics. The Highlands (including the Hebrides) still retained their own individuality. The other two regions were the eastern and western Lowlands, which, as industrialisation gathered pace in the west, became divided into a largely rural east and a largely industrial west. For most of the century, the east maintained its traditional political, legal and cultural dominance. Edinburgh the capital was on the east coast. Three of the four Scottish universities, Edinburgh, St Andrews and Aberdeen were in the east. The best land, which was now being 'improved' under the impact of the 'Agricultural Revolution', was also in the east. Edinburgh was very much the centre of the Scottish Enlightenment and though Adam Smith was a professor at Glasgow for a time he soon settled at Kirkcaldy, within reach of Edinburgh, and his friends. The *Edinburgh Review*, drawing much of its inspiration from the Enlightenment, provided intellectual leadership for the reform movement before and after 1832. (Thomas Babington Macaulay was a member for Edinburgh from 1839 to 1847 and 1852 to 1856.) It was not until the 1880s, after the Reform Acts of 1884 and 1885, that the west was in a position to exert the political power to which its economic and demographic growth entitled it. It was then that Glasgow showed itself to be a centre of Chamberlainite radicalism, aiming to assert itself against the 'Whiggish' east. If the history of England can be seen as a struggle between north and south, that of Scotland during this period revolves around the rivalry between west and east.

The division between the Gaelic-speaking Highlands and the English-speaking Lowlands continued to be a major cultural divide. In the course of the nineteenth century, however, the significance of the Highlands within a general Scottish context began to decline. In 1801 the highland counties contained nearly a fifth of the population. By 1901, even though some counties grew in population, this had dropped to 8 per cent and by 1939 to 6.5 per cent. The balance shifted inexorably in favour of the urbanised and industrialised Lowlands. By 1901 the population of the western Lowlands, with the Glasgow conurbation as their centre, rose from one fifth to just under half the total population of 4.5 million.

The history of the Highlands during this period closely resembled that of the west of Ireland, in so far as it was marked by a rapid growth of population, famine and heavy emigration. Like Ireland, Highland society became heavily dependent on the potato, a change in diet which made it possible to feed a larger population. In some parts of the Highlands the production of kelp, an alkaline ash made from burnt seaweed, became a major local industry and a source of temporary prosperity. With the coming of peace in 1815, however, the linen, glass and soap industries were able to turn to cheaper Spanish alkalis. The economic and demographic problems of the Highlands were now intensified and whereas at an earlier period landlords had opposed emigration they now began to encourage it. Estates were turned over to the more profitable activity of sheep farming. It was during these years that the notorious 'Highland Clearances' took place on the Sutherland estate where Patrick Sellar was the agent from 1810 to 1819. Sellar also acquired an estate of his own in Morvern, when the spendthrift sixth duke of Argyll was forced to sell part of his property. Emigration now became a way of life in the Highlands, whether as the result of conscious decision or as a consequence of eviction. Many went to Nova Scotia, Cape Breton Island or Prince Edward Island. Others made their way to Glasgow, where in such towns as Greenock there were Gaelic-speaking congregations.

The failure of the potato crop first in 1837 and then again in the blight-ridden years after 1846 added a further turn of the screw. There was no equivalent in the Highlands of the Irish Famine, however. The authorities were able to cope with the shortage more successfully, in part because the affected areas could be reached by steamship. The numbers of those affected were much smaller and the landlords, or most of them, seem to have played a more generous role than their counterparts in Ireland. Though emigration was heavy, the allocation of so much land to sheep farming meant that there was a chronic shortage of land. Beneath the surface there was a good deal of resentment among the crofters against landlords and graziers, which flared up into open hostility in the early 1880s. The crofters were hard-pressed in the lean years following 1879, and they turned to the example of the Irish League in an attempt to gain security of tenure. In 1882 the Highland Land League was founded and in 1885 five crofter candidates were returned to parliament. The result was the Crofters Act of 1886 giving some measure of security on the lines of the Irish Land Act of 1881. There was to be no equivalent in Scotland of the decline of the landed ascendancy in Ireland or Wales, however. The great landed estates survived, more often than not as large-scale game preserves.

Profound cultural changes also occurred in the Highlands as a consequence of the missionary activities of the evangelicals. What the Methodists achieved in Wales and what was denied to Protestant missionaries in the west of Ireland, the evangelical wing of the Church of Scotland accomplished in the Highlands. Gaelic oral culture gave way to a biblically-orientated literacy, also in Gaelic. Of the 474 ministers who left the Church at the 'Disruption' of 1843, 101 used the Gaelic language in public worship. A ship run by the evangelicals, the *Breadalbane*, which was used to ferry ministers between the islands, played a prominent part in famine relief work in the late 1840s. The temperance movement and the strict Sabbath took root. Despite the survival of Gaelic, it may be argued that the Lowlands radically transformed the culture of the Highlands. By a curious turn of events, while this was taking place, a romanticised version of Highland culture was making headway in the Lowlands. In the wake of the Ossianic forgeries of James Macpherson and of the novels of Walter Scott, the cult of the Highlander achieved extraordinary success. The newly invented kilt and tartan were taken over by Lowland families as emblems of ethnic identity. For many, Scottish Romanticism replaced Scottish Enlightenment.

In the Highlands, conflict of interest between grazier and crofter created a situation which in many ways resembled that of the west of Ireland. In the rural areas of the eastern Lowlands, a very different social structure developed, under the impact of the Agricultural Revolution. During the 'Age of Improvement', which lasted well into the nineteenth century, changes occurred which involved the disappearance of traditional rural units. The shared farming arrangements of 'runrig', which in some ways resembled the strip system of the middle ages, gave way to individual farms run by hired labour. In the Lothians, labour was provided by the 'hind' whose family were expected to serve as additional helpers ('bondagers'). In the north-east the use of unmarried labourers, hired for six months at a time, was more common and barrack-like bothies were built to accommodate them. One Aberdeenshire labourer complained that 'Feeing markets [sc. hiring fairs] always remind me of the old days when slaves were bought and sold by their general physical appearance, as one would buy a horse at St. Sair's Fair. I myself have had my wrists examined by farmers, to see what appearance of strength there was about them.'

The political reforms of 1832 had little effect upon this social structure. The Reform Act increased the Scottish electorate from c. 5,000 to c. 60,000 but the main beneficiaries were the urban and rural middle class. In the counties, the electorate remained very small, most notoriously in the case of Sutherland, which with under 150 electors was in effect a rotten borough for the duke of Sutherland. Until the 1880s Liberalism tended to reflect the interests of the lairds, graziers and wealthy small-town merchants of the east, who were against 'landlordism' but hostile to trade unions. Profound economic and social changes were taking place in the western Lowlands but for the most part the Liberal party was controlled by the 'Whiggish' east. The Conservative party was the party of the large landowners and the Established Church but the Liberals, though less conservative on some issues, also had landlords among their leaders. In the Lothians, the Elliotts, wealthy 'Liberal' landlords, contested elections with their traditional rivals, the Douglases of Buccleuch, as they had done since the fifteenth century. The wealthy landlord, Lord Rosebery, with his estate near Edinburgh, became leader of the Liberal party. It was against this type of landlord dominance that the crofters rebelled in the 1880s.

The social conservatism of eastern Liberalism was revealed perhaps most clearly in attitudes towards education. The traditional view of Scottish education had been that it encouraged the rise of a 'Scottish democracy' since the parochial system placed no obstacle in the way of a 'lad of parts' from passing from local school to university. In practice, fee-paying schools of an exclusively middle-class character made their appearance during the nineteenth century. When the Edinburgh Academy was founded in 1824, the reformer Henry Cockburn commented that this would be 'an important day for education in Scotland, in reference to the middle and upper classes'. In 1870, the charitable endowments of Edinburgh hospitals were taken over by the Merchant Companies to found five fee-paying schools catering for the middle class. In both town and countryside the evidence suggests a hardening of class boundaries. In nineteenth-century Edinburgh there was a sharp social divide between the New Town occupied by the professional middle class and the 'colonies' of artisan dwellings to the north and east. Educational arrangements merely reflected this fact of Edinburgh life.

In due course, the dominance of the east was to be challenged by an expanding west. The 'rise of the west' had its origins in the late eighteenth century with the establishment of cotton-spinning factories in New Lanark, Catrine and elsewhere. But it was not until the 1830s that the growth of heavy industry on a significant scale began to take place. In 1801, the population of Glasgow was still only 77,000 inhabitants compared to Edinburgh's 83,000. In 1881, Glasgow with 587,000 inhabitants was almost double the size of Edinburgh, with its 295,000 inhabitants. In 1911, Greater Glasgow had reached the million mark. Edinburgh, with 401,000, had less than half Glasgow's population. More was involved than the growth of Glasgow itself since it was surrounded by a network of substantial industrial towns, Hamilton, Paisley, Kilmarnock, Greenock, Dumbarton and others, which helped to make it the Scottish equivalent of Birmingham. The relative decline of Edinburgh was comparable with that of Dublin in relation to Belfast. The counties of Lanarkshire and Renfrewshire, which together had well over a million inhabitants in 1881 were the Scottish equivalent of Glamorgan and Monmouth. In 1830 the Lowland iron industry produced 40,000 tons of iron. By 1844 this had risen to c. 400,000 tons. In 1855 Scotland was producing a quarter of the total output of the United Kingdom. The Bairds factory at Gartsherrie was the largest iron works in the world after Dowlais in south Wales.

The ability of the western Lowlands to compete successfully with Welsh and English iron was largely due to the introduction of the Neilson hot blast process, patented in 1828, which made it possible to exploit the blackband ore of the Monklands areas near Glasgow. The Scottish lead did not last long, however, and by the 1860s the Lowlands were taking second place to the Cleveland field in the English north-east. By then, the growth of shipbuilding on the Clyde more than compensated for the changes. During the period 1850–70 Glasgow shipbuilders were in a position to meet the rapid growth in world demand for steam ships, and during the 1860s Glasgow's share of launchings in the United Kingdom rose from 30 per cent to 70 per cent, compared with a meagre 5 per cent earlier in the century. Glasgow also competed successfully in marine engine technology during this period and in the building of railway locomotives.

It was this rapidly expanding industrial economy which from the 1830s became a vast melting pot for migrants from neighbouring rural counties as well as from the Highlands and Ulster. In the east there was a steady flow of migrants from the eastern Highlands into Aberdeen and Edinburgh but the only industrial city on the east coast which matched the experience of the west was Dundee whose expanding jute industry attracted immigrants, many of them female, from Ireland. The flow of Ulster immigrants became a flood during the famine years 1846–51. It has been estimated that 1,000 immigrants a week arrived in Glasgow from Ireland in 1848. The result was to transform the religious and social composition of the western Lowlands, and to a lesser extent of the east, in Fife and Dundee. The number of Irish migrating into England and Wales was two or three times larger than that entering Scotland but in relation to the size of the Scottish population the proportion was much higher. It has been estimated that Irish-born inhabitants accounted in 1851 for 7.9 per cent of the population of Scotland, compared with 2.9 per cent for England and Wales. An additional complicating factor was that nearly half congregated in nine towns, Glasgow accounting for nearly 30 per cent. The result was that in western towns like Glasgow, Paisley and Kilmarnock the Irish-born amounted to between 10 and 18 per cent of the population. (Dundee had 18 per cent, Edinburgh only 6 per cent.) What has been described as the most Calvinist society in Europe, was confronted with the problem of absorbing a largely Catholic, often Irish-speaking, immigrant population. This was the plantation of Ulster in reverse which had the effect of creating a new sub-culture in the Scottish Lowlands.

The long term result of Irish immigration into the western Lowlands was to raise ethnic and religious tensions to a pitch unequalled elsewhere in the British Isles outside Belfast and Liverpool. Here, as in Ulster and Liverpool, the Orange Lodge took root. The Irish, like the Slavs in nineteenth-century Pennsylvania, were looked upon as a source of cheap labour. On the whole (Dundee excepted) the east escaped the problems presented by ethnic diversity. As a consequence, in the 1880s, when the 'No Popery' card was played in politics as a counter to Home Rule, it had much less success in the east than in the west. Gladstonian Liberalism survived in the east when it was being defeated in the west.

Another source of contrast between east and west had its origins in the 'Disruption' within the Church of Scotland. In 1843, over 470 ministers, representing some two-fifths of the total, left the Established Church, taking with them a similar proportion of elders and laity. It was an extraordinary event, which to some extent was an expression of Scottish nationalism against the control of Westminster symbolised by Sir Robert Peel. It was also a protest against the power of ecclesiastical patronage exercised by landlords. Perhaps also it was something of a middle-class movement drawing support from shopkeepers and skilled artisans. Certainly the speed with which the Free Church was able to organise and finance a rival organisation to the Church of Scotland indicates that it was able to draw upon local resources of wealth and expertise. Above all it drew upon the evangelical revival of the late eighteenth and early nineteenth centuries.

Resentment against state control and patronage was of long-standing and had already led to secessions from the Established Church during the eighteenth century. The Covenanting tradition with belief in a 'gathered' Church as opposed to an all-embracing establishment was still strong in the west where memories of Claverhouse and Drumclog were kept alive. But the 'Disruption' in numbers and organisation represented a division of much greater proportions. It had its origins in the rivalry between 'Moderates' and 'evangelicals' from the late eighteenth century onwards, which grew in intensity in the 1830s. A trial of strength took place in the courts over such issues as the control of the 'quoad sacra' chapels which had been built largely by the evangelicals to supplement the parish church in some areas. The right of patrons to present ministers to a living over the wishes of the presbytery was another key question.

The verdict of the courts went against the evangelicals and the 'Disruption' took place, led by Thomas Chalmers, whose views were Tory and who still believed in the desirability of an establishment. Chalmers himself may have believed this, but increasingly the logic of events took over and the Free Church, after Chalmers' death in 1847, moved towards the position of the dissenting churches on disestablishment. The Free Church had found itself in conflict with the state. After the 'Disruption', it also met with active opposition from many of the landlords, who refused sites for churches and schools. Tenants without written leases found themselves threatened with eviction. Shopkeepers were told that 'they would forfeit the custom and countenance of the wealthy and influential in the country'. It was said about Cromarty that 'the spirit in this part of the country is bitterness itself. Servants dismissed, labourers thrown out of employment, angry interviews between landlord and tenant – we hear of little else in this corner.' Chalmers complained that 'the upper classes looked on us [the Free Church] as so many Radicals or revolutionaries'.

During the first half of the nineteenth century, what we may call, following Immanuel Wallerstein, the 'peripheral' cultures of the British Isles were exposed to forces of change, emanating, in the main, from the 'centre'. The onset of industrialism in south Wales, the north of Ireland and the south of Scotland occurred largely in response to the demands of the English market or as a consequence of English investment. Hence, during this period, the individual histories of Wales, Ireland and Scotland can only be understood in relation to a wider British Isles context in which England, by virtue of its demographic and economic superiority, took a leading role.

Ireland, newly incorporated within the United Kingdom, experienced government intervention most during these years. During the 1830s, in particular, the Whig government introduced a series of reforms in education (the National Schools), poor relief, the abolition of tithes, municipal government and policing. In the 1880s Gladstone was to look back to these years, when Thomas Drummond had been Under-Secretary for Ireland (1835–40), as a model to follow.

In general, it may be said that the 'periphery' was restricted to a passive role during these years. Resistance to pressures which were perceived as coming from England were sporadic and localised. In Wales, serious unrest was confined to the Merthyr Rising of 1831, the Chartist attack on Newport in 1839 and the local outbreaks of 'Rebecca'. In Ireland, the agrarian violence of the Ribbonmen, though endemic, was of a local character. In Scotland, the troubles of the 1820s were confined to the Glasgow area. For much of the time the pattern of government within the United Kingdom rested upon tacit alliances between Westminster and the local ascendancies of Wales, Ireland and Scotland. This situation began to change in mid-century when Irish Catholicism, Welsh nonconformity and the Free Churches of Scotland formed an alliance with English dissent to bring pressure to bear upon the English establishment. It was this working entente, whose basis lay in a common antagonism to the English establishment and its local allies, which led to the formation of the Liberal party towards the end of the 1850s. The 'centre' was now to be exposed to political pressures from the 'periphery'.

10

The rise of ethnic politics

By the mid-nineteenth century a system of road, rail and sea communications brought the various communities of the British Isles more closely together than had ever been the case hitherto. To the network of roads built by Telford in the years after 1815 were added regular services of steam packets linking Britain and Ireland and a well-developed railway system. Road and rail routes from London to Dublin via Holyhead across the Menai Straits became a matter of routine. Ireland, Wales and Scotland were now open more than ever to English influences. Ireland in particular became more anglicised than either Wales or Scotland and the number of 'native' Gaelic-speakers declined drastically in the second half of the nineteenth century. The culture of southern England seemed destined to reach a position of total dominance throughout the British Isles.

In fact, however, this period (c. 1860–1914) witnessed a remarkable growth of 'ethnic' consciousness throughout the British Isles. During the first half of the nineteenth century 'class' issues had predominated in such movements as Chartism in England, Ribbonism and the Tithe War in Ireland, the Rebecca Riots in Wales and the Highland Clearances in Scotland. From mid-century, however, it was the dominance of England, particularly that of the south-east, which came to seem objectionable to influential groups in Ireland, Wales and Scotland. In Ireland, the catastrophic death toll of the Famine, accompanied as it was by massive emigration, was blamed, by and large, on the failure of the English government to provide adequate relief. Enforced emigration came to be seen as tantamount to eviction. In Wales, the affair of the Blue Books (1847) gave rise to outbursts of anti-English sentiment. Welsh critics of the Blue Books, in which the quality of Welsh education had been censured for its narrow biblicism, spoke of the 'Night of the Long Knives', a reference to the popular belief that in c. A.D. 600 Welsh princes had been massacred by Saxons. In Scotland, the 'Disruption' of 1843, when the Church of Scotland split into two bitterly hostile factions, led to the rise of nationalist feelings among those who left the establishment. It was they, with their memories of the Covenanters, who seemed truer at least by their own lights to the Scottish past.

There was, finally, the growing power of English nonconformity. In 1851 a census taken on church attendance indicated that dissent in England (and Wales) had gained a position of near-equality with the Established Church. During the second half of the century, nonconformity, despite its divisions, came to play an increasingly prominent role in English national life. More obvious examples of discrimination against the nonconformists had been done away with during the 1830s. In several fields, however, particularly that of higher education, nonconformists could feel that they were treated as second-class citizens.

The Crimean War (1854–6) distracted attention from domestic issues, and during the long ascendancy of Palmerston who was Prime Minister for most of the decade 1855–65 a strident English nationalism took the centre of the political stage. After Palmerston's death in 1865, however, the 'ethnic communities' of Ireland, Scotland and Wales together with those of English nonconformity began to express their grievances more vocally. It was the combination of these various ethnic (or quasi-ethnic in the case of northern England) groups which made possible the rise of the Liberal party under Gladstone. In 1868 after his victory in the election of that year Gladstone declared that 'our three corps d'armee, I may almost say, have been Scottish Presbyterians, English and Welsh Nonconformists and Irish Roman Catholics'.

During the second half of the nineteenth century and the first years of the twentieth century, ethnic issues became of immense importance in the politics of the British Isles. Ireland in particular presented problems which no government, Liberal or Conservative, was able to ignore. The slow rise of the Home Rule party in Ireland began after the general election of 1874, the first election when the secret ballot was normal practice in all three kingdoms. Irish issues, particularly land reform, raised implications for landlord–tenant relations elsewhere in the British Isles.

During this period, as we have seen for earlier periods, the course of English history cannot be understood purely in narrowly national terms, a judgment which applies with equal validity to the histories of Wales, Ireland or Scotland. Despite the impact of the various improvements in transportation and communications during the nineteenth century, ethnic divisiveness became a dominant characteristic of the British Isles during this period.

In England itself, during the second half of the nineteenth century, the pattern of politics was transformed by the emergence during the 1860s of the Liberal party. The issues which led to the creation of the party from an alliance of Whig landlords and radicals were in large measure English in character. In particular, the social divide separating Church and Chapel helps to explain the dominance of nonconformity in the new party. As Augustine Birrell put it, the cultural split between Anglicans and dissenters was like 'Offa's Dyke – broad, deep and practically impassable, cutting clear through social life'. Montagu remarked to Asquith about the Liberal party: 'There is no getting away from the fact that ours is a Nonconformist Party with Nonconformist susceptibilities and Nonconformist prejudices.' Such issues as the disestablishment of the Church of England, the removal of educational grievances and the pressure for control of the drink trade derived from the English nonconformist heritage of the Liberal party. The English past, especially from the seventeenth century, looked very different from a nonconformist vantage point than it did from an Anglican one.

But the Liberal party was something more than an English political party. The reform of the franchise in England, Wales and Scotland in 1867 and in Ireland in 1868 made possible a more effective popular approach to British Isles politics than had been the case hitherto. Irish Catholic grievances in particular came to occupy a central position in Liberal policy. Under Palmerston the Whigs had been the party of the Protestant ascendancy. Lord Palmerston was an Anglo-Irish landlord descended from the Sir John Temple who had written so eloquently about the 1641 massacre. Under Gladstone, however, the Liberal party made an Irish Catholic issue, the disestablishment of the Church of Ireland, the main plank of its platform during the 1868 election. Another Irish issue, university education for Irish Catholics, brought the government down.

For the next fifty years Irish issues were to influence the course of English politics. Irish 'reforms' were not seen as of localised significance: they were considered to have serious implications for the rest of the British Isles and for the British empire at large. This had already been the case during Gladstone's first administration when the disestablishment of the Church of Ireland and the 1870 Land Act were looked upon as the Irish end of a large British wedge. Gladstone's Irish Land Act of 1881 which was designed to undermine the basis of political agitation by making concessions to Irish farmers caused serious misgiving at the Whig end of Gladstone's Liberal coalition, particularly among those landlords with large Irish or Scottish estates.

Political reforms which were aimed primarily at changing the character of the English electorate were also looked upon as having wider implications. The Reform Acts of 1884–5, involving redistribution of seats and an extension of a wider franchise to include the counties as well as the boroughs, are normally discussed in terms of a purely English context. In fact, however, unlike 1832 and 1867 the reforms of 1884–5 attempted to deal with Ireland as uniformly as the rest of the United Kingdom. English politicians were well aware of the possible effects of these changes. Hartington declared at one stage that 'if this franchise [is] now given [we shall] be forced to concede Home Rule'. He spoke of

> a system which will exclude ... more than a million protestants ... [all those] opposed to Home Rule ... the owners of landed property and the great majority of capitalists, manufacturers, merchants, men of business and professional men in Ireland – and will not only exclude them but will misrepresent them by a body ... hostile to every interest they possess and every opinion they hold.

In this passage we may recognise the voice of an Anglo-Irish landlord, possessor of estates which originated in the Elizabethan plantation. As a Whig aristocrat Hartington had been a follower of the Anglo-Irish landlord Palmerston. The marquess of Lansdowne, descendant of Sir William Petty, was another prominent Whig, with Anglo-Irish connections.

Of all these issues, it was Irish Home Rule which had the most profound influence upon the course of English politics during this period. Any threat to the stability of the Union during the early and middle decades of the nineteenth century had been contained by successive British governments. O Connell had campaigned for 'Repeal' during Tory administrations while compromising with Whig governments for redress of specific grievances. The attempted rebellion of the Young Irelanders in 1848 had been a fiasco. Politically the Ireland with which British governments had to deal was the Ireland of the Protestant ascendancy. The situation began to change during the 1860s when Gladstone in response to the threat posed by the Fenians attempted to woo middle-class Catholic Ireland. Disestablishment, land reform and educational reform proved insufficient, however, to meet the challenge of a growing nationalism, and Home Rule became an important political issue after the 1874 election. It was to become even more important during the 1880s when Parnell leading a disciplined Irish party, made it impossible for the British government to ignore.

Home Rule in the eyes of many Liberals and most Conservatives was an imperial issue as much as an Irish one. During the second half of the nineteenth century England became the centre of a world-wide empire of which the centrepieces were the settlement colonies of Canada, Australia and New Zealand and the Indian empire together with a number of colonies in East, West and South Africa. For a mixture of strategic and economic reasons this imperial commitment led to an extension of responsibilities in the Near East where the Suez Canal became an indispensable link between the Indian Ocean and Britain. Alongside the formal empire lay a wide commercial network in Central and South America and the United States.

It was the new significance of empire, with England at its centre, which made Irish Home Rule much more than a matter of administrative reorganisation. Gladstone's decision in December 1885 to take up the cause of Home Rule raised issues of 'empire' and 'race'. Within the confines of the Liberal party, Gladstone's conversion to Home Rule was seen by some as a means of continuing his personal dominance of the party, and no doubt resentment against this helps to explain the decision of his colleagues, Hartington and Chamberlain to dissociate themselves from him. Professor John Vincent has suggested (in *The Governing Passion* (1974)) that the significance of the Home Rule issue as a matter of principle has been misunderstood. In his view politicians sought out policies not because they believed in them but as a means of gaining political power. The extraordinary impact which the Home Rule issue had for three decades after 1886, however, suggests that something more was at work than political machination. The Home Rule issue refused to go away. It survived the downfall of Parnell in 1891 and returned to haunt English politics in 1910. During the crisis years of 1912–14 English politicians were forced to confront the possibility of a rebellion by Ulster Unionists against the Home Rule Bill.

The Home Rule crisis of 1886 led to bitter divisions within the Liberal party, culminating in the formation of a separate group of 'Liberal Unionists' who in due course joined the Conservative party. Among them was the Cambridge historian Sir John Seeley, who wrote: 'In talking with a Home Ruler I am obliged to close my lips on almost all topics that interest me. I cannot trust myself to speak for I can scarcely speak with common civility.' About Gladstone he declared: 'I seriously think that if all the wicked men in England were rolled into one wicked man, he would be a mere muffer and bungler in mischief compared to Gladstone as Gladstone is now.' Seeley's hostility to Home Rule was typical of most prominent academics in Cambridge. The moral philosopher Henry Sidgwick noted that at Cambridge 'Unionists [were] gaining slowly but steadily. [I] Dined in Hall and was surprised to find the great preponderance of Unionist sentiment among the Trinity fellows – a body always, since I have known Trinity, preponderantly Liberal.' Sidgwick was utterly critical of the Home Rule Bill:

> to abandon the landowners of Ireland to the tender mercies of the people who for eleven years carried on an unscrupulous private war against their rights of property – rights which those of us who supported the Land Bill of 1881 morally pledged ourselves to secure to them – this is a national crime and deep moral disgrace in which I can have no part. (Quoted in J. Roach, 'Liberalism and the Victorian Intelligentsia', *Cambridge Historical Journal*, XIII (1957), 83, 80.)

The departure of the Whig landlords from Gladstone's government was perhaps not unexpected. The Land Act of 1881 and the Reform Acts of 1884–5 had placed a severe strain upon the loyalty of Hartington to his leader. What could hardly have been foreseen was the decision of the radical politician Joseph Chamberlain to place loyalty to the Union above his commitment to the politics of 'class conflict'.

Within the Liberal party, the future had seemed to many to lie with Joseph Chamberlain (1836–1914) who was to his generation of northern radicals what John Bright, his fellow-member for Birmingham, had been for the 1850s and 1860s. Indeed his attacks upon the aristocracy recalled those of Bright. In 1883, in a famous speech, he launched a fierce attack upon the Conservative party leader, Lord Salisbury.

> Lord Salisbury [he said] constitutes himself the spokesman of a class – of the class to which he himself belongs who toil not neither do they spin; whose fortunes – as in his case – have originated in grants in times gone by for the services which courtiers have rendered kings, and have since grown and increased while they have slept, by levying an increased share on all that other men have done by toil and labour to add to the general wealth and prosperity of the country.

Chamberlain's political reforms by extending the franchise to the rural labourers were intended to undermine the political power of the landed proprietors. In fact, the later 1880s ushered in twenty years of dominance by the Conservative party,

During the sixteenth and seventeenth centuries, university education expanded throughout the British Isles, though it was not open equally to all religious groups. In England and Ireland entry was confined to episcopalians. In Scotland, after 1690, Presbyterians were in control. Wales had no university. The illustration below is of Trinity College, Dublin, established during the reign of Elizabeth.

34 Trinity College, Dublin, was the academic embodiment of the Anglo-Irish ascendancy during the eighteenth and nineteenth centuries. It was a Church of Ireland institution in its overall membership. Catholics and dissenters attended it in the early nineteenth century, though without being able to take degrees or become fellows.

35 The University of Edinburgh, founded in 1583 as the 'tounis college', was a pillar of the Presbyterian Established Church after 1690. In the late eighteenth century, the university, housed in this handsome quadrangle (left centre), was a base for the 'Moderate' anti-Covenanting party in the Church of Scotland. The modern university buildings (right top) have been named after the figures of the Scottish Enlightenment, thus to some extent obscuring the heavily evangelical character of Edinburgh society in the nineteenth century.

THE RISE OF RELIGIOUS SUB-CULTURES

Throughout the British Isles during the nineteenth century, dissenters and Catholics (and in Scotland, episcopalians) improved their political and social status. This important change (carried out with the support of the Whig and Liberal parties) was reflected in their ecclesiastical architecture, which became more imposing than it had been during the years of discrimination.

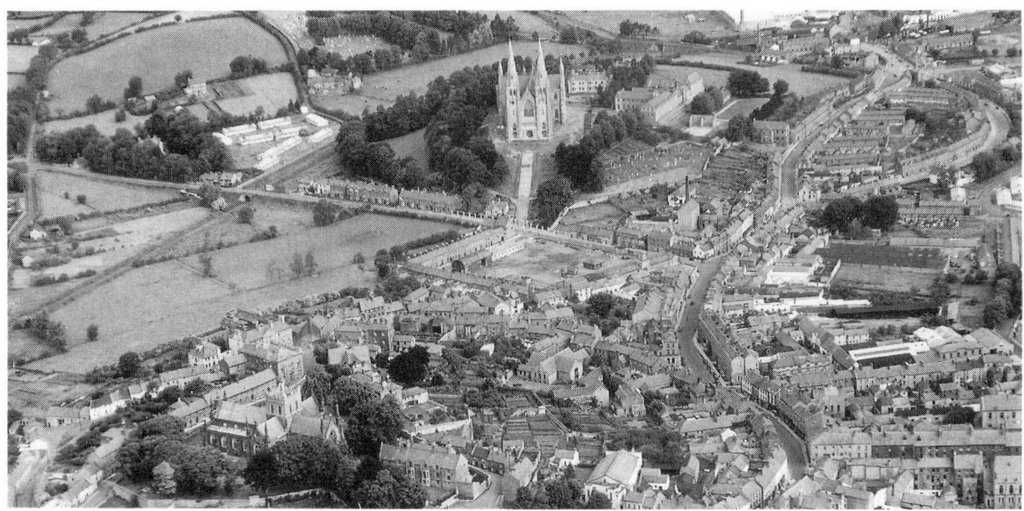

36 The Church of Ireland cathedral of St Patrick, in Armagh (bottom left in photograph), which dates from the medieval period, was restored in the 1830s. St Patrick's Catholic cathedral was begun in 1840 and completed in 1873 after a long delay during the Famine years. In its 'triumphalism' and confident choice of site, it marks the growing confidence of the Catholic population (see top half of photograph).

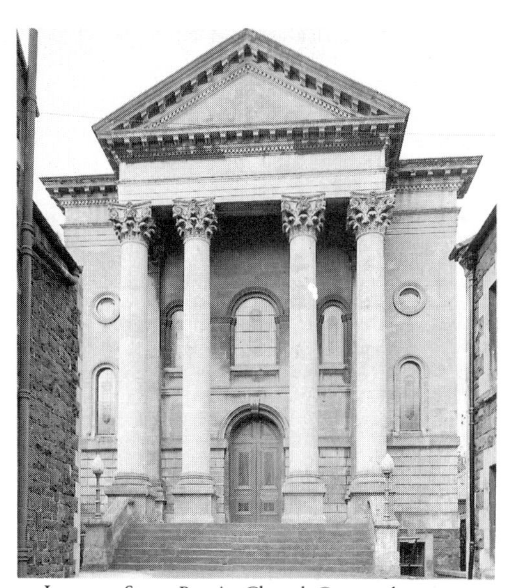

37 Lammas Street Baptist Chapel, Carmarthen (1872): the imposing, confident façade of this chapel indicates a change of mood among the Welsh dissenting bodies, whereby they came to see themselves, rather than the Established Church, as the religion of Wales.

38 It was not until the last decade of the nineteenth century that this statue of Oliver Cromwell was erected outside parliament. The event was a victory for the forces of English dissent within the Liberal party, though the actual donor was Lord Rosebery. Cromwell was the symbol of a non-Anglican view of English history.

39 New College, Edinburgh, was built in the aftermath of the 'Disruption' of 1843 by the Free Church. It occupies a spectacular site on Princes Street, where it stood as a challenge to the establishment. In the late nineteenth century the Free Church provided solid political support for the Liberal party.

40 St Mary's episcopalian cathedral, Edinburgh. The plans were drawn up in 1874. The building, which was completed in 1890, marked the re-emergence of Scottish episcopalianism. It stands at the opposite end of the city from the Presbyterian church of St Giles.

41 The column to the memory of George Walker in Derry (officially 'Londonderry' in British eyes) was erected in 1828 during the constitutional crisis over Catholic Emancipation. Walker, a figure of heroic legend, was remembered for closing the walls of Derry against the army of James II in 1688. The Protestant Prentice Boys march commemorates the event annually. Within the Catholic area of Derry is to be found the popular shrine of Columb's Well, a reminder of Derry's pre-colonial past.

42 St Patrick's College, Maynooth, was established by the British government in 1795 as a politically inspired gesture towards Irish Catholics during the wars with revolutionary France. In the 1840s the Maynooth Grant became a highly charged issue for the 'No Popery' wing of the Conservative party, led by Disraeli.

43 This statue of Cuchulain was erected in the General Post Office, Dublin, in 1935. It represents an attempt to link the rising of 1916 with a remote Gaelic past. Cuchulain was the hero of the Irish epic, The *Táin*.

44 Knock (Co. Mayo), the site of an apparition of the Virgin Mary in 1878. Today all roads lead to Knock. It has an international airport and attracts many thousands of pilgrims each year. The phenomenon of Knock provides some indication of the strength of Catholicism in the culture of the Irish Republic.

45 A nineteenth-century Welsh painting of *The Marriage of Rowena and Vortigern*, a prelude to 'The Night of the Long Knives', when the Anglo-Saxons were believed to have massacred their British guests. The episode received a new lease of life in Welsh consciousness after the 'Blue Books Affair' of 1844, when Welsh education was severely criticised by a government commission.

46 Boadicea, known in Welsh as Buddug, stands in Cardiff's City Hall. She is seen in this collection as part of Welsh history and a symbol of British resistance to the Roman legions. Other figures in the national pantheon include St David and William Williams, Pantycelyn.

47 The Royal National Eisteddfod (literally 'session') is an attempt to recreate in modern times the culture of the Celtic druids.

48 A modern stone circle erected at Holyhead (Anglesey) during the present century.

49 Though Britain is in practice a democratic, secular society, the ritual of the state revolves around the symbolism of a Protestant hereditary monarchy in which the Crown heads an Established Church and a peerage. The history of Britain tends to be written in terms of the kings of England. The illustration depicts the role of the monarchy in the state opening of Parliament, a splendid piece of ritual, which in fact conceals the political power of the House of Commons and of political parties.

50 The adoption of the kilt as a prime symbol of Scottish identity took place in the early nineteenth century in the wake of the Romantic movement. In the eighteenth century, tartan in some form was the dress of the Highlands. Its acceptance by the Lowlands was an extraordinary cultural shift, which implied that Scotland, despite its Anglo-Saxon, viking and Norman heritage, was a 'Celtic' nation. The illustration depicts the acceptance of the kilt in the heart of 'Hanoverian' Edinburgh (Police Band, 1968).

which, once based upon the support of the rural areas and the small agricultural boroughs, transformed itself into a city-based party.

Chamberlain's 'fiefdom' of Birmingham was lost to the Liberals when he broke with Gladstone over Home Rule. In the Birmingham area a mixture of imperialism and protectionism proved to be more potent as a vote-catcher than Home Rule. In Lancashire, as Peter Clarke has written, 'the greatest single mainstay of the Conservative party was the presence in the towns of an Irish immigrant community living uneasily among the indigenous population' (*Lancashire and the New Liberalism* (1971), p. 37). Disraeli had already played the 'ethnic' card with some success in the 1874 election. The rise of Irish Home Rule as a key issue in politics further consolidated the position of the Conservatives. The politics of 'nativism' triumphed in Preston, St Helens and other Lancashire towns. Manchester, once a Liberal stronghold, went Conservative. The issue of Home Rule made it possible for the Conservatives to divide the north by appealing to a potent combination of nationalism, imperialism and anti-immigrant feeling. In the early twentieth century, party, pamphlets criticised 'the present mongrel combination of teetotallers, Irish revolutionists, Welsh demagogues, Small Englanders, English separatists and general uprooters of all that is national and good'. They attacked a government which allowed 'foreign blacklegs and every other foreign undesirable to come in hundreds ... Any numbers of ships may now land parties of ... diseased and criminal aliens on our shores.'

To this was now added a stress on national unity:

> Shoulder to shoulder, strong in pride of race
> What fire shall thrust us from our ancient place
> The union safe ruled with an even hand
> The sister isle once more a prosperous land.

The Liberals (termed Radical-Socialists) by their opponents were described as

> A mob of factions, taught to shirk and steal
> But not to fight awaits the Conqueror's heel.
> The union sold, a British Isle no more,
> Ireland breeds treason at the Empire's core.

The Liberal party which won the election of 1906 was different in some striking ways from the party of Gladstone. The nonconformist north still remained the heartland of the party. In the Methodist mining villages of the north-east, temperance was a live issue in 1906. As one Sunday school teacher commented: 'After the Wilderness the Promised Land. And we have entered Canaan at last.' The *Sunday School Journal* declared 'No Christian patriot can, on reflection afford to stand idly by in supine indifference or pharisaic cynicism while the Drink Scourge, which combines in itself the evils of war, famine and pestilence put together, rolls its fiery tide of destruction o'er the land.' Among the leadership of the party, however, the balance of power was shifting towards those who argued that fundamental social reforms involving the intervention of the state was the answer to social evils and not individual regeneration on the lines advocated by Samuel Smiles. In the eyes of the 'Progressives', the politics of 'class' was the answer to the politics of 'empire'.

When the new Liberal government was formed, traditional issues such as Welsh disestablishment, Irish Home Rule and licensing reform were very much part of its agenda. Increasingly, however, the initiative was seized by the progressives. Social reforms such as old age pensions, unemployment and health insurance, the reform of the Poor Law and the introduction of labour exchanges now came to the fore under pressure from Asquith, who became Prime Minister in 1908, and Lloyd George who was Chancellor of the Exchequer from 1908 to 1915. There was no individual item in this programme of reform to which the Unionists could object. Indeed, it could be argued that the Liberals, once the party of laissez-faire, had taken over the mantle of Tory Paternalism. What was at stake, however, was the means by which the changes were to be financed. Chamberlain had seen indirect taxation as the main source of new revenue. The New Liberals, from the 1907 budget onwards, proposed to tax the wealthy, especially those who had benefited from the huge rise in urban land values. As Churchill put it, the Chancellor wanted to know 'How much have you got? and how did you get it?'

The voice of the Progressives was the *Manchester Guardian*, which, under the editorship of C. P. Scott (1846–1932), achieved a national importance. The success of the *Guardian* indicated that the Liberals were still very much a northern party; Scott himself was a Manchester man. Other writers for the paper such as C. E. Montague and J. A. Hobson were also from the north. But 'Progressivism' was more than a northern movement event though most of its leaders came to write for the *Guardian*. Though some of its members such as R. H. Tawney remained Christian others were influenced by the wave of agnosticism which swept the intelligentsia in post-Darwinian England. The 'New Liberals', as the Progressives were also termed, were in many ways nearer to Socialism than to the old-style Liberalism of Gladstone. As L. T. Hobhouse declared, 'The Old Liberalism, we thought, had done its work ... What was needed was to build a social democracy on the basis so prepared and for that we needed new formulas, new inspirations. The old individualism was standing in our way and we were for cutting it down' (quoted in S. Collini, *Liberalism and Sociology* (1979), p. 60–1).

The Unionists, now in a minority in the Commons, turned to the House of Lords as their main line of defence. The battle was joined over Lloyd George's 'People's budget' of 1909 in which he sought to raise extra revenue by such measures as 'super tax' on incomes over £5,000, higher rates for death duties and a levy on land values. The constitutional crisis which followed in 1910 was marked by two general elections fought on the issue of the right of the Lords to veto the budget. What was at stake, however, was the social policy of the 'New Liberalism'.

Victory went to the New Liberals in 1910. The future seemed to lie with the politics of class. The social cleavage, in Hobson's view, lay with 'organised labour against the possessing and educated classes on the one hand against the public house and unorganised labour on the other'. He argued that the contrast between north and south was between a Producer's England, which was Liberal, and a Consumer's England which was Conservative.

The actual facts of the political situation proved to be more complex. Religion and ethnicity returned once more in the shape of Irish Home Rule, as they had done in 1886. Liberal leaders had turned lukewarm on Home Rule after Gladstone's death. Asquith had argued in 1905 that a Home Rule Bill 'would wreck the fortunes of the party for another 20 years'. Haldane believed that 'it was vital that there should be a Liberal party that was completely independent of the Irish'. The election results of 1910, however, made the Liberals dependent upon the Irish parliamentary party.

The United Kingdom in 1914 may well have been on the brink of civil war on the key issue of the Union with Ireland. Other questions, the violent strikes of 1911 and the challenge offered by women suffragettes, took second place to the Home Rule issue. From 1911 onwards, Unionist party leaders encouraged the Ulster Unionists to make a show of force. Bonar Law, the leader of the party, declared his support in unambiguous terms. In 1914, the army entered on the political scene, when in the so-called 'Mutiny on the Curragh', officers stationed in Ireland made clear their unwillingness to be used in operations against Ulster. What changed the whole situation was the outbreak of war in August 1914. When hostilities ended in November 1918 a new set of factors had come into play which may be said to mark the beginning of a new period in the history of England, and of the British Isles.

The Ireland whose grievances this legislation was intended to redress was virtually an unknown country to most English politicians. As Professor Vincent has pointed out (in *Gladstone and Ireland* (1977)), Gladstone went to Ireland only once on a short visit and while there stayed largely in the company of Anglo-Irish landlords. From the vantage point of Westminster, Ireland appeared to be a simpler society than it was in fact. Political issues in Ireland were presumed to be essentially religious in character.

Religious issues were, of course, important. In the 1852 election in Ireland, the anti-Catholic riots in Stockport became a key electoral question in Co. Mayo and an electoral placard read

> Massacre and Sacrilege at Stockport!
> Irish Catholics murdered in their beds!
> Twentyfour houses wrecked and plundered!
> The priest's house burnt!
> The Chapel sacked and pillaged!
> Catholics of Ireland! Whoever votes for a supporter of Lord Derby's government votes for a massacre of his countrymen!
> The violation of the House of GOD; and
> The pollution of the BODY and BLOOD OF HIS REDEEMER!!!
> Down with Derby and McAlpine!

Such religious issues could override internal social divisions within the Catholic body. The fact remains, however, that the 'Catholic' south, though it might appear to be united behind its priests, was torn by internal social conflict for much of this period. Before the Famine, serious antagonisms could, and did, develop between farmers and labourers (both Catholic) over the price of potato land (termed 'conacre') on which the labourer depended for his very survival. It was this rather than landlord–tenant conflict which seems to lie behind much of the rural violence in southern Ireland during the pre-Famine period. The underground movement known as 'Ribbonism' (from the ribbon worn by its members) seems to have originated in the resentment of labourers and cottiers against the mainly Catholic 'strong farmers'. It survived in spite of repeated denunciation by bishops and clergy. Demographic pressures lay behind such unrest. The population of Ireland rose from over four million in 1781 to over eight million in 1841.

In the north, industrialisation acted as a safety valve, preserving its social fabric from overpopulation and famine. In the south, by contrast, the social structure was transformed in the late 1840s, by the Great Famine, a cataclysm which led to the deaths of nearly one million people and the emigration under appalling conditions of one and a half million more. Many died of starvation but the chief cause of death, it appears, was disease in the form of typhus, relapsing fever and dropsy, brought on by lack of nourishment. How much of this suffering was avoidable is still very much a matter of debate. Malthusians looked upon it as the inevitable consequence of overpopulation. Other commentators believed that government aid came too little and too late. Nationalists like John Mitchel put the blame directly on the British government. It seems clear, however, that the dependence of so many upon the potato as their main item of diet involved great risk of famine, which had indeed occurred on a lesser scale several times before 1845. It is worth pointing out that the incidence of mortality was much less while the Tories, with their paternalist traditions, were in power, than under the laissez-faire Whigs, who insisted until too late in the day that any long-term solution must be found in the laws of supply and demand.

The impact of the Famine was not felt equally throughout the south. Its main effect was upon the poorer, heavily populated areas of the west and south-west, where dependence upon the potato was high. The chief victims came from the labouring class who had fewer resources to fall back on in time of crisis. Emigration was heaviest among the small farmers, many of whom held on until the third failure of the potato crop before deciding to leave. The north, where oats rather than potatoes formed the main item of diet, was unaffected by the trauma, whereas in the south population control became a major cause for concern. A distinctive culture developed, marked by late marriage and strict sexual taboos which had the result of controlling the growth of population. The arranged marriage or 'match' had been a feature of 'strong farmer' society before the Famine. It now became more widespread. At the same time the proportion of unmarried men and women in the population rose.

In this as in so much else north and south drew apart. In the north there seems to have been more sexual permissiveness in rural society (e.g. in Island Magee where one fifth of women getting married were pregnant or believed themselves to be). Labourers also survived as an important segment of the population of the north, a fact which was to have important consequences in the 1880s when the landlords appealed over the heads of the tenant farmers to their labourers.

If the contrast between north and south was accentuated as a result of the Famine, there were other, cultural, factors at work in the same direction after mid-century. In the south, the post-Famine decades were marked by what Professor Emmet Larkin has termed the 'Devotional Revolution' (in 'The Devotional Revolution in Ireland, 1850–75, *American Historical Review*, XXVII (1972)), a movement of ecclesiastical reform introduced with papal backing by Paul Cullen, archbishop of Dublin (1803–78). The 'Devotional Revolution' was in part a response to missionary endeavours by the Established Church, with the backing of such Ulster landlords as the duke of Manchester and the earl of Roden. It also may be seen as the continuation of attempts made before the Famine, to 'reform' a still vigorous popular culture which in many respects was at variance with Catholic orthodoxy. Institutions such as the 'wake', where games with an obvious sexual implication were played, and the 'pattern' (the celebration of the feast day of local saints), which was an accepted occasion for courting, came under attack. Until the Famine, the campaign enjoyed only partial success. After the Famine, the task of reform was made much easier since the areas affected by depopulation were in many cases the poorer Irish-speaking sectors where popular culture had been strongest. Cullen went much further than had been attempted earlier. Under his leadership, clerical discipline was tightened, and new churches built. He was also responsible for introducing Italian-style devotions such as Quarante Ore, Benediction, Devotions to the Sacred Heart and the Immaculate Conception. Rosary beads, the scapular, holy pictures and holy medals also became part of the routine of religious life. The apparition of the Blessed Virgin at Knock (Co. Mayo) in 1879 may well have been one of the fruits of 'Devotional Revolution'.

While this was happening in the south (and among Catholics in the north) northern Protestantism was taking a more evangelical direction. The 1850s saw the rise of a 'Protestant Crusade' which had the backing of such Ulster landlords as the duke of Manchester and the earl of Roden. The aim of the enterprise was to bring biblical Christianity to the west of Ireland and though the intentions of its backers were, no doubt, laudable, the effect was to create religious tensions between themselves and the Catholic bishops, led by John MacHale. In the north itself the preaching of the Reverend Thomas Drew about the menace of 'Popery' led to several days of rioting in Belfast in 1857.

The real Protestant equivalent of the Devotional Revolution was the Second Great Awakening in 1859. That year, the 'Year of Grace', was marked by an extraordinary religious revival which began at the village of Kells near Ballymena (Co. Antrim), and spread throughout Ulster. The Presbyterian Church in Ulster reported an accession of 10,000 new members in the first three months of the revival, which later spread to Wales, Scotland and part of England. Unusual physical manifestations were seen by its participants as a sign of divine grace, though critics maintained it was religious hysteria. There were obvious links between this movement and the American Great Awakening of 1858. Professor William Gibson, soon to be moderator of the General Assembly of the Presbyterian Church of Ireland, visited the United States and wrote about his experiences under the title *Pentecost or the Work of God in Philadelphia.*

The effect of the religious revivals in both north and south was to accentuate already existing cultural and economic differences. More and more in the south the distinguishing feature of Irish identity was seen to lie in Catholicism. Father Tom Burke, a Dominican preacher, said in 1872:

> Take an average Irishman – I don't care where you find him – and you will find that the very first principle in his mind is 'I am not an Englishman because I am a Catholic.' Take an Irishman wherever he is found all over the earth and any casual observer will at once come to the conclusion 'Oh he is an Irishman, he is a Catholic.' The two go together.

Attitudes like this, though not universal, seem to have become more common, no doubt in part because they corresponded to the experience of emigrants in the United States, where segregation took place between the Catholic Irish and the Protestant 'Scotch-Irish'. The financial contribution of Irish-Americans was directed inevitably towards the cause of Catholic nationalism. Protestant Ulster could count upon the sympathy and active help of Orange groups in Canada, especially Toronto.

The difference between the two cultures was also revealed in contrasting attitudes towards the past. A 'Catholic' interpretation was likely to single out Hugh O Neill, Owen Roe O Neill, the penal laws and Daniel O Connell for emphasis, though some might stress 1798, and 1848. A 'Protestant' interpretation of Irish history would almost certainly centre upon the massacre of 1641, the battle of the Boyne in 1690 and the foundation of the Orange Order. Political songs became the vehicle for these interpretations in popular culture.

To the effect of religious revival as a cause of division should be added that of 'Fenianism'. The 'advanced' nationalism of the 1860s drew much of its inspiration from the Italian nationalist movement of Mazzini. Cullen looked upon the Fenians as the Irish counterparts of those who had driven Pius IX from Rome in 1848 and later had led the campaign for Italian unification, to the detriment of the Papal States. The Fenians themselves also looked back to 1798 and to the Young Ireland movement which had inspired the abortive 1848 insurrection in Tipperary. The founders of the Fenian movement hoped to find support for their ideas among the post-Famine exiles of the United States as well as in Ireland itself. Where they differed from O Connell and those, like Cullen, who took him as a model for Irish politicians was in their intention to establish a republic, if necessary by force. Cullen in 1864 declared 'it is foolish, it is wicked to speak of having recourse to violence and bloodshed or to expect anything good from illegal combinations and secret societies ... It is our duty to walk in the footsteps of the great Liberator, Daniel O Connell.' In spite of such condemnation, the Fenians did make headway in southern Ireland. Their attempted invasion of Canada misfired and the insurrection in Ireland was a failure, but what they lost in the field they gained in publicity. The execution of the 'Manchester Martyrs' in 1869 undoubtedly helped the Fenian cause. A leading Fenian, O Donovan Rossa, was elected to parliament in 1873. Michael Davitt, who had experienced hostility towards the Irish as an immigrant in Lancashire, joined the movement and was imprisoned.

Not the least important effect of Fenianism was to drive yet another wedge between north and south. The very events which led to a growth of sympathy towards the Fenians in the south discredited them in the north. The Fenians were by no means typical of the general attitude of Irish Americans, many of whom, under the influence of their clergy, steered clear of secret organisations. In the eyes of the north, however, the Fenians seemed to be the most active of Irish-American groups. When in 1882, Lord Frederick Cavendish, the newly appointed Chief Secretary and Thomas Burke, his Under-Secretary, were murdered in Phoenix Park, this merely confirmed northern suspicions about the immoral methods and aims of Fenianism.

The Famine left bitter memories, but the middle decades of the nineteenth century were a period of prosperity for many Irish farmers, as they were for those in Britain also. In 1855 Michael Donohoe, a Co. Carlow farmer, wrote to his brother in the United States:

> All the accounts that I have seen represent America to be in a bad state, particularly the working class Irish. Well, when America is getting bad, Ireland is getting good. The last two years were the best perhaps that were in Ireland for the last twenty years. The price of every description of agricultural produce was very high and the crops were pretty good, so that farmers and indeed everyone recovered the shock they received since 45. I believe old times are returning to us again.

In the late 1870s, however, again as in Britain, Irish farmers were hard hit by a combination of bad harvests, competition from American wheat and a drop in demand in England. The worst year was 1879–80 especially among the smallholdings of the west, where Michael Davitt and a group of local Fenians organised what was in effect a rural trade union, known as the Irish National Land League. The movement might well have remained of largely western significance but it was brought into the mainstream of national politics by Charles Stewart Parnell. Parnell, a Protestant landlord from Co. Wicklow, was a member of the loosely organised group of 'Home Rule' members of parliament but not yet its leader. The land question, together with a policy of parliamentary obstruction, provided him with a platform which eventually gave him the leadership in 1880.

Parnell spoke at Westport in June 1879 and told his audience of small farmers 'You must show the landlords that you intend to hold a firm grip on your homesteads and lands. You must not allow yourselves to be dispossessed as you were dispossessed in 1847.' During the same year he also managed to win the support of influential Irish-American groups, including the Fenians. However, the 'Parnellites' in the House of Commons after the 1880 general election numbered only twenty-four. The Church was still at this date suspicious of those who had a whiff of Fenianism about them. Sometime between 1880 and 1885, however, the Catholic bishops, or most of them, came down on Parnell's side. The results were to be seen in the election of 1885 when Parnell's Home Rule party, now much more of a 'machine' than it had been in 1880, won eight-five seats, putting it in a position to hold a balance between the Liberal and Conservative parties in the House of Commons.

Parnell's success is normally seen, and rightly, as a major change in the history of Irish nationalism. Of not less significance, however, was the reaction which it evoked in the north, as well as among southern landlords. If Parnell united the disparate elements in the south, he also made possible a counter-coalition in the north. Northern Protestants were divided by class, ethnicity and religion. There was little in common between the Orange Lodges drawing their membership from rural and urban labourers and the Presbyterian tenant farmers. Fear of Home Rule drew varied social and religious groups together.

The Home Rule populist coalition had called into existence a populist coalition against it. The extension of the parliamentary franchise in 1884 which made possible Parnell's victory also gave the vote to the Orange Lodges of the north. Serious divisions still remained between Liberal Unionists and Conservatives and, within the Conservative party, between the official leadership and the Orange Lodges, but the threat of Home Rule in 1886 led to the creation of the Ulster Loyalist Anti-Repeal union. Unionists controlled the north-east as completely as the Home Rulers controlled the south.

Class conflict, between tenant and landlord, provided much of the impetus behind Home Rule in the south. It was countered in the north by an appeal to religion and ethnicity. Clerical leaders in Ulster made contact with the Scottish Protestant Alliance and the Protestant Institute of Great Britain. As James Henderson, owner of the *Belfast News Letter*, put it: 'It is greatly to be desired that we should stir up the feeling of Scotland in favour of this movement ... I believe that if we can stir up religious feeling in Scotland we have won the battle.' On a visit to Belfast in February 1886, Lord Randolph Churchill assured the Unionists of the support which they enjoyed in England and a little later coined the phrase 'Ulster will fight and Ulster will be right.' Here was the equivalent of Parnell's equally stirring sentence 'No man has the right to fix the boundary of the march of a nation.'

In the 1860s Gladstone and Bright had planned to unite Irish Catholics and Irish Presbyterians. The disestablishment of the Church of Ireland in 1869 was calculated to please both groups and the Land Act of 1870, though unsatisfying in many respects, was intended to appeal to tenant farmers of each denomination. As a consequence the Liberals who had lacked support in Ulster began to build up a base there as the anti-landlord party. In the nine Ulster counties, the number of Liberal seats rose from two in 1868 to fourteen in 1880. Gladstone must also have hoped that he would do even better in the 1885 election after the extension of the franchise. In the event, however, the Conservatives won twenty-one seats in the counties compared to nine for the Liberals. The results were even worse in 1886 when Gladstonian Liberals won only three seats in the counties. Elsewhere in Ireland the Home Rule party took every seat. Outside the north-east the political power of the ascendancy had been wiped out. The 1880s thus brought into the open a polarisation which had existed for many decades. In the south, a largely Catholic middle class now held power, a shift which had been first revealed decisively in the elections to the Poor Law Boards in the late 1870s. It remained now to see what the long-term consequences of this division would be.

The years since 1879 had been full of incident. In 1879 there had been the spectacular murder of Lord Leitrim. In 1880 the 'Boycott' had been invoked against Captain Boycott, the agent of the earl of Erne, and an expedition of fifty Orangemen left the Farnham estate to give him aid. The year 1880 had been marked by hundreds of rural outrages in the west. In 1882, the Phoenix Park murders took place. Gladstone's Land Act had been passed in 1881 with the intention of detaching land agitation from general political issues. It had enjoyed some success. But agitation among leaseholders, who were not covered by the Act, continued. There was further radical development with the so-called 'Plan of Campaign', from 1885 onwards, which directed hostile attention towards particular estates. Gladstone's decision to bring a Home Rule Bill before the House of Commons should be seen against this background. What seemed like statesmanship in the eyes of the south appeared more like capitulation to anarchy in the view of northerners, Liberal and Conservative alike.

As suggested above, though there may not have been two nations in Ireland, there are clear grounds for believing that there were two cultures. Home Rule did not come about in 1886 but the cultural gap continued to exist and even to widen. The 1880s saw the growth of the Gaelic Athletic Association in the south while association football spread in the north. With the foundation of the Gaelic League in 1893 an interest in the Irish language became one of the symbols of southern Irish identity, though only a minority were involved. Not least, the Church came to favour Home Rule on moral grounds. If Home Rule meant Rome Rule for the Ulster Unionist, the Union came to stand for a type of modernity which the Catholic clergy found equally threatening from its own standpoint. For some Irish clergy, the Irish mind which had once been 'chaste, idealistic, mystical' had been sullied by 'an invading tide of English ideas'. The young Fr Lethaby in Canon Sheehan's novel *My New Curate* warned his rural parishioners against the perils of infidelity, from which Jews and freemasons benefited. The old parish priest of *My New Curate* also mocked the dangerous doctrines of religious modernism which the Higher Criticism was bringing in its wake. Home Rule promised moral as well as economic regeneration.

The elections of 1910 which left Redmond's Irish parliamentary party holding the balance in the House of Commons once more raised the spectre of Home Rule before the eyes of the northern Unionists. Threats of violence had been made in 1886. They were now renewed under the leadership of the Dubliner, Edward Carson, and with the backing of the Conservative party under Bonar Law, whose father had been an Ulster Presbyterian minister. The importation of arms into Ulster and the drilling of Ulster Volunteers was answered by similar demonstrations in the south, though Redmond who had everything to gain from constitutionality kept matters under control. The Home Rule Bill in fact became law in September 1914 with the proviso that Ulster should be allowed to opt out for six years. Early in 1916 the British administration in Dublin fully expected to be handing over power to Redmond in the near future. Though there was still rural unrest in certain western counties against encroachment by large graziers, the passing of Wyndham's Land Act in 1903 had made possible the creation of a 'peasant proprietorship' and, with it, agrarian peace. 'Landlordism' had been undermined in the south though cynics suggested 'gombeenism' (from the Irish word *gamba* 'a little portion' – of interest) had replaced it. With the land question solved and Home Rule on the statute book, it seemed not unlikely that the post-war years in Ireland would be peaceful.

After the outbreak of war most of the Ulster Volunteers and the Irish National Volunteers joined the British army and went off to fight on the Western Front or at the Dardanelles. Elsewhere in the British Isles, the common experience of the war seems to have reduced the intensity of religious and ethnic divisions. In Ireland, a similar development was ruled out by the Rising of Easter 1916. The extent of Irish-American involvement in the decision to attempt a rebellion with German aid is still unclear but it was certainly the Fenian-linked organisation, the Irish Republican Brotherhood, which took the decision to rise in 1916, against the wishes of the Volunteer commander, Eoin MacNeill. The surge of sympathy for the rebels after the executions of 1916 made possible the success of the Sinn Fein party in 1918. But '1916' also made partition, already a possibility in 1914, far more likely. Unionists were in key posts in Lloyd George's coalition government when the Home Rule Act was repealed in 1920 and the Government of Ireland Act substituted. Six of the nine counties of Ulster were partitioned from the rest and given the equivalent of Home Rule, with their own parliament under Westminster sovereignty. It was a 'solution' which the Treaty of 1922 with the Sinn Fein forces left unaltered.

It was during these years (1850–1914) that Welsh politicians came to the forefront of British Isles politics, so much so that historians have been tempted to speak of the 'Rebirth of a Nation'. In fact, however, Wales remained almost as deeply divided between two cultures as did Ireland. The prominence of Welsh nonconformity within the Liberal party tended to conceal the extent of these divisions. Thus, in 1881, the temperance lobby achieved their first real victory with the passing of the Welsh Sunday Closing Act. But this success revealed the extent of the rift which was growing between rural Wales and the industrial south-eastern counties of east

Carmarthen, Glamorgan and Monmouth. A Merthyr workman wrote a letter to the *Merthyr Express* in which he put forward a very different point of view to that of the temperance reformers.

> How would these very good people like to live days, weeks and months underground without a sight of the pub and then on a wet Sunday to keep within doors all the sunless hours, except while attending divine worship? Oh, these very generous people have their nice cosy clubs or homes which they enjoy every day. But the collier has to live in discomfort in a small home, and for nearly six months in every year never sees the sun, except on the first day of the week.

There were other signs that temperance was not seen in the same light in the south as it was in the north. Between mid-1882 and mid-1883 over 3,000 workingmen became members of clubs in Cardiff, an increase of 90 per cent over the year before. In 1889 there were nearly 500 shebeens in Cardiff. By the 1890s drunkenness was much more common in Glamorgan, Monmouthshire and Pembrokeshire than it was in Merioneth, Radnorshire and the rural counties. There were also indications that the number of supposedly 'bona fide' travellers markedly increased, since a journey of 3 miles entitled the thirsty wayfarer to be served a drink.

The second half of the nineteenth century had seen the great expansion of the south Wales coal fields, in particular those of the Rhondda valley. This was a 'boom' period during which the population of Cardiff rose from 18,000 in 1851 to 164,000 in 1901. By 1911, two-thirds of the population of Wales lived in Glamorgan and Monmouth and the industrial area of east Carmarthen. During the same period, there was a net loss of 400,000 from the rural counties. The vast modern pubs of the Rhondda valley were one indication that this was a very different world from that of the rural counties. The distinction was not as sharp in all areas of the south. In the Welsh-speaking valleys of the anthracite-mining area, conditions were more settled. It was not uncommon for miners to 'set out' potatoes on the land of a nearby farmer in return for help at harvest time. In general, however, the contrast between rural and industrial cultures was clear-cut. A miner from these areas commented that

> Life to us in the Rhondda was exceedingly artificial ... There is not a farm to be seen anywhere ... The tink of the damn pit, the tink of the tramcars on the road, that's all you would hear. Rhondda people are acclimatised to what I would say is a very uncouth proletarian life ... in the sense that there is nothing natural about it. (Quoted in D. Smith, *A People and a Proletariat* (London, 1980), p. 175.)

The social problems which the miners faced could hardly be alleviated by exhortation to temperance and self-help.

Despite the growing imbalance in favour of the south, the political leadership of the Welsh Liberals remained with the rural counties, where Welsh-speaking dissent was strong. To the small farmers, the example of Ireland seemed to provide a possible answer to their difficulties. In June 1886 an assembly of tenant farmers at Rhyl in north Wales, pressed for a Land Act on the lines of Gladstone's 1881 Irish Land Act. Tom Ellis, member for Merioneth, and descendant of a tenant evicted in 1859, was described as the 'Parnell of Wales'. Ellis' movement Cymru Fydd (Young Wales) put forward a programme in 1886, advocating tenant rights, disestablishment and the abolition of tithes. The young David Lloyd George ran successfully as a Home Ruler for the Caernarfon borough in 1890. In 1892, Welsh members imitated the earlier obstructionist tactics of Parnell in the House of Commons. These developments are often seen as signs of a growing rift between Welsh and English Liberalism. Equally important, however, was the fact that 'Young Wales' focussed its attention exclusively upon the problems of the rural counties. It was the agrarian crisis of the years following 1879 which engaged their energies. They seemed to be uninterested in the problems of industrial Wales. There were the possibilities here of a division between industrial and rural areas comparable to that which came about in Ireland during the 1880s. That it did not occur was due in large measure to Lloyd George, who, more than Tom Ellis, deserves the title the 'Parnell of Wales' for his skill in keeping an uneasy coalition together.

Signs that the south might try to go its own way came after the failure of the coal strike of 1898. The decision to go on strike had been a defeat for the established leader of the miners, William Abrahams (nicknamed 'Mabon'), who preferred to use a sliding scale based upon the relationship between wages and the price of coal as the basis for negotiation with the mineowners. Mabon, a Welsh-speaking dissenter, strongly committed to Welsh cultural causes, represented a traditional Liberal approach to industrial relations. The failure of the strike brought a new departure. Influences from outside Wales began to make themselves felt. The Independent Labour party (independent from the Liberal party) sent organisers to south Wales. The English radical newspapers, Blatchford's *Clarion*, was placed on sale. The Scottish socialist Keir Hardie made regular trips to south Wales and denounced the leadership of 'Mabon'. In the 'Khaki' election of 1900, Keir Hardie was elected for one of Merthyr's two seats and became the first Labour member of parliament. Labour also ran against a Liberal candidate at Gower, though without success. In the 1905 local elections Labour did well, and in the 1906 general election miners' representatives were elected for Merthyr, Gower and South Glamorgan. In 1905 Mrs Snowden predicted that Wales, 'a hot bed of Liberalism and Nonconformity in the past ... would become a hot bed of Socialism and real religion in the future', (K. O. Morgan, ed., *Wales in British Politics 1868–1922* (1963), p. 210).

This was the language of faith. The great majority of Welsh M.P.s were still Liberal. Indeed, the 1906 general election was an overwhelming victory for the very forces which Mrs Snowden condemned. Lloyd George's 'People's budget' of 1909 brought him great popularity in Wales and the social democracy of the 'New Liberalism' was clearly directed to the problems of an industrial society. Labour candidates were defeated by Liberals in mid-Glamorgan and east Glamorgan in 1910 despite the bitter strikes of 1909 and the violence at Tonypandy in 1910, when a miner had been killed. The signals coming from south Wales were ambiguous. At Swansea the dockers' candidates came bottom of the poll. At Merthyr, the Scot, Keir Hardie, though duly elected, polled fewer miners' votes than Edgar Jones, a Welsh-speaking Baptist. Syndicalism with its emphasis on direct industrial action was making some headway in the eastern valleys but there were few signs of the 'Strange Death of Liberal Wales'.

In Wales, as in Ireland, it was the war years which produced a decisive shift of direction, but the direction in which the two societies moved was very different. In southern Ireland, popular reaction to the 1916 Rising set in motion the rise of 'Sinn Fein' which in turn evoked the counter-nationalism of the Protestant north-east. At the end of the war Ireland was divided not by class but by culture. In Wales, by contrast, class became increasingly important and the ethnic and religious issues of the past moved into relative insignificance. Mounting tension in the coal fields in 1917 evoked pessimistic comments from the Commission of Enquiry set up to look into the problem. The success of the Russian revolution inspired enthusiasm among those whom critics termed the 'Bolsheviks of the south'. In the general election of 1918, however, Lloyd George Liberals with twenty-one seats still enjoyed a comfortable majority over Labour which won ten seats. But the old Liberal issues had lost their hold. In 1919 a Welsh Disestablishment Act was passed which took this once emotional question out of politics. The tithe problem was solved at much the same time. The break-up of the great estates, which paralleled similar changes in England, removed one of the main targets of traditional Welsh Liberalism. The war also seems to have reduced the power of organised dissent and along with it the emotive power of the cause of temperance. The issues which had enabled the rural west to maintain its political dominance had lost their potency.

To all this must be added the sharp decline in the influence of Lloyd George. In 1918 as the architect of victory his position seemed almost unchallengeable, but his political power in south Wales was soon to be undermined by his handling of the problems of the coal fields. During the war the mines had been under government control and the miners hoped that this would lead to nationalisation. The Sankey Commission which was set up in 1919 to discuss the matter did not reach a clear-cut decision and in March 1921 the Lloyd George government decided to hand back the mines to the owners. By this time the post-war boom was over. Unemployment had doubled between December 1920 and March 1921. The government decision not to nationalise the mines marked the end of Lloyd George's personal fluence in south Wales. The miners went on strike and though they were defeated, the Labour party reaped the benefits of Liberal decline in the elections of the 1920s. By 1929 Labour held twenty-five seats in Wales. After the war, the politics of class proved to be more important than the politics of religion and ethnicity. The balance shifted away from rural, Welsh-speaking counties to the industrial areas where English was strong and which looked to the Socialism of the Labour party. The nationalism of the south was to be expressed in the symbolism of sport, especially rugby football. National sentiment was satisfied in the south with the ritual 'slaughter' of English teams at Cardiff Arms Park.

In Scotland, up to the late eighteenth century the most significant cultural divide was that between Highlands and Lowlands. With the coming of the Industrial Revolution and the consequent growth of population in the Lowlands, the Highlands dropped into relative insignificance, although south of the Highland line the kilt and the tartan became symbols of Scottish cultural identity. Within the Lowlands itself the main split was between the heavily industrialised west centred upon Glasgow and its satellite towns, and the largely rural east, in which Edinburgh and Aberdeen were the 'capitals' and Dundee and the mining areas of the east coast were industrial outposts.

Though the contrast must not be pressed too far, 'east' and 'west' also enjoyed different political outlooks. In the industrial west the Chamberlainite programme of disestablishment, free education and land reform carried a greater appeal than in the Whiggish east where the Liberal party was led by such landowners as Rosebery and Elgin. In the industrial cities of the west, the Free Church and the Voluntaries had coped more successfully than the 'Moderates' with the challenge of industrialisation. Liberalism, though dominant throughout Scotland for the period after 1832, was more radical in the 'west' than in the 'east', more 'Whiggish' in Edinburgh than in Glasgow.

As a corollary to this, 'No Popery' was stronger in the west where Irish immigration had been heaviest. The Maynooth Grant issue of 1845 carried as much resonance north of the border and especially in the west as it did in England. There was thus always the possibility later in the century that the 'No Popery' card could cause the Liberal party to become polarised along the west/east divide. Issues of class kept the Liberal party in existence in the sense that it was the anti-landlord and anti-establishment party. Issues involving ethnic hostility, such as were raised by Home Rule in the 1880s, were a source of division.

From 1868, the odds seemed to favour a permanent Liberal majority in Scotland. Even in 1874, the year of an overall Conservative majority throughout the United Kingdom, Scottish Liberals took more seats than the Conservatives. In 1885 only eight Conservatives were elected out of a total of seventy Scottish M.P.s. Gladstone seemed well able to handle the internal divisions which arose inevitably in such a miscellaneous alliance. His critics declared that 'the Church people have swallowed Gladstone's soothing syrup'.

Gladstone's acceptance of Home Rule for Ireland in December 1885 transformed the situation in Scotland as it did elsewhere. Home Rule proved to be an issue which distracted attention away from disestablishment to the fear that 'Home Rule would mean Rome Rule'. The *Glasgow Herald* had begun to give expression to these fears in December 1885. In the Glasgow Chamber of Commerce, the Liberal Unionist candidate for the College division expressed the view that, after Home Rule, Ireland might 'become the choice refuge of all the dynamitards of Europe'.

Fears were expressed about the future of 'the merchants, the manufacturers, the bankers, the traders of Ulster who have made the North of Ireland what it is, trusting to the protection of the United Kingdom of which they are proud to be subjects'. In May 1886, representatives of the Irish Presbyterian Church told a meeting of Glasgow Liberal Unionists that Home Rule would lead to 'a Romish ascendancy' and to 'the ultimate extinction of Protestantism [in Ireland]'. In April, a collection was taken up at a huge Orange demonstration against Home Rule 'to assist men such as Dr. Hanna to stir up the people'. A Catholic chapel nearby was stoned and the Good Friday services were interrupted. In the election of 1886 the Unionists gained eleven seats in the west of Scotland, the Liberal Unionists, nine. A mixture of ethnic, religious and economic issues had led to the defeat of Gladstonian Liberalism in the west of Scotland.

Home Rule remained an emotional issue in the 1890s. In 1893 the eighth duke of Argyll made a speech attacking Gladstone's second Home Rule Bill in which he declared:

> I have been spending the last few weeks in a part of Scotland whence we can look down on the hills of Antrim. We can see the colour of their fields and in the sunset we can see the glancing of the light upon the windows of their cabins. This is the country, I thought the other day, which the greatest English statesman tells us must be governed as we govern the Antipodes. Was there ever such folly?

In this and other speeches Argyll played the card of ethnicity. 'Mr Gladstone says we are foreigners to the Irish. I say we are flesh of their flesh and blood of their bone. We are responsible for their liberties and will not betray them ... Above all remember your duty to your fellow countrymen across the Channel.'

Ethnic issues remained important in certain areas of industrial Scotland such as Greenock where the Orange Order was closely linked with the Conservatives. Increasingly, however, class issues came to the fore. In 1906 the number of Unionist seats fell from thirty-six to ten. In 1911 it was declared that 'Scotland has stood by the Liberal Government so solidly because it hates the House of Lords and the landlords.' With the advantage of hindsight, however, it is possible to see that given the right circumstances, the radical Liberalism of the west and the Whiggish Liberalism of the east might divide.

Many thousands of miles away from Scotland and Ireland, the cultural tensions of the British Isles were reproduced in parts of the empire. As we have seen, the English empire in North America achieved independence from the mother country, leaving only Canada and the West Indies tied formally to the United Kingdom. During the course of the nineteenth century, however, emigration took place on a grand scale from the British Isles. The United States was the most popular destination for British Isles emigrants but Canada, Australia, New Zealand and the South African colonies of Cape Province, Natal and, eventually, parts of the Transvaal, also came to attract many thousands of settlers. In the early twentieth century, Rhodesia and Kenya also became colonies controlled by white settlers from the British Isles. India and West Africa drew only civil servants or missionaries, and the direct impact of the cultures of the British Isles as distinct from government policy was correspondingly much less. Nonetheless, it could be a matter of some significance for the future whether the missionaries were Irish Catholics, Scottish Presbyterians or Anglicans from England.

In Canada the cultures of the British Isles were all strongly represented, from the Gaelic-speaking Highlanders of Prince Edward and Cape Breton islands to the Waterford fishermen of St Johns, Newfoundland. Ontario which was exposed to the threat of Fenian invasion in the 1860s became a centre of 'Orangeism' and anti-Gladstone feeling. Such figures as Bonar Law, leader of the Conservative party from 1911 to 1923, and Lord Beaverbrook who was born in New Brunswick were products of this Canadian Unionist tradition. J. H. Galbraith in his autobiography, *The Scotch* (1963), has described the outlook of a rural Ontario culture which had its roots in Ulster. Tension between English-speaking Ontario and French-speaking Quebec provides a major theme of Canadian history but political and religious differences deriving from the cultural history of the British Isles also formed an essential element in the 'Canadian Mosaic'.

The history of Australia during the nineteenth and twentieth centuries was also strongly influenced by attitudes which originated in the interaction of the cultures of the British Isles. New South Wales was founded as a penal colony in 1788 and together with Tasmania became the reception area for thousands of convicts, among whom were many Irishmen sentenced to transportation after the 1798 rebellion or the many outbreaks of rural disorder in Ireland during the early nineteenth century. In view of this it was inevitable that Irish nationalism should find a second home in Australia. It was almost equally inevitable that Unionism or 'Orangeism' should reach a sympathetic audience among other sections of the population.

Most of the cultures of the British Isles were represented in nineteenth-century Australia. English culture was dominant but the popularity of St Patrick's Day as a public holiday in many areas indicated a significant Irish presence. In proportion to the population, there were twice as many Catholics, mainly of Irish descent, in Australia as in England. In New South Wales in the mid-nineteenth century, the Irish amounted to one third of the population. In 1842 the governor of New South Wales wrote in support of the appointment of an English Catholic bishop: 'It is most important that an Englishman should have the preference, the Catholics being, I believe, all Irish.'

The rise of Fenianism had some repercussions in Australia especially after the attempted assassination of the duke of Edinburgh in 1867. It was widely believed at the time that the assassin, Patrick O Farrell, was part of a Fenian network, and in Melbourne particularly this gave rise to anti-Irish demonstrations, and the establishment of a Protestant Political Association. The rise of the Home Rule issue in the United Kingdom from the 1880s onwards also had political effects in Australia. At an Orange Lodge meeting in 1914 at Melbourne Town Hall during the Home Rule crisis at Westminster one speaker declared that 'The victory on the Boyne had been a victory, not only for Ireland, but the civil and religious liberty throughout the world.' Edward Carson was seen as 'another William III'. In 1916, government attempts to introduce conscription were defeated by the pro-Irish lobby. Mannix, the Irish-born archbishop of Melbourne was regarded as so dangerous that he was refused permission to land in Ireland during the post-war 'Troubles'. It is clearly impossible to understand the *mentalité* of Australia during this period without adopting a British Isles approach.

The same point may also be made about New Zealand, where emigrants from England, Scotland and Ireland set the tone. The Anglican and Presbyterian religious traditions were both strongly represented. The Catholic bishop of Dunedin declared 'In Otago it is Presbyterian Protestantism: in Canterbury, Anglican Protestantism: and in Wellington, Protestantism of any and every kind.' In the province of Otago, the Free Church of Scotland predominated, as the name of Port Chalmers, commemorating the leader of the 'Disruption', suggested. But throughout New Zealand, the Irish, of either Catholic or Protestant background, were also an important element in society. The problems of Ireland after 1916 led to the formation of a Protestant Political Association in New Zealand which was pledged to fight 'Rum, Romanism and Rebellion'. The election of 1919 was fought on sectarian issues and the Conservative 'Reformer' Massey, who had negotiated an informal alliance with the P.P.A., gained an overall majority over his Liberal and Labour opponents.

Apart from political issues relating to Ireland, temperance, Sabbatarianism and the place of Bible-teaching in the schools were as important in New Zealand politics as they were in the United Kingdom itself. The Protestant Churches repeatedly mounted moral crusades which were designed to preserve 'the fitness of the race ... the safety of the streets and the security of the family'. In all this the influence of the cultural divisions of Ireland loomed large. 'Well into the twentieth century', it has been said, 'the Anglo-Irish, the Scots-Irish and the Catholic Irish [in New Zealand] viewed each other suspiciously through the kaleidoscope of Irish history.'

In August 1914 a European war broke out which was expected to be over within a short time but which in the event lasted for over four years. Inevitably such a prolonged conflict carried with it immense political, social and economic consequences for the United Kingdom as it did for the British empire. Broadly speaking throughout most of the British Isles, the war had the effect of reducing the importance of ethno-religious issues and placing 'class' at the centre of politics. In Wales and Scotland, after 1918, disestablishment was carried out without fuss. The creation of the Irish Free State in 1922 removed the highly emotional issue of 'Home Rule' from British politics. Ethnic hostility remained strong at the local level in such cities as Glasgow and Liverpool. In national politics, however, the Irish issue in the sense that it had existed since the Act of Union of 1800 ceased to exist.

Wales and Scotland found themselves caught up within the general pattern of class politics. The industrialised areas of south Wales and of west Scotland provided solid support for a rejuvenated Labour party which took over the political inheritance of Liberal radicalism in Wales and Scotland as it did in England.

The great exception to this shift from ethno-religious to class politics was Ireland, where north and south divided upon largely ethnic lines. In 1914, the Protestants of Ulster had been willing to go to the brink of civil war in order to preserve the Union. In September 1914, however, the Home Rule Bill became law, though it was not put into effect because of the war. Home Rule, within a United Kingdom, seemed to be the most likely future for Ireland. In 1916, however, the Sinn Fein rebellion set in train a course of events which led to the overthrow of John Redmond's moderate nationalist party and ultimately, after three years of military struggle (1919–22), to the partition of Ireland between the six counties of Northern Ireland and the twenty-six counties of the Irish Free State.

Within each polity, ethno-cultural issues took precedence over class. Socialists had taken part in the Irish Rising of 1916 but Socialism found no place in the Irish Free State. Within the six counties of Northern Ireland the supremacy of the Unionist party rested upon the war cry of 'No Surrender' which could be relied upon to outflank any appeal to class issues among the electorate. For fifty years the politics of Northern Ireland remained frozen in an ethno-religious mould, with a two-thirds majority of Protestants maintaining its unity against the supposed threat presented by the Catholic minority.

In England itself the affluent south-east provided a secure basis of Conservative political power. The Liberal party, divided between its radical and its 'Whiggish' wings gradually ceased to exist as a serious political force. English politics, like those of Wales and Ireland, were increasingly based upon class issues, although the Conservatives were always able to draw upon working-class Toryism in areas such as Liverpool and Glasgow where ethno-religious issues still had some life. Even here however class unity on occasion could outweigh ethnic diversity. In Liverpool during the transport strike of 1911 an observer noted how 'from Orange Garston, from Roman Catholic Bootle and the Scotland Road area, they come. Forgotten were their religious feuds . . . The Garston band had walked five miles and their drum-major proudly whirled his sceptre twined with orange and green ribbons as he led his contingent band, half out of the Roman Catholic, half out of the local Orange band.' In broad terms, however, one of the most lasting effects of the First World War was the creation of a system of British politics in which Irish issues, northern or southern, ceased to count.

11

Between the wars

The World War of 1914–18 undoubtedly had a profound impact upon Great Britain and Ireland and it is tempting to see it as a watershed of revolution. On balance, however, despite the undoubted changes which occurred, the period between 1918 and 1939 appears more as an interlude in which old and new elements were still intermingled and the future of Britain and Ireland was still unclear. It was still presumed, for example, that Britain was a great world power, an attitude which seemed persuasive because of the fact that the United States and the Soviet Union largely retreated from their full roles in world affairs. The real weakness of the British empire was not to be exposed until 1940 when it became clear that Britain was dependent upon American aid for the continuance of the war.

Of the internal changes which occurred within the British Isles during this period one of the most important was the victory of Sinn Fein in Ireland. The election of 1918 saw the destruction of John Redmond's Irish parliamentary party. It was replaced by the more 'advanced' nationalist party of Sinn Fein whose members refused to take up its seats in the Westminster parliament. In 1919, there was open violence. The result of three years of guerrilla warfare was the partition of Ireland into the Irish Free State consisting of twenty-six counties including three belonging to the traditional province of Ulster (Monaghan, Cavan and Donegal) and six counties of 'Northern Ireland', which were given a measure of 'Home Rule'.

The Irish crisis of 1919–21 rarely receives its due from English historians. In fact, however, the prolonged and bitter struggle between the British government and the forces of Sinn Fein had wide repercussions not merely within the British Commonwealth but also throughout the empire and the United States. The conflict of 'Orange and Green' was revived once more.

Within the Conservative party a split developed between the official leadership headed by F. E. Smith and Austen Chamberlain who came to accept, reluctantly, the need for compromise with Sinn Fein, and the 'Die-hards' who regarded the Treaty as a 'Scuttle'. In June 1922, Field Marshall Sir Henry Wilson, an Anglo-Irishman who in 1914 had been involved in the 'Mutiny on the Curragh', was assassinated by a splinter group of Irish nationalists. Leo Amery, who had been sympathetic to the Die-hards, wrote:

> Down to the House hearing, just before the end of questions, of Henry Wilson's assassination. The whole House very much upset and adjourned at once. I have lost one of my best friends and his death raises in my mind again all the doubts I have felt about the whole hateful Irish business. I cannot help feeling that it is to these very men that we have handed over Ireland.

The ethno-cultural issues raised by the prospect of Irish independence undoubtedly strengthened the hand of the 'Die-hards' within the Conservative party and helped to bring down the Lloyd George Liberal–Conservative coalition at the end of 1922. The way was clear for a Conservative party in which men sympathetic to business, such as Stanley Baldwin and Neville Chamberlain, would have a much greater say. Salisbury's cabinet in 1895 was filled to overflowing with marquesses, dukes, earls and barons. With the victory of Baldwin over his noble rival, Lord Curzon, the balance tilted towards the world of business.

Perhaps more important than the Irish crisis itself was the long-term effect of Irish withdrawal from Westminster. Since 1801 there had been an active Irish presence in parliament and Irish issues possessed a centrality which successive British governments had been unable to ignore. From 1922, however, after the signing of the Anglo-Irish Treaty, Ireland, north and south, in effect dropped below the political horizon. There were periods, notably during the 1930s and the war years, when the British government and the Free State were at loggerheads, but Irish political questions no longer dominated the political scene as they had done at intervals since the Union. The absence of eighty-plus Irish nationalist members deprived the Liberals of their 'natural' allies and made a Liberal recovery more difficult.

The full implications of the establishment of an independent Irish Free State were slow to appear, however. 'Ireland' was still a member of the British Commonwealth and even Mr De Valera when he drew up a new Irish constitution in 1937 left room for Ireland's 'external association' with the Commonwealth. The Treaty itself had been drawn up on the assumption that the partition of Ireland would not be permanent. It was perhaps not until 'Eire' adopted a neutral stance during the war of 1939–45 that attitudes finally hardened.

The Irish revolution of 1916–22 brought political changes which were the nearest approximation within the British Isles to those of central and eastern Europe. Ireland, however, remained very much the political exception. In England, Scotland and Wales, the war did not have the social repercussions which many anticipated. A wave of strikes in the immediate post-war years had little effect and the General Strike of 1926 petered out after a week. The two decades before the outbreak of the Second World War were on the whole an age of isolationism, in which Stanley Baldwin was the British equivalent of President Coolidge. The majority of the population wanted at almost all costs to avoid a recurrence of the mass slaughter on the Western Front. Another wartime event, the Russian revolution of 1917, also had lasting consequences during the post-war period. Conservatives were able to play as successfully upon the general fear of 'Bolshevism' as they had upon 'Home Rule' in the 1880s.

In 1923 Stanley Baldwin became leader of the Conservative party, in succession to Bonar Law. Baldwin self-consciously created the image of a politician more interested in domestic tranquillity (the equivalent of America's 'normalcy') than in world politics. In so doing, his aim was to counter the main asset upon which his Liberal rival Lloyd George relied, i.e. his status as a key figure in international politics, organiser of victory in the war and of the peace which followed. Baldwin won most seats in the 1923 election but was forced to yield power to Labour. In 1924, however, he won a resounding victory and remained in power until 1929. During the 1930s he onec more became Prime Minister, during the troubled years which followed the 1931 financial crisis.

The Conservative party which Baldwin and later Chamberlain led was very much the party of south-eastern England. Here lay its electoral strength, in the suburban middle class of outer London and the Home Counties. One of the long-term effects of the war, indeed, had been to upset the economic balance of power within the British Isles. Northern England, south Wales and Clydeside (and Belfast) were no longer the 'booming' areas of Britain. As was to become clear during the rest of the twentieth century, the First World War marked the beginning of yet another period of dominance by London and the south-east, a dominance symbolised by the decision of the Bank of England to restore the Gold Standard in 1925, thus impeding economic recovery in the north and west.

Stanley Baldwin may have led a party whose strength lay in the suburban middle class. His own rhetoric, however, revealed in the volume of his speeches *On England* which ran into six editions during the year 1926–7, struck a note of English nationalism. He recalled Disraeli in a speech made in 1924: 'I want to see the spirit of service to the whole nation [as] the birthright of every member of the Unionist Party – Unionist in the sense that we stand for the union of those nations of which Disraeli spoke two generations ago ... to make one nation of our people.' In a speech made after Curzon's death in 1925 he spoke of 'the same spirit that would have been welcomed by Young England in the days of Disraeli's youth, of which period, in many ways he seemed to be a member'. In another speech he stated: 'My party has no political bible. Possibly you might find our ideals expressed in one of Disraeli's novels.' Repeatedly his rhetoric referred to an exclusively English past in a way which would have been impossible for the Welshman Lloyd George or for the Scot, Ramsay MacDonald (or Campbell-Bannerman). In Baldwin's speeches the most consistent note is that of English nationalism.

The power of managing our own affairs in our own way is the greatest gift of Englishmen.

Nowhere was the village community so real and so enduring a thing as it was in England for at least three centuries of its history ... to these twelve centuries of discipline we owe the peculiar English capacity for self-government.

But though Baldwin spoke in the name of England the strength of the Unionist party lay in the south of England. When it came to the point of a trial of strength between south and north, as it did in the General Strike of 1926, Baldwin acted in the interests of the south.

The rhetoric of the Conservative party during these years was based upon a three-fold appeal – to English nationalism, to the fear of Socialism and to pride in the British empire. Labour was portrayed by Baldwin as a party dominated by foreign ideas. 'Many of those [he declared] who have been eager for the progress of our country have only succeeded in befogging themselves and their fellow countrymen, by filling their bellies with the east wind of German Socialism and Russian Communism and French Syndicalism.'

Within the Labour party itself there was a struggle for dominance between its leader, Ramsay MacDonald, who favoured a 'gradualist' approach to social change and the 'Clydesiders' led by Maxton and Wheatley, who pressed for radical socialist solutions to the problem of unemployment. During the months leading up to the 1929 election MacDonald came off best. In drawing up the party manifesto he was helped by R. H. Tawney, Professor of Economic History at the London School of Economics and a former member of the progressive wing of the Liberal party in the pre-war period.

In Tawney's approach to English history, there was a clear contrast with that of Stanley Baldwin. In a series of studies of which the most notable were *The Acquisitive Society* (1921), *Religion and the Rise of Capitalism* (1926) and *Equality* (1931) he produced an interpretation of history in which exploitation rather than freedom was seen as the chief characteristic of English history. Of the Church of England he wrote: 'Deprived of its vitality, it had allowed its officers to become by the eighteenth century the servile clients of a half-pagan aristocracy, to whose contemptuous indulgence they looked for preferment. It ceased for some 200 years to speak its mind and, as a natural consequence, it ceased to have a mind to speak.' About nonconformity he was equally dismissive: 'The personal piety of the Nonconformist could stem that creed – ("a persuasive self-confident and militant Gospel proclaiming the absolute value of economic success") [but] with a few individual exceptions they did not try to stem it, for they had lost the spiritual independence needed to appraise its true moral significance.' Tawney's vision of an ideal society was one which approximated in some way to that of the medieval social order when moral restraints had been placed upon economic appetites.

Behind the rhetoric of Baldwin and Tawney there lay the inescapable fact of mass unemployment in northern England, south Wales, Clydeside and Belfast. All of these had been areas of economic expansion before the war and it was presumed at first that any setbacks would be temporary. Looking back from 1929 one Lancashire observer recalled the extraordinary confidence of the period before 1914. He quoted a cotton manufacturer's views about Lancashire superiority.

My lad, never again let anybody in Lancashire hear you talk all this childish stuff about foreign competition. It's right enough for Londoners and such like but it puts a born Lancashire man to shame as an ignoramus. It's just twaddle. In the first place, we've got the only climate in the world where cotton pieces in any quantity can ever be produced. In the second place, no foreign Johnnies can ever be bred that can spin and weave like Lancashire lasses and lads. In the third place, there are more spindles in Oldham than in all the rest of the world put together. And last of all, if they had the climate and the men and the spindles – which they never can have – foreigners could never find the brains Lancashire cotton men have for the job. We've been making all the world's cotton cloth that matters for more years than I can tell and we always shall.

This outlook did not survive the post-war depression when unemployment in the cotton industry became endemic, rising to over 40 per cent in 1930. What happened to cotton happened also in shipbuilding. Towns such as Barrow and Jarrow were particularly hard hit.

Culturally, Walter Greenwood's novel *Love on the Dole* (1933) reflects the mood of depression in northern England. The songs of Gracie Fields in *Sing as We Go* (1934) were an attempt to raise morale in the north, but observers such as George Orwell and J. B. Priestley on their visits to the northern cities found a deep-seated malaise. The hunger marches made by the Jarrow unemployed in 1936 were one way of attempting to cope with the situation. Another was to emigrate to the prosperous industrial areas of the south.

The politics of the inter-war period revolved around the contrast between the south-east and the depressed areas of the north and west. The north (and its associated areas) had been the product of an age of coal and iron. It was these industries which were hit by the new technology of oil, electrical power and chemical engineering. During the First World War the new industries found a home in the south, where they were nearer to the Channel ports and the Western Front. As a consequence, it was southern towns such as Bristol, Gloucester, Oxford, Luton and Slough which became centres of the automobile and aircraft industries and the new light industries. Coventry became part of the 'new south'. Statistics relating to unemployment during the 1920s and 1930s indicate that rates were much higher for the older industries of the north than the new industries of the south. In the coal-mining areas unemployment was well over 30 per cent in 1932 and 1933 and over 20 per cent for much of the time. In 1939 it was still over 12 per cent. In the shipbuilding industry, there was 62 per cent unemployment in 1932 and it was still at the rate of 20 per cent in 1939. Similar rates applied to dockworkers, and to workers in linen and cotton textiles. The new southern industries were more fortunate. For much of the period unemployment among the electrical engineers was under 10 per cent. From 1936 it was under 5 per cent. The same was true of the industries involving the construction and repair of cars, aircraft and cycles. Service industries

North, Scotland and Wales		The south	
Jarrow	67.8%	Coventry	5.1%
Merthyr	61.9%	Luton	7.7%
Maryport	57.0%	Oxford	5.1%
Motherwell	37.4%	St Albans	3.9%

also did well in the south. Statistics relating to unemployment in individual towns tell the same story.

Economically the period after the First World War was marked by substantial change, when what had once been 'boom' areas were effected by economic depression. Politically also the post-war scene was markedly different from what it had been before 1914. After the signing of the Anglo-Irish Treaty in 1922, the Irish dimension in British politics ceased to occupy its once central position. Religious issues also became of marginal importance. In particular, nonconformity, for so long a major force in the Liberal politics of northern England and Wales, increasingly lost ground. The bitter split within the Liberal party between the followers of Asquith and Lloyd George left many nonconformists without obvious political allegiance. For some, Conservatism became increasingly attractive in the face of the growth of Socialism, and Stanley Baldwin, in his speeches, went to some pains to stress his nonconformist background. In 1924 he spoke to the National Free Church Conference, stating that 'I owe a great deal of my public and private life to my Nonconformist ancestry.' 'No less than half my great grandfathers' he declared 'were Presidents of Conference [and] one was a follower of John Wesley.' In 1926 he appealed to the Wesleyans, saying that 'There is nothing this country needs so much as another Wesley or Whitefield.'

Many nonconformists, such as Kingsley Wood, a Wesleyan, gravitated towards the Conservative party, out of fear of Socialism. Others found a home in the Labour party. Ernest Bevin was a Baptist lay preacher, as was Arthur Cook, the miners' leader. Aneurin Bevan was the son of Welsh Baptists. Arthur Henderson was a Wesleyan lay preacher, Philip Snowden was a Wesleyan. Within the context of the British Isles, the Labour party thus inherited part of the mantle of the Liberal party in the sense that it drew far more for its support upon 'Outer Britain'. If the Conservative heartland was the south-east, that of Labour was northern England, south Wales and Clydeside, all of them heavily industrialised areas. Pre-war Liberalism, however, as the party of the 'Left' possessed a broader appeal than did the post-war Labour party. In Scotland, the Liberal party had been able to rely upon the rural east as well as the industrialised west, and in Wales upon the rural north as well as the industrialised south. During the post-war years, however, Labour found it difficult to make headway in the rural areas. In Scotland from 1924 the Conservatives did well in the east, where farmers reacted against the growth of trade unionism among the farm labourers. In north Wales, the Liberal party maintained its position in part at least because of nonconformist fears about the growth of Socialism in south Wales.

The tensions between 'Inner Britain' (i.e. the south-east) and 'Outer Britain' (northern England, south Wales and Clydeside) reached a climax in the General Strike of 1926. Large-scale strikes had already occurred before the war and they continued after it in industries such as mining and shipbuilding which were seriously affected by the post-war depression. The General Strike was made possible, though not inevitable, by the deflation which followed upon the Conservative government decision to return to the Gold Standard in 1925.

The General Strike, so often viewed in purely English terms, was very much a struggle between Inner and Outer Britain. The strength of the government rested in large measure upon its control of the communication network of Inner Britain, with its centre in London. The strike drew its support in the main from the industrial north, Clydeside and south Wales, with the East End of London as an additional bastion. In Scotland there was a contrast between the east, exemplified by Edinburgh, where the strike failed disastrously, and the west, where such towns as Motherwell, Hamilton and the Vale of Leven were solidly behind it. In Wales, the north remained aloof from the strike, while the south, in contrast, was largely in favour. In south Wales, however, there were clashes in the coastal cities of Cardiff, Swansea and Newport between pro- and anti-strike groups.

The General Strike collapsed after a week, leaving bitter memories, especially among the miners, who continued their resistance long after the other unions had capitulated. Within the Labour party the failure of the strike helped the cause of the 'gradualists' led by MacDonald. The General Strike may also be seen as highlighting in dramatic fashion the tensions which existed within Britain between an increasingly prosperous and powerful south-east and a depressed north and east. It was a pattern which was temporarily reversed during the Second World War when Britain depended for its survival upon its Atlantic ports and its traditional industries, especially shipbuilding and mining. After the war the victory of Labour restored the influence of the periphery, in the persons of such cabinet ministers as Emmanuel Shinwell (of Glasgow Jewish background), Aneurin Bevan (from Tredegar in south Wales) and Harold Wilson (of Yorkshire nonconformist background). With the victory of the Conservatives, however, in 1951 the drift to the south-east once more picked up momentum, accentuated by the decision to apply to enter the European Economic Community in 1962.

For much of the inter-war period Ireland, both north and south, remained largely insulated from the course of events on the other side of the Irish Sea. Economically, Ireland, north and south, was as depressed as Wales, Scotland and northern England. In Belfast, employment in the shipbuilding yards, heavily dominated by a Protestant labour force, fell from 20,000 in 1924 to 2,000 in 1933. The linen industry enjoyed some degree of prosperity in the early 1920s as a result of American demand but after 1927 it also declined. In 1937 there were only 15,000 linen workers in Belfast, less than one third of the numbers in 1927. The Irish Free State was also badly hit during the depression though the extent of unemployment was concealed to some extent by underemployment in the rural areas, where the great majority of the population lived. When De Valera came to power in 1932 a tariff war broke out with Britain over the payment of annuities due under the Land Acts of an earlier period. The decision of the Irish Free State to remain neutral during the Second World War acted as an obstacle to economic development.

Culturally also both the Free State and Northern Ireland remained isolated. Within the Free State, Church and state were in general agreement about the need to keep Ireland uncontaminated from the pressures of 'modernity'. Divorce and contraception were prohibited and a stringent system of literary censorship was enforced. Partition, though rejected in theory, was tacitly accepted on the grounds that it made possible the development of Ireland as a 'Catholic' society. Neutrality during wartime accentuated the trend towards cultural isolation. In a wartime broadcast De Valera spoke eloquently of how 'That Ireland which we dreamed of would be the home of a people who valued material wealth only as a basis for right living, of a people who were satisfied with frugal comfort and devoted their leisure to the things of the spirit.' In 1972, however, this pre-industrial vision was to be decisively rejected when the population of the Republic voted overwhelmingly in favour of joining the E.E.C.

In the Irish Free State Catholicism was the religion of the great majority. In Northern Ireland, two-thirds of the population were Protestant and one third Catholic. As it became clear that partition was likely to be a permanent feature of Irish life for the foreseeable future, a situation was created in which the two cultures lived side by side with a minimum of social contact. Each had its own churches, schools, newspapers and forms of recreation. In small towns, Protestant and Catholic grocers had their own clientele. For one community, soccer and rugby were appropriate games, for the other, Gaelic football and hurling. Each had its own interpretation of Irish history. At Queen's University, Belfast, Irish history began with Elizabeth. In Catholic colleges, the Gaelic past received its share of attention. In mixed rural areas, as Rosemary Harris' study of Ballygawley has shown, a complex and subtle system of relationships came into existence in which both sides took great pains to avoid causing offence.

From time to time, the I.R.A., a legacy from the day of Fenianism, attempted 'offensive' operations to overthrow partition. The main consequence of these episodes was to confirm the Unionists in their entrenched position, backed by a Special Powers Act and an armed constabulary. At times of general elections to the Northern Ireland parliament official rhetoric ('A Protestant Parliament for a Protestant People') easily overcame any attempt to introduce class-based politics on the British model.

In Wales and Scotland, after the end of the war, legislative reforms removed the sense of grievance which had provided support for the Liberal party. In 1920, with the backing of Lloyd George, the Church of Wales was disestablished, in a reform which marked the culmination of a series of changes which had begun in 1881 with the Welsh Temperance Act. Anti-landlordism, linked with anti-English feeling, also ceased to be a live political issue as the large landed estates in Wales were split up and sold. Over a quarter of the land in Wales changed hands, a social shift of the highest importance. Specifically Welsh issues lost much of their appeal. Chapel membership declined. In effect the Welsh had been granted a large measure of 'Home Rule' under the aegis of a Welsh-speaking, temperance-minded, non-conformist middle class, with which power and status now rested.

There was little support during these years for the Welsh Nationalist party (Plaid Cymru) which had emerged during the 1920s. Its leader Saunders Lewis became a Roman Catholic in 1932, hardly a sure recipe for political success in nonconformist Wales. The party itself admired the conservative French group Action Française and looked back to an idealised medieval social order as a model for Wales to follow. In some ways, Saunders Lewis was the Welsh equivalent of Eamonn De Valera.

If Wales enjoyed a considerable degree of 'Home Rule' during this period so also did Scotland. The Scottish legal and educational systems retained their traditional distinctiveness. The Church of Scotland also remained influential. In 1929 prolonged negotiations between the Church of Scotland and the United Free Churches ended in agreement, leaving only a minority group, the 'Wee Frees', outside the main Presbyterian fold. The 'Disruption' had come to an end. In law, religion and education national symbols existed, acceptable to the great majority. The Education Act of 1918, providing state assistance for building and maintaining Roman Catholic schools, met the grievances of the immigrant minority. Insistence upon teachers at secondary level possessing a four-year degree effectively excluded immigration of English-trained teachers. The symbolic independence of Scotland was recognised by the formal visits of the Royal Family to Holyroodhouse. In England, the Queen was head of the Church. In Scotland, she was merely a member of the Church of Scotland.

In such circumstances it was not surprising that a more 'advanced' nationalism should have little appeal. A Scottish National party was formed in 1934 on the basis of two groups founded earlier, the Scottish party and the National party. It failed to make much headway in the 1935 election, its best result being in the Western Isles with 28 per cent of the vote, its worst in Greenock with 3.3 per cent. The Labour party did toy with the idea of Home Rule in the early 1920s but by 1925 had moved away from it. The labour leader, Ramsay MacDonald, though himself a Scot, displayed a distinct lack of enthusiasm for the nationalist cause. Labour in Scotland as in Wales saw its future as part of a wider socialist movement in Britain.

In Scotland throughout this period political issues revolved largely round questions of class rather than ethnicity. After the recognition of the Irish Free State in 1922, Scottish Catholics of Irish background turned towards the Labour party. Ethnic rivalries remained of some significance, notably in football where Celtic and Rangers represented differing religious affiliations. In the Glasgow constituency of Kelvingrove, politics still had ethnic overtones and in Edinburgh during the 1930s, 'No Popery' once again became a live issue. In contrast with the pre-1914 period, however, Catholics, who amounted to 25 per cent of the population in some areas, voted consistently for Labour. During the 1960s when the S.N.P. showed signs of revival, Catholics showed little enthusiasm for the nationalist programme.

The majority of Scots lived in the central Lowlands and it was there that the main clash of labour and Unionist took place. The Highlands may be seen as the Scottish equivalent of north Wales. It was there, as in north Wales, that nonconformity in the shape of the 'Wee Frees' predominated, and that issues of language, temperance and Sabbatarianism were central. The borders also had their own distinctive character. Elsewhere in Scotland, class issues were decisive with a broad contrast still existing between a 'Whiggish' east and a radical west.

The reality of 'Home Rule All Round' in Ireland, Scotland and Wales helps to explain why ethnic questions which had exercised so powerful a gravitational pull upon the politics of the British Isles during the late nineteenth century began to lose ground. The Liberal party had drawn much of its strength from the sense of 'relative deprivation' which various groupings in Ireland, Scotland and Wales experienced. In one way or another these grievances had been met in the immediate post-1918 period. For their part, the English nonconformists no longer felt discriminated against.

Perhaps the one great exception to the rise of class-based politics in England was Liverpool where the politics of ethnicity survived until after the Second World War. A Catholic did not become Lord Mayor of Liverpool until 1944. T. P. OConnor, the Irish nationalist M.P. for the Scotland division of Liverpool, thought that the likelihood of this happening was as good as the chance of a Christian becoming Caliph of Baghdad. A tacit alliance between the Conservative 'Tammany Hall'-style organisation and Protestant party led by H. D. Longbottom, long-serving chaplain to the Orange Order, led to a split in the working-class vote, comparable to that which occurred in Belfast. As late as 1948, Dr Heenan, Catholic archbishop of Liverpool, was stoned in the Scotland Road area. But the ethnic politics of Liverpool were increasingly untypical of the rest of England. For this period at least, Peter Pulzer's uncompromising generalisation is justified: 'the basis of [English] politics is class – all else is embellishment and detail! (*Political Representation and Politics in Britain* (1972), p. 44), though what was true of England was not necessarily the case in other parts of the British Isles.

12

Withdrawal from empire

Winston Churchill once declared that he had not become the King's chief minister to preside over the dissolution of the British empire. In fact, however, the process of decolonisation which had begun before 1939 with the Statute of Westminster (1931), and perhaps even earlier with the Anglo-Irish Treaty, gathered momentum after 1945. The granting of independence to India, Pakistan, Ceylon and Burma in the late 1940s was accompanied by withdrawal from Palestine in 1948 and in 1954 from the Suez Canal Zone. An attempt to restore British influence in the Middle East with the Suez expedition of 1956 broke down in the face of American opposition.

During the 1960s, withdrawal from empire continued apace under Harold Macmillan and his colonial secretary Iain MacLeod. It was accompanied by a policy of drawing closer to the European Economic Community. Macmillan made the first application to enter Europe in 1962 but it was not until 1973 that Britain, together with the Republic of Ireland was finally admitted to membership. Looked at in retrospect, this apparently inexorable process of moving from overseas empire to European community would seem to be the most significant trend of post-war Britain.

Within Britain the long-term impact of commitment to Europe was to intensify the drift to the south-east. The economic decline of the north and west which had been halted during the Second World War was resumed. As they had been during the 1920s and 1930s, rates of unemployment were much higher in 'Outer Britain'. The core prospered, the periphery languished. A. J. P. Taylor concluded his study *England 1914–45* with the reflection 'Few even sang "England Arise". England had risen all the same.' His point was wrongheaded in relation to England, but may be allowed to stand in relation to the south-east.

Alongside the currents of change there were elements of continuity. The key to Welsh attitudes as so often before lay in the division between the largely rural north (in which industrial Flintshire was an exception) and the largely industrial south. The attempt of Plaid Cymru to create a unified nationalist movement ran into great difficulties in the face of this divide. It was not until 1966 in a by-election at Carmarthen that Plaid Cymru won its first parliamentary seat, only to lose it in the general election of 1970. The cruellest blow which Welsh nationalism received was in the referendum of 1979 when there was an overwhelming vote against devolution (46.5 per cent against, 11.8 per cent for).

The most powerful force in Wales, the Labour party, set its face against nationalism. Aneurin Bevan (1897–1960) throughout his political career spoke out against any concession to Welsh nationalist sentiment. It was only with the greatest reluctance that he accepted a proposal to establish a Secretary of State for Wales on the Scottish model, backed by the more nationally minded James Griffiths. In the 1979 election Plaid Cymru came a poor third with two seats compared to eleven for the Conservative party and twenty-two for Labour.

There was indeed no national issue which was capable of uniting north and south. In 1960, debates on the question of Sunday opening of public houses aroused old antagonisms. The northern counties in which Welsh-speaking nonconformity was strong voted heavily against the sale of drink on Sundays. The southern counties voted in favour. Though the voting was largely symbolic since alcoholic refreshment was available throughout Wales in innumerable small social clubs, the results did point to the continued influence of Sabbatarian attitudes in the north which went back to the heyday of Gladstonian Liberalism and the 1881 Sunday Closing Act.

In Scotland, Scottish nationalism also remained surprisingly weak. Discontent with the dominance of south-eastern England took the form of an increased vote for Labour. Scottish nationalism hit the newspaper headlines but the realities of power remained with Labour. The contrast between east and west remained important though the balance shifted increasingly towards the west in the sense that Labour, the party of the industrial west, continued to make headway. In the 1959 election the east returned twelve Conservatives to thirteen Labour. On Clydeside Labour won nineteen seats, the Conservatives eight, a better result for the Conservatives than it was to be seven years later. In the 1966 election, which marked a high point for labour, the east stretching from Aberdeen to Edinburgh still returned ten Conservative seats to Labour's fourteen. In the industrial west, however, it was a different story. On Clydeside, Labour won twenty-four seats, Conservatives, three.

There were some signs in the 1960s that the system of informal Home Rule was beginning to break down. In November 1967, with a Labour government in power, Hamilton, the second safest Labour seat in Scotland, was won by an S.N.P. candidate, Mrs Winifred Ewing. From late 1970, the discovery of a series of important oil fields off the east coast of Scotland provided an issue on which the S.N.P. capitalised. The demand that 'Scottish Oil' should be used for the benefit of the Scottish people gave new life to Scottish nationalism. In the first general election of 1974, the S.N.P. gained seven seats with 22 per cent of the Scottish vote. In the second general election of that year they gained eleven seats with 30 per cent of the vote. Devolution became an issue which the labour government could not ignore and in 1979, in Wales as well as Scotland, it was put to a referendum. In Wales, to the consternation of Plaid Cymru, devolution was decisively rejected with less than 12 per cent of the votes cast. In Scotland it attracted 52 per cent of the votes cast but this amounted to only 33 per cent of the total electorate, short of the 40 per cent which the government had laid down as an essential prerequisite. In the 1979 election, there was a decisive swing against the S.N.P., which was left with only two seats. Labour, though losing the general election in the United Kingdom as a whole, regained its position as the main party of protest in Scotland.

Despite the importance of class and of nationalism, religious issues still remained very much alive in some areas of Scottish life. In this respect the central Lowlands and especially the Clydeside area resembled Northern Ireland. As J. G. Kellas stated in his study of modern Scotland (*Modern Scotland* (1968)), it is still possible to see graffiti urging passers-by to 'F--k the Pope' (an anti-Irish sentiment rather than an anti-papal one). Ulster Unionists found a more sympathetic audience on Clydeside than they found elsewhere in the British Isles.

In Ireland, as in Wales and Scotland, long-standing historical patterns continued to reveal themselves. The Republic of Ireland was an independent state. Culturally and politically and economically, however, its affairs remained inextricably intertwined with those of the United Kingdom. The relationship of Ireland and Britain was full of paradoxes. Many of the leading figures in 'English' literature during the twentieth century, Yeats, Joyce, Synge, O Casey, Heaney, were Irishmen. In certain sports, such as golf and rugby, the difference between the republic and Northern Ireland was virtually ignored and 'Ireland', a non-existent political entity, fielded a united team. In horse-racing also there were the closest of ties between English and Irish communities. Irish actors such as Cyril Cusack and T. P. MacKenna were familiar figures on the London stage.

Profound tensions remained, however, in the relationship between the Republic and the United Kingdom. Each had different interpretations of the recent past. The Sinn Fein rebellion of 1916 was heroic in nationalist eyes, an act of treachery to unionists. Irish neutrality in the Second World War continued to be a source of resentment in Britain long after the war ended. In Ireland, Churchill's criticism of De Valera in 1945 was looked upon as a piece of spite against a small nation by a victor lacking in magnanimity. During the northern crisis of 1969 and the years following relations between Britain and the Irish Republic continued to reflect deep-seated historical emotions.

Irish emigration to England had been low during the depressed 1930s and during the war years. After the war Irish men and women once more made their way to England in search of a job. During the 1950s an 'Irish presence' in the south-east became noticeable after the emigration of 375,000 Irish men and women to the United Kingdom. These were figures higher than any period since the 1880s and were a consequence of the depressed state of the Irish economy.

In Ireland itself partition itself was in some respects more notional than real. Trinity College, Dublin, continued to draw many of its students from the 'north'. The archbishopric of Armagh, north of the border, was the primatial see both for the Catholic Church and for the Church of Ireland. During the 1960s, indeed, it seemed as though good relations between Stormont and Dublin were about to make the border irrelevant. In 1965, Sean Lemass, the Irish Taoiseach, and Terence ONeill, Prime Minister of Northern Ireland met.

Cultural divisions within Northern Ireland itself, however, proved to be less amenable to resolution. The Protestant community in Northern Ireland had been badly hit by the collapse of the linen industry in the face of competition from man-made fibres and by the decline of the Belfast shipbuilding industry. In contrast, among northern Catholics, there was a sense of rising expectations, fuelled in part by the long-term effects of the 1944 Education Act which made higher education more accessible to poorer sections of the population. Terence ONeill's promises of reform aroused further hopes. In 1967 members of the newly articulate Catholic middle class protested against discrimination and founded a Civil Rights Association on the model of similar movements in the United States. The largely unanticipated consequence of Terence ONeill's reform proposals and the Catholic response was a fierce Protestant backlash which led to violence in 1969. A prolonged crisis began which was partially resolved in 1972 when the British government took-over direct responsibility for Northern Ireland. A fifty-year period of 'Home Rule' had come to an end.

The 'Irish Question' once more entered British politics, and the 'British Question' re-entered Irish politics. Violence in Northern Ireland had the consequence of bringing the Republic of Ireland into closer contact with the United Kingdom. After a long period of mutual isolation the governments of the two states were once more involved with each other. In 1973 both countries became members of the E.E.C.

The Northern Ireland crisis of 1969 and the years following illustrate once again the difficulty of treating the different national units of the British Isles in isolation. The influence of history, since the plantation of Ulster in the early seventeenth century and the battle of the Boyne in 1690, was too powerful to be ignored. Historians of Britain since 1922 have dealt with the problem of the 'Irish dimension' by ignoring it. To resort to this solution, however, is to oversimplify. The cultural influence of Ireland is still strong in Glasgow and Liverpool and in the new Irish communities of London and Birmingham. The politics of Northern Ireland itself cannot be understood in a specifically six-county context. The I.R.A. itself adopts an interpretation of Irish history which takes it back at least to Wolfe Tone and the rebellion of 1798. There is, in addition, the British Isles dimension of the dominions of Canada, Australia and New Zealand.

Twentieth-century British history (especially in the south-east) has been complicated by an additional 'ethnic' factor. As has been indicated earlier, ethnic diversity had been a characteristic of the newly industrialised areas of the British Isles during the nineteenth century, with the Irish and, to a lesser extent the Jews, making up the bulk of the new immigrants. Between the wars, emigration rather than immigration was a more typical phenomenon. Between 1921 and 1930, for example,

261,000 British emigrants arrived in Australia, four-fifths of them on government-assisted passages. After the war, the situation changed. There was now a huge demand for unskilled labour in Britain and in western Europe generally. London Transport set up a recruiting office for bus drivers in Barbados. Mills in Yorkshire despatched representatives to the Punjab to recruit labour for night shift work and for dirtier, lower-paid jobs. In Bradford by 1971 there were 30,000 Pakistanis out of a total working population of 300,000.

The earliest post-war immigrants were from the West Indies, many of them ex-servicemen from Jamaica, who arrived on the *Empire Windrush* in 1948. West Indian immigration on a large scale did not begin, however, until 1953, after restrictions were imposed on entry into the United States by the MacCarran Act of 1952. A second phase began in the early 1950s after the granting of independence to Britain's East African colonies. Indians had settled there in large numbers with the encourage-ment of the British government. In 1901 the British Special Commissioner in Uganda declared that 'East Africa is, and should be, from every point of view, the America of the Hindu.' Fifty years later the wheel had come full circle. The newly independent colonies began to implement policies of 'Africanisation', which placed the Indians under pressure. It was this 'push' factor which led to a mass exodus of Indians from East Africa to the United Kingdom from 1967 onwards.

After the 1971 census it was estimated that over one and a half million immigrants of 'New Commonwealth' ethnic origins were resident within the United Kingdom. Of these, over half were from India and Pakistan or were East African Asians. Between a quarter and a third were from the West Indies. These bald statistics, however, do not convey any sense of the wide variety of internal cultural differences, particularly among Indians and West Indians.

Immigrants from the New Commonwealth made up only a small proportion (between 2 and 3 per cent) of the total population of the United Kingdom. They tended to congregate in specific areas, however, drawn there partly by the prospect of employment and partly by cheap housing. In 1971, statistics for certain London boroughs, especially Brent, Haringay, Hackney, Islington and Lambeth, indicate that new immigrants accounted for between 20 and 30 per cent of the entry into local schools. The largest concentration of Commonwealth immigrants was in the south-east, especially in Greater London. Other towns such as Derby, Huddersfield, Bradford and Wolverhampton attracted large numbers of immigrants. Other areas, Scotland and most of northern England, were largely untouched.

Mention should also be made of 'New Irish' immigration which was much higher than that of any single group of new Commonwealth immigrants. In 1969 it was estimated that there were c.750,000 immigrants from the Irish Republic, as well as many thousands from Northern Ireland. The New Irish did not settle in the depressed areas of Liverpool and Glasgow where there were old-established Irish populations but in London (especially Kilburn), Bristol and Birmingham.

Many of these newcomers, the Irish excepted, were highly visible because of their colour and, in the case of such groups as the Sikhs, because of their costume. It was thus not surprising that legislation was passed to restrict entry in 1962 and again after the arrival of other Indians from East Africa in 1968. But attempts which were made to whip up 'nativist' hysteria against the immigrants on lines which recalled anti-Irish and anti-Jewish propaganda in the nineteenth century fell largely on deaf ears. In April 1968, Mr Enoch Powell, perhaps in an attempt to challenge Edward Heath's leadership of the Conservative party, made a speech which has been compared to Randolph Churchill's playing of the 'Orange Card' in 1886. Powell, a former Professor of Classics, declared that 'Those whom the gods wish to destroy they first make mad. We must be mad, literally mad, as a nation, to be permitting the annual flow of some 50,000 dependents .... It is like watching a nation busily engaging in heaping up its own funeral pyre.' He spoke in highly emotional terms of a formerly 'quiet street' which had become 'a place of noise and confusion' and where 'a single white old lady, had been shouted at by her coloured neighbours' and had 'excreta pushed through her letter box'. Ironically, after playing the 'Orange Card', Powell found himself consigned to the relative obscurity of an Ulster constituency.

As with Britain's entry into the E.E.C., it remains to be seen what the long-term impact of the New Commonwealth immigration upon British society will be. Clearly, important distinctions must be drawn between the different immigrant groups. One West Indian stated that 'We are not immigrants in the true technical sense: after all we are members of the Realm. We are British.' A prominent Trinidadian observed, 'Like every West Indian, I am part Englishman. I mean this, of course, in the sense that, having acquired the English language, the traditions and institutions of this country, it is natural for me to want to be here. The West Indian is essentially what British culture and influences have made him.'

We may conclude this brief survey of post-war trends by stressing once again the continuing dominance of the south-east. In the field of higher education, many of the new universities, Sussex, East Anglia, Essex, Kent, Surrey, Brunel and others, were situated in the southern and eastern counties in an arc with Greater London as its centre. The public schools, heavily concentrated in the south and east, were attacked during the first Labour government but successfully beat off the challenge. The 'Media' in broadcasting, publishing and the press remained based upon London. The 'City' continued to grow in importance. It was thus not surprising that the finest sight in the north, as in Scotland and Wales, continued to be the High Road to the south. Even Ireland was not immune from the cultural influence of London. One of the most striking sights of the Dublin area is the forest of high-rising T.V. aerials, constructed to receive British television programmes from across the Irish Sea. 'Sinn Fein' had broken down with a vengeance in the newly urbanised Ireland of the 1960s.

South Wales drew closer to south-eastern England during the post-war period, as new high-speed trains and motorways made communication easier. North Wales became a culture under pressure, partly as a consequence of unemployment, partly owing to the influence of tourism.

In western Scotland, Clydeside was particularly hard hit by unemployment in shipbuilding and mining. The shipbuilding industry in particular found it difficult to compete with competition from Japan, South Korea and Germany. Eastern Scotland, after the discovery of North Sea oil, enjoyed something of a 'boom' period. Of all the peripheral areas of the United Kingdom, Scotland may well have retained its autonomy more successfully than any other.

As this concluding paragraph is written (1988), a channel tunnel is under construction with the aim of linking London and Paris by road. The consequence will surely be to intensify the drift to southern England. House prices are rising in the south-east at the rate of 25 per cent a year compared to 7 per cent in the periphery. The flood to the south-east seems destined to become a torrent with a 70-mile area around London linked to the metropolis by high-speed trains for the benefit of daily commuters. The balance between 'core' and 'periphery' has shifted unmistakably in favour of the core.

In 1985, a Cambridge tutor told me that it was the custom of his college to steer his students away from Scottish, Irish or Welsh history should they show unhealthy signs of interest in such peripheral topics. For him, British history was English history. The problem about this, as has been suggested repeatedly throughout this study, is that the history of 'England' has overlapped repeatedly with that of other cultures within the British Isles (a term which should include the Isle of Man, the Channel Islands, Shetland and Orkney, as well as the larger islands of Britain and Ireland). It would, no doubt, have simplified the historian's task had England, Ireland, Scotland and Wales been distinctive, stable historical units over long periods of time. In fact, however, the history of the British Isles, for at least a thousand years, resembles that of the Italian peninsula, the Iberian peninsula or the Swiss Confederation more than is generally supposed. In modern times English culture has achieved a general dominance much as German culture did within the dominions of the Habsburgs. The advance of the English language has squeezed Celtic to the periphery of the British Isles. It is as possible for an English-based historian to view history through English eyes as for a German historian to do the same for the Habsburg empire. It is possible, but undesirable, since it removes elements of complexity and paradox from the historical process.

During the past millennium, 'England', 'Ireland', 'Scotland' and 'Wales' have not lived in mutual isolation. Since the viking invasions, if not earlier, the cultures of the British Isles have reacted with each other. In 1973 a new historical page was turned when the United Kingdom and the Irish Republic entered the Common Market. Clearly this was a new beginning, the implications of which are being worked out. Clearly also, Britain and Ireland are exposed to powerful cultural influences from across the Atlantic. When all this is said, however, the influence of history itself cannot be left out of account. The conflict between Celtic and Germanic cultures, the Norman Conquests, the impact of Reformation and Counter-Reformation, the effect of migration within the British Isles, the consequences of imperial expansion – all these have left a lasting mark upon cultural relationships within these islands.

The story did not end in 1973 with British and Irish entry into the Common Market, nor can it be confined merely to the relationship between Britain and Ireland. The impact of new ethnic groups began to be felt in 1989 after the publication of Salman Rushdie's *The Satanic Verses* which was publicly burned in Bradford by Islamic fundamentalists. The possible entry into Britain of Hongkong Chinese after the return of Hongkong to China in 1997 also showed signs of becoming an important political issue in 1990. The debate about what constituted 'British identity' continued in 1990 against the background of governmental involvement in a national history curriculum. Scottish and Welsh nationalism simmered. The Northern Ireland issue, which involved Dublin as well as London, Belfast and Washington, D.C., refused to go away. Class issues were still dominant in British politics but ethnicity remained as a factor of great political significance for the future.

Conclusion

In this book I have argued that the 'British Isles' constituted a historical unit comparable to the valley of the Danube, the Iberian peninsula or the Italian peninsula in which various cultures struggled for supremacy or survival over a thousand years and more. In the case of the British Isles an enduring pattern was set after the withdrawal of the Roman legions c.410 A.D. It was then, during the fifth, sixth and seventh centuries that a frontier was drawn between Celtic and Germanic cultures. But, as was the case with the valley of the Danube, other cultural and political patterns came to overlay the enduring linguistic divide between Celtic and Teutonic. Over the course of the four centuries between c.800 and c.1200 A.D. Viking and Norman cultures added to the complexity of the pattern. At the end of the thirteenth century a 'Norman' ascendancy seemed to have established itself throughout the British Isles with some prospect of permanence. The Scandinavian future which once seemed a likely outcome for the British Isles had been replaced by one which linked these islands to western Europe. The crisis of the fourteenth and fifteenth centuries, culminating in the failures of the Hundred Years War and the Wars of the Roses, enabled the varied cultures of the British Isles, including Gaelic Ulster and the Lordship of the Isles to achieve some form of autonomy. It was only in the first half of the sixteenth century that the modern period began, in which the English monarchy established a political and cultural hegemony throughout the area. Beneath the political unity symbolised by the Crown, however, distinctive cultures and religious identities survived, as they did also in the Habsburg empire. During the nineteenth century nationalist movements made some headway, particularly in the case of Ireland and Wales, but the internal cultural differences in those countries prevented any single national solution from being arrived at. In Ireland, the divide between north and south proved to be too deep for any nationalist leader to overcome. In Wales the gap between the rural north and the industrialising south prevented the achievement of any real 'national' unity. In Scotland, also, the historic divisions between Highlands and Lowlands remained. To them were added new religious divisions beween Catholic immigrants and Protestant 'nativists', and within the Established Church between the establishment and the Free Church.

During the crisis of the Great War, 1914–18, the English empire of the British Isles did not break up as completely as the Habsburg empire. It did, however, suffer a deep wound, when the Irish Free State was established in 1922. In due course, after the Second World War during which Eire remained neutral, the Republic of Ireland was established (1949). Other ethnic divisions within the United Kingdom led to demands for political independence but when it came to the test of a plebiscite in the late 1970s, the political and cultural balance of power remained unaltered. During the 1980s, however, it was possible to discern a shift of population and wealth to the south-east and a growing centralisation based upon London. The history of the British Isles did not come to an end in 1973, the year with which this study concludes. Writing in 1990, however, there is no sign that the British Isles is ceasing to be an enduring historical unit, of which the Republic of Ireland forms part, and to which new, non-European ethnic groups are now making a contribution.

It is the complexities of this geographical area which have been projected against the screen of world history. An ethnocentric absorption with 'the Englishman and his history' hinders any real understanding of the contribution which has been made by migrants from the British Isles to the histories of the United States, Canada, Australia and New Zealand. In a reverse direction, Irish-American involvement in the politics of Ireland has been a factor which successive British and Irish governments have been unable to ignore. The shadow of the Great Famine may still be said to fall across the course of Anglo-American relations. The history of the 'English-speaking peoples' has interacted continuously with that of the 'Celtic-speaking peoples', for at least a thousand years, not always to their mutual benefit.

All except those marked

Selected reading list

GENERAL WORKS WITH A BRITISH ISLES APPROACH

Pre-Roman

Childe, V. G., *The Prehistoric Communities of the British Isles*, Edinburgh 1947.
Dillon, M. and Chadwick, N. K., *The Celtic Realms*, 2nd edn rev. by D. A. Binchy, Dublin 1972.
Laing, L., *The Archaeology of Late Celtic Britain and Ireland*, London 1975.
Moore, D., *The Irish Sea Province in Archaeology and History*, Cardiff 1970.
Piggott, S., *Early Celtic Art*, Edinburgh 1970.
Pocock, J. G. A., 'The Limits and Divisions of British History: In Search of an Unknown Subject', *American Historical Review*, LXXXVII (1982), 311–36.
Ross, A., *Pagan Celtic Britain*, London 1967.

Roman

Barley, M. W. and Hanson, R. P. C., eds., *Christianity in Britain 300–700*, Leicester 1968.
Sawyer, P. H., *From Roman Britain to Norman England*, London 1978.
Thomas, C., *Christianity in Roman Britain to A.D. 500*, London 1981.

Post-Roman

Morris, J., *The Age of Arthur: A History of the British Isles from 350 to 650*, London 1973.
Thomas, C., *Britain and Ireland in Early Christian Times A.D. 400–800*, London 1972.

The Norman Conquest

Davies, R. R., *Lordship and Society in the March of Wales 1282–1400*, Oxford 1978.
Le Patourel, J., *The Norman Empire*, Oxford 1976.
Warren, W. L., *Henry II*, University of California Press 1973.

The Reformation and its aftermath

Kearney, H. F., *Scholars and Gentlemen: Universities and Society in Pre-Industrial Britain*, London 1970.
Lecky, W. E. H., *A History of England in the Eighteenth Century*, 8 vols., London 1878–90.
A History of Ireland in the Eighteenth Century, 5 vols., London 1892.
Mathew, D., *The Celtic Peoples and Renaissance Europe*, London 1933.
Pocock, J. G. A., *The Ancient Constitution and The Feudal Law*, Cambridge 1957.
Trevor-Roper, H. R., *Religion, the Reformation and Social Change*, London 1967.

'The Unity of the Kingdom: War and Peace with Wales, Scotland and Ireland', in *The English World*, ed. R. Blake, London 1982, pp. 100–10.
Catholics, Anglicans and Puritans, London 1987.

The Industrial Revolution

Curtis, L. P. Jr, *Anglo-Saxons and Celts*, New York 1968.
Durkacz, V. E., *The Decline of the Celtic Languages: A Study of Linguistic and Cultural Conflict in Scotland, Wales and Ireland from the Reformation to the Twentieth Century*, Edinburgh 1983.
Flanagan, T., *The Irish Novelists 1800–1850*, New York 1958.
Gash, N., *Politics in the Age of Peel*, London 1953.
Halévy, E., *A History of the English People in the Nineteenth Century*, 6 vols., London 1924–34.
Hanham, H. L., *Elections and Party Management: Politics in the Time of Disraeli and Gladstone*, London 1959.
Hechter, M., *Internal Colonialism: The Celtic Fringe in British National Development*, Berkeley 1975.
Lunn, K., *Hosts, Immigrants and Minorities: Historical Responses to Newcomers in British Society 1870–1914*, London 1980.
Pelling, H., *Social Geography of British Elections 1885–1910*, London 1967.
Vincent, J., *The Formation of the Liberal Party 1857–68*, London 1966.

Geographical

Baker, A. R. H. and Butlin, R. A., *Studies of Field Systems in the British Isles*, Cambridge 1973.
Roberts, B. K., *Rural Settlement in Britain*, London 1977, repr. 1979.

NATION-BASED HISTORIES

Briggs, A., *A Social History of England*, London 1983.
Haigh, C., *The Cambridge Historical Encyclopedia of Great Britain and Ireland*, Cambridge 1985.
Mitchison, R., *A History of Scotland*, London 1982.
Morgan, K. O., *The Oxford Illustrated History of Britain*, Oxford 1984.
Stubbs, W., *The Constitutional History of England*, 3 vols., Library edn, Oxford 1880.
Whittington, G. and Whyte, I. D., *An Historical Geography of Scotland*, London 1983.
Williams, D., *A History of Modern Wales*, London 1950, repr. 1977.

PRE-ROMAN

Binchy, D. A., 'The Linguistic and Historical Value of the Irish Law Tracts', *Proceedings of the British Academy*, XXIX (1943), 195–227.
'The Fair of Tailtiu and the Feast of Tara', *Eriu*, xvii (1958), 113–38.
ed., *Crith Gablach*, Dublin 1941.
Byrne, F. J., 'Tribes and Tribalism in Early Ireland', *Eriu*, XXII (1971), 128–66.
Irish Kings and High Kings, London 1973.
Cunliffe, B., *Iron Age Communities in Britain: An Account of England, Scotland and Wales from the Seventh Century B.C. until the Roman Conquest*, London 1974.
Dillon, M., ed., *Early Irish Society*, Dublin 1954.
Greene, D., *The Irish Language*, Dublin 1966.
MacCana, P., *Celtic Mythology*, London 1970.
Rivet, A. L. F., *The Iron Age in North Britain*, Edinburgh 1966.
Taylor, J. A., *Culture and Environment in Prehistoric Wales*, Oxford 1980.

ROMAN

Breeze, D. J. and Dobson, B., *Hadrian's Wall*, London 1976.
Collingwood, R. G. and Myres, J. N. L., *Roman Britain and the English Settlements*, Oxford 1937.
Dudley, D. R. and Webster G., *The Roman Conquest of Britain A.D. 43–57*, London 1965.
Frere, S. S., *Britannia*, London 1967.
Johnson, S., *Later Roman Britain*, London 1980.
Nash-Williams, V. E., *The Roman Frontier in Wales*, 2nd edn, Cardiff 1969.
Rivet, A. L. F., *Town and Country in Roman Britain*, London 1958.
Salway, P., *Roman Britain*, Oxford 1981.
Wacher, J., *The Towns of Roman Britain*, London 1974.

POST-ROMAN

The Anglo-Saxons

Bonser, W., *Anglo-Saxon and Celtic Bibliography 450–1087*, Oxford 1957.
Bruce-Mitford, R. L. S., *The Sutton Hoo Ship Burial: A Handbook*, London 1979.
Campbell, J., ed., *The Anglo-Saxons*, London 1982.
Finberg, H. P. R., *Lucerna*, London 1964.
ed., *Agrarian History of England and Wales*, vol. 1, Cambridge 1972.
Hill, D., *An Atlas of Anglo-Saxon England*, Toronto 1981.
Hunter Blair, D., *An Introduction to Anglo-Saxon England*, Cambridge 1956.
John, E., *Orbis Britanniae*, Leicester 1966.
Loyn, H. R., *Anglo-Saxon England and the Norman Conquest*, London 1962.
Mayr-Harting, H., *The Coming of Christianity to Anglo-Saxon England*, London 1972.
Myres, J. N. L., 'The Teutonic Settlement of Northern England', *History*, xx (1935), 250–62.
Sherley-Price, L., *Bede – A History of the English Church and People*, Harmondsworth 1955.
Stenton, F. M., *Anglo-Saxon England*, 2nd edn, Oxford 1947.
Taylor, H. M. and J., *Anglo-Saxon Architecture*, 2 vols., Cambridge 1965.
Whitelock, D., ed., *English Historical Documents, c.500–1042*, vol. 1, London 1955.
Wilson, D. M. *The Anglo-Saxons*, London 1960.
The Archaeology of Anglo-Saxon England, London 1976, repr. Cambridge 1981.

Ireland

Binchy, D. A., 'The Background of Early Irish Literature', *Studia Hibernica*, I (1961), 7–18.
'St. Patrick and his Biographers: Ancient and Modern', *Studia Hibernica*, II (1962), 7–173.
Celtic and Anglo-Saxon Kingship, ODonnell Lectures 1967–8, Oxford 1970.
DePaor, M. and L., *Early Christian Ireland*, London 1958.
Flower, R., *The Irish Tradition*, Oxford 1947.
Greene, D., 'The Celtic Languages', in *The Celts*, Thomas Davis Lectures 1960, ed. J. Raftery, Cork 1964, pp. 9–22.
Henry, F., *Irish Art in the Early Christian Period to A.D. 800*, London 1965.
Hughes, K., *The Church in Early Irish Society*, London 1966.
Kenney, J. F., *The Sources for the Early History of Ireland*, vol. 1: *Ecclesiastical*, New York 1929, repr.
Ó Corráin, D., *Ireland before the Normans*, The Gill History of Ireland, vol. 2, Dublin 1972.

Scotland

Anderson, A. D. and Ogilvie, M. *Adomnan's Life of Columba*, London and New York 1961.
Anderson, M. O., *Kings and Kingship in Early Scotland*, Edinburgh and London 1980.

Jackson, K. H., 'The Britons in Southern Scotland', *Antiquity*, XXIX (1955), 77–88.
Ritchie, J. N. G., *Scotland, Archaeology and Early History*, London 1981.

Wales

Davies, W., *Wales in the Early Middle Ages*, Leicester 1982.
Dumville, D. N., 'Sub-Roman Britain: History and Legend', *History*, n.s., LXII (1977), 72–104.
Rees, W., *An Historical Atlas of Wales, from Early to Modern Times*, London 1959.

THE VIKING PERIOD

Binchy, D. A., 'The Passing of the Old Order', in *Proceedings of the Dublin Congress of Celtic Studies*, ed. B. O Cuiv, Dublin 1962, 119–32.
Davis, R. H. C., 'Alfred the Great: Propaganda and Truth', *History*, LVI (1971), 169–82.
Stenton, D. M., ed. *Preparatory to Anglo-Saxon England Being the Collected Papers of Frank Merry Stenton,* Oxford 1970.
Wainwright, F. T., *Scandinavian England*, ed. H. P. R. Finberg, Chichester 1975.

THE NORMAN CONQUEST

England

Ashley, W., *An Introduction to English Economic History*, London 1909.
Beresford, M. W. and St Joseph, J. K. S., *Medieval England: An Aerial Survey*, Cambridge 1979.
Brown, R. A., *English Castles*, London 1976.
Clanchy, M. T., *England and its Rulers 1066–1272*, London 1983.
DuBoulay, F. R. H., *An Age of Ambition: English Society in the Late Middle Ages*, London 1970.
Hallam, H. E., *Rural England*, London 1981.
Homans, G. C., *English Villagers of the Thirteenth Century*, Cambridge, Mass., 1941.
Hoskins, W. G., 'The Domesday Book in the Highland Zone', in *Provincial England*, London 1963.
Kapelle, W. E., *The Norman Conquest of the North: The Region and its Transformation, 1000–1135*, Chapel Hill 1979.
Keen, M. H., *England in the Later Middle Ages*, London 1973.
Kirby, D. P., *The Making of Early England*, London 1967.
Knowles, M. D., *The Monastic Order in England*, 2nd edn, Cambridge 1949.
Lander, J. R., *Conflict and Stability in Fifteenth Century England*, London 1969.
Lennard, R., *Rural England*, Oxford 1959.
Le Patourel, J., *The Norman Empire*, Oxford 1976.
Platt, C., *The English Medieval Town*, London 1976.
Medieval England: A Social History and Archeology from the Conquest to 1600 A.D., New York 1978.
Pollock, F. and Maitland, F. W., *The History of English Law*, 2 vols., 2nd edn, Cambridge 1898.
Postan, M. M., *The Medieval Economy and Society*, London 1975.
Reynolds, S., *An Introduction to the History of English Medieval Towns*, Oxford 1977.
Thrupp, S. L., *The Merchant Class of Medieval London*, Ann Arbor 1948.
Vinogradoff, P., *Villeinage in England*, Oxford 1892.

Ireland

Frame, R., *Colonial Ireland*, Dublin 1981.
Lydon, J., ed., *The English in Medieval Ireland*, Dublin 1984.
Nicholls, K., *Gaelic and Gaelicised Ireland in the Middle Ages*, Dublin 1972.
Orpen, G. H., *Ireland Under the Normans*, Oxford 1911, repr. 1968.
Watt, J.A., *The Church and the Two Nations in Medieval Ireland*, Cambridge 1970.

Scotland

Barrow, G. W. S., *The Kingdom of the Scots: Government, Church and Society from the Eleventh to the Fourteenth Century*, London 1973.

The Anglo-Norman Era in Scottish History, Oxford 1980.

Kingship and Unity: Scotland 1000–1306, London 1981.

Brown, J. M., *Scottish Society in the Fifteenth Century*, New York 1977.

Dodgshon, R. A., *Land and Society in Early Scotland*, Oxford 1981.

Duncan, A. A. M., *Scotland: The Making of a Kingdom*, Edinburgh 1975.

Nicholson, R., *Scotland: The Later Middle Ages*, London 1974.

Wormald, J., *Lords and Men in Scotland: Bonds of Manrent 1442–1603*, Edinburgh 1985.

Wales

Davies, R. R., 'Colonial Wales', *Past and Present*, LV (1974), 3–23.

'Kings, Lords and Liberties in the March of Wales', *Transactions of the Royal Historical Society*, 5th series, XXIX (1979), 41–61.

Conquest, Co-existence and Change: Wales 1063–1415, Oxford 1987.

ed., *The British Isles: 1100–1500 Comparisons, Contrasts and Connections*, Edinburgh 1988.

Jones, Pierce T., *Medieval Welsh Society*, ed. J. Beverly Smith, Cardiff 1972.

Lloyd, Sir John Edward, *A History of Wales from the Earliest Times to the Edwardian Conquest*, London 1939.

Richter, M., 'The Political and Institutional Background to National Consciousness in Medieval Wales', in *Nationality*, ed. T. W. Moody, Belfast 1978, pp. 37–55.

Williams, G., *The Welsh Church from Conquest to Reformation*, Cardiff 1962.

Religion, Language and Nationality in Wales, Cardiff, 1979.

THE REFORMATION AND ITS AFTERMATH

England

Bossy, J., *The English Catholic Community 1570–1850*, London 1975.

Clark, J. C. D., *English Society 1688–1832: Ideology, Social Structure and Political Practice during the Ancien Regime*, Cambridge 1985.

Collinson, P., *The Religion of Protestants: The Church in English Society 1559–1625*, Oxford 1982.

Dickens, A. G., *The English Reformation*, London 1964.

Elton, G. R., *Reform and Reformation*, London 1977.

Hill, C., *The World Turned Upside Down*, London 1981.

James, M. E., *Family, Lineage and Civil Society: A Study of Society, Politics and Mentality in the Durham, Region 1500–1640*, Oxford 1974.

Malcolmson, R. W., *Life and Labour in England 1700–80*, London 1981.

Stone, L., *The Crisis of the Aristocracy 1558–1641*, Oxford 1965.

Tawney, R. H., *The Agrarian Problem in the Sixteenth Century*, London 1912, repr. 1967.

Thirsk, J., ed., *Agrarian History of England and Wales*, vol. 4, Cambridge 1967.

Thomas, K., *Religion and the Decline of Magic*, London 1971.

Wrightson, K., *English Society 1580–1680*, London 1982.

Ireland

Bradshaw, B., *The Irish Constitutional Revolution of the Sixteenth Century*, Cambridge 1979.

Brady, C. and Gillespie, R., *Natives and Newcomers: Essays on the Making of Irish Colonial Society 1534–1681*, Dublin 1986.

Reformation to Restoration: Ireland 1534–1660, Dublin 1987.

Canny, N., *The Elizabethan Conquest of Ireland*, Hassocks 1976.

Cullen, L. M., *An Economic History of Ireland since 1660*, Dublin 1972.
Ellis, S., *Tudor Ireland 1470–1603*, London 1985.
Ford, G. A., *The Protestant Reformation in Ireland, 1590–1641*, Frankfurt 1985.
Kearney, H. F., *Strafford in Ireland 1633–41*, Manchester 1959. Reprinted 1989.

Scotland

Campbell, R. H. and Skinner, A. S., *The Origins and Nature of the Scottish Enlightenment*, Edinburgh 1982.
Chitnis, A. C., *The Scottish Enlightenment: A Social History*, London 1976.
Cowan, I. B., *The Scottish Covenanters 1660–1688*, London 1976.
Regional Aspects of the Scottish Reformation, London 1978.
Cullen, L. M. and Smout, T. C., *Comparative Aspects of Scottish and Irish Economic and Social History 1600–1800*, Edinburgh 1977.
Davie, G. E., *The Democratic Intellect*, Edinburgh, 1961.
The Scottish Enlightenment, London 1981.
Devine, T. M. and Dickson, D., *Ireland and Scotland 1600–1850: Parallels and Contrasts in Economic and Social Development*, Edinburgh 1983.
Donaldson, G., *The Scottish Reformation*, Cambridge, 1960.
Scotland James V – James VII, Edinburgh 1965.
All the Queen's Men: Power and Politics in Mary Stewart's Scotland, New York 1983.
Dwyer, J., Mason, T. A. and Murdoch, A., *New Perspectives in the Politics and Culture of Early Modern Scotland*, Edinburgh 1982.
Graham, H. G., *The Social Life of Scotland in the Eighteenth Century*, 2 vols., London 1899.
Hont, I. and Ignatieff, M., *Wealth and Virtue: The Shaping of the Political Economy in the Scottish Enlightenment*, Cambridge 1983.
Makey, W., *The Church of the Covenant 1637–1651: Revolution and Social Change in Scotland*, Edinburgh 1979.
Philipson, N. T. and Mitchison, R., eds., *Scotland in the Age of Improvement*, Edinburgh 1970.
Smout, T. C., *A History of the Scottish People 1560–1830*, Edinburgh 1969.
Stevenson, D., *Alisdair MacColla and the Highland Problem in the Seventeenth Century*, Edinburgh 1980.
Scottish Covenanters and Irish Confederates: Scottish–Irish Relations in the Mid-Seventeenth Century, Belfast 1981.
Trevor-Roper, H. R., *George Buchanan and the Ancient Scottish Constitution*, London 1966.
Whyte, I., *Agriculture and Society in Seventeenth Century Scotland*, Edinburgh 1979.
Williamson, A. H., *Scottish National Consciousness in the Age of James VI: The Apocalypse, the Union and the Shaping of Scotland's Public Culture*, Edinburgh 1979.
Wormald, J., *Court, Kirk and Community: Scotland 1470–1625*, London 1981.
Youngson, A. J., *After the Forty-Five*, Edinburgh 1973.

Wales

Jenkins, G. H., *Literature, Religion and Society in Wales, 1660–1730*, Cardiff 1978.
Jones, G. J., *The Gentry and the Elizabethan State*, Swansea 1977.
Lloyd, H. A., *The Gentry of South-West Wales, 1540–1640*, Cardiff 1968.
Morgan, P., *The Eighteenth Century Renaissance*, Llandyhie, Dyfed, 1981.
Roberts, P. R., 'The Union With England and the Identity of "Anglican" Wales', *Transactions of the Royal Historical Society*, 5th series, XXII (1972), 49–70.

The Atlantic empire

Bailyn, B., *The Ideological Origins of the American Revolution*, Cambridge, Mass., 1967.
The Origins of American Politics, New York 1968.

Greene, J. P., *The Re-interpretation of the American Revolution*, New York 1968.
Greene, J. P. and Pole J. R., *Colonial British America: Essays in the New History of the Early Modern Era*, Baltimore 1984.
Henretta, James A., *The Evolution of American Society*, London 1973.
Marshall, P. and Williams, G., *The British Atlantic Empire before the American Revolution*, London 1980.
Pocock, J. G. A., ed., *Three British Revolutions 1641, 1688, 1776*, Princeton 1980.

THE INDUSTRIAL REVOLUTION AND ITS IMPACT

England

Blake, R., *Disraeli*, London 1966.
Briggs, A., *Victorian People*, London 1954.
The Age of Improvement 1783–1867, London 1959.
ed., *Chartist Studies*, London 1959.
Chambers, J. D. and Mingay, G. E., *The Agricultural Revolution 1750–1880*, London 1966.
Crouzet, F., *The Victorian Economy*, trans. A. S. Forster, London 1982.
Ensor, R. C. K., *England 1870–1914*, Oxford 1936.
Jones, Maldwyn A., 'The Background to Emigration from Great Britain in the Nineteenth Century', in Fleming, D., and Bailyn, B., eds., *Perspectives in American History* (Cambridge, Mass.), VII (1973), 1–94.
Joyce, P., *Work, Society and Politics: Culture of the Factory in Later Victorian England*, Hassocks 1980.
Mathias, P., *The First Industrial Nation: An Economic History of Britain*, London 1969.
McKenzie, R. and Silver, A., *Angels in Marble: Working Class Conservatives in Urban England*, Chicago and London 1968.
Norman, E. R., ed., *Anti-Catholicism in Victorian England*, London 1968.
Thomas, B., *Migration and Economic Growth: A Study of Great Britain and the Atlantic Economy*, Cambridge 1954.
Thompson, F. M. L., *English Landed Society in the Nineteenth Century*, London 1963.
Webb, R. K., *Modern England*, 2nd edn, New York 1980.

Ireland

Beckett, J. C. and Glasscock, R. E., eds., *Belfast: The Origin and Growth of an Industrial City*, London 1967.
Clark, S. and Donnelly, J. S., eds., *Irish Peasants: Violence and Unrest, 1780–1914*, University of Wisconsin Press 1983.
Connell, K. H., *Irish Peasant Society*, Oxford 1968.
Connolly, S. J., *Priests and People in Pre-Famine Ireland 1780–1845*, Dublin 1982.
Cruise OBrien, C., *Parnell and his Party*, Oxford 1957.
Cullen, L. M., *The Emergence of Modern Ireland 1600–1900*, New York 1981.
Hoppen, K. T., *Elections, Politics and Society in Ireland 1832–1885*, Oxford 1984.
Kennedy, R. E. Jr, *The Irish: Emigration, Marriage and Fertility*, University of California Press 1973.
Larkin, E., 'The Devotional Revolution in Ireland, 1850–75', *American Historical Review*, XXVII (1972), 625–52.
Lee, J., *The Modernisation of Irish Society 1848–1918*, Dublin 1973.
McDowell, R. B., *Public Opinion and Government Policy in Ireland, 1801–1846*, London 1952.
O Tuathaigh, G., *Ireland before the Famine 1798–1848*, Dublin 1972.

Scotland

Bumsted, J. M., *The People's Clearance: Highland Emigration to British North America*, Edinburgh 1982.

Campbell, R. H., *Scotland since 1707: The Rise of an Industrial Society*, New York 1965.

Davie, G. E., *The Democratic Intellect: Scotland and her Universities in the Nineteenth Century*, Edinburgh 1962.

Drummond, A. L. and Bulloch, J., *The Church in Victorian Scotland 1843–74*, Edinburgh 1975.

Ferguson, W., *Scotland: 1689 to the Present*, Edinburgh 1968.

Flinn, M., ed., *Scottish Population History*, Cambridge 1977.

Gray, M., 'Scottish Emigration: The Social Impact of Agrarian Change in the Rural Lowlands, 1775–1875', in Fleming, D. and Bailyn, B., eds., *Perspectives in American History* (Cambridge, Mass.), VII (1973), 95–176.

Handley, J. E., *The Irish in Scotland 1798–1845*, Cork 1945.

Meikle, H. W., *Scotland and the French Revolution*, New York 1969.

Saunders, L. J., *Scottish Democracy 1815–40: The Social and Intellectual Background*, Edinburgh 1950.

Smout, T. C., *History of the Scottish People 1830–1950*, London 1986.

Wales

Conway, A., 'Welsh Emigration to the United States', in Fleming, D. and Bailyn, B., eds., *Perspectives in American History* (Cambridge, Mass.), VII (1973), 177–274.

Davies, E. T., *Religion and Society in the Nineteenth Century*, Llandyhie, Dyfed, 1981.

Dodd, A. H., *The Industrial Revolution in North Wales*, Cardiff 1971 (repr.)

Howell D. W., *Land and People in Nineteenth Century Wales*, London 1977.

John, A. H., *The Industrial Revolution of South Wales*, Cardiff 1950.

Jones, D., *Before Rebecca: Popular Protest in Wales 1793–1835*, London 1973.

Jones, I. G., *Explorations and Explanations*, Gomer 1981.

Lambert, W. R., *Drink and Sobriety in Victorian Wales c.1820–1895*, Oxford 1983.

Morgan, K. O., *Re-Birth of a Nation: Wales 1880–1980*, Oxford 1981.

ed., *Wales in British Politics 1868–1922*, Cardiff 1963, rev. edn 1970.

Smith, D., ed., *A People and a Proletariat: Essays in the History of Wales 1780–1980*, London 1980.

Williams, D., *The Rebecca Riots*, Cardiff 1955.

WITHDRAWAL FROM EMPIRE

England

Marwick, A., *Britain in the Century of Total War: War, Peace, and Social Change 1900–1967*, Boston 1968.

Rose, E. J. B., *Colour and Citizenship: A Report on British Race Relations*, Oxford 1969.

Taylor, A. J. P., *English History 1914–1945*, Oxford 1965.

Townsend, P., *Poverty in the United Kingdom: A Survey of Household Resources and Standards of Living*, London 1978.

Ireland

Brown, T., *Ireland: A Social and Cultural History 1922–79*, London 1981.

Brown, T. N., *Irish-American Nationalism*, New York 1966.

Farrell, M., *Northern Ireland the Orange State*, London 1979.

Finnegan, R. B., *Ireland: The Challenge of Conflict and Change*, Boulder, Colorado, 1983.

Lyons, F. S. L., *Ireland since The Famine*, London 1971.

Culture and Anarchy, Oxford 1979.

Meenan, J., *The Irish Economy since 1922*, Liverpool 1970.
Miller, D. W., *The Queen's Rebels: Ulster Loyalism in Historical Perspective*, New York 1978.
Murphy, J. A., *Ireland in the Twentieth Century*, Dublin 1975.
OMalley, P., *The Uncivil Wars: Ireland Today*, Boston 1983.
Rose, R., *Governing Without Consensus*, London 1971.

Scotland

Campbell, R. H., *The Rise and Fall of Scottish Industry 1707–1939*, Edinburgh 1980.
Gallagher, Tom, *Glasgow: The Uneasy Peace: Religious Tension in Modern Scotland*, Manchester 1988.
Edinburgh Divided: John Cormack and No Popery in the 1930s, Edinburgh 1988.
Harvie, C., *No Gods and Precious Few Heroes: Scotland 1914–80*, Toronto 1981.
Henderson, R. A., *The Location of Immigrant Industry Within a U.K. Assisted Area: The Scottish Experience*, Oxford 1980.
Lenman, B., *An Economic History of Modern Scotland 1660–1976*, Hamden, Conn., 1977.
Lewis, T. M. and McNicoll, I. H., *North Sea Oil and Scotland's Economic Prospects*, London 1978.

Wales

Cooke, P., *Department Development in the United Kingdom Regions with Particular Reference to Wales*, Oxford 1980.
Smith, D., *Wales, Wales*, London 1984.
Smith, David B. and Williams, Gareth W., *Fields of Praise*, Cardiff 1980.
Williams, G., *Social and Cultural Change in Contemporary Wales*, London 1978.

SELECTED LOCAL STUDIES

Much of the best recent historical work has been produced by historians with a local perspective.

England

Ashby, M. K., *Joseph Ashby of Tysoe 1859–1919*, Cambridge 1961.
Blythe, R., *Akenfield: Portrait of an English Village*, London 1969.
Hoskins, W. G., *The Midland Peasant: Economic and Social History of a Leicestershire Village*, London 1957.
Roberts, R., *The Classic Slum: Salford Life in the First Quarter of the Century*, Manchester 1971.
Spufford, M., *Contrasting Communities: English Villagers in the Sixteenth and Seventeenth Centuries*, Cambridge 1974.
Waller, P. J., *Democracy and Sectarianism: A Political and Social History of Liverpool 1868–1939*, Liverpool 1981.

Ireland

Akenson, D. H., *Between Two Revolutions Islandmagee: County Antrim 1798–1920*, Hamden, Conn., 1979.
Arensberg, C. M. and Kimball, S. T., *Family and Community in Ireland*, Cambridge, Mass., 1940.
Fox, R., *The Tory Islanders: A People of the Celtic Fringe*, Cambridge 1978.
Harris R., *Prejudice and Tolerance in Ulster: A Study of Neighbours and 'Strangers' in a Border Community*, Manchester 1972.
Nolan, W., *Fassadinin: Land, Settlement and Society in South-East Ireland, 1600–1850*, Dublin 1979.

Scotland

Buchan, D., *The Ballad and the Folk*, London 1972.

Cregeen, E. R., 'The Changing Role of the House of Argyll in the Scottish Highlands', in *History and Social Anthropology*, ed. I. M. Lewis, London 1968.

Gaskell, P., *Morvern Transformed: A Highland Parish in the Nineteenth Century*, Cambridge 1968.

Wales

Rees, A. D., *Life in a Welsh Countryside*, Cardiff 1950.

IMPERIAL HISTORY

Australia

Blainey, G., *The Tyranny of Distance*, Melbourne 1975.

Clark, C. M. H., *A History of Australia*, vols. 1–4, Melbourne 1962–81.

Day, David, *The Great Betrayal: Britain, Australia and the Onset of the Pacific War, 1939–42*, London 1988.

Inglis, K. S., *The Australian Colonists: An Exploration of their Social History*, Melbourne 1974.

Ward, R., *The History of Australia: The Twentieth Century*, New York 1977.

New Zealand

Oliver, W. H., with Williams, B. R., *The Oxford History of New Zealand*, Oxford 1981.

Canada

Brebner, J. B., *Canada: A Modern History*, new edn, rev. and ed. by D. C. Masters, Ann Arbor 1970.

Galbraith, J. K., *The Scotch*, London 1964.

Innis, H. A., *The Fur Trade in Canada*, rev. edn, Yale 1962.

Senior, H., *Orangeism: The Canadian Phase*, Toronto 1972.

United States

Thernstrom, S., ed., *Harvard Encyclopedia of American Ethnic Groups*, Cambridge, Mass., 1980.

A lucid survey of recent literature is to be found in Jonathan Clark, 'English History's Forgotten Context: Scotland, Ireland, Wales', *The Historical Journal*, xxxii, 1 (1989), 211–228.

ADDITIONS TO THE READING LIST (1990)

Cahill, G. A., 'Irish Catholicism and English Toryism', *Review of Politics*, XIX (1957), 62–76.

Clark, J. C. D., 'English History's forgotten context: Scotland, Ireland, Wales', *Historical Journal*, XXXII (1989), 211–28.

Donovan, R. K., *No Popery and Radicalism: Opposition to Roman Catholic Relief in Scotland 1778–1782*, New York 1987.

Gunnin, G. C., *John Wheatley, Catholic Socialism and Irish Labour in the West of Scotland 1906–1924*, New York 1987.

Johnson, M. D., *The Dissolution of Dissent 1850–1918*, New York 1987.

Karsten, P., *Patriot Heroes in England and America: Political Symbols and Changing Values over Three Centuries*, Madison, London, 1978.

Lubenow, W. C., *Parliamentary Politics and the Home Rule Crisis: The British House of Commons in 1886*, Oxford 1988.

MacDonagh, O., *States of Mind: Study of Anglo-Irish Conflict 1780–1980*, London 1983.
Neal, F., *Sectarian Violence: The Liverpool Experience 1819–1914*, Manchester 1988.
Phillips, P. T., *The Sectarian Spirit: Sectarianism, Society and Politics in Victorian Cotton Towns*, Toronto 1982.
Rich, P. B., *Race and Empire in British Politics*, Cambridge 1986; rev. edn 1990.
Robbins, K., *Nineteenth Century Britain: England, Scotland and Wales – the Making of a Nation*, Oxford 1988.
Russell, C., 'The British Background to the Irish Rebellion of 1641', *Historical Research* LXI (1988), 166–72.
Samuel, R., 'In search of Britain', *New Statesman and Society* (25 Aug. 1989) 21–4.
ed., *Patriotism: The Making and Unmaking of British National Identity*, 3 vols., London and New York 1989.
Smith, D., *North and South: Britain's Economic Social and Political Divide*, London 1989.
Thomas, B., ed., *The Welsh Economy: Studies in Expansion*, Cardiff 1962.
Westerkamp, M. J., *Triumph of the Laity: Scots-Irish Piety and the Great Awakening, 1625–1760*, New York 1988.

Index